TECHNICAL ANALYSIS
OF STOCK TRENDS

TECHNICAL ANALYSIS

OF

STOCK
TRENDS

BY

ROBERT D. EDWARDS

AND

JOHN MAGEE

PUBLISHED BY JOHN MAGEE INC.
BOSTON, MASSACHUSETTS

FIRST EDITION, 1948
SECOND EDITION, 1951
THIRD EDITION, 1954
FOURTH EDITION, 1957
FIFTH EDITION

First Printing, December 1966
Second Printing, June 1967
Third Printing, February 1968
Fourth Printing, June 1968
Fifth Printing, April 1969
Sixth Printing, January 1970
Seventh Printing, May 1971
Eighth Printing, June 1972
Ninth Printing, January 1973
Tenth Printing, September 1975
Eleventh Printing, September 1977
Twelfth Printing, June 1979
Thirteenth Printing, April 1981
Fourteenth Printing, February 1983
Fifteenth Printing, May 1984

International Standard Book Number 0-910944-00-8
Library of Congress Catalog Card Number: 66-29742

Printed in the United States of America

PREFACE TO SECOND EDITION

It is, needless to say, gratifying to the authors of this treatise to report that not only has a large first edition been exhausted (although it was originally assumed that it would suffice for many years), but also that the demand for copies has been increasing at a rather astonishing pace during the past six months without any "promotion" except word-of-mouth recommendation from one investor to another.

In preparing this new edition, a careful perusal of everything that was written in the previous printing, checked by the market events of the past twenty-four months and compared with all of the additional chart data accumulated during that period, resulted in the not unexpected but nevertheless mildly surprising conclusion that nothing whatever of real consequence needed to be changed or amplified. Hence, only minor revisions of an editorial nature have been made.

It would have been interesting to augment our already copious illustrations with a number of charts from current and recent months of market action, but costs of engraving and printing have risen to such a distressingly high level that any additions of that sort would, it was found, be prohibitively expensive. Aside from their novelty, they would add nothing to the book; they would only be substituted for other charts of precisely the same nature and significance and fully as pertinent to present-day conditions.

The stock market, as I wrote in the original Foreword, "goes right on repeating the same old movements in much the same old routine. The importance of a knowledge of these phenomena to the trader and investor has been in no whit diminished." We see the same forecasting patterns developing on the charts today that we have seen over and over again for the past twenty years. Neither the mechanics nor the "human element" of the stock market have changed, and there is no reason to think that they will.

ROBERT D. EDWARDS

May 1, 1951

PREFACE TO FOURTH EDITION

In the several years since publication of the first edition of this work, "the stock market goes right on repeating the same old movements in much the same old routine." Nearly all of the technical phenomena outlined in the first edition have appeared many times since then; and we see no reason to expect that these habits of stocks will change materially in the years ahead, barring revolutionary changes in the economy such as the abolishment of the free market entirely.

Since the basic nature of the market has not changed appreciably, it has been unnecessary to make sweeping alterations in the text of PART ONE; TECHNICAL THEORY. The previous edition has been very carefully re-studied, and revisions have been made where they were called for to bring the material up-to-date. In PART TWO; TRADING TACTICS, more extensive changes were needed, due to the more specific nature of the material and some differences in the present margin requirements, trading rules, etc. Also, there have been some improvements in the application of technical methods at the tactical level, and these have been incorporated in this section.

Somewhat less emphasis has been put on the use of stop-loss orders, since their need is not so great in the case of the experienced trader as it might be with the novice. The principle of always following the Major trend has been modified to achieve better protection of capital through balance and diversification. In line with avoiding "all-out" situations, with their consequent dangers the idea of using an Evaluative Index has been introduced; and this concept has modified somewhat the tactics of following the Major trend. It also has a bearing on the Composite Leverage or determination of total risk.

Type for the entire book has been re-set in this edition. The illustrative charts originally used have been, in the main retained, since they demonstrate the various points very well, but a new chapter includes a number of additional charts taken from the market history of recent years, showing how the same phenomena continue to appear again and again.

The appendix on the Sensitivity Indexes has been completely re-computed, and extended to cover a broad list of the more important issues. The arduous labor of determining these index figures was undertaken by Frank J. Curto and Marcella P. Curto. Material help in proof-reading and revision for this edition was given by Beverly Magee and Elinor T. Magee.

JOHN MAGEE

January 1, 1957

PREFACE TO FIFTH EDITION

During the sixteen printings of the Fourth Edition of "TECHNICAL ANALYSIS OF STOCK TRENDS" very few changes have been made in the original text, mainly because the lucid presentation of market action by the late Robert D. Edwards covered so thoroughly the basic and typical market action of common stocks. There has seemed no reason, for example, to discard a chart picture illustrating some important technical phenomenon merely because it occurred several or many years ago.

Instead, over the various printings of the book pages have been added showing similar examples, or in some cases entirely new types of market action taken from recent history; but these demonstrate mainly that the inherent nature of a competitive market does not change very much over the years, and that "the same old patterns" of human behavior continue to produce much the same types of market trends and fluctuations.

The principal change in this Fifth Edition, and it is a spectacular improvement, is that practically all of the chart examples drawn to the TEKNIPLAT scale have been redrawn and new plates of these have been substituted. In the course of this work several minor errors of scaling, titling, etc., previously undiscovered, came to light and have been corrected.

The difficult work of revision was initiated in our charting room by two ambitious teen-agers, Anne E. Mahoney, and Joseph J. Spezeski, who took on the entire job of preparing the finished drawings and making necessary corrections. This enormous project was undertaken and carried through by these two young people spontaneously. In order to free them entirely from other distractions their regular charting work was taken over for a period of months by the rest of the chart-room staff; so that a great deal of credit is due to the fine efforts of the entire chart-room group.

JOHN MAGEE

December 3, 1966

CONTENTS

ILLUSTRATIONS

Regarding the illustrations in this book:—Except for those which are marked as adapted from other sources, the charts listed as FIGURES below have been reproduced from the authors' own "working" charts. As such they were made up originally for private use only and without a thought to their eventual reproduction, much less their publication. They are not and do not pretend to be works of art, but it is hoped that they will, despite their "home-made" appearance, serve the purpose of illustrating the various formations, patterns, market phenomena and trading principles discussed in the text. That they do not show the clean line and expert lettering of a professional drafts-man's work is regretted. The reader will, we trust, make allowances.

As for their selection, it should be stated most emphatically that it was not necessary to search through thousands of charts in order to find good examples of all these various technical formations. Many dozens—even hundreds—were available for practically every type of pattern. Anyone who has learned to recognize them can find for himself plenty of good technical pictures in a quick examination of even as small a portfolio as fifty or a hundred charts. In other words, the illustrations in this book are in no sense unique. In selecting them we have tried only to show as much variety as possible and also samples from previous as well as more recent market history.

Perhaps it is not necessary, but it is at least in accord with custom, to add that the information as to specific market prices, volume of transactions, etc., used in preparing our illustrations (or cited in the text of this book) has been derived from sources believed to be reliable but is not guaranteed.

PART ONE

TEXT DIAGRAMS

The charts listed above as FIGURES all represent actual market history. In distinction, the DIAGRAMS listed below do not depict real trading history but have been specially drawn as simplified, hypothetical market situations to facilitate the explanation of certain trading principles.

TEXT DIAGRAMS

The charts listed above as FIGURES all represent actual market history. In distinction, the DIAGRAMS listed below do not depict real trading history but have been specially drawn as simplified, hypothetical market situations to facilitate the explanation of certain trading principles.

TECHNICAL ANALYSIS
OF STOCK TRENDS

PART ONE

———

TECHNICAL
THEORY

FOREWORD

This book has been written for the layman rather than for the Wall Street professional. But, it assumes that the reader is already possessed of at least an elementary knowledge of the nature of stocks and bonds, that he has had some dealings with a broker and some familiarity with the financial pages of his newspapers. Hence, no attempt is made herein to define common stock market terms and procedures. Every effort, however, has been exerted to explain in full the theories and the terminology of our specific subject, Technical Market Analysis.

Part One is based in large part on the pioneer researches and writings of the late Richard W. Schabacker. Students of his *Technical Analysis and Stock Market Profits* (the latest revision of which—now out of print—was made in 1937 by the present writer and Albert L. Kimball) will find in the pages of this section much that is familiar and, except for the illustrations, only a little that is really novel. It has been a matter of surprise, in fact, to the authors and other students of market technics that all the new controls and regulations of the past several years, the new taxes which have placed a heavy handicap on successful investors, the greatly augmented and improved facilities for acquiring dependable information on securities, even the quite radical changes in certain portions of our basic economy, have not much altered the "pattern" of the stock market.

Certain of the evidences of pool manipulation which used to appear on the charts are now seldom seen. A few of the price formations which formerly were quite common, now appear rarely or may have lost much of their practical utility for the trader; they have been omitted from this text. Others have altered their habits slightly, or their consequences to a degree (but not their fundamental nature), which has, of course, been noted herein. The distressing thinness of the market at times—one of the undoubted effects of regulation—has resulted in a few more "false moves," more spells of uninteresting (and unprofitable) inactivity. But, in the main, the market goes right on repeating the same old movements in much the same old routine. The importance of a knowledge of these phenomena to the trader and investor has been in no whit diminished.

Part Two, which has to do with the practical application of these market patterns and phenomena, with the *tactics* of trading, is all new. For more than fifteen years (his total market experience extends back for nearly thirty years),

I

John Magee has invested and traded exclusively via the technical theory, kept thousands of charts, made hundreds of actual trades, tested all sorts of applications, audited and analyzed methods, tactics and results from every conceivable angle, depended on his profits for his living. His contribution is that of one who has tried and knows.

It may well be added here—and will be often repeated in the following pages —that the technical guides to trading in stocks are by no means infallible. The more experience one gains in their use, the more alive he becomes to their pitfalls and their failures. There is no such thing as a sure-fire method of "beating the market"; the authors have no hesitancy in saying that there never will be. Nevertheless, a knowledge and judicious application of the principles of technical analysis does pay dividends—is more profitable (and far safer) for the average investor than any other of the presently recognized and established approaches to the problems of buying and selling securities.

ROBERT D. EDWARDS

CHAPTER I

THE TECHNICAL APPROACH TO TRADING
AND INVESTING

FEW human activities have been so exhaustively studied during the past fifty years, from so many angles and by so many different sorts of people, as has the buying and selling of corporate securities. The rewards which the stock market holds out to those who read it right are enormous; the penalties it exacts from careless, dozing or "unlucky" investors are calamitous—no wonder it has attracted some of the world's most astute accountants, analysts and researchers, along with a motley crew of eccentrics, mystics and "hunch players" and a multitude of just ordinary hopeful citizens.

Able brains have sought, and continue constantly to seek, for safe and sure methods of appraising the state and trend of the market, of discovering the right stock to buy and the right time to buy it. This intensive research has not been fruitless—far from it. There are a great many successful investors and speculators (using the word in its true sense which is without opprobrium) who, by one road or another, have acquired the necessary insight into the forces with which they deal and the judgment, the forethought and the all-important self-discipline to deal with them profitably.

In the course of years of stock market study, two quite distinct schools of thought have arisen, two radically different methods of arriving at the answers to the trader's problem of What and When. In the parlance of "the street," one of these is commonly referred to as the *fundamental* or statistical, and the other as the *technical*. (In recent years a third approach, the cyclical, has made rapid progress and, although still beset by a "lunatic fringe," it promises to contribute a great deal to our understanding of economic trends.)

The stock market fundamentalist depends on statistics. He examines the auditors' reports, the profit-and-loss statements, the quarterly balance sheets, the dividend records and policies of the companies whose shares he has under observation. He analyzes sales data, managerial ability, plant capacity, the competition. He turns to bank and treasury reports, production indexes, price statistics and crop forecasts to gauge the state of business in general, and reads the daily news carefully to arrive at an estimate of future business conditions. Taking all these into account, he evaluates his stock; if it is selling currently below his appraisal he regards it as a buy.

3

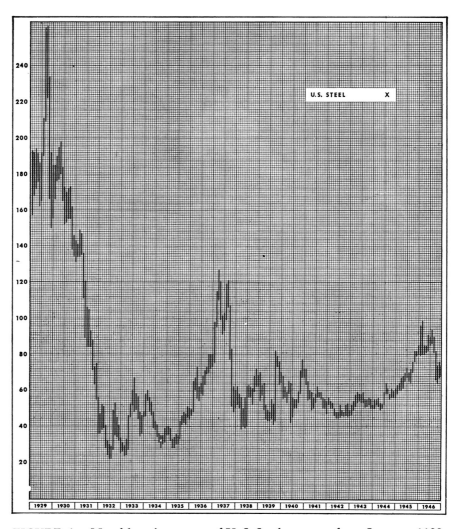

FIGURE 1. Monthly price ranges of U. S. Steel common from January, 1929 to December, 1946. Compare the great swings in the market price for this stock—from 1929 (extreme high, 261¾) to 1932 (extreme low, 21¼), from 1932 to 1937, from 1937 to 1938, from 1942 to 1946—with its book values for those years as cited on page 5.

As a matter of fact, aside from the greenest of newcomers when they first tackle the investment problem, and to whom in their inexperience any other point of view is not only irrational but incomprehensible, your pure fundamentalist is a very rare bird. Even those market authorities who pretend to scorn charts and "chartists" utterly, are not oblivious to the "action" chronicled by the ticker tape, nor do they conceal their respect for the Dow Theory which, whether they realize it or not, is in its very essence purely technical.

Definition of Technical Analysis

The term *technical* in its application to the stock market has come to have a very special meaning, quite different from its ordinary dictionary definition. It refers to *the study of the action of the market itself* as opposed to the study of the goods in which the market deals. *Technical Analysis* is the science of recording, usually in graphic form, the actual history of trading (price changes, volume of transactions, etc.) in a certain stock or in "the averages" and then deducing from that pictured history the probable future trend.

The technical student argues thus: It is futile to assign an intrinsic value to a stock certificate. One share of United States Steel, for example, was worth $261 in the early Fall of 1929, but you could buy it for only $22 in June of 1932! By March, 1937, it was selling for $126 and just one year later for $38. In May of 1946 it had climbed back up to $97 and ten months later in 1947 had dropped below $70 although the company's earnings on this last date were reputed to be nearing an all-time high and interest rates in general were still near an all-time low. The book value of this share of U. S. Steel, according to the corporation's balance sheet, was about $204 in 1929 (end of the year), $187 in 1932, $151 in 1937, $117 in 1938 and $142 in 1946. This sort of thing, this wide divergence between presumed value and actual price, is not the exception; it is the rule; it is going on all the time. The fact is that the real value of a share of U. S. Steel common is determined at any given time solely, definitely and inexorably by supply and demand, which are accurately reflected in the transactions consummated on the floor of the New York Stock Exchange.

Of course, the statistics which the fundamentalists study play a part in the supply-demand equation—that is freely admitted. But there are many other factors affecting it. The market price reflects not only the differing value opinions of many orthodox security appraisers but also all the hopes and fears and guesses and moods, rational and irrational, of hundreds of potential buyers and sellers, as well as their needs and their resources—in total, factors which defy analysis and for which no statistics are obtainable, but which are nevertheless all synthesized, weighed and finally expressed in the one precise figure at which a buyer and seller get together and make a deal (through their agents, their respective stock brokers). This is the only figure that counts.

Moreover, the technician claims with complete justification that the bulk of the statistics which the fundamentalists study are past history, already out of date and sterile, because the market is not interested in the past or even in the present! It is constantly looking ahead; attempting to discount future developments, weighing and balancing all the estimates and guesses of hundreds of investors who look into the future from different points of view and through glasses of many different hues. In brief, the going price as established by the market itself comprehends all the fundamental information which the statistical analyst can hope to learn (plus some which is perhaps secret from him, known only to a few insiders) and much else besides of equal or even greater importance.

All of which, admitting its truth, would be of little significance were it not for the fact, which no one of experience doubts, that *prices move in trends* and trends tend to continue until something happens to change the supply-demand balance. Such changes are usually detectable in the action of the market itself. Certain patterns or formations, levels or areas, appear on the charts which have a meaning, can be interpreted in terms of probable future trend development. They are not infallible, it must be noted, but the odds are definitely in their favor. Time after time, as experience has amply proved, they are far more prescient than the best informed and most shrewd of statisticians.

The technical analyst may go even further in his claims. He may offer to interpret the chart of a stock *whose name he does not know,* so long as the record of trading is accurate and covers a long enough term to enable him to study its market background and habits. He may suggest that he could trade with profit in a stock knowing only its ticker symbol, completely ignorant of the company, the industry, what it manufactures or sells, or how it is capitalized. Needless to say such practice is not recommended, but if your market technician is really experienced at his business he could, in theory, do exactly what he claims.

Should the reader at this point find the technical approach to trading or investing, as explained in the foregoing, completely abhorrent, perhaps he had better close the book now. For it is primarily the technical approach, the science of technical analysis, with which the remainder of it deals.

CHAPTER II

CHARTS

CHARTS are the working tools of the technical analyst. They have been developed in a multitude of forms and styles, to represent graphically almost anything and everything that takes place in the market or to plot an "index" derived therefrom. They may be monthly charts on which an entire month's trading record is condensed into a single entry, or weekly, daily, hourly, transaction, "point-and-figure," etc. They may be constructed on arithmetic, logarithmic or square-root scale, or projected as "oscillators." They may delineate moving averages, proportion of trading volume to price movement, average price of "most active" issues, odd-lot transactions, the short interest, and an infinitude of other relations, ratios and indexes—all technical in the sense that they are derived, directly or indirectly, from what has actually been transacted on the exchange.

With most of these, fortunately, we shall not need to concern ourselves at all; they are of interest only to the full-time economic analyst.* Many of them have derived from a (so far at least) completely futile endeavor to discover some one "mechanical" index or combination of indexes which will always, automatically, without ever failing or going wrong, give warning of a change in trend; such in our experience are often confusing and sometimes downright deceptive at a most critical juncture. This book, however, is designed for the layman, the business or professional man who cannot spend all his hours on his investing or trading operations but to whom these operations are nevertheless of sufficient importance or interest to warrant his devoting at least a few minutes a day to their study and management. The theories and methods outlined herein will require only the simplest form of stock chart—a record of the price range (high and low), closing price and volume of shares traded each day. These daily graphs will be supplemented, for certain purposes which will be discussed farther on, by weekly or monthly charts, which for most stocks can be purchased ready-made.

Nearly all the illustrations throughout the following pages are examples of such daily charts. They are easy to make and maintain, requiring only a supply

---

* An exception should perhaps be made for the Odd-Lot Indexes developed by G. A. Drew. The reader who wishes to delve deeper in market technics will find these explained in Mr. Drew's book "New Methods for Profit in the Stock Market" the latest edition of which was published in 1955 by The Metcalf Press.

of graph or cross-section paper (almost any kind can serve), a daily newspaper which gives full and accurate reports on stock exchange dealings, a sharp pencil and a few minutes of time.

It is customary in preparing ordinary daily stock charts to let the horizontal axis represent time, with the vertical cross-lines (or as some prefer, the spaces between them) from left to right thus standing for successive days. The vertical scale is used for prices, with each horizontal cross-line then representing a specific price level. Space is usually provided at the bottom of the sheet to plot volume, i.e. the number of shares which change hands each day. The newspapers publishing complete stock market reports give the day's turnover or volume (exclusive of odd-lot transactions which may for our present purpose be disregarded), the highest and lowest price at which each stock sold during the day, the closing price (which is the price at which the last sale effected during the day was made) and usually the opening or first sale price. On our charts, the daily price range is plotted by drawing a vertical line connecting the points representing the high and the low. Then a short horizontal "tick" is added, either crossing the vertical range line or extending out to the right from it, at the level of the closing price. Sometimes all transactions in a stock during a day take place at one and the same price; the high, low and close are thus all on a level and the only mark on our chart will then be the horizontal dash representing the closing figure. Volume is depicted by drawing a vertical line up from the base line of the chart.

The opening price need not be recorded. Experience has shown that it seldom if ever has any significance in estimating future developments, which is all that ordinarily should interest us. The closing price is important, however. It is, in fact, the only price which many casual readers of the financial pages ever look at. It represents the final evaluation of the stock made by the market during the day. It may, of course, be registered in the first hour of trading, provided no other sales are subsequently effected, but, it becomes, nevertheless, the figure upon which a majority of prospective traders base their plans for the following day. Hence its technical significance, which will appear in various connotations in later chapters.

DIFFERENT TYPES OF SCALES

Many specific suggestions as to the details of charting are deferred for discussion in the second section of this book, but there is one chart feature which may well be considered here. Until recent years nearly all stock price charts were kept on the common form of graph paper ruled to what is known as plain or arithmetic scale. But, more and more chartists have now come to use what is known as semi-logarithmic paper, or sometimes as ratio or percentage paper. Our own experience indicates that the semi-logarithmic scale has definite advantages in this work; most of the charts reproduced in this book employ it.

The two types of scale may be distinguished at a glance by the fact that on arithmetic paper equal distances on the vertical scale (i.e. between horizontal lines) represent equal *amounts* in dollars, whereas on the semi-logarithmic paper they represent equal *percentage changes*. Thus, on arithmetic paper the distance between 10 and 20 on the vertical scale is exactly the same as that from 20 to 30, and from 30 to 40. On the logarithmic scale the difference from 10 to 20, representing an increase of 100%, is the same as that from 20 to 40, or from 40 to 80, in each case representing another 100% increase.

Percentage relations, it goes without saying, are important in trading in securities. The semi-logarithmic scale permits direct comparison of high and low priced stocks and makes it easier to choose the one offering the greater (percentage) profit on the funds to be invested. It facilitates the placing of stop-loss orders. Area patterns appear much the same on either type of paper but certain trend lines develop more advantageously on the ratio scale. Almost anyone can quickly become accustomed to making entries on semi-logarithmic paper. *We recommend its use.* However, its advantages are not so great as to require one to change who because of long familiarity and practice prefers an arithmetic sheet. Such percentage calculations as may seem to be required can, after all, be made on another sheet or in the head and the results then entered on the arithmetic chart if a record is desired.

Several firms specializing in the manufacture of graph paper and other engineers' and architects' supplies, now offer sheets specifically designed for stock charting, on which heavier lines to define the business week mark each sixth day on the time scale, and the price scale is subdivided into eighths to represent the standard fractions of the dollar in which stocks are traded on all American exchanges. These sheets are available in various sizes and with either arithmetic or logarithmic price and volume scales.

On weekly charts each vertical line represents a week's trading. The price range for the week is plotted thereon and usually the total volume, but the closing price may be omitted. The range extends, of course, from the highest price at which the stock sold on any day during the week to the lowest price at which it sold on any day; these two extremes might, and sometimes do, occur on the same day but the weekly chart makes no distinction as to day. Monthly charts are prepared in the same way but do not, as a rule, record volume. These two—often referred to as long-term or major charts—are used chiefly for determining important support and resistance levels and marking long-term trends. Weekly charts—if the reader prefers to keep his own—can be posted easily from the Sunday morning editions of those daily newspapers (e.g., the New York *Times* or Barron's Business and Financial Weekly) which publish a summary therein of the previous week's transactions.

In concluding this chapter on the construction of the charts which we shall study in succeeding chapters, it can well be said that there is no special virtue, certainly no magic, in the chart itself. It is simply a pictorial record of the trading history of the stock or stocks in which we may be interested. To the man possessed of a photographic memory no paper chart work is necessary; his mind records all the necessary data—he carries his charts in his head. Many of the expert "tape-readers" who have no use for charts are gifted with that rare memory talent which renders reference to graphic records unnecessary. But most of us are not so blessed; to us the chart is necessary and useful because it lends itself conveniently to the type of analysis which indicates future probabilities.

There is a saying in Wall Street to the effect that "there is nothing wrong with charts—the trouble is with the chartists." Which is simply another way of expressing the truth that it is not the chart itself but its interpretation that is important. Chart analysis is certainly neither easy nor fool-proof. Yet it is not at all uncommon for some casual investor who has no idea whatever of market technics to pick up a chart by chance and see in it something which he had not hitherto suspected—something perhaps which saves him from making an unfavorable commitment.

If you have never used stock charts, never paid much attention to them, you may be surprised at some of the significant things you will quickly detect as soon as you begin to study them seriously.

CHAPTER III

THE DOW THEORY

THE DOW THEORY is the granddaddy of all technical market studies. Although it is frequently criticized for being "too late," and occasionally derided (particularly in the early stages of a Bear Market) by those who rebel at accepting its verdicts, it is known by name to nearly everyone who has had any association with the stock market, and respected by most. Many who heed it in greater or less degree in determining their investment policies never realize that it is purely and simply "technical." It is built upon and concerned with nothing but the action of the stock market itself (as expressed in certain "averages"), deriving nothing from the business statistics on which the fundamentalists depend.

There is much in the writings of its original promulgator, Charles H. Dow, to suggest that he did not think of his "Theory" as a device for forecasting the stock market, or even as a guide for investors, but rather as a barometer of general business trends. Mr. Dow founded the Dow-Jones financial news service and is credited with the invention of stock market averages. The basic principles of the theory, which was later named after him, were outlined by him in editorials he wrote for the *Wall Street Journal*. Upon his death in 1902, his successor as editor of the *Journal*, William P. Hamilton, took up Dow's principles and, in the course of 27 years of writing on the stock market, organized them and formulated them into the Dow Theory as we know it today.

Before we proceed to any explanation of the theory itself, it will be necessary to examine the stock *averages* which it employs. Long before the time of Dow, the fact was familiar to bankers and business men that the securities of most established companies tended to go up or down in price together. Exceptions —stocks which moved against the general financial tide—were rare, nor did they as a rule persevere in that contrary course for more than a few days or weeks at a time. It is true that when a boom was on, the prices of some issues rose faster and farther than others, and when the trend was toward depression some stocks declined rapidly while others would put up considerable resistance to the forces that were dragging the market down—but the fact remained that most securities tended to swing together. (They still do, needless to say, and always will.)

This fact, as we have said, has long been commonly known and accepted— so completely taken for granted that its importance is usually overlooked. For it is important—tremendously important from many angles in addition to those which come within the province of this volume. One of the best of all reasons for a student of market technics to start with the Dow Theory is because that theory stresses the *general market trend*.

Charles Dow is believed to have been the first to make a thoroughgoing effort to express the general trend (or, more correctly, level) of the securities market in terms of the *average price* of a selected few representative stocks. As finally set up in January of 1897, in the form which has been continued to date, and used by him in his studies of market trends, there were two Dow-Jones averages. One was composed of the stocks of 20 railroad companies only, for the railroads were the dominant corporate enterprises of his day. The other, called the Industrial average, represented all other types of business, and was made up at first of only 12 issues. This number was increased to 20 in 1916 and to 30 on October 1, 1928.

THE DOW AVERAGES

The stocks included in these two averages have been changed from time to time in order to keep the lists up-to-date and as nearly representative as possible of their respective groups. It is interesting to note that the only railroad stock which has been included in the Rail average continuously from 1897 to 1956 is New York Central. Only General Electric of the present 30 industrial stocks was included in the original Industrial average and that was dropped at one time (in 1898) and subsequently reinserted. In 1929, all stocks of public utility companies were dropped from the Industrial average and a new Utility average of 20 issues was set up; in 1938 its number was reduced to 15. The 20 rail, 30 industrial and 15 utility stocks are now averaged together to make what is known as the Dow-Jones 65-Stock Composite. The history of these averages, the various adjustments that have been made in them and their method of computation, is an interesting story in itself which the reader may want to look up elsewhere. For our present purpose, it remains only to add that the Dow Theory pays no attention to the Utility or Composite averages; its interpretations are based on the Rail and Industrial averages only. (Although the specific Dow-Jones averages are always used in this connection, the Theory would presumably work just as well with any other equally representative indexes of railroad and industrial stocks.)

In recent years the values of the Dow-Jones averages have been computed for the end of each hour of trading as well as the end of the day. These hourly figures are published in the *Wall Street Journal* as well as on the Dow-Jones news ticker service. The *Wall Street Journal* also prints in each issue a summary of the important highs and lows of each average by date for the preceding two or three years. Their daily closing prices are reported in many other metropolitan daily newspapers.

Basic Tenets

To get back to the Dow Theory, itself, here are its basic tenets:—

1. *The Averages Discount Everything* (*except "Acts of God"*)—Because they reflect the combined market activities of thousands of investors, including those possessed of the greatest foresight and the best information on trends and events, the averages in their day-to-day fluctuations discount everything known, everything foreseeable, and every condition which can affect the supply of or the demand for corporate securities. Even unpredictable natural calamities when they happen are quickly appraised and their possible effects discounted.

2. *The Three Trends*—The "market," meaning the price of stocks in general, swings in trends of which the most important are its *Major or Primary Trends*. These are the extensive up or down movements which usually last for a year or more and result in general appreciation or depreciation in value of more than 20%. Movements in the direction of the Primary trend are interrupted at intervals by *Secondary* swings in the opposite direction—reactions or "corrections" which occur when the Primary move has temporarily "gotten ahead of itself." (Both Secondaries and the intervening segments of the Primary trend are frequently lumped together as Intermediate movements—a term which we shall find useful in subsequent discussions.) Finally, the Secondary trends are composed of *Minor* trends or day-to-day fluctuations which are unimportant.

3. *The Primary Trends*—These, as aforesaid, are the broad over-all up and down movements which usually (but not invariably) last for more than a year and may run for several years. So long as each successive rally (price advance) reaches a higher level than the one before it, and each secondary reaction stops (i.e., the price trend reverses from down to up) at a higher level than the previous reaction, the Primary Trend is *Up*. This is called a *Bull Market*. Conversely, when each intermediate decline carries prices to successively lower levels and each intervening rally fails to bring them back up to the top level of the preceding rally, the Primary Trend is *Down,* and that is called a *Bear Market*. (The term *bull* and *bear* are frequently used loosely with reference, respectively, to any sort of up or down movements, but we shall use them in this book only in connection with the Major or Primary movements of the market in the Dow sense.)

Ordinarily—theoretically at least—the Primary is the only one of the three trends with which the true long-term investor is concerned. His aim is to buy stocks as early as possible in a Bull Market—just as soon as he can be sure that one has started—and then hold them until (and only until) it becomes evident that it has ended and a Bear Market has started. He knows that he can safely disregard all the intervening Secondary reactions and Minor fluctuations. The trader, however, may well concern himself also with the Secondary swings, and it will appear later on in this book that he can do so with profit.

4. *The Secondary Trends*—These are the important reactions that interrupt the progress of prices in the Primary direction. They are the Intermediate declines or "corrections" which occur during Bull Markets, the Intermediate rallies or "recoveries" which occur in Bear Markets. Normally they last for from three weeks to as many months, and rarely longer. Normally they retrace from one third to two thirds of the gain (or loss as the case may be) in prices registered in the preceding swing in the Primary direction. Thus, in a Bull Market prices in terms of the Industrial average might rise steadily, or with only brief and minor interruptions, for a total gain of 30 points before a Secondary correction occurred; that correction might then be expected to produce a decline of not less than 10 points and not more than 20 points before a new Intermediate advance in the Primary Bull trend developed.

Note, however, that the one-third—two-thirds rule is not an unbreakable law; it is simply a statement of probabilities. Most Secondaries are confined within these limits; many of them stop very close to the halfway mark, retracing 50% of the preceding Primary swing; they seldom run less than one third but some of them cancel nearly all of it.

Thus we have two criteria by which to recognize a Secondary trend. Any price movement contrary in direction to the Primary trend which lasts for at least three weeks and retraces at least one third of the preceding net move in the Primary direction (from the end of the preceding Secondary to the beginning of this one, disregarding minor fluctuations) is labeled as of Intermediate rank, i.e. a true Secondary. Despite these criteria, however, the Secondary trend is often confusing; its recognition, its correct appraisal at the time it develops and while it is in process, poses the Dow Theorist's most difficult problem. We shall have more to say about this later.

5. *The Minor Trends*—These are the brief (rarely as long as three weeks —usually less than six days) fluctuations which are—so far as the Dow Theory is concerned—meaningless in themselves, but which in toto make up the Intermediate trends. Usually, but not always, an Intermediate swing, whether a Secondary or the segment of a Primary between successive Secondaries, is made up of a series of three or more distinguishable Minor waves. Inferences drawn from these day-to-day fluctuations are quite apt to be misleading. The Minor trend is the only one of the three trends which can be "manipulated" (although it is, in fact, doubtful if under present conditions even that can be purposely manipulated to any important extent). Primary and Secondary trends cannot be manipulated; it would strain the resources of the U. S. Treasury to do so.

Right here, before we go on to state a sixth Dow tenet, we may well take time out for a few minutes to clarify the concept of the three trends by drawing an analogy between the movements of the stock market and the movements of the sea. The Major (Primary) trends in stock prices are like the tides. We can compare a Bull Market to an incoming or flood tide which carries the water farther and farther up the beach until finally it reaches high-water mark and begins to turn. Then follows the receding or ebb tide comparable to a Bear Market. But all the time, during both ebb and flow of the tide, the waves are rolling in, breaking on the beach and then receding. While the tide is rising, each succeeding wave pushes a little farther up onto the shore and, as it recedes, does not carry the water quite so far back as did its predecessor. During the tidal ebb, each advancing wave falls a little short of the mark set by the one before it, and each receding wave uncovers a little more of the beach. These waves are the Intermediate trends—Primary or Secondary depending on whether their movement is with or against the direction of the tide. Meanwhile, the surface of the water is constantly agitated by wavelets, ripples and "catspaws" moving with, or against or across the trend of the waves—these are analogous to the market's Minor trends, its unimportant day-to-day fluctuations. The tide, the wave and the ripple represent, respectively, the Primary or Major, the Secondary or Intermediate, and the Minor trends of the market.

TIDE, WAVE AND RIPPLE

A shore dweller who had no tide-table might set about determining the direction of the tide by driving a stake in the beach at the highest point reached by an incoming wave. Then if the next wave pushed the water up beyond his stake he would know the tide was rising. If he shifted his stake with the peak mark of each wave, a time would come when one wave would stop and start to recede short of his previous mark; then he would know that the tide had turned, had started to ebb. That, in effect (and much simplified), is what the Dow Theorist does in defining the trend of the stock market.

The comparison with tide, wave and ripple has been used since the earliest days of the Dow Theory. It is even possible that the movements of the sea may have suggested the elements of the theory to Dow. But the analogy cannot be pushed too far. The tides and waves of the stock market are nothing like as regular as those of the ocean. Tables can be prepared years in advance to predict accurately the time of every ebb and flow of the waters, but no time-tables are provided by the Dow Theory for the stock market. We may return to some points of this comparison later, but we must proceed now to take up the remaining tenets and rules of the Theory.

MAJOR TREND PHASES

6. *The Bull Market*—Primary up trends are usually (but not invariably) divisible into three phases. The first is the phase of *accumulation* during which far-sighted investors, sensing that business although now depressed is due to

turn up, are willing to pick up all the shares offered by discouraged and distressed sellers, and to raise their bids gradually as such selling diminishes in volume. Financial reports are still bad—in fact, often at their worst—during this phase. The "public" is completely disgusted with the stock market—out of it entirely. Activity is only moderate but beginning to increase on the rallies (minor advances). The second phase is one of fairly steady advance and increasing activity as the improved tone of business and a rising trend in corporate earnings begin to attract attention. It is during this phase that the "technical" trader normally is able to reap his best harvest of profits. Finally comes the third phase when the market boils with activity as the "public" flocks to the boardrooms. All the financial news is good; price advances are spectacular and frequently "make the front page" of the daily papers; new issues are brought out in increasing numbers. It is during this phase that one of your friends will call up and blithely remark, "Say, I see the market is going up. What's a good buy?"—all oblivious of the fact that it has been going up for perhaps two years, has already gone up a long ways and is now reaching the stage where it might be more appropriate to ask "What's a good thing to sell?" In the last stage of this phase, with speculation rampant, volume continues to rise but "air pockets" appear with increasing frequency; the "cats and dogs" (low-priced stocks of no investment value) are whirled up but more and more of the top-grade issues refuse to follow.

7. *The Bear Market*—Primary down trends are also usually (but again not invariably) characterized by three phases. The first is the *distribution* period (which really starts in the later stages of the preceding Bull Market). During this phase far-sighted investors sense the fact that business earnings have reached an abnormal height and unload their holdings at an increasing pace. Trading volume is still high though tending to diminish on rallies and the "public" is still active but beginning to show signs of frustration as hoped-for profits fade away. The second phase is the *panic* phase. Buyers begin to thin out and sellers become more urgent; the downward trend of prices suddenly accelerates into an almost vertical drop while volume mounts to climactic proportions. After the panic phase (which usually runs too far relative to then existing business conditions) there may be a fairly long Secondary recovery or a sidewise movement and then the third phase begins. This is characterized by discouraged selling on the part of those investors who held on through the panic or, perhaps, bought during it because stocks looked cheap in comparison with prices which had ruled a few months earlier. The business news now begins to deteriorate. As the third phase proceeds the downward movement is less rapid but is maintained by more and more distress selling from those who have to raise cash for other needs. The "cats and dogs" may lose practically all their previous Bull advance in the first two phases. Better grade stocks decline more gradually, because their owners cling to them to the last, and the final stage of a Bear

Market in consequence is frequently concentrated in such issues. The Bear Market ends when everything in the way of possible bad news, the worst to be expected, has been discounted, and it is usually over before all the bad news is "out."

The three Bear Market phases described in the preceding paragraph are not the same as those named by others who have discussed this subject but the writers of this study feel that they represent a more accurate and realistic division of the Primary down moves of the past thirty years. The reader should be warned, however, that no two Bear Markets are exactly alike, and neither are any two Bull Markets. Some may lack one or another of the three typical phases. A few Major advances have passed from the first to the third stage with only a very brief and rapid intervening mark-up. A few short Bear Markets have developed no marked panic phase and others have ended with it, as in April 1939. No time limits can be set for any phase; the third stage of a Bull Market, for example, the phase of excited speculation and great public activity, may last for more than a year or run out in a month or two. The panic phase of a Bear Market is usually exhausted in a very few weeks if not in days, but the 1929-1932 decline was interspersed with at least five panic waves of major proportions. Nevertheless the typical characteristics of Primary trends are well worth keeping in mind. If you know the symptoms which normally accompany the last stage of a Bull Market, for example, you are less likely to be deluded by its exciting atmosphere.

PRINCIPLE OF CONFIRMATION

8. *The Two Averages Must Confirm*—This is the most often questioned and the most difficult to rationalize of all the Dow principles. Yet it has stood the test of time; the fact that it has "worked" is not disputed by any who have carefully examined the records. Those who have disregarded it in practice have, more often than not, had occasion to regret their apostasy. What it means is that *no* valid signal of a change in trend can be produced by the action of one average alone. Take, for example, the hypothetical case shown in Diagram 1 on next page. In this we assume that a Bear Market has been in effect for several months and then, starting at "a," the Industrial average rises (along with the Rails) in a Secondary recovery to "b." On their next decline, however, the Industrials drop only to "c," which is higher than "a," and then turn up to "d," which is higher than "b." At this point the Industrials have "signaled" a change in trend from down to up. But note the Rails during this period; their decline from "b" to "c" carried them lower than "a" and their subsequent advance from "c" to "d" has not taken them above "b." They have (so far) refused to *confirm* the Industrials and, hence, the Major trend of the market must be regarded as *still Down*. Should the Rails

DIAGRAM 1.   A hypothetical daily market chart to show how one
average may fail to confirm the other's Dow signal.   Closing prices,
indicated by short horizontal dashes, are connected with vertical
lines to make the day-to-day trend easier to follow.

go on to rise eventually above their "b," then and then only would we have
definite signal of a turn in the tide.   Until such a development, however, the
chances remain that the Industrials will not be able to continue their upward
course alone, that they will ultimately be dragged down again by the Rails.
At best the direction of the Primary trend is still in doubt.

The above illustrates only one of the many ways in which the principle of
confirmation applies.   Note also that at "c," it might have been said that
the Industrials had thus far not confirmed the Rails in continuing the down
trend—but this had to do only with the continuation or reaffirmation of an
existing trend, regarding which more later.   It is not necessary that the two

averages confirm on the same day. Frequently both will move into new high (or low) ground together, but there are plenty of cases in which one or the other lags behind for days, weeks or even a month or two. One must be patient in these doubtful cases and wait until the market declares itself in definite fashion.

9. *"Volume Goes with the Trend"*—Those words, which you may often hear spoken with ritual solemnity but little understanding, are the colloquial expression for the general truth that trading activity tends to expand as prices move in the direction of the prevailing Primary trend. Thus, in a Bull Market, volume increases when prices rise and dwindles as prices decline; in Bear Markets, turnover increases when prices drop and dries up as they recover. To a lesser degree, this holds for Secondary trends also, especially in the early stages of an extended Secondary recovery within a Bear Market when activity may show a tendency to pick up on the Minor rallies and diminish on the Minor setbacks. But to this rule again there are exceptions, and useful conclusions can seldom be drawn from the volume manifestations of a few days, much less a single trading session; it is only the over-all and relative volume trend over a period of time that may produce helpful indications. Moreover, in Dow Theory, *conclusive* signals as to the market's trend are produced in the final analysis only by price movement. Volume simply affords collateral evidence which may aid interpretation of otherwise doubtful situations. (We shall have much more to say in later chapters about volume in specific relation to other technical phenomena.)

10. *"Lines" May Substitute for Secondaries*—A *Line* in Dow Theory parlance is a sidewise movement (as it appears on the charts) in one or both of the averages, which lasts for two or three weeks or, sometimes, for as many months, in the course of which prices fluctuate within a range of approximately 5% or less (of their mean figure). The formation of a Line signifies that pressure of buying and selling is more or less in balance. Eventually, of course, either the offerings within that price range are exhausted and those who want to buy stocks have to raise their bids to induce owners to sell, or else those who are eager to sell at the "Line" price range find that buyers have vanished and that in consequence they must cut their prices in order to dispose of their shares. Hence, an advance in prices through the upper limits of an established Line is a bullish signal and, conversely, a break down through its lower limits is a bearish signal. Generally speaking, the longer the Line (in duration) and the narrower or more compact its price range, the greater the significance of its ultimate breakout.

Lines occur often enough to make their recognition essential to followers of Dow's principles. They may develop at important tops or bottoms, signalizing periods of distribution or of accumulation, respectively, but they come more frequently as interludes of rest or consolidation in the progress of established Major trends. Under those circumstances, they take the place of normal Secondary waves. A Line may develop in one average while the other is going through a typical Secondary reaction. It is worth noting that a price movement out of a Line, either up or down, is usually followed by a more extensive additional move in the same direction than can be counted on to follow the "signal" produced when a new wave pushes beyond the limits set by a preceding Primary wave. The direction in which prices will break out of a Line cannot be determined in advance of the actual movement. The 5% limit ordinarily assigned to a Line is arbitrarily based on experience; there have been a few slightly wider sidewise movements which by virtue of their compactness and well-defined boundaries could be construed as true Lines. (Farther on in this book we shall see that the Dow Line is in many respects similar to the more strictly defined patterns known as Rectangles which appear on the charts of individual stocks.)

11. *Only Closing Prices Used*—Dow Theory pays no attention to any extreme highs or lows which may be registered during a day and before the market closes, but takes into account only the closing figures, i.e., the average of the day's final sale prices for the component issues. We have discussed the psychological importance of the end-of-day prices under the subject of chart construction and need not deal with it further here except to say that this is another Dow rule which has stood the test of time. It works thus: Suppose an intermediate advance in a Primary up trend reaches its peak on a certain day at 11 a.m. at which hour the Industrial average figures at, say, 152.45, and then falls back to close at 150.70. All that the next advance will have to do in order to indicate that the Primary trend is still *up* is register a daily close above 150.70. The previous intra-day high of 152.45 does not count. Conversely, using the same figures for our first advance, if the next up swing carries prices to an intra-day high at, say, 152.60, but fails to register a closing price above 150.70, the continuation of the Primary Bull trend is still in doubt.

In recent years, differences of opinion have risen among market students as to the extent to which an average should push beyond a previous limit (top or bottom figure) in order to signal (or confirm or reaffirm, as the case may be) a market trend. Dow and Hamilton evidently regarded any penetration, even as little as .01, in closing price as a valid signal, but some modern commentators have required penetration by a full point (1.00). We think that the original view has the best of the argument, that the record shows little or nothing in practical results to favor any of the proposed modifications. One incident in June of 1946, to which we shall refer in the following chapter, shows a decided advantage for the orthodox "any-penetration-whatever" rule.

12. *A Trend Should Be Assumed to Continue in Effect Until Such Time as Its Reversal Has Been Definitely Signaled*—This Dow Theory tenet is one which, perhaps more than any other, has evoked criticism. Yet when correctly

understood, it, like all the others we have enumerated, stands up under practical test.   What it states is really a *probability*.   It is a warning against changing one's market position too soon, against "jumping the gun."   It does not
imply that one should delay action by one unnecessary minute once a signal of
change in trend has appeared, but it expresses the experience that the odds are
in favor of the man who waits until he is sure, and against the other fellow
who buys (or sells) prematurely.   These odds cannot be stated in mathematical
language such as two-to-one or three-to-one; as a matter of fact they are
constantly changing.   Bull Markets do not climb forever and Bear Markets
always reach a bottom sooner or later.   When a new Primary trend is first
definitely signaled by the action of the two averages, the odds that it will be
continued despite any near-term reactions or interruptions are at their greatest.
But as this Primary trend carries on, the odds in favor of its further extension
grow smaller.   Thus, each successive reaffirmation of a Bull Market (new Intermediate high in one average confirmed by a new Intermediate high in the other)
carries relatively less weight.   The incentive to buy, the prospect of selling new
purchases at a profit, is smaller after a Bull Market has been in existence for
several months than it was when the Primary up trend was first recognized,
but this twelfth Dow tenet says, "Hold your position pending contrary orders."

A corollary to this tenet, which is not so contradictory as it may at first
seem, is:—A reversal in trend can occur *any time* after that trend has been confirmed.   This can be taken simply as a warning that the Dow Theory investor
must watch the market constantly so long as he has any commitment in it.

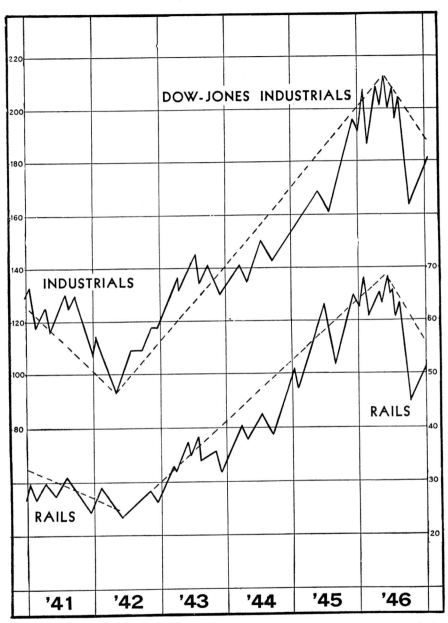

FIGURE 2. "Swing" chart showing all the Intermediate and some of the more extensive Minor trends of the Dow-Jones Industrial and Rail averages, January, 1941 to December, 1946. Industrial price scale left; Rails right.

CHAPTER IV

THE DOW THEORY IN PRACTICE

A T THIS point, the reader, if he has little previous knowledge of the stock
market, may be suffering a mild attack of mental indigestion. The Dow
Theory is a pretty big dose to swallow at one sitting. We departed deliberately in the foregoing chapter from the order in which its principles are usually stated, in an effort to make it a little easier to follow and understand.
Actually, not all of the twelve tenets we named are of equal import. The
essential rules are contained in 2, 3, 4, 5, 8, 10 and 11. Number 1 is, of
course, the basic assumption, the philosophical justification for these rules. The
other points (6, 7, 9, and 12) furnish "background material," as the news
reporters might put it, which aid in interpretation. Theoretically one should,
by strict adherence to the essential rules alone, accomplish just as much as he
could with the added collateral evidence.

But the utilization of Dow Theory is, after all, a matter of interpretation.
You may memorize its principles verbatim and yet be confounded when you
attempt to apply them to an actual market situation. We can better organize
our knowledge of the Theory and acquire some understanding of its interpretation by following through a few years of market action and seeing how it looked
at the time through the eyes of a Dow Theorist. For this purpose we may well
take the period from late 1941 to the beginning of 1947, since this covers
the end of one Bear Market, an entire long Bull Market and part of another
Bear Market, and includes examples of most of the market phenomena with
which the Dow Theory has to deal.

FIVE YEARS OF DOW INTERPRETATION

Figure 2 is a condensed chart of the course of the two Dow-Jones averages
from January 1, 1941 to December 31, 1946, on which most of the Minor trends
have been disregarded but all the recognized Intermediate swings (Primary and
Secondary) have been indicated. Certain portions of this history will be supplemented by complete daily charts in connection with our detailed discussion
which follows.

The year 1941 opened with the stock market in a Minor rally. A Primary
Bear Market had been signaled when prices collapsed in the Spring of 1940, and
that Bear Market was still in effect. After the May panic had ended, a Secondary recovery swing, which lasted for more than five months, had regained more

FIGURE 3. Closing price levels of the Dow-Jones Industrial and Rail averages, February 1 to August 31, 1941, and total daily market volume. Vertical lines show net daily change from one closing level to next.

than half of the ground previously lost by the averages, carrying the Industrials from their closing price of 111.84 on June 10 to 138.12 on November 9 and the Rails from 22.14 on May 21 to 30.29 on November 14.   (During this long Bear Market Secondary, incidentally, volume tended to increase on rallies, which encouraged many who did not hold strictly to first principles to believe that this rise was the beginning of a new Bull trend—illustrating the point we cited under "Volume" in Chapter III.)   From the November highs, however, the trend turned down again.   Then a Minor rally developed, as we have said, at the end of the year, reaching its peak on January 10 at 133.59 in the Industrials and 29.73 in the Rails.   From there prices fell again to 117.66 and 26.54, respectively, on February 14.

The First Severe Test

The next few months will be particularly interesting for us to trace because they put the Dow Theory to a real test.   Figure 3 shows the daily ranges and closing prices of the two averages and total daily market volume for the seven months from February 1 to August 31, 1941.   Before we examine it in detail, however, let us first review the situation on February 14.   The Bear Market lows to date had been registered in May-June, 1940.   Thereafter an extended Intermediate recovery had advanced the Industrial average 26.28 points and the Rail average 8.15 points.   This had been followed by a three-month decline of 20.46 and 3.75 points, respectively, and this decline, incidentally, had consisted of three well defined Minor waves.   In duration and in extent of price change with respect to the previous swing—46% in the Rails and nearly 78% in the Industrials—this down swing qualified as an Intermediate trend—and now prices were turning up again.   Dow Theorists were on the alert.   If both averages could continue their rise to levels above their high closes of the previous November (138.12 and 30.29), that action would constitute a signal of a new Primary Bull Market, and re-investment of funds withdrawn from stocks in May, 1940 would be at once in order.   Also, it would then be necessary to go back and label the May-June lows of 1940 as the end of a Bear Market, the advance to November as the first Primary swing in the new Bull Market, and the decline to February as its first Secondary reaction.   But note that Rule 12 of our preceding chapter applied here; the presumption was that it was still a Bear Market until a definite signal to the contrary appeared.

Let us now turn again to Figure 3 and see what actually did happen.   The Industrials rallied for six weeks, reaching 124.65 on April 3.   The Rails got up to 29.75 on the same date, registering double the percentage gain of the Industrials, but both averages were still below their November highs.   Then the Industrials slipped off, within two weeks had broken down below their February low and drifted down to close at 115.30 on May 1.   This average was, therefore, still in an Intermediate down trend.   But the Rails meanwhile were staging a different sort of performance. They dropped back from their April 3 high for two weeks but held at 27.72, rallied smartly and then sold off again to 27.43 on May 31. The picture became at once even more interesting. Here was a *divergence* between the two averages, a failure to confirm; the Rails after two opportunities were refusing to confirm the Industrials in the latter's down trend.

FAILURE TO CONFIRM

When prices began to work upward in June, many commentators seized upon this "failure to confirm" as a bullish omen and the wishful thinkers again talked Bull Market. There is an unfortunate tendency in "the street" to over-stress any such divergence, particularly when it can be twisted into a favorable sign. The fact is that, in Dow Theory, the refusal of one average to confirm the other can never produce a *positive* signal of any sort. It has only negative connotations. Divergences sometimes occur at reversals in the Major trend— there have been several instances in market history of which perhaps the most remarkable occurred way back in 1901 and 1902, and we shall soon inspect another—but they also occur with at least equal frequency at times when no Major reversal is developing, and the instance we are here discussing was one of the latter.

So the situation at the end of May in 1941 was precisely the same to the Dow Theorist, insofar as the Major trend was concerned, as it had been on February 14. The June-July rally topped out in the Rails at 30.88 on August 1, and in the Industrials at 130.06 on July 28 (compare these figures with their 1940 November highs) and prices then declined at an accelerating pace which culminated, temporarily, in the "Pearl Harbor" panic. This took the Industrial average below its previous Bear Market low (111.84 on June 10, 1940), although the Rails again did not follow. They had, however, by this time broken below their previous (February 14) Intermediate bottom by a liberal margin.

The next period of importance began in April, 1942. We can skip any detailed chart of the months between December and April because they posed no Dow Theory problems. After a Minor rally in the Rails in January, prices simply drifted lower and lower but it was increasingly evident that trading volume did not expand on the dips (minor declines). Liquidation was drying up; the boardrooms were void of customers; the atmosphere was typical of the last stages of a Bear Market.

Our next chart (Figure 4) shows the daily action of the averages from March 2 to October 31, 1942. New lows (since 1940) were registered in both in late April, at 23.72 on April 24 in the Rails and at 92.92 on April 28 in the Industrials. Shortly thereafter another notable divergence developed, when after rallying for only seven days, the Railroad index began to slip off while the other average kept right on going up. Trading activity remained at a low ebb

FIGURE 4. Daily closing price levels of the Dow-Jones Industrial and Rail averages from March 2 to October 31, 1942, and total daily market volume. This period saw the beginning of a four-year Major Bull Market.

(there was no sustained volume increase, in fact, until late September). On June 1, the Rails dropped to another new low and on the 2d closed at 23.31. On June 22 it looked as though the Industrials were going to be pulled down again, but only a few days later the best rally in months got started, taking the Industrials to new highs and more than recovering all of the April-May loss in the Rails. Activity also speeded up briefly, with one day registering a greater turnover than the market had enjoyed in any session since early January.

Signs of Major Turn

Again the Dow Theorists were very much on the alert. An advance of Intermediate proportions was obviously under way. Until proved otherwise it had to be labeled a Secondary within the Bear Market which was still presumably in effect, but that Major down trend had by now run for nearly three years— nearly as long as any on record—and its last decline had shown no selling pressure whatever, simply a dull drift. This presumed Secondary might turn out to be instead a new Primary; hopes for such a denouement had been blighted twelve months earlier under somewhat similar circumstances but this time prices were lower and there was a different "feel" to the market. The general news offered little encouragement but the Dow Theory does not concern itself with any news other than that made by the market itself (which discounts all other kinds of news). In any event, there was nothing to do but wait and see —let the market in its own time and way state its own case.

In early July, the Industrials started to "mark time"; for eleven weeks they fluctuated within a 5-point range, building a typical Dow Line from which they emerged on the *up side* in late September. The Rails pushed up to a new high for the move at the same time, and by November 2 both averages had surpassed their rally tops of the preceding January. At this stage some Dow Theorists were willing to announce that a Bull Market had been signaled. Their arguments, aside from points of a non-technical nature or having nothing to do with Dow Theory, were:—

1. The conspicuously low level of volume at the April-June bottom, typical of the end of a Bear swing. (*True and cogent.*)

2. The Rail average had refused to follow the Industrials into new *Major* low ground at that time. It had held above its closing level of May, 1940. (*Also true, but of questionable significance. More about this later.*)

3. The Industrials had constructed a Line and gone up out of it. (*Again true, but the Line was somewhat short to have, beyond doubt, Major purport.*)

4. The Rail average had for four months produced successively higher Minor tops and bottoms. (*And this also was true but did not permit of positive differentiation from a Bear Market Secondary.*)

The more conservative Dow Theorists were not yet convinced. They maintained that this up trend had yet to undergo the test, bound to occur sooner or later, of an Intermediate reaction. They admitted that the picture was most encouraging but called attention to the fact that, except for Point 1, it was no better than that of November, 1940. Let's follow along through the next five months. Our next chart (Figure 5) shows the daily market action from November 1, 1942 to June 30, 1943.

THE BULL SIGNAL

After reaching 29.28 at their close on November 2, the Rails declined in almost a straight line for six weeks to 26.03 on December 14. This move indubitably rated as an Intermediate in duration and it had "given up" more than half of that average's entire advance from the June 2 low point. The industrial index, however, held stoutly in another narrow Line throughout November, December and January. From December 14, the Rails turned up and finally, on February 1, 1943, closed at 29.55, out above their previous Intermediate top of 29.28 recorded the previous November. By then the Industrials had also moved up into new high ground. This development at last satisfied every strictest requirement of Dow Theory; a new Primary Bull Market was in force. Trading volume had also been expanding on each Minor advance during the Fall and Winter months but its evidence was not needed; the price action alone was conclusive. The Rails had produced the necessary sequence of higher Intermediate tops and bottoms. In the Industrials, Lines had served the purposes of the Theory as substitutes for Intermediate reactions.

It was necessary now to re-label the up move from April-June to November of 1942 as the first Primary swing in a Bull Market. The decline of the Rails from November 2 to December 14 was now recognized as the first Secondary within that Major up trend.

We may turn back for a moment at this point to comment on the performance of the Rail index in June, 1942. Because it held then above its low of May, 1940, some commentators have maintained that the Bull Market should really have been dated from that former year as representing the last "confirmed" lows. This strikes us as rather impractical hair-splitting. Regardless of the 1.17 higher level in the Rail average in June, 1942, a genuine Bull move did not start until that time. We suspect that before many years have passed, Dow Theorists will have occasion greatly to regret the importance which has since been assigned to the Rails' "failure to confirm" in the Spring of 1942. Remember, such a divergence does not and cannot produce a positive signal; at the time of its occurrence it can serve merely to negative or cast in doubt the implications of the other average; only subsequent action in the opposite direction can establish the existence of a change in trend. If the Rails' decline in May, 1942 had carried them below 22.14 but their subsequent action had followed the course which it actually did, point for point but at a lower level, a

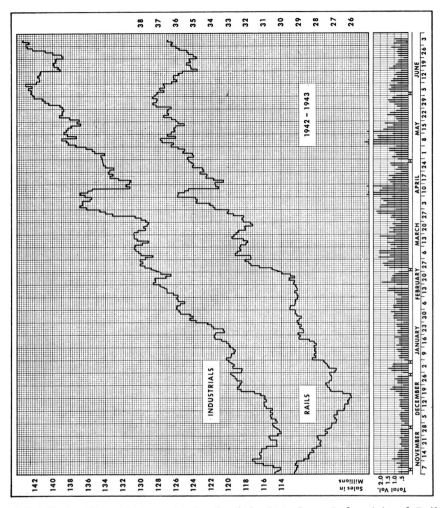

FIGURE 5. Daily closing price levels of the Dow-Jones Industrial and Rail averages from November 2, 1942 to June 30, 1943, and total daily market volume. This chart follows and should be compared with Figure 4. The decline in the Rail average during November and early December produced the first test of the Major trend since the preceding June. When this index recovered and, on February 1, 1943, closed above its November 2 high, a Primary Bull Market was thereby signaled according to Dow Theory.

Bull Market signal would nevertheless have been given at the very same time, not one day later and not one day sooner.

Moreover, a divergence does not necessarily imply that a move of consequence in the opposite direction will ensue. We have already examined one comparable instance (in the Spring of 1941) which resulted otherwise. Logically, also, if a failure to confirm such as occurred in 1942 is to be taken as an indication of a turn in trend, then its opposite, i.e., confirmation or reaffirmation by both averages, should argue with equal force *against* a turn in trend. Yet the simple truth is that many more Major reversals have come when the averages were in agreement than when they were divergent. We have no wish to belabor the point or waste the reader's time but we do feel that he should be warned against the wishful thinking which every "failure to confirm" seems to inspire when the market is in a Bear trend.

To return to our history, the averages closed at 125.88 and 29.51, respectively, on the day following our conclusive Bull Market signal in February, 1943. Theoretically, there is where an investor who followed the Dow Theory strictly would have bought his stocks. (Those who were satisfied that the Primary trend was up in November, 1942, bought with the averages around 114.60 and 29.20.) It was reasonable to assume that this Bull Market, which as yet showed few of the usual characteristics of the second phase and none whatever of the third phase, would continue for some time to come. The next four months produced no market developments that required interpretative attention and we can move on to the events of July. Figure 6 charts the action from July 1, 1943 to January 31, 1944.

THE FIRST CORRECTION

After closing at 145.82 on July 14, 1943, the Industrial average drifted off. The Rails pushed up to a new high (38.30) ten days later but the Industrials refused to join in the rally and then both indexes cracked down sharply for seven sessions. Turnover increased and the decline was the greatest that had occurred in the Bull Market up to that date, but everyone realized that the market after several months of quite persistent advance was "entitled to a correction." In neither duration nor extent could this down move be qualified as more than a Minor trend. Next ensued three months of desultory fluctuation with little net progress in either average. The Industrials pulled up to 141.75 on September 20 and then drifted off again, while the Rails struggled back to 35.53 on October 27. Another quick break developed in early November, culminating in a high-volume shake-out which cut the value of the Industrials by 3.56 points and the Rails by 1.75 on November 8. Prices rallied a little and sold off again, reaching new lows (since early Spring) on November 30—Industrials 129.57 and Rails 31.50.

There was no question now but what a full-fledged Secondary reaction had

FIGURE 6. Daily closing prices of Dow-Jones Industrial and Rail averages, and total market volume, July 1, 1943 to January 31, 1944.

developed. The problem for Dow interpreters was whether more than that was involved. If the first drop in July could be construed as an Intermediate trend in itself, and the August-October action as another Intermediate swing, then the November break would signal a Bear Market. As a matter of fact, no Dow Theorist, so far as we know, gave very serious consideration to any such interpretation. The July break, as aforesaid, did not rate as an Intermediate in either duration or points re-traced; the whole move from July to November, 1943, had to be regarded as all-of-a-piece, all one Secondary reaction. The real Major trend test would come on the next advance whenever that should develop; if that failed to top the July peaks and prices thereafter declined to new lows, a Bear Market would indeed be in effect.

The decision was long deferred. Prices began again to move up, but the advance in the Industrials was slow and grudging. The Rails forged ahead more rapidly and pushed through their July top on February 17, 1944, going on to a Minor peak at 40.48 on March 21. The Industrial average attained 141 on March 13, but still nearly 5 points below its "signal" level, faltered and fell back. Here was another striking case of "failure to confirm." For those who chose to assign grave significance to such developments, it could have only a very bearish meaning. But all it did mean in fact was that continuation of the Primary Bull move had not *as yet* been confirmed. Only if both averages now declined and closed below their respective November 30 bottoms would the new high registered by the Rails alone in February have to be disregarded and a Primary Bear Market announced. In brief, the situation at the end of March was no whit different, so far as its Major trend implications were concerned, from what it had been in early January before the Rails pushed through.

(If our reader here finds the constant repetition of terms—Major, Intermediate, Rails, Industrials, etc.—beginning to dull his interest and clog his understanding, we can only plead that we know of no way to avoid it. Skip along, if you wish, to another chapter and then turn back later to resume this study.)

BULL TREND REAFFIRMED

The situation remained in doubt (but subject always to that basic presumption of the Dow Theory which we named as Number 12 in the preceding chapter) until June 15, 1944, when the Industrials finally came through to close at 145.86. It had taken them four months to confirm the Rails, almost a full year to reaffirm the Primary up trend. The effect of this "signal" on traders was electric; trading volume increased by 650,000 shares on the following day as prices jumped another full point.

The following twelve months need no detailed discussion as they produced nothing in the way of market action to give a Dow Theorist any concern. Prices drifted off irregularly for nine weeks after mid-July but their net loss was

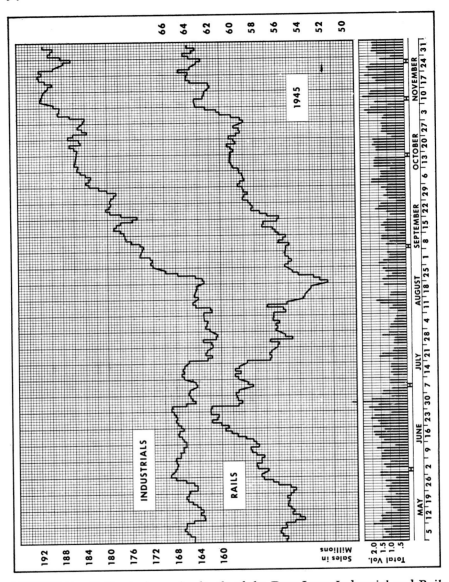

FIGURE 7.   Daily closing price levels of the Dow-Jones Industrial and Rail averages from May 1 to November 30, 1945, and total daily market volume. This period, which saw the end of World War II, produced only a moderate Secondary correction in the Primary Bull Market which had already run for three years from its beginnings in April-June, 1942.

of minor proportions, and they then climbed with only brief interruptions to 169.08 in the Industrial index on May 29, 1945 and 63.06 in the Rail index on June 26, 1945. We should take a brief look at the period which followed, not because it illustrates anything new in our study but because it takes in the surrender of Japan and the end of fighting in World War II.

Our next chart (Figure 7) covers the seven months from May 1 to November 30, 1945. The Industrials held steady for four weeks while the Rails were making the spurt to their June 26 top. On June 28, with nothing in the newspaper headlines to account for such a radical trend change, prices broke sharply and turnover climbed to nearly three million shares, the highest day's total for the Bull Market up to that time. But the Industrial average gave ground reluctantly thereafter and by July 26, at 160.91, had given up less than 5% of its top price. The Rails shook down rapidly, however. The Hiroshima bomb was dropped on August 5 and Japan surrendered on the 14th. The Industrials were now rallying up from their July 26 low but the Rails couldn't hold and plunged again, hitting bottom finally (for this move) on August 20 at 51.48, for a loss of more than 18% of their June peak value.

THE RAILS FALTER

Before we go on with our examination of the market action here, it is interesting to note that up to this point the Rail average has been the "hero" of our story. Starting with its refusal to go down to a new Bear Market low in June of 1942, it was the spearhead of each important advance, had staged the most spectacular rallies, had gained 170% in value as compared with the Industrials' 82%. In retrospect, the explanation is obvious: The railroads were the chief business beneficiaries of the war. They were rolling up profits, paying off indebtedness and reducing their fixed charges at a rate unheard of in this generation (and probably never to be seen again). While the "public's" eye was on the traditional and better publicized "war industries," the market began as far back as Pearl Harbor shrewdly to appraise and discount this unprecedented harvest for the Rails. But from here on the picture changes and the Rails become the laggards. As we look back now it is just as obvious that with equal shrewdness the market began in July of 1945 to discount a change in their fortunes. An illuminating demonstration of the basic assumption (Tenet Number 1) in Dow Theory!

Turning back to our chart, prices began to push up again with renewed vigor after August 20. Both averages had experienced a Secondary reaction and now Dow Theorists had to watch closely to see if the Primary up trend would again be reaffirmed by their going to new highs. The Industrials "made the grade" when they closed at 169.89 on August 24, but the Rails had much more ground to recover and were running into offerings as they came up in succession to each of the Minor bottom levels of their June-August down trend (a phenomenon to which we shall devote some attention later on in the chapter on "Support and Resistance"). Not until early November, 1945 were they able to confirm the signal of the Industrials by closing above 63.06. At this point, the averages had once again announced that the Primary Bull Market was still in force. It had now lasted for three and a half years—longer than most Bull Markets, and "third phase" signs were rapidly appearing. The public was buying, the boardrooms were crowded, stock market news was making the front pages of even small city newspapers, the "cats and dogs" were being whooped up, business was booming.

With both averages in new high ground and the Bull Market reaffirmed, all previous low points could now be disregarded. For example, the 160.91 bottom of July 26 in the Industrials and the 51.48 of August 20 in the Rails had no further significance *in Dow Theory*. This is a point we have not stressed heretofore, but it is important. It might, indeed, be added to our set of rules in the preceding chapter were it not implicit in the basic tenets. Once a Primary trend has been confirmed or re-confirmed, the past is forgotten and everything hinges on future action. At the end of 1945, with "third phase" symptoms rife, the action of the market had to be followed with redoubled vigilance. The third phase could last for two more years (as it did in 1927-1929) or be concluded at any moment. Our next chart (Figure 8) carries us through May, 1946.

THE SPRING OF 1946

The market went through a minor setback in late December—a development which has come to be expected as the normal pattern for that month and which is usually attributed to "tax selling"—and stormed ahead again in January, 1946. Daily volume on January 18 exceeded three million shares for the first time in more than five years. During the first week of February, prices "churned" with little net change. Extreme high closes were registered during this period by the Rail average at 68.23 on February 5, and by the Industrial average at 206.97 on February 2. On February 9, both started to slide off, pulled back sharply from the 13th to the 16th, and then broke in a selling wave that ran to a climax on February 26 with closings at 60.53 and 186.02, respectively. The loss in the Industrials was the greatest in points (20.95) they had suffered during the entire Bull Market; in the Rails it was exceeded only by their July-August decline of the previous year. It amounted to a little more than 10% in the former and 11% in the latter, and gave up a little less than half of their advances from the 1945 Summer lows. The decline was three weeks old on February 26. It was an unqualified Intermediate—in Dow Theory a Secondary reaction presumptively within the still existing Major up trend.

Labor troubles were dogging the steel and motor industries in 1946 from

FIGURE 8. Daily closing price levels of the Dow-Jones Industrial and Rail averages from December 1, 1945 to May 31, 1946, and total daily market volume. Noteworthy features of this period included the extremely high volume which prevailed during January and February as compared with lower turnover in April and May, and the laggard performance of the Rails when the Industrial average pushed up to a new high in April and again at the end of May. At the latter date the February lows were still the critical down-side "signal" levels according to the Dow Theory.

early January on, and a coal strike was looming. The February break was attributed to those news developments but the ruling cause was more likely the discontinuance of margin trading. The Federal Reserve Board had announced in January that after February 1 stocks could be bought only for full 100% cash. The late January up-fling was featured by the "little fellow" seizing his last chance to buy on margin. (Those who participated in this scramble will doubtless regret it for a long time yet to come.) Professionals seized the opportunity to unload their trading commitments but the "little fellow" was now temporarily out of funds; his brokerage account was quickly "frozen." Under the circumstances, as we look back, it is amazing that a more extensive panic did not then eventuate.

But the Dow Theorist was not concerned with causes. The Bull Market had been reaffirmed by both averages in early February, canceling all previous "signal" levels. Bullish forces were still evidently in effect because the February 26 lows held and prices began to recover. The Industrials came back quickly and by April 9 had closed in new high ground at 208.03. The Rails dragged. When the market showed signs of weakening at the end of April, the Rail average was still nearly 5 points below its early February high. Was this another "failure to confirm" to worry about?

FINAL UP THRUST

The late February bottoms were now the critical points on the down side; if both averages should decline below the Intermediate low closes then recorded, before the Rails could make a new high above 68.23 (in which event the bullish signal of the Industrials would be canceled), a Bear Market would thereby be signaled. But, despite a miners' strike and an imminent rail workers' strike, the market turned firm again in mid-May and put forth a surprising rally which swept the Industrial index up to 212.50 on May 29, 1946—a new Bull high by nearly six points. The Rails failed in May by only .17 to equal their February high close, slid back a trifle and then pushed through at last on June 13 to close at 68.31, thereby confirming the Industrials in their announcement that (as of that date) the Primary trend was still Up. The February lows (186.02 and 60.53) now ceased to signify in Dow Theory, but keep those figures in mind because they are involved in an argument which raged among Dow students for months thereafter.

Our next chart (Figure 9) overlaps the preceding picture, taking up the market's action on May 4 and carrying it forward to October 19, 1946. Trading volume, it may be noted, in late May and early June did not come up to the levels of either the late January-early February top or the late February bottom; the market appeared to be losing vitality, an ominous although by no means a decisive manifestation. Prices began to fall off rapidly immediately after the Rail confirmation on June 13. The Industrials rallied for two weeks in early

FIGURE 9.   Daily closing price levels of the Dow-Jones Industrial and Rail averages from May 4 to October 19, 1946, and total daily market volume. This chart overlaps Figure 8.   Compare the closing price of the Rail average on June 13 with its February 5 high close.   This June action nullified the previous Dow Theory importance of the February lows.   Note significant change in volume pattern after May, especially during August rally.

July but the Rails continued to decline; the Industrials broke again on July 15 and the two averages continued their slide until they stood at 195.22 and 60.41 at the close on July 23.

There, as it subsequently developed, was the end of that particular Intermediate swing—one which in accord with our Rule 12 had to be labeled a Secondary reaction in a Bull Market until proved otherwise. The market swung up again. It climbed slowly and steadily, but with turnover running well under a million shares, until exactly three weeks later the Industrials at 204.52 (August 13) had regained a little more than half of their June-July loss and the Rails at 63.12 (August 14) a little more than a third of theirs. This advance, therefore, had met the minimum requirements of an Intermediate trend. If prices could continue to rise and eventually push through their May-June tops, the Major Bull trend once again would be re-affirmed. But, if they should now turn down and fall below the July 23 closing levels, that action would signalize a *reversal of the Primary Trend*.

THE BEAR MARKET SIGNAL

That the situation was critical was evident in the volume chart. Ever since the end of May, turnover had tended not only to increase on the declines but, what was much more important, to dry up on the rallies. Compare Figure 9 with 7 and 8 and you can see how conspicuous this phenomenon had become by mid-August. Prices did turn down, with activity increasing on the breaks, and on August 27 the closing prices—191.04 for the Industrials and 58.04 for the Rails—told a sad story. The averages had spoken: a four year Bull Market had ended and a Bear Market was under way. A Dow investor should have sold all his stocks on the following day (at approximately 190 and 58 in terms of the two averages).

To clear the record it was necessary for the Dow Theorist now to go back and mark the May 29 and June 13 highs in the Industrials and Rails, respectively, as the end of the Bull Market. The June-July decline then became the first Primary swing in the new Bear trend, and the July 23-August 14 advance became the first Secondary recovery within the Major Down trend. A second Primary swing was now in process of development.

You will have noted in the foregoing that a Bear Market was signaled as soon as both averages penetrated their July 23 lows. Let us return now and take up that argument which we mentioned on the preceding page. Some students of Dow Theory refused to recognize the new high of June 13 in the Rail average as a decisive reaffirmation of the Bull trend. The previous close should be bettered by at least a full point (1.00), many argued, in order to confirm the signal previously given by the Industrials; the margin of only .08 was inconclusive. But this opinion, if accepted, had logical consequences which later proved embarrassing. For, if the Bull Market had not been reaffirmed in June, then the critical levels on the down side remained at 186.02 in the Industrials and 60.53 in the Rails, the February 26 bottoms. Therefore, a Bear Market could not be "called" until those prices had been penetrated down-side by both averages. This view acquired a large following, especially among those who were not interested in "hair splitting" theory but wanted "to give the market every chance *in view of the still improving fundamentals.*"

The market did, of course, proceed to break its February lows and by that time the panic (second phase) was on. Obviously, in this case the orthodox "any-penetration-whatever" school had all the best of it; they had sold out at least 13 points higher up in terms of the Industrial index (at least 6 in the Rails). Six weeks later, on October 9, 1946 to be exact, this second Primary Intermediate swing ended at Industrials 163.12, Rails 44.69, and another Intermediate recovery move started.

Before closing this history of six years of Dow Theory interpretation, we might note that the June 13 high in the Rail average furnishes a perfect illustration of the rule that a trend can change *any time* after it has been confirmed or reaffirmed, also of the diminishing odds in favor of continuance with each successive reaffirmation of the Primary trend.

CHAPTER V

THE DOW THEORY'S DEFECTS

OUR readers, we suspect, heaved a deep sigh of relief when they closed the preceding chapter on a difficult, tedious and at times confusing subject. Some may even wish at this point that the Dow Theory had never been conceived. Others doubtless spotted one or more of its real or supposed defects and have questions to ask. Before we proceed to more interesting chart matters, we had better devote a few pages to clearing them up.

First, let's take up the charge of "second guessing" which is so often flung at writers on Dow Theory. It is a charge which will continue to crop up so long as opinions differ among Dow Theorists at critical periods (which unfortunately is often the case). Even the most experienced and careful of Dow analysts find it necessary occasionally to change their interpretations when a stand first ventured is rendered untenable by some subsequent action of the market. They would not attempt to deny it—but, they say, in the long run surprisingly little is lost by such temporary misinterpretations. Many of them publish their comments regularly and can refer you to the printed files of opinions and advices expressed before and during the event, as well as after it. As for the preceding chapter of this book, the reader, if he cares to check such records, will find that the interpretations given therein (aside from the remarks made "in retrospect" and so labeled) were precisely the interpretations published at the time by the best established Dow analysts.

The Dow Theory is "too late."

This is a more valid objection. It is sometimes expressed in the rather intemperate statement that "The Dow Theory is a sure-fire system for depriving the investor of the first third and the last third of every Major move, and sometimes there isn't any middle third!" Or, to give a specific example:—A Primary Bull Market started in 1942 with the Industrial average at 92.92 and ended in 1946 at 212.50, for a total gain of 119.58 average points, but strict Dow Theorists could not buy until the Industrials were up to 125.88 and couldn't sell until prices had already declined to 191.04, thus capturing at best only about 65 points or not much more than half of the total move. This specific statement cannot be disputed. But the answer to the general objection is: "Try and find a man who first bought his stocks at 92.92 (or even within 5 points of that level) and stayed 100% long throughout the intervening years, and finally sold out at 212.50, or within 5 points thereof."

The reader is welcome to try; he will, in fact, find it very difficult to locate even a dozen who did as well as the Dow Theory.

A still better answer, since it comprehends all of the hazards of every known kind of Bull and Bear Market to date, is the over-all dollars and cents record of the past sixty years. We are indebted to Mr. Richard Durant* for permission to reprint the following computation of what would, in theory, have resulted if a fund of only $100 could have been invested in the stocks of the Dow-Jones Industrial average on July 12, 1897 when a Primary Bull Market was signaled by the Dow Theory, and those stocks were thereafter sold and repurchased when and only when the Dow Theory had definitely confirmed a change in the Major trend.

THE DOW THEORY'S SIXTY-YEAR RECORD

Original Fund $100.00	Date	Industrial Average Price	% Gain	Proceeds
Invested	July 12, 1897	44.61		
Stocks sold	Dec. 16, 1899	63.84	43.1	$ 143.10
Proceeds re-invested	Oct. 20, 1900	59.44		
Stocks sold	June 1, 1903	59.59	0.3	143.53
Proceeds re-invested	July 12, 1904	51.37		
Stocks sold	April 26, 1906	92.44	80.0	258.35
Proceeds re-invested	April 24, 1908	70.01		
Stocks sold	May 3, 1910	84.72	21.0	312.60
Proceeds re-invested	Oct. 10, 1910	81.91		
Stocks sold	Jan. 14, 1913	84.96	3.7	324.17
Proceeds re-invested	April 9, 1915	65.02		
Stocks sold	Aug. 28, 1917	86.12	32.5	429.53
Proceeds re-invested	May 13, 1918	82.16		
Stocks sold	Feb. 3, 1920	99.96	21.7	522.74
Proceeds re-invested	Feb. 6, 1922	83.70		
Stocks sold	June 20, 1923	90.81	8.5	567.17
Proceeds re-invested	Dec. 7, 1923	93.80		
Stocks sold	Oct. 23, 1929	305.85	226.1	1,849.54
Proceeds re-invested	May 24, 1933	84.29		
Stocks sold	Sept. 7, 1937	164.39	95.0	3,606.61
Proceeds re-invested	June 23, 1938	127.41		
Stocks sold	Mar. 31, 1939	136.42	7.2	3,866.29
Proceeds re-invested	July 17, 1939	142.58		
Stocks sold	May 13, 1940	137.50	(Loss 3.6)	3,727.10
Proceeds re-invested	Feb. 1, 1943	125.88		
Stocks sold	Aug. 27, 1946	191.04	51.9	5,653.71
Proceeds re-invested	Oct. 2, 1950	228.94		
Stocks sold	April 2, 1953	280.03	22.3	6,911.01
Proceeds re-invested	Jan. 19, 1954	288.27		
Stocks sold	Oct. 1, 1956	468.70	62.6	$11,236.65

* WHAT IS THE DOW THEORY? by Richard Durant. Durant & Co., Detroit.

In brief, an investment of $100 in 1897 would have become $11,236.65 in 1956 simply by buying the Industrial average stocks each time the Dow Theory announced a Bull Market and holding them until the Dow Theory announced a Bear Market. During this period, the investor would have made 15 purchases and 15 sales, or about one transaction every two years on the average.

The record is not perfect. It shows one losing transaction and three instances where re-investment would have been made at a higher level than the preceding liquidation. But, at that, it hardly needs defending! Also, it takes no account of commissions and transfer taxes but neither does it include the dividends the investor would have received during the time he held his stocks; the latter would, needless to say, have added many more dollars to the fund.

For the enlightenment of the man who believes in "just buying good stocks and putting them away," compare the above results with the best that could have been done by buying shares only once at the lowest price recorded by the Industrial average during these entire fifty years and selling them only once at the highest. $100 invested at the all-time low, 29.64 on August 10, 1896, would have become only $1,757.93 at the all-time high, 521.05, sixty years later on April 6, 1956, as against the $11,236.65 derived from the straight Dow Theory program.

The Dow Theory is not infallible.

Of course, it isn't. It depends on interpretation and is subject to all the hazards of human interpretive ability. But, again, the record speaks for itself.

The Dow Theory frequently leaves the investor in doubt.

This is true in one sense and not in another. There is never a time when the Dow Theory does not afford a *presumptive* answer to the question of the direction of the Primary trend. That answer will be wrong for a relatively short time at the beginning of each new Major swing. There will also be times when a good Dow analyst should say, "The Primary trend is still presumably Up but it has reached a dangerous stage and I cannot conscientiously advise you to buy now. It may be too late."

Frequently, however, the above objection simply reflects the inability of the critic mentally to accept the fundamental concept that the averages discount all the news and statistics. He doubts the Dow Theory because he cannot reconcile its message with his own ideas, derived from other sources, of what stocks should do. The Theory, needless to say, is usually more nearly right.

This criticism in other cases reflects nothing but impatience. There may be weeks or months (as, for example, during the formation of a Line) when the Dow Theory cannot "talk." The active trader quite naturally rebels. But patience is a virtue in the stock market as elsewhere—in fact, essential if serious mistakes are to be avoided.

The Dow Theory does not help the Intermediate trend investor.

This is perfectly true. The Theory gives little or no warning of changes in Intermediate trend. Yet, if a fair share of these can be captured, the profit amounts to more than can be derived from the Primary trend alone. Some traders have worked out supplementary rules based on Dow principles which they apply to Intermediate movements but these have not proved to be altogether satisfactory. The remainder of our book is devoted to a better approach to this problem.

A man cannot buy or sell the "averages."

Also perfectly true. The Dow Theory is a mechanical device, designed to tell the direction of the Primary market trend which is important because, as we said at the beginning of this study, most stocks tend to go with the trend. The Dow Theory does not and cannot tell you what stocks to buy. That again is a problem for the remainder of this book.

CHAPTER VI

IMPORTANT REVERSAL PATTERNS

IN OUR discussion of certain deficiencies in the Dow Theory from the point of view of the practical trader, we mentioned the fact that it did not tell us what specific stocks to trade in. We cannot buy or sell "the averages." A conservative and wealthy investor, more interested in safety than maximum profit, can solve this problem by making up a comprehensive and thoroughly diversified list of sound, well-seasoned "blue chip" issues and handing his broker an order to buy the lot when the Dow Theory signals a Bull trend. Some of his selections will do better than others; some may "go sour," but wide diversification will ensure his getting a fair average result. Better results should be obtained if we can find a way to select for purchase the most favorably situated issues at any given time, and can manage to sell them promptly and switch to others whenever the prospects for the first have been fully discounted.

There is the possibility, too, of increasing our gains if we can at times buy with safety earlier in an up trend than the Dow Theorist does, and sell before the market has reacted far enough to give a Dow Bear signal.

We mentioned also the fact that the Dow Theory is of little or no assistance in trading on the Intermediate trends. There is obviously more money to be made if we can get the benefit of all of each up move without having to write off some of our profits in each reaction. Or if we can profit both ways by trading on both the "long side" and "short side" of the market.

Finally, although all stocks *tend* to move with "the market" as typified in the averages, there are in fact wide variations in the price paths of individual issues. An average, after all, is just that—a device for expressing in one figure a diversity of other figures. A Primary Bull Market ended in the Dow-Jones Industrial average on May 29, 1946; but United Air Lines registered its highest price in December, 1945; General Motors saw its peak in January, 1946; Goodyear in April, Du Pont in June and Schenley in August. Is there a way of capitalizing on these divergences?

Technical analysis of the charts of individual stocks definitely answers the first and most important of these four problems, the matter of selection. It frequently, but not always, gives us a running start on the Dow Theory; it also in large part takes care of the question of the Intermediate trend, although there are certain reservations as to policy and risk in connection with both these

46

points which will be taken up in due course. Finally, careful technical analysis should in nearly every case get us out of a stock that "tops out" ahead of the averages long before it has suffered any considerable decline, often in time to transfer funds to other issues which have yet to complete their advances.

Just as the averages constantly discount all known and foreseeable factors affecting the future of security prices in general, in the same way does the market action of an individual issue reflect all the factors affecting its individual future. Among these factors and expressed in its chart are the general market conditions which influence all stocks to a greater or less degree as well as the particular conditions applying to the particular stock, including the operations of "insiders."

Let us assume right from the start that you, the reader, are not a member of that mysterious inner circle known to the boardrooms as "the insiders." Such a group—genuinely entitled to be called insiders, thoroughly informed on every fact, figure and development that might determine the fortunes of a certain corporation—may exist from time to time, may influence the market price of its stock. But it is fairly certain that there are not nearly so many "insiders" as the amateur trader supposes, and that they do not cause one tenth of the market movements for which the public blames them. It is even more certain that insiders can be wrong; they would, in fact, be the first to admit it. Frequently their plans are upset by some development which they could not foresee, or by some blind force which puts to scorn all expert estimates of value. Any success they have, however, can be accomplished only by buying and selling on the floor of the exchange. They can do neither without altering the delicate poise of supply and demand which governs prices. Whatever they do is sooner or later reflected on the charts where you, the "outsider," can detect it. Or detect, at least, the way in which the supply-demand equation is being affected by insiders' operations plus all other prevailing market factors. So, you don't need to be an insider in order frequently to ride with them.

IMPORTANT REVERSAL PATTERNS

Stock prices move in trends. Some of those trends are straight, some are curved; some are brief and some are long-continued; some are irregular or poorly defined and others are amazingly regular or "normal," produced in a series of action and reaction waves of great uniformity. Sooner or later, these trends change direction; they may reverse (as from up to down) or they may be interrupted by some sort of sidewise movement and then after a time proceed again in their former direction.

In most cases, when a price trend is in process of reversal, either from up to down or from down to up, a characteristic "area" or "pattern" takes shape on the chart, becomes recognizable as a *reversal formation*. Some of these chart pictures are built and completed very quickly while others may require several weeks to reach a stage where one can surely say that a reversal of trend is definitely indicated. Speaking in broad generalities, the greater the reversal area—the wider the price fluctuations within it, the longer it takes to build, the more shares transferred during its construction—the more important its implications. Thus, roughly speaking, a big reversal formation suggests a big move to follow and a small pattern, a small move. Needless to say, the first and most important task of the technical chart analyst is to learn to know the important reversal formations and to judge what they may signify in terms of trading opportunities.

There is one recognized reversal pattern which appears and is completed within a single day's trading, and is, in consequence, named the "One-Day Reversal." There are times when it has great significance as calling a halt, at least temporarily, to any up or down move, but in its ordinary manifestations it does not imply much of an immediate move in the opposite direction. It is a useful pattern and we shall have more to say about it later. But the price formations from which extensive new trends proceed take time to build. One does not bring instantly to a stop a heavy car moving at seventy miles an hour and, all within the same split second, turn it around and get it moving back down the road in the opposite direction at seventy miles an hour.

Time Required to Reverse Trend

But we do not need to lean on racing automobile analogy to explain why it takes time (and volume and price action) to produce an important trend reversal. The logic of it is plain enough, if we take but a moment to examine it. We can do so most easily by describing what might have (and doubtless many times has) happened in specific terms. Suppose a certain well-informed and well-financed coterie decides that the shares of a certain company, now selling around 40, are cheap, that this company's affairs are progressing so satisfactorily that before long it will attract the attention of many investors and its stock will be in demand at much higher levels, perhaps at 60 or 65. Our group realizes that if they manage their market operations skillfully, if nothing unforeseen intervenes to upset their calculations, they can "take" 20 points out of the situation. So they proceed to buy in all offerings, going about this business as quietly as possible, until they have accumulated their "line" which may run to several thousand shares and represent practically all of the current floating supply of the issue. Then they wait. Presently, professionals become suspicious and the rumor circulates that there is "something doing in PDQ," or other canny bargain hunters discover the company's bright prospects, or chart analysts detect the signs of accumulation in the stock's action. Buyers now find that the stock is scarce; there are few offerings on the books and they have to raise their bids to get it. An advance starts.

The up move gathers momentum as more and more traders are attracted by rising prices. It is helped along by the good reports (higher earnings, increased dividend, etc.) which our group knew were to be expected. Eventually prices approach the level at which they had planned to take profits. But this operation—the "distribution" of their holdings—may require even more patient and skillful handling than did the accumulation. Suppose they have 20,000 shares to unload. They cannot throw all on the market at once; to do so would defeat their own ends immediately and, perhaps, permanently. They must feed their line out little by little, trying to avoid attention, feeling their way along and never permitting a surplus of offerings to kill the demand. If activity in their stock has reached a level of, say, 2,000 shares transferred daily, they may be able to dispose of 500 shares a day from their holdings without breaking the price down. (They will be competing, sooner or later, with others who have followed their play, who bought lower down and will be ready to take profits as soon as the advance shows signs of weakening.) So they start to sell when the rising trend appears to have attained maximum momentum, or as it nears their price objective, but well before it has reached its probable limit, and they push out their shares as rapidly as buyers will take them.

Before long, as a rule—before they have distributed their entire line—a lull in demand will occur. Perhaps prospective buyers sense the increase in supply. A reaction develops. Our group quickly ceases selling, withdraws its offers, perhaps even buys back a few shares to support prices if they threaten to drop too far. With supply temporarily held off the market, the decline halts and the advance resumes. Our group lets it proceed this time until it carries prices into new high ground; this reassures other holders and brings in more buyers. As soon as the pot is once again merrily boiling, distribution is started anew and, if the maneuver has been well directed, completed in perhaps two or three weeks, before the second wave of demand has been exhausted.

Our group is now out of its stock with a nice profit; its 20,000 shares have passed into other hands. If they gauged the market correctly and distributed their line at a price about as high as the situation would bear, demand will have been satiated for a long time to come. Prices will probably first drift back to somewhere near the level where they were supported on the previous dip, then rally feebly on the strength of a little new buying from traders who were waiting for just such a minor reaction, meet sales from other traders who failed to seize the opportunity to take their profits on the preceding volume top and are now anxious to get out, and then break down into a decline of Intermediate or Major proportions.

You can see now why, under one specific set of circumstances, a top area, a chart pattern of distribution, takes time and volume to complete. But, it doesn't matter whether we have to deal with the highly organized operations of a single group of insiders or of an investment syndicate or, as is more often the case, with the quite unorganized activities of all the investors variously interested in an issue. The result is pretty much the same. Distribution, which is simply the "street's" way of expressing the process of supply overcoming demand, takes time and a change in ownership (turnover) of a large number of shares. And it is amazing to see how these patterns of distribution, which hereafter we shall find it simpler to refer to as "tops," tend to assume certain well-defined forms. Most of the same pattern forms appear also as "bottoms," in which manifestation they signify accumulation, of course, instead of distribution.

THE HEAD-AND-SHOULDERS

If you followed closely and were able successfully to visualize how the foregoing example of distribution would appear on a chart, you saw a *Head-and-Shoulders Top* formation. This is one of the more common and, by all odds, the most reliable of the major reversal patterns. Probably you have heard it mentioned, for there are many traders who are familiar with its name but not so many who really know it and can distinguish it from somewhat similar price developments which do not portend a real reversal of trend.

The typical or, if you will, the ideal Head-and-Shoulders Top is illustrated in Diagram 2. You can easily see how it got its name. It consists of:—

A.—A strong rally, climaxing a more or less extensive advance, on which trading volume becomes very heavy, followed by a minor recession on which volume runs considerably less than it did during the days of rise and at the top. This is the "left shoulder."

B.—Another high volume advance which reaches a higher level than the top of the left shoulder and then another reaction on less volume which takes prices down to somewhere near the bottom level of the preceding recession, somewhat lower perhaps or somewhat higher but, in any case, *below the top* of the left shoulder. This is the "head."

C.—A third rally, but this time on decidedly less volume than accompanied the formation of either the left shoulder or the head, which fails to reach the height of the head before another decline sets in. This is the "right shoulder."

D.—Finally, decline of prices in this third recession down through a line (the "neckline") drawn across the bottoms of the reactions between the left shoulder and head and the head and right shoulder, respectively, and a close below that line by an amount approximately equivalent to 3% of the stock's market price. This is the "confirmation" or "breakout."

Note that each and every item cited in A, B, C and D is essential to a valid Head-and-Shoulders Top formation. The lack of any one of them casts in doubt the forecasting value of the pattern. In naming them, we have left the way clear for the many variations which occur (for no two Head-and-Shoulders are exactly alike) and have included only the features which must be present if we are to depend upon the pattern as signalizing an important reversal of trend. Let us examine them in greater detail.

DIAGRAM 2. A hypothetical daily stock chart—price in the upper part and volume at bottom—drawn to show how an ideal Head-and-Shoulders top reversal formation would develop. A, B, C and D refer to essential features listed on preceding page.

VOLUME IS IMPORTANT

First, the matter of *volume*. It is always to be watched as a vital part of the total picture. The chart of trading activity makes a pattern just as does the chart of price ranges. The two go together and each must conform to the requirements of the case. But note also that volume is relative. When we speak of *high* volume, we mean a rate of trading notably greater than has been customary in that particular stock during that particular period under examination. The exact number of shares traded is not important, nor will it ordinarily signify anything for our purposes to compare a daily volume of, say, 6,500 shares in Radio Corporation with 500 in Bohn Aluminum and Brass. The former may be very low and the latter very high as judged by the proper technical criterion which is in each case the average recent activity *in the same issue*. In the case of a Head-and-Shoulders Top, we have said that high volume attends the making of the left shoulder, so this means that activity on the rise to, and at the top of the left shoulder should be greater than on the preceding rally waves in the same issue. Then a minor recession on dwindling activity and then a new advance on high volume. The action thus far does not differ from what we should expect of normal wave development within a continuing up trend. In these respects any two typical, successively higher waves in an advance may, as you can see, become the left shoulder and head, respectively, of a Head-and-Shoulders reversal.

FIGURE 10. Small but typical Head-and-Shoulders formation which reversed the Intermediate recovery of early 1947 in American Power & Light. Neckline (line of dashes at 15 level) was broken by decisive margin on March 17. Note particularly relative volume on two shoulders (S and S) and rally back to neckline March 28 (see page 58). Intermediate up trendline (see Chapter XIV) was broken by decline from head, SC indicates Selling Climax on May 19 (see Chapter X). Triangular patterns of the type which appeared here in April-May are discussed in Chapter VIII.

The first suggestion that a Head-and-Shoulders is really developing may come when the volume record shows that activity accompanying the most recent top was somewhat less than on the one preceding it. If this volume disparity is conspicuous, and if it becomes evident from the way prices are receding that the second and higher rally has ended, then the chart should be tabbed with a "red" signal and further developments closely scrutinized. But such a preliminary warning does not always appear, nor should it be taken as conclusive when it does appear. Roughly estimated, about one third of all confirmed Head-and-Shoulders formations show more volume on the left shoulder than on the head, another third show about equal volume, and the final third show greater volume on the head than on the left shoulder.

Another warning—or more often the first—comes when prices drop in the course of the second reaction (i.e., from the head) below the level of the top of the left shoulder. Such action, as we shall see later on in our specific study of support and resistance levels, is significant of weakness in the price structure. So far it is minor; it may be only temporary; it is certainly not conclusive. Nevertheless, when this occurs put a double red tab on your chart.

FIGURE 11. Daily chart of Chicago, Milwaukee, St. Paul & Pacific common from January 1 to June 29, 1946. Head-and-Shoulders which topped this issue's Primary advance in February was unmistakable despite small size of shoulders (S S). Note volume pattern. Measuring implication (see page 60) of this formation was carried out by April. Rectangular price congestion of March 30–May 4 is subject of Chapter IX. "ST" fell to 11½ in October.

FIGURE 12.   Bull Market top of Westinghouse Electric in 1946 was the "wide-swinging," powerful type of Head-and-Shoulders (S-H-S).   Decline which broke neckline (NL) on February 13 produced a Breakaway gap (G) discussed in Chapter XII.   Measuring formula (see page 60) called for initial decline to 33.   The possible bottom Head-and-Shoulders pattern (S?- H?- S?) formed in March was never completed (see Chapter VII).   Note failure of prices to push up through neckline of latter at any time, despite several rally efforts in late Spring while general market averages were actually reaching new high levels.   By the following November "WX" had broken on down to 21½.   Study in detail the change in volume pattern after the end of January.

BREAKING THE NECKLINE

The real tip-off appears when activity fails to pick up appreciably on the third rally, the right shoulder.   If the market remains dull as prices recover (at which stage you can draw a tentative "neckline" on your chart) and if as they approach the approximate level of the left shoulder top, and begin to round over, volume is still relatively small, your Head-and-Shoulders Top is at least 75% completed.   Although the specific application of these pattern studies in trading tactics is the province of the second part of this book, we may note here that many stock traders sell or switch just as soon as they are sure a low-volume right shoulder has been completed, without waiting for the final confirmation which we named under D as the breaking of the neckline.

Nevertheless, the Head-and-Shoulders is not complete, and an important reversal of trend is not conclusively signalized until the neckline has been penetrated down-side by a decisive margin.   Until the neckline is broken, a certain percentage of Head-and-Shoulders developments—perhaps 20%—are "saved"· i.e., prices go no lower but simply flounder around listlessly for a period of time in the general range of the right shoulder, eventually firm up and renew their advance.

Finally, it must be said that in rare cases a Head-and-Shoulders Top is confirmed by a decisive neckline penetration and still prices do not go down much farther.   "False Moves" such as this are the most difficult phenomena with which the technical analyst has to cope.   Fortunately, in the case of the Head-and-Shoulders they are extremely rare.   The odds are so overwhelmingly in favor of the down trend's continuing, once a Head-and-Shoulders has been confirmed, that it pays to believe the evidence of the chart no matter how much it may appear to be out of accord with the prevailing news or market psychology.

FIGURE 13.   A "perfect" Head-and-Shoulders which developed in Republic Steel in 1936—except that prices never broke down through the neckline (NL).   Hence, no signal to sell was given.   This uncompleted reversal attempt was, nevertheless, a warning; the final Bull Market top was made only three months later.   See comment above and on following page.

FIGURE 14.   Every Bull Market produces its share of Head-and-Shoulders tops.   Mack Trucks built an ideal pattern in 1937.   Note typical volume on S, H and S; low volume on right shoulder was a storm warning not to be ignored.   Two pull-backs to neckline (on April 13 and 20) are not uncommon, although the second usually occurs after a more extensive Minor reaction has been completed. Late January price pattern is a Flag (Chapter XI).

There is one thing that can be said and is worth noting about Head-and-Shoulders formations which fail of completion or produce false confirmations. Such developments almost never occur in the early stages of a Primary advance. A Head-and-Shoulders which does not "work" is a warning that, even though there is still some life in the situation, a genuine turn is near.   The next time something in the nature of a reversal pattern begins to appear on the charts it is apt to be final.

VARIATIONS IN HEAD-AND-SHOULDERS TOPS

There is a tendency, surprising when one thinks of all the vagaries of news and cross-currents which may influence day-to-day trading, for Head-and-Shoulders patterns to develop a high degree of symmetry.   The neckline tends to be horizontal and the right shoulder tends to resemble the left in price confirmation (although not, of course, in volume); there is a sort of satisfying balance to the over-all picture. But symmetry is not essential to a significant Head-and-Shoulders development. The neckline may slope up (from left to right) or down. The only qualification on an up-sloping neckline is that the bottom of the recession between the head and right shoulder must form appreciably below the general level of the top of the left shoulder. It is sometimes said that a down-sloping neckline indicates an unusually weak situation. This is so obvious that it is apt to be given even more weight than it deserves. A share of that excessive weakness, it should be noted, will have already been discharged by the time the down-sloping pattern is formed and prices have broken the neckline. The measuring formula which we shall discuss later applies to such situations.

Because of the tendency toward symmetry in shoulder development, some traders, as soon as the neckline has formed, will draw on their charts a line parallel to the neckline, extending from the top of the left shoulder through the head and on to the right. This furnishes a guide as to the approximate height which the right shoulder rally should attain and, consequently, a selling level. But

FIGURE 15. Reversal formations which develop in important stocks while the general market is still apparently in a strong trend are often difficult to believe, much less act upon. But they may be highly significant. Du Pont topped out in 1936 four months ahead of the averages. Despite its extended right shoulder (but note volume), reversal implications were clear on December 19. The pull-back of January, meeting supply at the old neckline level, and the second try in March were interesting and typical of such a general market situation. Compare with Figure 12.

FIGURE 16. Another 1937 Bull Market top of Head-and-Shoulders form, with only one quick pull-back (February 10). In this case volume increased sharply on February 5 with the initial break through the neckline (NL). Measuring formula was satisfied in March. Study this picture in connection with "ED's" long-range chart (Figure 89) in Chapter X, and turn back to it later when you come to Support-Resistance study in Chapter XIII.

you will not see very many formations as perfect and symmetrical as our ideal picture, a fact which the several actual examples accompanying this chapter amply illustrate. Either shoulder may, in fact, go higher or take more time than the other. Either or both may come up nearly to the level of the head (but *not* equal it, else no Head-and-Shoulders) or both may fall considerably short of it. If activity attending the right shoulder is abnormally dull, that shoulder is apt to be low but protracted in time. In general, there seems to be a balanced relation between the three elements of price pattern, time and volume which is practically impossible to express in words or figures but which one comes with experience to sense in their development. However, there are no "laws" beyond those stated in our A, B, C and D; within those limits, look for an infinity of minor variations.

PRICE ACTION FOLLOWING CONFIRMATION—THE MEASURING FORMULA

The final step—the down-side penetration of the neckline—may be attended by some increase in activity but usually isn't *at first*. If volume remains small for a few days as prices drift lower, a "pull-back" move frequently ensues which brings quotations up again to the neckline level (rarely through it). Normally this is the "last gasp"; prices then turn down quickly as a rule and break away on sharply augmented turnover. Whether or not a pull-back rally will occur after the initial penetration seems often to depend on the condition of the market in general. If the whole market trend is turning down at the same time as our individual issue which has just completed its Head-and-Shoulders, there will probably be no pull-back; prices instead will tend to accelerate their decline with activity increasing as they leave the vicinity of the top. If on the other hand the general market is still firm, then an attempt at a pull-back is likely. Also the odds seem slightly to favor a pull-back if the neckline has been broken before much of a right shoulder developed, but certainly no very sure rules can be laid down. In any event, the pull-back rally is of practical interest chiefly to the trader who wants to sell the stock short, or who has sold it short and has then to decide where he should place a stop-loss order.

FIGURE 17. The six months long Head-and-Shoulders top of Republic Aviation in 1946. Such a pattern became a possibility to be watched for when prices broke down in May below the level of the February high (first S). Refer back to requirement B on page 50. Note also how the Head-and-Shoulders measuring formula stated on page 60 is applied to patterns with up-slanting necklines. Minimum down-side requirement here was 12½, reached in November. The quick pull-back on July 27 gave a last good selling opportunity.

Now we come to one of the most interesting features of this basic reversal formation—the indication which it gives as to the extent (in points) of the move which is likely to follow the completion of a Head-and-Shoulders. Measure the number of points down vertically from the top of the head to the neckline as drawn on the chart. Then measure the same distance down from the neckline at the point where prices finally penetrated it following the completion of the right shoulder. The price level thus marked is the *minimum probable* objective of the decline.

Let us hasten to state one important qualification to the Head-and-Shoulders measuring formula. Refer back to our original set of specifications for a Head-and-Shoulders. Under A, we required "a strong rally *climaxing a more or less extensive advance.*" If the up move preceding the formation of a reversal area has been small, the down move following it may, in fact probably will, be equally small. In brief, a reversal pattern has to have something to reverse. So, we really have two minimums, one being the extent of the advance

FIGURE 18. Graham-Paige, which had come up from 50 cents a share in four years, ended its Bull Market in February, 1946 with a typical Head-and-Shoulders (S-H-S). Measuring formula (see above) called for initial decline to 10½, reached at end of April. Note return to neckline March 1 and again May 31. "GP" dropped to 4 a few months later. Three down-slanting lines drawn from right shoulder are "fan lines," discussed in Chapter XIV.

preceding the formation of the Head-and-Shoulders and the other that derived by our measuring formula; whichever is the smaller will apply. The measuring rule is indicated on several of the examples which illustrate this chapter. You can see now why a down-sloping neckline indicates a "weaker" situation than an up-sloping, and just how much weaker, as well as the fact that more than half of the *minimum* expected weakness has already been expended in the decline from the top of the head to the penetration of the neckline.

The *maximum* indications are quite another matter, for which no simple rules can be laid down. Factors which enter into this are the extent of the previous rise, the size, volume and duration of the Head-and-Shoulders formation, the general market Primary trend (very important), and the distance which prices can fall before they come to an established support zone. Some of these are topics for later discussion.

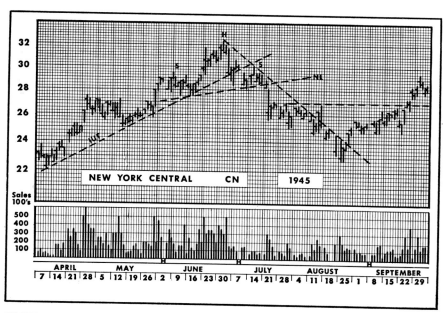

FIGURE 19. New York Central made a Head-and-Shoulders top in June, 1945. Intermediate up trendline (IUT) was broken by drop from head on July 5. Minimum measuring implication was carried out at 24 on August 18. Reaction ended a few days later at 22¾. Prices recovered to projected neckline (see September 25), dropped again to 26⅞ in October, and then pushed up, giving "re-buy" signal (on fan-line construction) at 30 in first week of November. Final Bull Market high was made in January at 35½. The period from August, 1945 to February, 1946 was difficult for technical traders in this stock. Those who sold at 26-27 in July, 1945 could, however, congratulate themselves in May, 1947 when "CN" hit 12.

FIGURE 20. The great 1929 Bull Market top was characterized by many impressive Head-and-Shoulders formations, of which this is an interesting example. Note the small Head-and-Shoulders pattern of September which became the head of a much larger formation of the same character. The pullback of October 9 to the upper neckline afforded a second chance to get out at 128 to those who did not sell immediately when this first line was decisively penetrated on September 28. The larger pattern "broke" on October 19, with a quick pull-back on October 22. Less than a month later "UK" had lost half its peak value. By 1932 it had fallen to 15½.

Although such a catastrophic decline as 1929-1932 may never come again, the moral is none the less plain: Never scorn a Head-and-Shoulders formation.

Patterns such as this merge into the "multiple" types discussed in Chapter VII. Although this example is selected from the 1929 portfolio, they are not at all uncommon today. Several modern examples appear in our later pages.

Relation of Head-and-Shoulders to Dow Theory

Without doubt, some of you have already suspected that the Head-and-Shoulders pattern is, in a sense, just an adaptation of the principles of Dow Theory to the action of an individual stock. So it is. The decline of prices from the head to the neckline, the rally to the right shoulder and then the ensuing decline which breaks the neckline, set up a sequence of lower tops and bottoms analogous to those which signalize a down trend in Dow Theory. This logical relation of the Head-and-Shoulders to Dow Theory is another reason, in addition to its basic importance, frequency and dependability, why we have placed it first in our study of reversal formations. But it is more definite, gives advance warnings which are relatively easier to detect, and is quicker with its signals in the case of up-sloping necklines. Also it requires no specified minimum time for any of its component moves, and no confirmation by another stock or average.

There are Head-and-Shoulders Bottoms as well as Tops, with equally important implications. The Bottom formation will be taken up in our next chapter.

CHAPTER VII

IMPORTANT REVERSAL PATTERNS—CONTINUED

HEAD-AND-SHOULDERS BOTTOMS

A FORMATION of the Head-and-Shoulders type may develop at an important reversal of trend from down to up. In that case it is, of course, called a Head-and-Shoulders Bottom and its price pattern (as compared with a Top) is turned upside down; i.e., it stands on its head. The volume pattern is somewhat the same (not turned upside down) as at a Top, but with some important changes in the latter half of the formation which we shall discuss in detail. We can lay down specifications for it in much the same words as we used for the Head-and-Shoulders Top. Here they are, with the portions which differ in principle from the Top printed in italics.

A.—A decline, climaxing a more or less extensive down trend, on which trading volume increases notably, followed by a minor recovery on which volume runs less than it did during the days of final decline and at the bottom. This is the "left shoulder."

B.—Another decline which carries prices below the bottom of the left shoulder, on which activity shows some increase (as compared with the preceding recovery) but *usually does not equal the rate attained on the left shoulder decline,* followed by another recovery which carries above the bottom level of the left shoulder and *on which activity may pick up,* at any rate *exceed that on the recovery from the left shoulder.* This is the "head."

C.—A third decline on decidedly less volume than accompanied the making of either left shoulder or head, which fails to reach the low level of the head before another rally starts. This is the "right shoulder."

D.—Finally, an advance *on which activity increases notably,* which pushes up through the neckline and closes above it by an amount approximately equivalent to 3% of the stock's market price, *with a conspicuous burst of activity attending this penetration.* This is the "confirmation" or "breakout."

The essential difference between top and bottom patterns, you can see, lies in their volume charts. Activity in Head-and-Shoulders Bottom formation begins usually to show up-trend characteristics at the start of the head and always to a detectable degree on the rally from the head. It is even more marked on the rally from the right shoulder. *It must be present on the penetration of the neckline,* else the breakout is not to be relied upon as a decisive confirmation.

There is an important basic principle of technics involved here which merits further discussion. Wall Street has an old saying which expresses it: "It takes buying to put stocks up but they can fall of their own weight." Thus we trust, and regard as conclusive, any price break (by a decisive margin) down through the neckline of a Head-and-Shoulders Top even though it occurs on light turnover, but we do not trust a breakout from a Head-and-Shoulders Bottom unless it is definitely attended by high volume. A low-volume breakout from a bottom pattern may only be premature, to be followed after more "work" around the bottom levels by a genuine advance, or it may be a "false" move entirely. It pays generally to wait and see. This same distinction in volume development applies to some of the other reversal patterns we shall take up farther on.

Other differences between top and bottom Head-and-Shoulders do not involve any new principles. It can be said that bottoms are generally longer and flatter; i.e. they take more time in relation to depth of pattern in points than do tops. This is particularly true when they occur at reversals in the Primary

FIGURE 21. After "rounding over" in October, 1943 in the last phase of a long decline from 41 in 1940, Lockheed made a conspicuous two-month Head-and-Shoulders bottom. Note especially on above chart the volume on the rally in early December and in the first week of January with reference to points B and D on the preceding page. "LK" dropped back to 15 again in June, 1944, then ran up quickly to 23 by November and finally reached 45 in January, 1946. One advantage of logarithmically scaled charts is that they expand and thus call attention to important formations which develop at low price levels and which would be obscured on an arithmetic scale.

FIGURE 22. Weekly charts are particularly useful for detecting Major bottom reversals, since bottom formations characteristically take longer to build than tops. Dome Mines made a typical Head-and-Shoulders base, thirteen months long, at its Primary trend reversal in 1942. Note volume pattern. (Volume detail, however, is better studied on daily charts—see page 84.) Dome's powerful H & S bottom was "high" enough to be conspicuous on an arithmetic monthly chart. Reached 25 in 1944.

trend. The over-all volume at bottoms tends to be less than at tops, and the turns more "rounded." In the construction of a Head-and-Shoulders top the activity that goes into the left shoulder usually exceeds that on any preceding rally in the entire up trend. In a down trend, on the other hand, there may be panic selling in some of the earlier phases of decline which runs the volume chart up to a mark higher than any that is subsequently registered in the final bottom formation. But none of these differences affect our essential Head-and-Shoulders specifications.

The measuring implications of the Head-and-Shoulders Bottom are the same in all respects and are applied in the same way as with Tops. Tendency to symmetry is again the rule with variations as to slope of neckline, relative size of shoulders about the same as in Tops. Reactions to the neckline following the initial breakout from the Bottom type appear in about the same frequency and proportions as do the pull-back rallies which follow initial breakdown from the Top type.

FIGURE 23. Do not trust or make trading purchases on a Head-and-Shoulders bottom formation in which activity does not plainly increase on the advance from the head to the neckline, and does not again pick up notably on the rise from the right shoulder through the neckline. The September, 1946 price pattern in Newport Industries lacked the essential volume confirmation for a good bottom. From early November prices dropped steadily to 26½ in January, 1947, and to 24½ by the following May.

MULTIPLE HEAD-AND-SHOULDERS PATTERNS

The Head-and-Shoulders formations we have examined up to this point have been, despite minor variations, relatively simple and clean-cut, consisting of three well-defined elements. We come now to a group of related patterns which carry much the same technical significance but have more elements and are much less clearly defined. These are the Multiple Head-and-Shoulders Tops and Bottoms, also known as Complex Formations. We need not take much of our space to define them or lay down specifications for them, since they may be described quite sufficiently as Head-and-Shoulders reversals in which either the shoulders or the head, or both, have been doubled or proliferated into several distinct waves.

Almost any combination is possible, of which only a few can be illustrated in the actual chart examples reproduced with this chapter. Formations of this type appear with fair frequency at Primary bottoms and tops, but more often at bottoms than at tops. They appear less frequently at Intermediate reversals.

A common form consists of two left shoulders of approximately equal size, a single head, and then two right shoulders again of approximately even size and balancing the two on the left. Another is made up of two heads with two or more shoulders on either side. Still another, of which you will usually find several good examples at any Major market turn, consists of double shoulders on either side of a head which is itself composed of a small but quite distinguishable Head-and-Shoulders development.

FIGURE 24. Marshall Field's Bull Market top in 1946 was a Multiple formation, best construed as a triple head with single shoulders. The "rounding" patterns (note volume trend particularly) of July and August were typical of rallies in a Primary Bear trend. "MF" was selling at 23 a year later.

FIGURE 25. An "ideal" Multiple top made by Budd in 1946, with two heads. Observe accompanying volume. Prices often break away from Complex formations more reluctantly than from the simple Head-and-Shoulders type (see page 72). The late March rally which went back through the old neckline, was greater than normal in that respect, but the general market averages were pushing to new highs at this time. Re-penetration of a neckline does not of itself alone cancel the implications of a reversal formation.

TENDENCY TO SYMMETRY

We have mentioned the tendency toward symmetry in the simple Head-and-Shoulders formation. Patterns of the Multiple or Complex type show an even stronger urge toward symmetry—so strong, in fact, that it may be counted on in determining trading policy. If there are two shoulders on the left, there are almost always two on the right of nearly the same size and duration. (Of course, one does not know that a Multiple is in process of formation until its right shoulder becomes evident.) Except in volume, the right-hand half of the pattern is in the great majority of cases an approximate mirror image of the left.

Necklines on Multiple Head-and-Shoulders formations are not always easy to draw, since the reactions between the shoulders and between shoulders and heads may not stop at levels which all fall on a single line. Up-sloping and down-sloping variants seldom appear in this class or patterns; necklines are almost always very close to the horizontal. Sometimes, it is possible to estimate by simple inspection where the critical line really lies. More often there are two necklines, an inner and an outer, and no price movement of consequence is to be expected until the outer has been penetrated (which, of course, is simply another expression of that tendency toward symmetry referred to above).

Curiously enough, the "power" of a Multiple Head-and-Shoulders pattern is more apt to be over- than under-estimated. One might think, in view of the length of time and amount of trading entering into its construction, that it would signalize a move (in reverse direction to the trend preceding it) of greater extent than the simple Head-and-Shoulders. Yet, in its immediate consequences at least, the Complex shows consistently less power. Minimum measuring rules for the two types of formations are the same and are applied in the same manner. The difference between the patterns appears in the price action after the minimum has been reached. The first down swing out of a plain Head-and-Shoulders Top, not counting any early pull-back rally, will frequently carry out the minimum measuring implications of that pattern quickly and run well beyond it. From a Multiple Top, the first down swing is often more leisurely and very seldom does it exceed the bare minimum—a probability well

FIGURE 26. The long Multiple H & S top made by American Locomotive in 1946 displays very well the sort of volume pattern—irregular but taking on definitely bearish character in its latter half—which is normal to this formation. The rounded Bear Market rally of August (compare price and volume trends) was unable to attain the old neckline but was stopped at a resistance (RL) created by earlier bottom levels (see Chapter XIII). G and G mark breakaway gaps which were not "covered" (see Chapter XII).

worth remembering when you are dealing with an Intermediate rather than a Primary Top. Of course, if the Complex does develop at a turn in the Primary trend, prices will eventually go much farther, but even then there is usually a strong recovery (or reaction in the case of a Bottom) from the "minimum rule" level.

A Leisurely Pattern

The volume attending the construction of Multiple Head-and-Shoulders conforms in general to the "laws" we have previously stated and explained for simple Head-and-Shoulders reversals. During the earlier stages of Multiple formation development, the volume chart may show much irregularity with little recognizable pattern, but in the latter stages its correspondence with the Head-and-Shoulders trend should be plainly seen.

There is something about Multiple Head-and-Shoulders patterns especially pleasing to technical chart followers. Because of their symmetrical tendencies

FIGURE 27. A Multiple H & S bottom with a single head and triple shoulders. Study the volume pattern. Note also the symmetry (see page 69) displayed by this formation as well as by those in preceding Figures 24 and 25. After advancing out of this base, "BO Pr" was turned back three times from an old resistance zone at 38-39 (see Chapter XIII) and then pushed up through with a Breakaway Gap (Chapter XII).

it is fascinating to watch them evolve to completion.   Once completed, however, they may try your patience by their seeming reluctance to "get going"
with the new trend.   On that account, it becomes easy at times to jump to the
conclusion that they have "blown out," i.e., produced a false signal.   Actually,
except in the matter of *extent* of move which we have already discussed, they are
fully as reliable as the plain Head-and-Shoulders.   False moves are relatively
rare with both.   And in those extraordinary cases when a Complex formation
does go wrong, it still stands, like the plain Head-and-Shoulders, as a warning
that the final reversal is near.

FIGURE 28.   Hybrid formations made up of a small Head-and-Shoulders
within the head of a larger Head-and-Shoulders are not uncommon at Primary
trend reversals.   Creole Petroleum (above) and Lone Star Cement (Figure 30,
opposite page) made bases of this type in 1942, both with down-sloping necklines.   These are weekly charts, each vertical line representing the price range
for an entire week.   Creole took ten months to complete its bottom pattern
and Lone Star, seventeen.   One great advantage of keeping supplementary
weekly charts is that it affords perspective on developments of Major import
which are obscured by the minor detail on the daily.   Study volume and
symmetry in these pictures.   (Compare with Figure 20.)

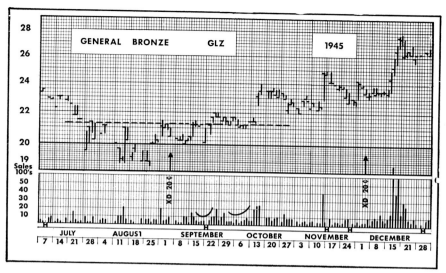

FIGURE 29. An Intermediate bottom of the Complex class, abnormal in its lack of symmetry but none-the-less easy to recognize. Low volume on reactions after head was completed gave usual (and essential) bullish confirmation. The sluggish start of the new trend is a common feature of Multiple H & S reversals.

FIGURE 30 (below). Refer to comment under Figure 28, page 72.

FIGURE 31. Another variant of the H & S within a Major reversal formation. The smaller Head-and-Shoulder pattern was easily overlooked on the
daily chart. Moreover, although it was six months long, this pattern in itself
did not necessarily imply Primary reversal. But when it pushed "PJ's" prices
up in October through the great supply which had been lodged at 12-13 the
previous December, something more than a Secondary advance could obviously be in prospect. An up move of consequence was not finally signaled,
however, until February, 1943 when the upper neckline was penetrated and
prices closed at 14. Public Service "threw back" to 12 in November, 1943 (to
the old neckline exactly) but then advanced steadily to 30.

Study this again when you take up Support-Resistance, Chap. XIII.

This chart reiterates the point that whereas top formations are often completed in a relatively short time, Major bottoms usually require many months,
and call for a great deal of patience. Allowing for the greater time needed,
however, most top patterns have their counterparts in bottom formations

FIGURE 32. Still another form which the Complex reversal may take. This can be described as an H & S pattern with two widely separated heads. Study its volume pattern, noting breakout June 20 and subsequent pull-back. Compare it with Bethlehem Steel's bottom reversal shown in Chapter XII, Figure 123.

ROUNDING TOPS AND BOTTOMS

The Multiple formations we have just examined are produced by a sort of extension or proliferation of the ordinary Head-and-Shoulders pattern. Carry this process still further and the Complexes merge into our next class of reversals, known as Rounding Turns.

In our first approach to the theory of chart reversal patterns we saw why it takes time and a considerable volume of trading to swing an established trend in prices from up to down or down to up. In the Head-and-Shoulders type of reversal, the trend surges, struggles, attacks again and again before it finally gives up and retreats. During this struggle the balance between the forces of supply and demand fluctuates, often wildly, until finally the one overcomes the other. In the Multiple formations a similar process goes on but rather less violently and, over a period of time, the progressive change in balance from one

FIGURE 33.   Major top reversal patterns in high-priced investment issues are frequently long and "flat."   The 1946 top of Phillips Petroleum could be classified as either a Multiple H & S or an irregular Rounding Top.   An important trendline (Chapter XIV) was broken down-side in July.

force to the other becomes clearly apparent.   The Rounding Turn is a much more simple and logical manifestation of this technical phenomenon.   It pictures simply and plainly a gradual, progressive and fairly symmetrical change in the trend direction, produced by a gradual shift in the balance of power between buying and selling.

If, for example, the buying has been stronger than the selling for some time past, we know that the result will have been a general upward trend in the price of our stock, as indicated by our pictorial chart record of its trading history. So long as the buyers of the stock remain more anxious, more numerous, more aggressive, more powerful than the sellers, that preceding upward trend will continue.   Now, however, suppose the selling grows a little stronger, while the buying either weakens slightly or remains stationary at its previous strength. This slight change in the technical balance will be indicated by a slowing up of the previous advance.   As the selling increases in relative power it will finally become equal to the buying power, with the result that the market level moves neither up nor down but remains for a time quite stationary (except for minor and insignificant fluctuations).

Assume that the new development continues and the selling pressure grows until it is finally stronger than buying power.   Now the balance is moving the other way.   There are now more sellers than buyers and the result will be a gradual decline in the market quotations for the stock.   If this change in the

FIGURE 34. The war-end reaction of 1945 in American & Foreign Power 2d Preferred, as well as in many other issues, took the form of a Rounding Bottom. Compare the price and volume trends. By October 4 the implications here were plain to see.

balance of power is fairly steady and continues to its logical conclusion, we can see, even without the aid of a chart, that our picture of the price movement for that stock would be one of long advancing trend slowly beginning to round off, holding in stationary suspense for a time, and then commencing a retreat, reversing the previous upward movement into a new and accelerating downward trend.

Rounding Bottoms are commonly referred to as *Bowl* or *Saucer* patterns. Rounding Tops are sometimes called *Inverted Bowls*. Despite the logic of their construction, neither types appear as frequently as Head-and-Shoulders formations. Rounding Bottoms occur most often in low-priced stocks, in an extended, flat-bottomed form which usually takes many months to complete. There was a host of such developments during 1942 and 1943 among issues selling under $10 a share. (It should be noted here that "saucer" bottoms of two or three months' duration also appear frequently, one right after another, in the charts of low-priced issues *during* an extended up movement. Their characteristics and denotations will be discussed later when we come to *Consolidation*.

FIGURE 35.   Monthly chart, on arithmetic scale.   American Safety
Razor's 1932 Major bottom was a Head-and-Shoulders, also its
1936 Bull top.   Its 1942-46 Bull Market started from a Rounding
Bottom nearly two and a half years long!   See page 84.   Monthly
chart study pays.

Tops of the Rounding type are very rare among stocks in the lower and medium price ranges, but are found occasionally in the charts of those high-priced
common stocks which command an AA rating among wealthy investors and
do not ordinarily interest the general public.   They also appear frequently in the
charts of high-grade preferred stocks, and quite naturally, because the demand
for their shares reflects chiefly two factors—supply of funds seeking conservative
investment and interest rates—both of which tend to change very slowly.   The
speculative appeal which produces wide-swinging price fluctuations is absent in

such issues. The same line of reasoning explains why Rounding Tops almost never develop in lower priced, speculative common stocks; Bull Markets in those are topped off by excited public buying which pays little or no heed to long-range investment considerations.

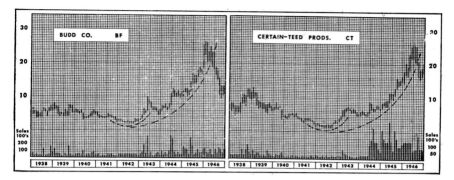

FIGURE 36 (left above). Monthly chart of Budd Co. Note that 1942 was the first year to produce a dull saucer-shaped pattern, a Rounding Bottom of Major import. "BF" climbed from below 3 in 1942 to above 26 in 1946.

FIGURE 37 (right above). Similar formation in Certain-teed Products, which rose from below 2 in 1942 to above 25 in 1946. Study volume 1940 to 1945. The up-curving type of Major Bull trend shown on these charts will be discussed in Chapter XV.

How Rounding Turns Affect Trading Activity

We have not as yet mentioned the volume half of the Rounding Turn picture. It is interesting as well as meaningful. In the case of Rounding Bottoms its pattern is usually as clean-cut and decisive as the price pattern. The first step in the gradual conquest of supply by demand which produces a Rounding Bottom appears as a lessening in selling pressure. Volume, which has been running high, gradually decreases; demand is still timid but the pressure on it less: so, while prices still decline, the pace is slower and the trend curves more and more to the horizontal. At the bottom, with the two forces technically in balance, relatively few transactions are recorded. Then demand begins to increase and as the price curve turns up trading becomes more active. Volume accelerates with the trend until often it reaches a sort of climactic peak in a few days of almost "vertical" price movement on the chart.

In such formations, the tips of the volume lines at the bottom of the chart when connected will describe an arc which often roughly parallels the arc formed by the price "bowl" above. These patterns, when they occur *after an extensive decline* are of outstanding importance, for they nearly always denote a change in Primary trend and an extensive advance yet to come.   That advance, however, seldom carries right on in a "sky-rocket" effect which completes the entire Major move in a few weeks.   On the contrary, the up trend which follows the completion of the pattern itself is apt to be slow and subject to frequent interruptions, tiring out the impatient trader but yielding eventually a substantial profit.

Let us repeat that trading volume should ebb to an extreme low at the bottom of a bowl pattern if its implications are to be trusted.   After prices have passed dead center, however, and begun their first gradual climb with as yet only a slight pick-up in activity, something in the nature of a premature breakout may occur.   Without warning, a burst of buying may shoot quotations straight up for a day or two.   These incidents are by no means rare, but almost invari-

FIGURE 38.   A classic example of Rounding Bottom at the Major trend reversal of 1932.   The jump out of line on June 10 and subsequent return to the saucer pattern is a common development in Rounding Bottoms.

ably prices will quickly drop back again into their former channel and the gradual rounding movement is resumed. There is no particular danger for the trader in these premature bursts but, if he is tempted to jump in on such a sudden showing of strength, he should realize that there probably will still be need for patience. A classic example of this type of premature break appears in one of our accompanying illustrations.

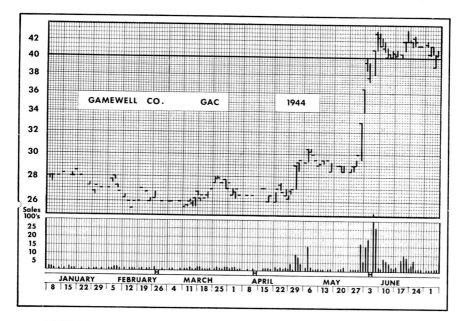

FIGURE 39. An extreme case of "Dormant Bottom." There were many days in first four months during which no shares were traded. A "buy" signal appeared on April 26. Note volume.

THE DORMANT BOTTOM VARIATION

There is one sort of Major Bottom chart picture which has been called a *Dormant Bottom* but which relates logically to our Bowl pattern, being in effect an extreme development of the "extended, flat-bottomed form" to which we have alluded above. It appears characteristically in "thin" stocks, i.e. those in which the total number of shares outstanding or, more particularly, the floating supply of shares is very small. In such issues a normal day's turnover may be only two or three hundred shares in an active rising market. After a severe sell-off, blank days begin to appear on the chart. Finally, weeks and sometimes months will pass during which no sales will be registered for days at a time, or only an occasional lot at a figure which fluctuates within a fractional range. The chart appears "fly specked."

Eventually, there may appear a sudden and usually quite inexplicable flurry of activity. Several hundred shares appear on the tape and prices advance sharply. This "break out of dormancy" can be a premature move, such as we have noted in connection with typical Rounding Bottoms, to be followed by several more weeks of inactivity, or it can be the first lift in a sort of step-up process with shorter and shorter intervals between each step until finally a consistent up trend develops. In any event, it is a signal that we are dealing with an important accumulation pattern.

What has happened to form these Dormant Bottoms is easy to guess. With relatively few shares outstanding, and only an occasional lot put up for sale "at the market," investors (perhaps insiders connected with the company) would succeed only in running the price up out of reach if they started to bid for the stock. So they simply "hold a basket under it," as the saying goes, quickly picking up anything that is offered but never reaching for it, until eventually the tree is shaken clean. Then they may raise their bids a point or so; if that seems to bring out a lot of stock for sale, they go back to their waiting tactics.

FIGURE 40. The March, 1935 reaction produced many Rounding Bottoms. This one verges on the "dormant" type. The gap (G), a breakaway through a resistance level, was not "closed" until late 1937 (Chapter XII).

FIGURE 41.   Brief (two to three months) Rounding Turns are fairly common patterns at Intermediate bottoms in Primary Bull trends.   Longer ones develop at Major bottoms.   This 1945 pattern in Gabriel is typical of "thin" stocks.   Horizontal dashes indicate support-resistance levels, discussed in Chapter XIII.

VOLUME PATTERN AT TOPS

The volume pattern on Rounding Tops is seldom as clearly defined as at Bottoms.   Indeed, it is apt to be rather high and irregular throughout the entire rounding over movement in prices.   Under close scrutiny one can usually see some signs of a change from bullish to bearish activity in the minor fluctuations after the peak has been passed but the volume warnings do not become conspicuous in most cases until the down trend has begun to accelerate toward the vertical.

We know of no measuring formula which can be applied to Rounding Turns (except for the minimum qualifications we mentioned in connection with Head-and-Shoulders: i.e., they cannot be counted upon to produce a greater move than the preceding price swing in the opposite direction).   But they *almost never deceive.*   Their implications can be roughly estimated from the magnitude of the trends which led to them and the length of time they take in the rounding over process. The Rounding Turns which often appear on weekly and monthly charts, thus, have major import.

Which leads us to the general consideration of weekly and monthly chart patterns. Thus far we have been speaking in detail of only daily chart developments, but all of the formations we have taken up appear as well in the much larger swings into which daily movements are condensed on weekly and monthly charts, and with identical significance. The volume record may not be quite so easy to read (climactic activity may occur on one day of a week and the other days run dull, which would not show at all in the week's total figure) but is less critical—may almost be disregarded. Head-and-Shoulders Tops are particularly plentiful on monthly charts and should be accorded due respect. In fact, any clearly defined pattern which is built to completion on a weekly or monthly chart is proportionately significant (bearing always in mind that "a reversal must have something to reverse").

FIGURE 42. In October, 1936, Vanadium Corp. appeared to be well on its way toward completion of a Rounding Top. The price pattern was typical of that formation and volume had declined notably as quotations rose in August and then "rounded over" through September. But note the volume pattern during late October, and then refer to Figure 43 on following page.

FIGURE 43. This chart carries the Vanadium picture of Figure 42 on through December. When prices dipped further on October 26, trading turnover should have increased if a genuine top reversal formation was being completed. Instead, volume remained at a minimum on that down day and then increased sharply on the following day which saw prices advance. This bullish rather than bearish volume trend was maintained for four weeks during which prices refused to break below their October 26 low point. On December 3 the whole picture quickly turned strong and active. By March, 1937, "VA" had climbed to 39.

If the volume trend does not curve around with prices when the latter appear to be making a Rounding Turn, take no action. Await further developments. Volume is an essential part of every technical formation.

CHAPTER VIII

IMPORTANT REVERSAL PATTERNS—THE TRIANGLES

WE COME next to an entirely different family of technical patterns, the Triangles—a group which has not been as well represented on the charts of the past ten years as it was during the twenties and early thirties. Their present scarcity is regrettable because they are an intriguing lot with excellent profit potentialities. Before we examine them in detail, however, a quick review of the basic theory which gives meaning and value to technical analysis, may be appropriate. That theory can be re-summarized in the following brief statements.

1. The market value of a security is determined solely by the interaction of supply and demand.

2. Supply and demand are governed at any given moment by many hundreds of factors, some rational and some irrational. Information, opinions, moods, guesses (shrewd or otherwise) as to the future, combine with blind necessities in this equation. No ordinary man can hope to grasp and weigh them all, but the market does this automatically.

3. Disregarding minor fluctuations, prices move in trends which persist for an appreciable length of time.

4. Changes in trend, which represent an important shift in the balance between supply and demand, however caused, are detectable *sooner or later* in the action of the market itself.

By this time, the fact expressed in the italicized words of the last statement may have begun to raise some misgivings in your mind. The complaint that the Dow Theory is often "later" has already been discussed. The reversal patterns studied in the two preceding chapters give no certain signal until *after* the trend has changed, usually "sooner" as compared with Dow Theory, but never at the absolute top or bottom price. The man who sells a stock as soon as, but not until, a Head-and-Shoulders Top has been completed on its chart may cash in on no more than half of the total decline from its extreme high to extreme bottom, since by the very terms of our measuring formula the first half of the decline can have taken place before the top reversal formation was finally confirmed.

Make up your mind that there is no help for it. Somebody, of course, managed to sell his shares at the very top eighth of a point on the peak of the "head" (and some poor devil bought them). The seller was just plain lucky!

His exploit can be truly compared with a "hole-in-one" in golf. Even a complete duffer occasionally enjoys that thrill. But the more experienced a player, the better satisfied he is to land safely on the green and not too far from the cup. The more experienced an investor, the less concerned he is with getting the last point, or even the last ten points, out of his market commitments.

No one can ever be sure *at the time* that he is selling at the final high. No rules or methods have ever been devised—nor ever will be—to ensure buying within fractions of the bottom, or selling within fractions of the top. Of course, a man can make certain of buying a stock at its absolute low provided he is prepared to take at that figure every last share offered, even to the entire outstanding issue if necessary. It might, in theory, require as much as $3,743,-000,000.00 to "put a bottom" under U. S. Steel at 70, in case you are tempted.

The reader, who at this point may think we "protest too much," will see more excuse for the foregoing remarks when we take up the habits of Triangles, for these formations are not always indicative of trend reversal. On the contrary, except in certain rather uncommon varieties, they are more apt to signalize what may most conveniently be termed *consolidation,* terminating an up or down move only temporarily and setting the stage for another strong move *in the same direction* later on. (Schabacker called such chart formations "Continuation Patterns.") The reason for including Triangles in this section of our studies under the general heading of Reversal Formations is that they do at times develop at periods of Major trend change, and those are, by all odds, the periods which it is most essential for the investor to recognize.

SYMMETRICAL TRIANGLES

The commonest form of Triangle is composed of a series of price fluctuations, each of which is *smaller than its predecessor,* each Minor top failing to attain the height of the preceding rally and each Minor recession stopping above the level of the preceding bottom. The result is a sort of contracting "Dow Line" on the chart—a sidewise price area or trading range whose top can be more or less accurately defined by a *down-slanting* boundary line and whose bottom can be similarly bounded by an *up-slanting* line. This type of Triangle is called a Symmetrical Triangle. If we wanted to make a more accurate application of the language of geometry, we might better call it an Acute Triangle, since it is not at all necessary that its top and bottom boundaries be of equal length or, in other words, make the same angle with the horizontal axis. However, there is a very strong tendency in these formations to approximate the symmetrical form, so the established name will do well enough. This pattern is also sometimes referred to as a "coil."

While the process of contraction or coiling which makes up the price action of the Symmetrical Triangle pattern is going on, trading activity exhibits a diminishing trend, irregularly perhaps but nevertheless quite noticeably as time goes on. The converging upper and lower boundary lines of the price formation come together somewhere out to the right (the future in the time sense) of the chart, at the *apex* of our Triangle. As prices work their way along in narrower and narrower fluctuations toward the apex, volume ebbs to an abnormally low daily turnover. Then, if we are dealing with a typical example, comes the action which first suggested the name "coil." For suddenly and without warning as though a coil spring had been wound tighter and tighter and then snapped free, prices break out of their Triangle with a notable pick-up in volume, and leap away in a strong move which tends to approximate in extent the up or down move which preceded its formation.

There is seldom any clue given on the one chart containing the Triangle to tell in which direction prices are going to break out of pattern until that action finally occurs. Sometimes you can get a pretty good idea of what is likely to happen by observing what is going on at the same time in the charts of other stocks (which is an important topic for later discussion) but often there is

FIGURE 44. A fine Symmetrical Triangle reversal formation on a weekly chart. Upper boundary sloping down from February, 1942 recovery high at 21 and lower boundary sloping up from "Pearl Harbor" bottom at 16⅜ converge to an apex at about 18⅝. From this Major bottom pattern, "HD" advanced to 45 in 1946. Note shrinkage in volume as pattern formed, and increase as price broke out through top in October, 1942. Breakout came not quite three quarters of way over from first top to apex (see page 90).

FIGURE 45. Sears Roebuck made a Symmetrical Triangle reversal at its Bull Market top in 1946 and then went into another long Triangle which turned out to be a consolidation rather than reversal formation. (Logarithmic volume scaling minimizes volume variations.) Sell signal was given at 44½ and again at 41. Decline continued to 30½.

nothing to do but wait until the market makes up its mind which way to go. And "making up its mind" is just what the market seems to be doing when it builds a Triangle; everything about this pattern appears to exemplify doubt, vacillation, stalling until finally a decision is reached.

SOME CAUTIONS ABOUT SYMMETRICAL TRIANGLES

A compact clean-cut Triangle is a fascinating picture, but it has its tricky features. The beginner in technical chart analysis is quite naturally prone to look for Triangles constantly, and will often think he has detected them when, in fact, something entirely different is in process of development. Remember that it takes *two* points to determine a line. The top boundary line of a price area cannot be drawn until two Minor trend tops have been definitely established, which means that prices must have moved up to and then down away from both far enough to leave the two peaks standing out clear and clean on the chart. A bottom boundary line, by the same token, cannot be drawn until two Minor trend bottoms have been definitely established. Therefore, before you can conclude that a Symmetrical Triangle is building, you must be able to see *four* reversals of Minor trend. If it comes after an advance in prices, you must have first a top, next a bottom, next a second top lower than the first, and finally a second bottom higher than the first bottom (and prices must move up away from the second bottom before you can be sure it is a bottom). Then, and only then, can you draw your boundary lines and proceed on the assumption that you have a Symmetrical Triangle.

Another point to remember—and one which does not conform at all to the "coil" simile—is that the farther out into the apex of the Triangle prices push without bursting its boundaries, the less force or power the pattern seems to have. Instead of building up more pressure, it begins to lose its efficacy after a certain stage. The best moves (up or down) seem to ensue when prices break out decisively at a point somewhere between half and three quarters of the horizontal distance from the base (left-hand end) to the apex. If prices continue to move "sidewise" in narrower and narrower fluctuations from day to day after the three-quarter mark is passed, they are quite apt to keep right on to the apex and beyond in a dull drift or ripple which leaves the chart analyst completely at sea. The best thing to do in such cases is go away and look for something more promising elsewhere in your chart book.

FIGURE 46. Johns-Manville's Primary trend reversal in 1942 developed out of a Symmetrical Triangle which had also some aspects of an H & S pattern with a long right shoulder. Although this is a weekly chart, the volume here is worthy of detailed study in connection with the price action. "JM" (old stock) advanced more than 100 points in next four years.

FIGURE 47. Logarithmic price scaling on weekly chart empha-
sizes important technical developments at low price levels. "DH's"
Symmetrical Triangle bottom started a Bull Market which reached
57 in 1945. Note throw-back to apex of Triangle, a not uncommon
development. The apex itself is a strong support (Chapter XIII).

And a third tricky point is that it becomes necessary sometimes to re-draw
one or both boundaries of a Triangle before it is finally completed (i.e., before
prices break out and move away from it in decisive fashion). This can happen,
for example, when, after the first two rally tops have established a down-slanting
upper boundary line, the third rally starting from the lower boundary pushes up
and *through* the original top line by a moderate margin and then, without developing recognizable breakout volume on this move, stops short of surpassing
the highest level of the preceding (second) pattern top. When prices subsequently drop back again into pattern, it is necessary to abandon the original
upper boundary line and draw a new one across the highs of the first and third
rally tops.

How Prices Break Out of a Symmetrical Triangle

Prices may move out of a Symmetrical Triangle either up or down. There is seldom if ever, as we have said above, any clue as to direction until the move has actually started; i.e., until prices have broken out of their triangular "area of doubt" in decisive fashion. In a very general way the precepts we have laid down for breakouts from Head-and-Shoulders formations apply here as well. For example, the margin by which prices should close beyond the pattern lines is the same, roughly 3%. It is equally essential that an *up-side* break in prices be confirmed by a marked increase in trading volume; lacking volume, do not trust the price achievement. But a *down-side* breakout, again as in the case of the Head-and-Shoulders, does not require confirmation by a pick-up in activity. As a matter of record, volume does visibly increase in most cases, but in a majority of down breaks not to any notable extent until after prices have fallen below the level of the last preceding Minor bottom within the Triangle, which as you can see, may be several points lower than the boundary line at the place (date) of the actual breakout.

The curious fact is that a down-side breakout from a Symmetrical Triangle

FIGURE 48. Triangles often form as a part of a larger and more important pattern of some other type. Here a Symmetrical figure constitutes the latter half of a Rounding Turn. Note premature breakout October 17, return to pattern, and then final breakaway on November 8.

which is attended right from the start by conspicuously heavy volume is much more apt to be a false signal rather than the start of a genuine down trend that will be worth following. Particularly is this true if the break occurs after prices have worked their way well out into the apex of the Triangle; a high volume crack then frequently—we might even say usually—develops into a two or three day "shake-out" which quickly reverses itself and is followed by a genuine move in the *up* direction.

All of which the reader will have undoubtedly found most disconcerting. Here is a very pretty technical pattern and it cannot always be trusted. Unfortunately, Symmetrical Triangles are subject to *false* moves to a far greater extent than the Head-and-Shoulders or any of the other formations we have discussed or will discuss later. Unfortunately, some of these false moves cannot be identified as such until after a commitment has been risked (although good trading tactics should prevent their occasioning much more than a trivial loss). And, unfortunately again, even a typical shake-out, such as we described in the preceding paragraph, may produce a double-cross—may proceed right on down

FIGURE 49. Prices in this Symmetrical Triangle squeezed away out into the apex before erupting. Breakout at that stage is unreliable; above is a fair sample of the false moves that occur there. Real move was down.

in a genuine decline.   No technical chart formation is 100% reliable, and of all, our present subject is the worst offender.

But, most Symmetrical Triangles—lacking an actual statistical count, our experience would suggest more than two thirds of them—behave themselves properly, produce no false signals which cannot be spotted before any damage is done.   Up-side breakouts on high volume may be premature in the sense that prices return to pattern and do some more "work" there before the genuine up trend gets under way, but they seldom are false.   We shall have a little more to say about false signals in this chapter and more later on that we trust will be helpful in developing the experience a trader needs to defend himself against them.

A Typical Triangle Development

The several actual chart examples of Symmetrical Triangles which illustrate this chapter will serve, we trust, to give the reader a working acquaintance with their appearance in various manifestations.   Yet it may help to clear up some of the more important points if we describe in detail just how a typical pattern develops, step by step.   Let us suppose that you are watching a stock on your charts which has climbed, with only the normal, brief hesitations and inconsequential reactions, from around 20 to 30, 32, 35 and is still moving up.   (Let's hope you bought it at 20!)   Lower down its turnover ran between 300 and 600 shares daily but now, above 30, it has attracted quite a following and daily volume has increased to around 1,000.   As it approaches 40, activity shoots up to nearly 2,000 shares, the market "churns" between 39 and 40, and then prices begin to drop.   As they fall back, you (especially if you own the stock) watch it with some concern but you know it is hardly likely that it is going to go right straight down again to 20; stocks don't act that way.   If the trend of this issue has actually been reversed it should nevertheless spend some more time and effort around its top levels, make some sort of a distribution pattern.

The decline continues for ten days with the turnover also declining quite appreciably.   By the time prices have worked back to 33, volume is running at only about 700 shares daily.   At 33 it may pick up again for a single day to 800 or 900 shares, but the reaction stops there and after a day or two prices begin to climb again with little change in their turnover rate.   In eight or nine days, quotations have gotten back into the upper thirties and activity increases and reaches, say, 1,200 shares on the day 39 is reached.   Instead of going on to 40 or beyond, however, a new reaction sets in and prices drift back to 37.   (Perhaps you will find this growing picture easier to visualize if you will pencil its development on a scrap of chart paper.)   Now it is evident that a second top has formed at 39; you can now draw a tentative pattern line (there are other names for this, as we shall see later) on your chart across the two extreme high ranges (not closing prices) which will slant downward from left to right. So far you have only one bottom point so you can draw no lines from that. But this second decline brings out even less trading activity than the first. Volume ebbs to 400 shares and the down move halts at 34; the price track "rounds out" and turns up again; trading is very dull but begins to pick up as 36 is reached.

This action defines a second Minor bottom and now you can draw a bottom "tangent"—an up-slanting line across the extreme low prices registered on the two reactions, the first at 33 and the second at 34. Your two pattern lines will converge, meeting near the 36½ level about four weeks ahead (i.e., to the right) on your chart. You have a Symmetrical Triangle—*but* you don't know whether prices are going to fall out of it eventually or shake off present doubts and push up in a new advance worth following. You can only watch further

FIGURE 50. Recovery rallies from "panic" bottoms are often capped by Triangles, for those are periods in which doubt and indecision (see page 89) are prevalent. The doubt in such cases, however, is usually resolved in favor of renewed decline. "Panic bottoms seldom hold." This chart shows a typical symmetrical pattern topping the recovery from the famous selling climax of October 19, 1937. Note pull-back to apex.

developments very closely and be prepared to take whatever action is in due time indicated thereby.

The second rally picks up a little in activity, attains a daily turnover of about 700 shares and pushes up to 38 and on for part of a day to 38½. This nudges through the previously drawn pattern line by perhaps a quarter of a point (since each swing is shorter in points traveled and accordingly in duration). But the volume on this minor penetration is less than on the preceding top (at 39) and buying again ebbs. As the price range line falls back to 37 and 36, you had best now draw a new upper tangent across the first top at 40 and the last top at 38½. There is the suggestion here in this slight "lift" that the balance may be swinging slightly to the demand side, but don't count on it. Pin-point accuracy is not to be expected; Triangles must be allowed some leeway.

On the third reaction, activity dwindles away to the lowest yet. The up-slanting bottom boundary will be reached at about 35 level if prices continue their present course. It is worth noting now if they will come all the way down to it this time—because if they don't—if their recession is halted half a point or so above it—that action would give some significance to the previous bulge

FIGURE 51. A Major Symmetrical Triangle top in which prices squeezed out into the apex and then produced a false move up side (cf. Figure 49). "VEC," as a matter of fact, is a bad actor technically, but this particular break-out would be suspect anyway (see page 90).

through the upper boundary. But this doesn't happen; the drift continues right on down to 35 and now volume is running at the rate of only 200 shares daily—less than it ran in the early stages of the original advance above 20. This is a critical spot. The price track flattens out momentarily, turns up feebly but keeps on hitching up, crosses 36½, picks up activity, reaches the (new) upper Triangle boundary at 37½ and, on the next day, punches through on a turnover of 1,500 shares to close at 39⅛. This is a breakout; the doubt is resolved and (barring a false move—unlikely at this point) the trend is once again up. Note that it was not necessary for prices to surpass the previous high at 40 to produce this signal—that is one of the interesting things about Symmetrical Triangles.

REVERSAL OR CONSOLIDATION

But, we started to discuss Symmetrical Triangles as reversal patterns and our example has turned out to be instead a *consolidation* pattern, i.e., only a sort of resting stage in a continued up trend. Well, three out of four, approximately, of these formations will turn out to be just that. The fourth is the dangerous one (if you own the stock). How would it differ?

The example described might have been a reversal instead of a consolidation formation any time up to the point of the decisive break through to 39. If it had been a *typical* Reversal the first change would probably have appeared shortly after the final rally started up from the third bottom at 35. That rally would have petered out at about 36½ and prices would have started to drift back again. Then, with activity increasing slightly, the bottom boundary would be penetrated. As quotations dropped to 34, daily volume might mount to 600 or 700 shares. Any further decline would constitute a down signal and would result in a further pick-up in turnover and an acceleration in the price decline as the stop-loss orders (to be discussed later) spotted under 34 were "touched off."

Before we leave our typical example, we might make some mention of the post-breakout reactions or pull-backs that sometimes occur. As in the case of the Head-and-Shoulders formation, the initial breakout move from a Symmetrical Triangle may halt before prices are carried very far away from the pattern and be followed by a minor reaction, usually lasting only two or three days, which will carry quotations back to the nearest pattern boundary. Thus, in our first example in which the break when it came took our stock up through the top side to 39⅛, the next day might have seen a push on to 40 and then prices might have backed off again in a couple of days of decreased activity to 37½ or 38. The up move would then normally be resumed with greater vigor. Down-side breakouts are sometimes followed in much the same manner by pull-backs to the lower boundary of the pattern, after which the decline is resumed

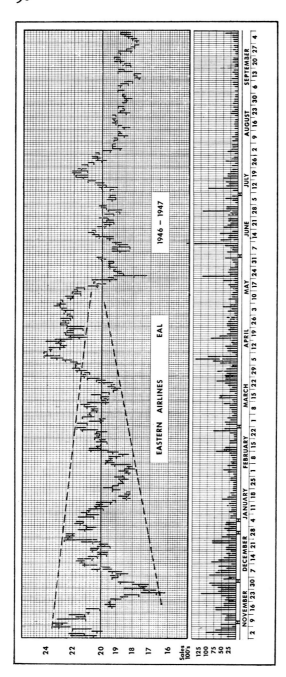

FIGURE 52. The other side of the story—an imposing Symmetrical Triangle which failed badly, although for the alert and experienced technician there were warnings of something amiss in March and April. Eastern Airlines built in late 1946 and early 1947 a formation which so far as price pattern was concerned left little to be desired. Prices broke out top-side decisively in late March. A throw-back in April met normal support at the upper Triangle boundary. But the subsequent advance fell short, weakened, and finally broke down, producing an "end run" around the apex. Warnings referred to were high and irregular volume, particularly on reactions, in February and March—not characteristic of valid Triangle development—and failure of prices to push up rapidly and vigorously after the April 14 throw-back.

with an increase in volume. However, these post-breakout reactions occur less often with Triangles than they do with Head-and-Shoulders.

Another matter we might take up, before going on to study the next formation, is the *rationale* of the Symmetrical Triangle. It may help to fix its characteristics in mind if we try to deduce what sequence of events might typically produce it. Of course, any effort of this sort can result only in a gross oversimplification which will not fit all of the Triangle's various manifestations, but it is an interesting mental speculation—and one not without benefit to our understanding of the general theory of chart formations. Let us turn back again to our typical example. We started with a stock that ran up rather steadily from around 20 to 40 and then reacted. It is fairly obvious what happened at

FIGURE 53. A weekly chart. The seven-month consolidation area of 1944 in "NG," undefinable at first, developed eventually into a typical Symmetrical Triangle. Two months after the high volume breakout in January, 1945, prices reacted nearly to apex level, then pushed away rapidly. Minimum measuring implications of this Triangle (see page 111) were satisfied at 16.

40: many investors had substantial paper profits, approaching 100%, at that price. (A "round figure such as 40, 50, 75 or 100 is apt to become a sort of mental profit objective and, hence, bring in increased selling.) Some of them were ready to cash in and did so, temporarily swinging the technical balance from demand to supply; they sold less freely, of course, as prices receded. Other would-be investors had been attracted to the same stock but too late to "get aboard" below 30. Unwilling to "chase" it-up to 40, they welcomed the reaction and, by the time prices had dropped back to 33, enough of them were now ready to buy to swing the balance back again to the demand side of the equation.

Watching the ensuing rally, however, were the owners of the stock who had failed to grab their profits near 40 on the previous advance and had made up their minds to be a little less greedy if given a second opportunity. Their offerings began to come in above 37, say, and were sufficiently copious at 39 to stem the advance at that level. Behind the scenes we can imagine this process repeated again and again, with new money constantly coming in and meeting supply from owners increasingly anxious to cinch their profits. Eventually the offerings of the latter are all absorbed, or perhaps withdrawn, and then professionals as well as hopeful investors suddenly discover that there is no stock ahead on the books and a rush to buy results.

Since the advance (or decline) which follows the completion of a Symmetrical Triangle usually runs to worth-while trading proportions (we shall discuss measuring implications later), there would be an evident advantage to the

FIGURE 54. A small Symmetrical Triangle which tended toward the "ascending" type (see page 102). Note that the higher volume which developed within this pattern in early January came on a rally. This sort of action is fairly typical of very "thin" stocks.

trader who could tell in advance of the breakout which way prices were going to move. The odds are, as we have already said, that the new move will proceed in the same direction as the one prior to the Triangle's formation. These odds are greatest, of course, in the *early* stages of either a Primary Bull or Bear Market, with the chances of reversal increasing as those Major trends mature. But the charts of other stocks often furnish valuable collateral evidence. Thus, if at the same time you detect a Symmetrical Triangle in process of formation in

FIGURE 55. An ascending Triangle ten months long which was the start of a Major Bull trend, carrying "ABN" to 45. Refusal of prices to react to the lower pattern boundary, as here in August, 1942, is a frequent development in strong formations, a warning of near completion and breakout.

"PDQ," a majority of your charts are showing Saucers or Head-and-Shoulders Bottoms or Ascending Triangles or some other pattern of typically bullish import, it is a fair assumption that your Symmetrical Triangle will break out top-side. There are times when advance indications of this sort are strong enough to justify taking a position on it.

FIGURE 56. Premature breakouts from Right-Angle Triangles, such as appeared in Celanese in March, 1946, are temporarily disappointing to the trader who buys on them, but work out all right eventually. Celanese before its 1946 split was subject to frequent and peculiar shake-outs, as here on March 9 and 26.

THE RIGHT-ANGLE TRIANGLES

We mentioned *Ascending* Triangles in the preceding paragraph. The Ascending and Descending are the bullish and bearish manifestations, respectively, of our next class of patterns, the *Right-Angle Triangles*. In many respects, in most in fact, they perform like their Symmetrical cousins, but with this very gratifying difference: they give advance notice of their intentions. Hence their names, for the supposition always is that prices will ascend out of the Ascending form and descend from the Descending form.

The Symmetrical Triangles as we have seen are constructed of a series of successively narrower price fluctuations which can be approximately bounded across their tops by a down-sloping line and across their bottoms by an up-sloping line. Right-Angle Triangles are distinguished by the fact that one of their boundaries is practically horizontal while the other slants toward it. If the top line is horizontal and the bottom line slopes up to meet it somewhere out to the right on the chart (at the apex), the Triangle is of the *Ascending* persuasion. If the bottom line is horizontal and the top line slopes down, the Triangle is *Descending*.

These formations are perfectly logical and easy to explain. The Ascending Triangle, for instance, pictures in the simplest and most normal form what happens when a growing demand for a certain stock meets a large block of shares for sale at a fixed price. If the demand continues, the supply being distributed at that price will eventually be entirely absorbed by new owners looking for still higher levels, and prices will then advance rapidly. A typical Ascending pattern starts to develop in much the same way as the "ideal" Symmetrical Triangle previously described, with an advance in our certain stock from 20 to 40 where sufficient supply suddenly appears on the market to fill the orders of all buyers and produce a reaction. Sensing the temporary satiation of demand some owners may dump their holdings on the decline but offerings are soon exhausted

FIGURE 57.   A steep recovery from a panic bottom (the "Pearl Harbor" selling) flattened out into a fine Ascending Triangle. Note horizontal supply line at 19, above a gradually rising demand line. The breakout at the end of September signaled initiation of an advance of some consequence. It turned out to be a Primary Bull Market which took Briggs up to 53.

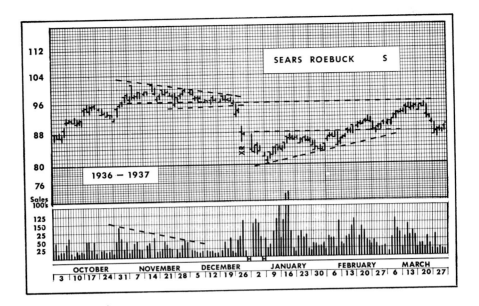

FIGURE 58.   Sears' 1936 Bull Market top was a Symmetrical Triangle, out of which it declined 15 points.   An Ascending Triangle then produced an Intermediate recovery to the supply zone (see Chapter XIII) at the lower side of the top Triangle.   Compare this chart with the 1946 top in Figure 45.

as prices drop back to, say, 34 and renewed demand then stimulates a new rally. This runs into supply again at 40 and again all buyers are accommodated at that level.   The second recession, however, carries quotation down only to 36 before another up move develops.   But the pool or inside group that is distributing at 40 still has some of its holdings left to sell, so it may take more time, another backing away and another attack at the 40 line, before the supply there is exhausted and the trend can push along up.

A PLANNED DISTRIBUTION

This type of market action evidences a planned campaign by owners of a fairly large quantity of shares to liquidate at a pre-determined price.   It contains little of the element of doubt which we mentioned as characterizing the Symmetrical pattern.   So long as demand persists, the distributing pool knows it can ultimately cash in its entire line at 40 and need not sell for less.   It is equally apparent, so long as demand keeps coming in at higher and higher

FIGURE 59. An Ascending Triangle at an Intermediate bottom. This chart runs from April through August, 1936. Extreme shrinkage in trading volume during this formation indicated a very strong situation technically.

levels, that, once the supply at 40 has all been absorbed, the market will advance rapidly and easily. As soon as prices break out above 40, those who took over the supply at that figure will feel their judgment has been vindicated and will not be disposed to sell until they in turn can register a good profit.

The crux of the matter is, of course, contained in the two preceding sentences. Demand must continue to come in at higher and higher levels; otherwise our formation will cease to be an Ascending Triangle. And the overhead supply must eventually be absorbed, permitting an up-side breakout. If demand begins to falter any time before the supply line (horizontal top boundary) has been broken through, the ensuing reaction may drop prices down "out of pat-

FIGURE 60. One of early 1947's disappointments (to the Bulls) was the failure of "AM" to break out top-side from the long Ascending Triangle depicted above. Here is a case (see page 105) where supply at 15 finally overwhelmed demand. A pattern such as this indicates a potentially strong underlying situation for the long pull. Ordinarily the consequence of an Ascending Triangle's "failure" of this sort is the development either of an extended rectangular base within the general range of the Triangle (in this case, 10 to 15), or formation of a Double Bottom at or near the earlier low (in this case near 10). However, "AM" dropped lower after several more attempts to overcome the Major supply at the 15 level, which was not substantially penetrated until 1955.

tern" and then the chart technician is faced with the necessity of revising his chart picture. One might think that such a development, blasting the earlier promise of the chart, would occur fairly often but, as a matter of experience, it is surprisingly rare. We say "surprisingly" because it is obvious that in many cases of Ascending Triangle development the group whose selling creates its top boundary or supply line must believe that level to be just about as high as the stock has any right to go. As holders of a large enough block to influence the market for several weeks, and sometimes for months, their judgment is hardly to be scorned. Yet, once it becomes evident that the lower boundary or demand line is slanting *up*, the odds are certainly somewhere in the neighborhood of nine to one that the new buyers will eventually have the best of it.

On occasion, the third reaction or fourth reaction within an Ascending

FIGURE 61. The 1942 Bear Market bottom in Socony Vacuum was an unusual Head-and-Shoulders formation, the head consisting of an Ascending Triangle. Note increase in volume on the breakout from the Triangle in July and again on the break through the H & S neckline in October.

Triangle formation will break down through the previously established up-slant-ing demand line (lower boundary) but will be halted at the same level as the previous reaction. The pattern from there on is apt to develop as a *Rectangle,* a formation to be discussed in our next chapter, and should be treated as such. (The *tactics* of trading on Ascending and Descending Triangles, including protection against the rare cases of collapse, will be taken up in the second section of this book.)

FIGURE 62. Because a dividend of $1.00 went ex on March 14, the lower boundary of this Descending Triangle top in "BIW" had to be dropped one point from 33 and re-drawn at 32. Despite the added leeway thus afforded, however, the original pattern implications were quickly carried out. Prices pulled back three times to the new lower boundary line of this Triangle—on April 4, April 16 and May 31—unusual, but explained by the existence of a strong general market up trend during this period.

Whenever a stock goes ex-dividend during the formation of an area pattern of any type, the lines bounding that pattern should immediately be adjusted to the new value by lowering them a distance corresponding to the amount of the dividend.

DESCENDING TRIANGLES

Descending Triangles have a horizontal lower boundary or demand line and a down-sloping upper boundary or supply line. It is evident that they are created by market conditions just the reverse of those responsible for the Ascending pattern. Their implications are equally strong and their failures equally rare. Development of a Descending formation hinges upon a campaign by a group or syndicate (often an investment trust) to acquire a large block of shares in a certain company at a predetermined price below the market. Their orders are placed and allowed to stand until executed at that level. If the successive rallies therefrom, which their buying generates, are stifled by new supplies of stock for sale at lower and lower levels (thus creating the typical

FIGURE 63. On the basis of "fundamentals," Revere was an attractive holding in 1946, which may account for its reluctance to "give up" when the market generally started downhill in earnest in June of that year. Its fluctuations from mid-May to late August constructed a fine, large Descending Triangle in which, however, bearish volume signals had already appeared in late June and on July 23. The breakout came (with a wide breakaway gap) on August 27. Prices clung to the edge of the pattern for four days, then collapsed. The small formations outlined in April and May are Flags, to be discussed in Chapter XI.

FIGURE 64. The 1937 Bull Market top in Westinghouse was this Descending Triangle which started in January and broke on February 15. Prices hung at the lower edge of the Triangle for four days, fell away and then pulled back to its lower line on March 4 at the time when the general market averages were making their final Bull highs.

This chart, and a number which have preceded it, illustrate an important point for the market technician which may well be stated here: When a large number of individual issues, after an extensive advance, make well-defined reversal patterns of plainly bearish import, break down out of them, and then succeed only in pulling back no farther than their lower boundaries or "resistance lines" at a time when the averages are going on up to new highs, *the whole market is in dangerous condition* and a Major down turn is imminent. Divergences of this particular sort between many important issues and the averages seldom develop at Intermediate turns.   The warning is particularly pointed when stocks of the caliber of Westinghouse, du Pont, General Motors, etc. fail to "confirm" new highs in the averages.

Refer back to Figures 12, 15, 18, 20 and 58, for example, and compare the "timing" in those with the trend of the averages for the same periods.

The saucer-like reaction pattern of October to January in the above chart analyzes into a complex Head-and-Shoulders *consolidation,* a formation which will be taken up in Chapter XI.

Incidentally, "WX" continued on down to 130 in April, 1937, made a Rectangle base there and recovered to 158 (cf. above Descending Triangle) in August, and then fell to 88 in November.   Compare this daily chart with the monthly chart of "WX" for 1935-1938 in Chapter XV.

Descending picture on the chart), orders to buy are eventually all filled and quotations break through and on down. The mere breaking of the critical line which many traders have seen function as a support under the market for a more or less extended period, often shakes the confidence of holders who had not previously considered selling. Their offerings now come on the market and accelerate the decline.

VOLUME CHARACTERISTICS SAME AS SYMMETRICAL TYPE

The volume section of the Right-Angle Triangle's chart requires little comment. It will ordinarily present a picture practically identical with that accompanying the development of a Symmetrical Triangle. Activity tends to lessen as prices move out toward the apex. In the Ascending formation there will usually be a pick-up on each rally and an ebb in turnover on each decline within the pattern; in the Descending formation the opposite is true, but sometimes not quite so evident. These minor fluctuations, however, do not affect the over-all diminishing trend of volume until the breakout point is reached.

As to breakouts also, practically everything we have said about the Symmetrical Triangle will apply as well to the Right-Angle type. Upside breakouts (from an Ascending pattern, of course) are attended by a conspicuous increase in trading volume; if not they should be treated as suspect. Downside breakouts (from Descending patterns) may not evince much of pick-up in activity, but turnover usually speeds up the second or third day out of pattern. Throwback reactions to the pattern's boundary line after a breakout are fairly common; their occurrence seems to depend largely on general market conditions. Thus, if prices break down out of a Descending Triangle in an individual stock at a time when the rest of the market is firm, a pull-back rally is fairly certain to intervene before any very extensive further decline takes place.

Good, reliable breakouts from Right-Angle Triangles usually occur at about the same stage of pattern completion as they do in Symmetrical Triangles. The earlier the breakout the less apt it is to be a false move (although false moves from Right-Angle formations are considerably rarer, it should be noted, than from Symmetrical). In those infrequent cases when prices "squeeze" right on out to the apex without producing a definite breakout the pattern seems to lose much of its power.

MEASURING IMPLICATIONS OF TRIANGLES

We have stated (in Chapter VI) a minimum measuring rule to apply to price movements developing from a Head-and-Shoulders formation, and we can lay down a somewhat similar rule for Triangles—one that applies to both the Symmetrical and the Right-Angle species. The method of deriving the Triangle formula is not easy to explain in words but the reader can familiarize himself with it quickly by studying its application on several of the actual examples

FIGURE 65.   A series of Triangles, Symmetrical and Descending, which
evolved during the 1929-32 Bear Market in Hudson Motors.   Note that at no
time during this decline did anything resembling a Major bottom appear.
Note also how each Triangle's measuring implications were carried out before any temporary halt or consequential rally developed.   Follow your daily
charts for the proper timing of your trading operations but keep an eye
always on the longer range pictures which evolve on weekly and monthly
projections, so as to maintain your perspective on the Major trend.

which illustrate this chapter.   Assuming that we are dealing with an up movement (upside breakout), draw from the top of the first rally which initiated
the pattern (in other words, from its upper left-hand corner) a line parallel to
the bottom boundary.   This line will slope up away from the pattern to the
right.   Prices may be expected to climb until they reach this line.   Also, as a
rule, they will climb, following their breakout from the pattern, at about the
same angle or rate as characterized their trend prior to their entering the pattern.   This principle permits us to arrive at an approximate time and level for

FIGURE 66.   The curious, and in its early stages confusing, Major bottom
formation which American Rolling Mills constructed in 1941-43.   The recovery from the "Pearl Harbor panic" of 1941 ran into a large Symmetrical
Triangle which broke out on the down side in April, 1942.   The subsequent
decline satisfied the measuring requirements of that Triangle, but did not
carry below the December low.   The rally of June and reaction of August-
September built the whole area out into another and larger Symmetrical
Triangle, out of which prices broke on the up side in September.   Then the
reaction to the apex of the latter, in December, 1942, and the following advance built up into a fifteen-month Ascending Triangle which constituted
the final Major bottom for a trend that carried prices up eventually to 42 in
1946.   The low volume on the June and August-September reactions, the
increase on the October mark-up and, even more, on the January, 1943 rise
and breakout in February, were unmistakably of Major bullish implications.
It takes time, remember, to build a foundation for a Bull Market.

FIGURE 67. A beautifully compact Ascending Triangle which turned out to be the Major Bear-to-Bull reversal in Goodrich in 1942. The breakout from this pattern (in April) was not signalized by any extraordinary pick-up in activity so far as this weekly record shows (but remember that significant volume detail is often hard to see in a weekly plotting). The Triangle's measuring implications were carried out by the first up swing which reached 18¼ at the end of May. Supply had to be absorbed in the 18-21 range (refer back to this chart when you study Support-Resistance in Chapter XIII), but a Major up signal was given in September when prices erupted through that zone with a conspicuous increase in trading volume.

them to attain the measuring line. The same rules apply (but measuring down, of course, from the lower left corner) to a descending move.

Although application of the above formula does afford a fair estimate of the extent of move to be expected from a Triangle, it is neither as definite nor as reliable as the Head-and-Shoulders formula. Do not forget the important qualification that a Triangle has somehow lost a part of its potential strength if the breakout is delayed until prices are crowded into the apex.

Triangles on Weekly and Monthly Charts

We have seen in preceding studies how Head-and-Shoulders formations may appear on the long-range (weekly or monthly) charts and will have importance commensurate with their size. Triangles also may develop. On weekly charts their implications are usually clear and dependable, but the coarse triangular patterns which can be found on graphs of monthly price ranges, especially the great, loose convergences which take years to complete, had better be dismissed as without useful significance.

Other Triangular Formations

There are other patterns of price consolidation or congestion that can be bounded by converging lines and might, therefore, be classified as Triangles. But they deviate from the true Triangles of this chapter so markedly in one or more important respects that they are best treated under other headings elsewhere. Such are the Flags, Pennants and Wedges. Still another group of chart patterns develops between *diverging* boundary lines, on which account they have sometimes been called Inverted Triangles. But their causes, characteristics and forecasting implications are so radically different that we have chosen to re-name them Broadening Formations and discuss them in a later chapter.

*   *   *   *   *

The reader may have become dismayed at this point by our frequent recourse to such qualifying adjectives as *usually, ordinarily,* and the like. It cannot be avoided if one wishes to present a true picture of what actually happens. No two chart patterns are ever precisely alike; no two market trends develop in quite the same way. History repeats itself in the stock market but never exactly. Nevertheless, the investor who familiarizes himself with the historical pattern, with the normal in market action, and refuses to be tempted into a commitment in the belief that "this time will be different," will be far and away ahead of his fellow who looks for the exception rather than the rule.

The beginner is proverbially lucky. He will find Triangles, Head-and-Shoulders or other significant patterns, one after the other, on his charts, watch

them develop and see them carry through with profitable moves right according
to rule.   And then the exception will come along—or he will overlook the larger
picture while concentrating on some minor pattern development—and suddenly
awake to the fact that he is caught in a very bad play.   Hence our constant
emphasis on the non-conforming movements.   Our words of qualification are
necessary because technical analysis of market action is not an exact science and
never will be.

CHAPTER IX

IMPORTANT REVERSAL FORMATIONS—CONTINUED

The Rectangles, Double and Triple Tops

THE triangular price formations which we examined in the preceding chapter can be either *reversal* or *consolidation* patterns. In the case of the Right-Angle Triangles, we know as soon as they have attained recognizable form in which direction the trend will (or should) proceed. With the Symmetrical Triangles, we have no way of knowing whether they point up or down until prices finally break away from them, although the odds are, as we have seen, that the previous trend will be continued rather than reversed. In this respect and in many others, our next class of technical formations, the *Rectangles*, resemble the Symmetrical Triangles. There are, in fact, so many points of similarity between them that we can forego any long and detailed discussion.

A *Rectangle* consists of a series of sidewise price fluctuations—a "trading area" as it is sometimes called—which can be bounded both top and bottom by *horizontal* lines. A glance at any one of the examples which illustrate these pages will show how it got its name. On rare occasions you may discover a chart pattern whose upper and lower boundary lines are parallel but either slightly down-sloping or up-sloping. So long as their departure from the horizontal is trivial, they may be treated as Rectangles. You will also find on occasion patterns whose boundaries, while nearly horizontal, tend somewhat to converge. These may be considered Rectangles or Symmetrical Triangles; it doesn't matter which since the "prognosis" will be the same in either case.

If you will give a quick mental review also to the Head-and-Shoulders, the Complex and the Rounding types of formations, you will see how, if you disregard the volume part of their charts, any one of these patterns might merge or grade into a Rectangle. As a matter of fact, however, you will seldom be left in doubt as to proper classification because the circumstances of trading, the type of buying and selling, which produce Rectangles are different and that difference is usually apparent.

We characterized the Symmetrical Triangle as a "picture of doubt." The Rectangle might, with even greater propriety, be called a picture of conflict. Of course, any fairly compact price formation represents conflict in the supply-demand sense. A Head-and-Shoulders Top, for example, portrays a conflict between "strong" sellers and "weak" buyers, with the outcome already clearly

to be seen before the combat has ended.   But a Rectangle defines a contest between two groups of approximately equal strength—between owners of the
stock who wish to dispose of their shares at a certain price and others who wish
to accumulate the stock at a certain lower figure.   They bat the ball back and
forth (up and down, that is) between them until ultimately, and usually quite
suddenly, one team is exhausted (or changes its mind) and the other then proceeds to knock the ball out of the lot.   Nobody (often not even the contestants
themselves) can tell who is going to win until one line or the other is decisively
broken.

   We speak of two groups operating in the development of a rectangular trading area because, under present-day conditions, that is what is usually the fact
behind the scenes.   This, it should be noted, does not imply "manipulation" in
any invidious sense.   An investment trust or an estate or, in some cases, an
individual heavy stockholder has good and sufficient reasons for selling at the
top price (the "supply line" of the Rectangle) with no intent to mislead the
public.   And another investment trust or a group of financiers interested in the
company may have equally good and, from their point of view, wise reasons for
buying at the bottom price ("demand line").   Such are the forces at work in
the market at the start of most rectangular chart patterns, but if the "spread"

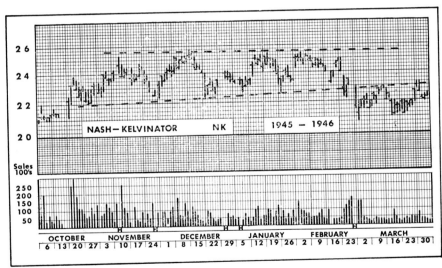

FIGURE 68.   Although its bottom boundary had a slight tendency to "lift,"
the formation which put a top on Nash-Kelvinator in 1946 was an unmistakable four-month distribution Rectangle.   Long and rather loose rectangular
patterns of the type shown here may not evince constantly and noticeably
diminishing volume, but note nevertheless the general though irregular down
trend in volume from mid-October to mid-February.

FIGURE 69. Consolidation Rectangles in up trends have been less common in recent years than during the twenties and early thirties. The large price gap (G) in this example is of the "last in pattern" type which we shall come to in Chapter XII. When a gap within a pattern area is followed by breakout from that pattern, as in this case, the gap is seldom quickly closed.

between top and bottom lines is wide enough (say 8 or 10% of the market value of the stock) the situation may quickly attract a following from quick-turn scalpers and the professional element. Thus, a syndicate holding a large block of U. S. Steel may decide to liquidate at 76, while another group decides to invest heavily in "Steel" at 69. The price of X will naturally fluctuate for a time between those two levels. Traders, seeing this, will try to "ride the play," buying at 69 and selling at 76 (perhaps also selling short at 76 and covering at 69). Their operations will tend to accentuate or extend the Rectangle, although the number of shares involved in such "parasitic" trading is seldom great enough to affect the final outcome. As a matter of fact, this type of trading *inside* a Rectangle can be quite profitable at times, especially if protected by doubling stops (see Part II).

POOL OPERATIONS

In times past, before the SEC outlawed the practice, Rectangles were frequently created by the well-organized operations of a *single* "pool" or syndicate. Such a pool might undertake to accumulate a large block of stock in a certain company with a view to marking it up and taking profits when some piece of good news of which they had inside knowledge eventually became public.   In order to acquire the desired "line," they would find it necessary first to shake out shares held by other traders and uninformed investors.   They might start their campaign by suddenly selling short a few hundred shares in order to quench any current demand and start a reaction.   Then, on that reaction to the previously determined accumulation level they would start to buy, scattering their orders carefully and avoiding any publicity.   Their buying would, sooner or later, engender a rally but then they would "plant" rumors around the boardrooms to the effect that such-and-such insiders were selling, or that a projected merger was being called off, or a dividend would have to be

FIGURE 70.   A perfect example of Consolidation Rectangle which formed in Loew's near the end of the 1932-37 Bull Market.   In this case, a large block of "inside" stock was distributed at 64-65 but taken over around 62 by other investors who had the satisfaction of seeing it go on up to 87 the following August.   Note throw-back following breakout in January.

passed—and, if necessary, they would ostentatiously let out a few of their own recently purchased shares to give color to the rumor. The process might be repeated several times, with the "pool" gradually securing more and more shares on balance until finally it had completed its intended line, or could shake out no more of the floating supply. Often what was going on was fairly evident to the alert chartist back in the twenties even before the operation was concluded, and perfectly evident, of course, as soon as prices broke out top-side from their Rectangle.

But such tactics are no longer permitted. "Wash sales" are strictly condemned. The constant policing of all exchange transactions and prompt investigation by the SEC of any suspicious news or activity in a stock, effectually deters the blatant "pool" manipulations of previous years. This probably is the chief reason why Rectangles are nowhere near so common on the charts of the fifties as they were in the twenties.

Perhaps we can clear up various details of the Rectangle formation most

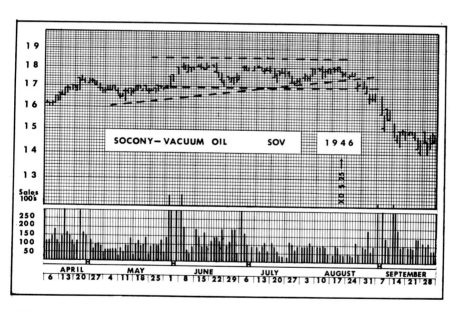

FIGURE 71. Here is a Rectangle in Socony-Vacuum, a low-priced stock characterized by fluctuations within a narrow range. After reaching a high of 18¾ in December, 1945, it fell back to 15¼ and then rallied in mid 1946 as shown above. In late August prices broke down through an Intermediate trendline (see Chapter XIV) and four days later fell out of the Rectangle. This formation in conjunction with the earlier and higher top, implied lower levels for "SOV" for some time to come. See also comment under Figure 72.

quickly and easily by comparison with that most nearly related chart pattern, the Symmetrical Triangle, as follows:—

Volume—Follows the same rules as in the Triangles, gradually diminishing as the Rectangle lengthens. Any contrary development, unless it be a momen-- tary news flurry, is suspect.

Breakouts—Here also the same rules apply as with Triangles. Review volume requirements, margin of penetration, etc., thereunder.

False Moves—Much less frequent from Rectangles than from Symmetrical Triangles. A clearly defined Rectangle is, in fact, almost as reliable as a Head- and-Shoulders, although not as powerful in its implications.

Premature Breakouts—Slightly more frequent, perhaps, from Rectangles than from Triangles.

(Note: Both *false moves* and *premature breakouts*, in the sense in which we employ these terms, are indistinguishable at the time they occur from genuine

FIGURE 72. Another long, loose Rectangle of Major reversal implications, somewhat similar to that pictured in Figure 68. Both an Intermediate and Major up trendline (to be discussed later) were decisively punctured by "YB" in August just before its Rectangle broke down. Under Figure 64 we dis- cussed one sort of warning of a Primary down turn which may be derived from the comparison of individual stock charts with the averages. Here is another hint: The better-grade Steels and Oils (see "SOV," Figure 71) fre- quently hold up, or make stronger Secondary recoveries, after the averages have turned down at Major tops. The "street" sometimes speaks of "distribu- tion under cover of strength in the Steels."

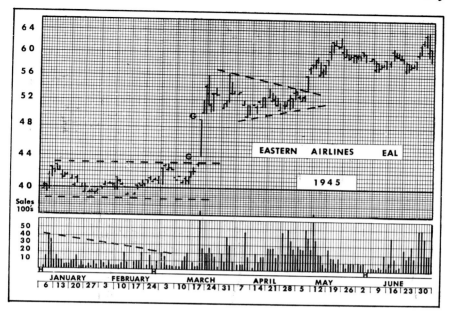

FIGURE 73. The Rectangle in early 1945 in "EAL" was actually the final stage of a nearly two-year consolidation in the rise which started around 17 in 1942 and ended above 125 in December, 1945. G, G mark gaps (Chapter XII), the first a breakaway and the second a measuring gap which marked the probable objective of the move as 55. When prices reached that level, another consolidation developed, a Symmetrical Triangle. Neither of these gaps was "closed" during the following two years.

breakouts. Following both false and premature breaks, prices return inside the pattern. But, in the case of a *false* move, the trend ultimately proceeds out of pattern in the *opposite* direction, while in the case of the *premature* move, the trend finally breaks out again and proceeds in the *same* direction.)

Pull-backs—Return of prices to the boundary of the pattern, subsequent to its initial penetration (breakout), takes place more frequently with Rectangles than with Symmetrical Triangles. Our estimate would be that a pull-back or throw-back (the first is the common term for a rally after a down-side breakout, and the second for a reaction following an up-side breakout) occurs within three days to three weeks in about 40% of all cases.

Directional Tendency—The Rectangle is more often a *Consolidation* formation than a *Reversal* formation, the ratio being about the same as with Symmetrical Triangles. As reversal patterns, Rectangles appear more frequently

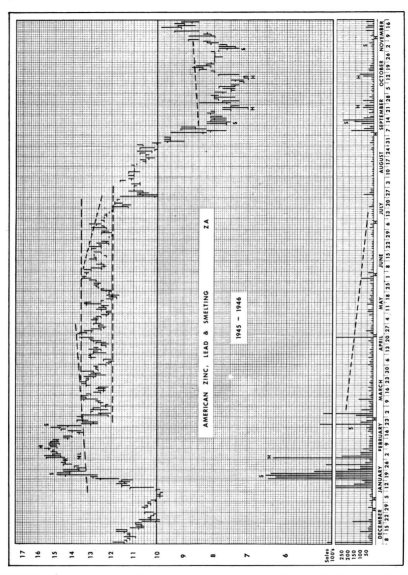

FIGURE 74. An extraordinary, fine, long Rectangle which developed after
"ZA" had broken down out of an H & S top in February, 1946. A perfect
opportunity to sell this stock short was given by its pull-back of July 17-18
after prices had broken out of the Rectangle on the 15th. The Multiple
H & S Bottom which it subsequently made from September to November produced a recovery to 11, but prices later fell to 6 in early 1947.

at bottoms (either Major or Intermediate) than at tops. Long, thin, dull Rectangles are not uncommon at Primary bottoms, sometimes grading into the type of flat-bottomed saucer or dormancy described in Chapter VII.

Measuring Implications—A safe minimum measuring formula for the Rectangle is given by its width. Prices should go at least as far in points beyond the pattern as the difference in points between the top and bottom lines of the pattern itself. They may, of course, go much farther. Generally speaking, the brief, wide-swinging forms, which appear nearly square in shape on the chart and in which turnover is active, are more dynamic than the longer and narrower manifestations. Moves out of the latter almost always hesitate or react at the "minimum" point before carrying on.

RELATION OF RECTANGLE TO DOW LINE

The resemblance of this individual stock chart formation, which we have discussed under the name of Rectangle, to the average formation known to Dow Theorists as a "Line" has doubtless occurred to you. Obviously, their rationale and forecasting implications are much the same. But true Rectangles with sharply delimited top (supply) and bottom (demand) boundaries are truly

FIGURE 75. In this weekly chart showing Sears Roebuck's 1942 Bear Market bottom, a consolidation Rectangle (June to November) forms the right shoulder of large "unbalanced" Double Head-and-Shoulders pattern.

characteristic only of trading in individual issues. Line formations in the averages are seldom rigorously defined, with successive Minor highs forming quite precisely at a certain horizontal tangent, and successive bottoms at a similarly precise horizontal level. If you will examine the separate charts of the issues composing an average at a time when that average is "making a line," you are pretty sure to find that some of them are showing an irregular up trend, others an irregular down trend, still others may be forming Triangles and a few may be constructing Rectangles, or what not, but it is the algebraic sum of all these more or less divergent pictures which makes up the average "Line."

To be sure, there is some tendency on the part of active traders to sell (or buy) stocks when a certain average reaches a certain figure, regardless of the status of individual issues involved. An investment counsel will occasionally advise his clients, for example, to "sell all speculative holdings when the Dow Industrials reach 500." But trading commitments based solely on general average levels are so seldom followed consistently that they have little effect.

FIGURE 76. After advancing to 16 in January, 1945, "BLL" dropped back to 13 and then constructed a fifteen-week Rectangle. Note that the down gap (G) on April 30 was caused by a $1.00 dividend going off. The revised bottom line of the pattern, drawn $1.00 lower, was not violated.

FIGURE 77. A brief and very "high" Rectangle formed in September, 1937 in the rapid Bear Market decline of "KN," followed by a Descending and then a Symmetrical Triangle consolidation.

RECTANGLES FROM RIGHT-ANGLE TRIANGLES

In the preceding chapter we referred to a type of partial "failure" in the development of a Right-Angle Triangle which necessitates re-classifying the Triangle as a Rectangle. Now that we have examined the latter pattern in detail, we need say little more about this phenomenon, except to note that the odds appear to be still somewhat in favor of ultimate breakout in the direction originally implied by the incipient Triangle. The fact that there is this slight presumption, however, certainly does not warrant disregard of an opposite breakout from the rectangular reconstruction.

DOUBLE AND TRIPLE TOPS AND BOTTOMS

To some of the old hands in "the street," our relegation of that good old by-word, the *Double Top,* to a minor position in our array of reversal formations may seem almost sacrilegious. It is referred to by name perhaps more often than any other chart pattern by traders who possess a smattering of technical "lingo" but little organized knowledge of technical facts. True Double Tops and Double Bottoms are exceedingly rare; Triple forms are even rarer. And the true patterns (as distinguished from chart pictures which might mistakenly be called such but are really assignable to some one of our other reversal formations) can seldom be positively detected until prices have gone quite a long way away from them. They can *never* be foretold, or identified as soon as they occur, from chart data alone.

But we are getting ahead of our story. We should first define what we are talking about. A *Double Top* is formed when a stock advances to a certain

FIGURE 78. This formation, constructed by United Aircraft in 1942, was not completed and could not be called a Double Bottom until prices rose above 31 in February, 1943. (See page 132.)

FIGURE 79. Climbing from 46 in August, 1945, "GN" reached a high price above 65 in November, dropped back to 55 in February, 1946 for a 15% loss, and then rose again to 64 in June, seven months after the first top. When prices thereafter broke down through 54 in August, a Major Double Top had been made, meeting all the specifications stated on pages 131 and 132.

level with, usually, high volume at and approaching the top figure, then retreats with diminishing activity, then comes up again to the same (or practically the same) top price as before with some pick-up in turnover but not as much as on the first peak, and then finally turns down a second time for a Major or consequential Intermediate decline. A *Double Bottom* is, of course, the same picture upside down. The Triple types make three tops (or bottoms) instead of two.

It isn't difficult to skim through a book of several hundred monthly charts and pick out two or three examples of Major Double Tops, perhaps one or two Double Bottoms. One will find cases where stocks made two successive Bull Market peaks, several years apart, at almost identical levels. Such phenomena stand out in distant retrospect like the proverbial sore thumb, which undoubtedly accounts for the undue awe with which the amateur chartist regards them. He neglects for the moment to consider the fact that a thousand other issues might

FIGURE 80.   Because of the long time-between-tops requirement for true Double Top reversals, these formations can seldom be seen to advantage on a daily chart, but here is a good 1946 example in Republic Steel.   Note five months and 20% decline between tops.   This chart contains many interesting lesser technical formations also.   The "broadening" swings (see Chapter X) in June and July, as the second top was made, and the rounding rally in August were extremely bearish in their implications.

have done the same thing but didn't—that some of these even acted for a time as though they were going to double-top but then went on through and higher.

Is there then any practical utility for the trader or investor in the Double Top concept? Yes, there is, but it will be easier for us to formulate it if we first consider what is *not* a Double Top. Refer back for a moment to the Ascending Triangles and the Rectangles previously studied. When these start to evolve, almost their first step is the construction of two tops at an identical level with an intervening recession, and with less volume on the second top than on the first. In the ordinary course of events, a third top will develop there and ultimately prices will break through and move on up to still higher levels. Thus, we see we must have some rule or criterion to distinguish a true Double Top reversal pattern from the double tops which do not imply reversal when they appear as a part of a consolidation area in an up trend.

Distinguishing Characteristics

No absolute and unqualified rule can be laid down to fit all cases involving stocks of different values and market habits, but one relative distinction quickly suggests itself when we study these different kinds of chart formations. It is: If two tops appear at the same level but quite close together in time and with only a minor reaction between them, the chances are that they are part of a consolidation area; or, if a reversal of trend is to ensue, that there will first be more pattern development—more "work" done—around those top ranges. If, on the other hand, there is a long, dull, deep and more or less rounding reaction after the initial peak has appeared, and then an evident lack of vitality when prices come up again to the previous high, we can at least be suspicious of a Double Top.

How deep is deep, and how long is long? Fair questions, to which, unfortunately, it is impossible to give simple, definite answers. But we can attempt approximations. Thus, if the two tops are *more than* a month apart, they are not likely to belong to the same consolidation or congestion formation. If, in addition, the reaction between the first and second high reduces prices by 20% of their top value, the odds swing toward a Double Top interpretation. But both of these criteria are arbitrary, and not without exception. There are cases in which the two peaks have occurred only two or three weeks apart, and others in which the "valley" between them descended only about 15%. Most true Double Tops, however, develop two to three months or more apart. Generally speaking, the time element is more critical than the depth of the reaction. The greater the time between the two highs, the less the need for any extensive decline of prices in the interim.

Given the conditions we have specified, viz., two tops at approximately the same level but more than a month apart on the chart, with somewhat less activity on the second advance than on the first, and a rather dull or irregular and rounding type of recession between them, we can then be suspicious that a Double Top reversal has actually evolved. Should a small Head-and-Shoulders or Descending Triangle start to develop at the second top, as is frequently the case, we can be on guard, to the extent of protecting long commitments at once with a close stop or switching to something else with a more promising chart picture.

Yet, even all these signs together are not final and conclusive. The situation can still be saved, and often is. Let us take a look at what is, presumably, going on behind the scenes to create our chart picture up to this point. The first top on relatively high volume was a normal incident and tells us little except that here, for the moment, demand met with sufficient supply to stop the advance and produce a reaction. That supply may have represented only traders' profit taking, in which event the trend is likely to push on up after a brief setback. But, when the reaction drifts off lower and lower until it has given up 15% and more of the stock's peak market value, and flattens out without any prompt and vigorous rebound, it becomes evident that either the demand was pretty well played out on the last advance or that the selling there represented something more than short-term profit cashing. The question then is: Did the first high give evidence of important distribution, and is there much more to meet at that same price range?

Nevertheless, as our chart picture shows, demand did finally come in and absorb enough of the floating supply to turn the trend around. When prices pushed up and began to run into selling again near the level of the first top, that was to be expected on "psychological" grounds; many quick-turn operators naturally would take profits at the old high (perhaps with the intention of jumping right back in at a still higher price if the old high should be exceeded). Hence a minor hesitation there was quite in order. But selling in sufficient quantity to produce another extensive reaction would be quite another matter. We have by now established a zone of supply or resistance at the peak levels and a zone of support or demand at the bottom of the valley between. The final and decisive question now is: Will the "valley" support re-appear and stop the second decline?

The conclusive definition of a Double Top is given by a negative answer to that last question. If prices on their recession from the second peak drop through the bottom level of the valley, a reversal of trend from up to down is signaled. And it is usually a signal of Major importance. Fully confirmed Double Tops seldom appear at turns in the Intermediate trend; they are characteristically a Primary reversal phenomenon. Hence, when you are sure you have one, do not scorn it. Even though prices may have already receded 20%, the chances are they have very much farther to go before they reach bottom.

As to measuring implications, the Double Top affords no formula comparable with that we have attributed to Head-and-Shoulders and Triangle formations, but it is safe to assume that the decline will continue *at least as far* below the valley level as the distance from peak to valley. It may not do so, of course, in one uninterrupted slide; on the contrary considerable time may be required to carry out the full descent in a series of waves. Pull-backs to the "valley" price range, following the first break-through, are not uncommon. (Bear in mind the general rule that a reversal formation can be expected to produce no more than a retracement of the trend which preceded it.)

One more point: We have said that the tops need not form at precisely the same level. Use here the 3% rule we have previously laid down as a measuring

FIGURE 81. Shares of "AMR," then selling for around 90, were split 5-for-1 in April, 1946, resulting in a quick rally to a new high. But the over-all aspect of a Double Top with the high made the previous December was nevertheless apparent, and was confirmed when prices broke down through the "valley" level on August 28. Popular buying brought in by "splits" is usually short-lived and only temporarily distorts the broad picture.

stick for breakouts.   A first top at 50, for example, and a second at 51½ would come within this limit.   Curiously enough, the second peak often does exceed the first by a fraction.   The important points are (1) that buying cannot push prices up into the clear *by a decisive margin* and (2) the support below is subsequently broken.

FIGURE 82.   The Major reversal formation in "CNR" at the start of a Primary advance which reached 54.   Note how an attempt at an Ascending Triangle turned into a Double Bottom.

DOUBLE BOTTOMS

In identifying a Double Bottom we can apply all of the precepts we have formulated for the Double Top pattern, but of course, upside down.   The differences between the two pictures are just what you might expect them to be, having in mind the characteristic differences between Head-and-Shoulders Tops and Bottoms, for example.   Thus, the second bottom is usually conspicuously dull (little trading volume) and is apt to be quite rounded, whereas the second top in a Double Top is moderately active and nearly as sharp and "spiky" in contour as the first. The rally up from the second bottom shows an increase in turnover and volume should pick up to a marked degree as the valley level, or more properly in this case the *height* between the two bottoms, is surpassed. Double Bottoms appear just about as frequently as do Double Tops at Primary trend reversals, and Double Bottoms also occur sometimes at the end of Intermediate corrections in a Major up trend.

If you are familiar with some of the jargon of "the street," it has probably occurred to you that the second low of a Double Bottom is an example of the market action so often referred to as a "test." In a sense that is just what it is —a test or corroboration of the support (i.e., demand) which stemmed the first decline at the same level. The *success* of that test is not *proved,* however—and this is a point to remember—until prices have demonstrated their ability to rise on increasing volume above the preceding high (the height of the rally between the two bottoms). Until such time as that has happened there is always the possibility that a second test (third bottom) may be necessary, or even a third, and that one of these will fail, with prices then breaking on down into further decline. Which thought leads us to our next type of reversal formation.

FIGURE 83. Great Northern's 1942-46 Bull Market originated in a Triple Bottom which was completed in February, 1943. (See following page.)

FIGURE 84. Publicker made its Bull Market high only a few
weeks after it was listed on the "big board." Then it started to
build a Descending Triangle, but pulled up out of it. Final outcome was a Triple Top, completed in August. (Cf. Figures 60 and
82.)

TRIPLE TOPS AND BOTTOMS

Logically, if there are Double Tops, then we might expect that there will
also be Triple Tops which will develop in somewhat similar fashion. Fact is
that reversal formations which can only be classed as Triple Tops do occur,
but they are few and far between. Of course, there are many patterns evolved
at an important turn from up to down in the trend which contain three top
points, but most of these fall more readily into the category of Rectangles. For
that matter, any Head-and-Shoulders formation, particularly if it be rather "flat"
with the head not extending much above the level of the two shoulders, might be
called a sort of Triple Top.

The true Triple Top (as distinct, that is, from other types of three-peak
formations) carries a recognizable family resemblance to the Double Top. Its
tops are widely spaced and with quite deep and usually rounding reactions between them. Volume is characteristically less on the second advance than on

the first, and still less on the third which often peters out with no appreciable pick-up in activity. The three highs need not be spaced quite so far apart as the two which constitute a Double Top, and they need not be equally spaced. Thus, the second top may occur only about three weeks after the first and the third six weeks or more after the second. Also, the intervening valleys need not bottom out at exactly the same level; the first may be shallower than the second and vice-versa. And the three highs may not come at precisely the same price; our 3% tolerance rule is again useful here. Yet, despite all these permissible variations, there should be and generally is something suspiciously familiar about the over-all picture, something which immediately suggests the possibility of a Triple Top to the experienced chartist.

The *conclusive* test, however, is a decline from the third top which breaks prices down through the level of the valley floor (the lower one, if the two valleys form at different levels). Not until that has occurred can a Triple Top be regarded as confirmed and actually in effect, since so long as demand persists at the valley price range, the trend can be turned up again. Only in those cases where activity is conspicuously lacking on the third peak and then begins to show bearish characteristics by accelerating on the ensuing decline, is one justified in "jumping the gun."

Triple Bottoms are simply Triple Tops turned upside down, with the same qualifications we noted when we were discussing Double Bottoms. The third low should always be attended by small volume, and the rise therefrom must show a decided increase in turnover and carry prices decisively above the tops of the rallies that formed between the bottoms. One is never justified in "jumping the gun" on a presumed Triple Bottom formation unless nearly every other chart in the book is in an unmistakably bullish position. The risk of premature buying is expressed in a saying one sometimes hears in the boardrooms to the effect that "a triple bottom is always broken." This is not a true saying. Once a true Triple Bottom has been established and confirmed by the necessary up-side breakout, it seldom fails—almost always produces an advance of distinctly worth-while proportions. But an uncompleted "possible" Triple Bottom chart picture must be regarded as treacherous. Stick to the breakout rule and you will be safe.

Triple Tops are sometimes referred to as "W" patterns because of their occasional resemblance to that capital letter on the chart. There is a sort of hybrid between the Double and Triple Top, in which the middle one of the three tops does not attain the height of the first and third, and thus even more strikingly resembles a "W." For the same reason, Double Tops are sometimes called "M" formations.

Because the elements in Double and Triple patterns are normally spaced well apart in time, they are often easier to detect and appreciate on a weekly chart than on a daily. Monthly graphs disclose numbers of wide spread Double and

FIGURE 85. In the ordinary course of events at the time this bottom pattern developed in "NG," consisting as it did of fluctuations for ten long months within a range of only one full point, most traders would pay no attention to it. Certainly it suggested very little opportunity for short-term profits. On an arithmetically scaled chart the pattern could hardly be seen. Logarithmic price scaling, however, as we have remarked in an earlier chapter, has the great advantage of bringing to light the percentage importance of significant market action at very low price levels.

Note that this formation qualifies in every detail—spacing between bottoms, extent in percent of intervening rallies, volume—as a Triple Bottom. Of course, its completion, in October, 1942, did not necessarily forecast that "NG" would climb to 33, as it ultimately did. But the fact that many other stocks were making sound Major bottom formations at higher price levels at the same time certainly warranted the conclusion that "NG" was on its way up, and that it was a bargain at 5.

Triple Bottoms but, on the other hand, are too coarse to reveal many good Double and Triple Top patterns.

         *   *   *   *   *

In our foregoing discussion of the Triple Top we referred to a sort of intuition which comes with experience and enables a technical analyst to recognize the potentialities for reversal of a certain chart development, sometimes long before it has reached a conclusive stage. This is a not uncommon talent but it is one that is seldom attained except through searching study and long experience (which latter usually involves a few expensive mistakes). The reader of this book need not despair of acquiring "chart sense"—and without undue cost—if he will concentrate on his study, watch, check and double-check every new development on his charts, and "keep score" on himself.

It has been said that chart interpretation is not a *science* but an *art*. It is not an exact science, to be sure, because it has no rules to which there are not exceptions. Its finer points defy expression in rule or precept. It requires judgment in appraisal of many factors, some of which may seem at times to conflict radically with others. But to call it an Art, which implies the need for genius or at least for a high degree of native talent, is certainly improper. Say rather that it demands skill, but a skill that can be acquired by anyone of ordinary intelligence.

CHAPTER X

OTHER REVERSAL PHENOMENA

W E HAVE considered so far seven classes of chart patterns which appear at more or less important reversals of direction in the trend of prices. They were:—

1. The Head-and-Shoulders
2. Multiple or Complex Head-and-Shoulders
3. Rounding Turns
4. Symmetrical Triangles
5. Right-Angle Triangles
6. Rectangles
7. Double and Triple Tops and Bottoms

Of these, 1, 2, 3 and 7 develop most often at *Major* turns, while 4, 5 and 6 occur more frequently at Intermediate stages. Numbers 1, 2, 3 and 5 give indication *before* they are completed as to which way the price trend is likely to proceed from them. Numbers 4 and 6 give no such indication and, as we have seen, are rather more apt to signalize consolidation or continuation than reversal. But all of them can, and on occasion do, appear at both Major tops or bottoms.

We have yet to take up a few other technical patterns which because of their limited significance, or their rarity, or their doubtful utility to the long-term traders, have been relegated to the end of our reversal studies.

THE BROADENING FORMATIONS

In concluding our discussion of Triangles in Chapter VIII we mentioned certain types of price congestion or trading areas which have sometimes been called "Inverted Triangles" because, starting with very narrow fluctuations, they widen out between diverging rather than converging boundary lines. Herein, we have chosen to classify them instead as *Broadening Patterns* because, except for that inverted resemblance in superficial appearance, they are quite different in their nature and trend implications.

If the Symmetrical Triangle presents a picture of "doubt" awaiting clarification, and the Rectangle a picture of controlled "conflict," the Broadening Formation may be said to suggest a market lacking intelligent sponsorship and out of control—a situation usually in which the "public" is excitedly committed and which is being whipped around by wild rumors. Note that we say only that it *suggests* such a market. There are times when it is obvious that those are precisely the conditions which create a Broadening pattern in prices, and there are other times when the reasons for it are obscure or undiscoverable. Nevertheless, the very fact that chart pictures of this type make their appearance as a rule only at the end or in the final phases of a long Bull Market lends credence to our characterization of them.

Hence, after studying the charts for some twenty years and watching what market action has followed the appearance of broadening price patterns, we have come to the conclusion that they are definitely bearish in purport—that, while further advance in price is not ruled out, the situation is nevertheless approaching a dangerous stage. New commitments (purchases) should not be made in a stock which produces a chart of this type and any previous commitments should be switched at once, or cashed in at the first good opportunity.

The Broadening Formation may evolve in any one of three forms, comparable, respectively, to inverted Symmetrical, Ascending or Descending Triangles. The "Symmetrical" type for example, consists of a series of price fluctuations across a horizontal axis, with each minor top higher and each minor bottom lower than its predecessor. The pattern may thus be roughly marked off by

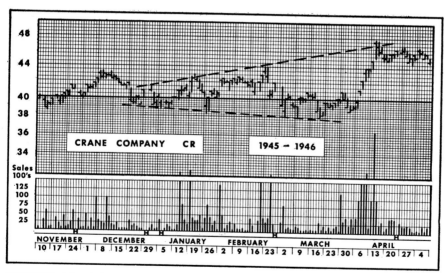

FIGURE 86. The symmetrical type of Broadening Formation, which develops most frequently in the later and more "excited" stages of a Primary Bull Market, is perfectly exemplified in this Crane Co. chart. Note that the broadening pattern here started to form in December, 1945 *after a 10% reaction;* if it had formed on top of a rally it would have been suspect as a possible Broadening Top (see page 145). Nevertheless, it carried the usual bearish implications. "CR" topped out at 49½ in June.

two diverging lines, the upper sloping up (from left to right) and the lower sloping down. But these broadening patterns are characteristically loose and irregular, whereas Symmetrical Triangles are normally regular and compact. The converging boundary lines of a Symmetrical Triangle are clearly defined as a rule, and the tops and bottoms within the formation tend to fall with fair precision on those boundary lines. In a Broadening Formation, the rallies and declines usually do not all stop at clearly marked boundary lines.

Volume During Broadening Formations

Another distinction between Triangle and Broadening Formation is in the volume chart. The construction of a true Triangle is attended, as we have seen, by diminishing activity, starting with high volume on the first Minor reversal which initiates the pattern but growing less and less as prices fluctuate in ever smaller waves out toward the apex. Then activity picks up again after prices have broken out of the Triangle, immediately and sharply if the breakout is through the top side. With the Broadening Formation, on the other hand, trading activity usually remains high and irregular throughout its construction. If it develops after an advance, as is almost always the case, the first Minor reversal which starts the pattern will occur on large turnover, but so will the second rally in the pattern, and the third, and high volume also frequently develops on one or more of its minor bottoms. The whole picture —both price and volume—is thus one of wild and apparently "unintelligent" swings.

As can easily be seen, under such circumstances a true breakout from the area may be difficult, if not impossible, to detect at the time it eventuates. The volume part of the chart obviously furnishes no clue, while the very looseness and lack of definition of the price pattern prevents the drawing of any line which surely says, "thus far and no farther." (We are referring now to the "symmetrical" type only of Broadening Formation.) Of course, once prices have run well away, either up or down, from the pattern area it becomes plain that a breakout has occurred but by that time it may be too late to risk a trade on the situation; the move may already have gone too far. What can we do about Broadening Formations then? Well, we have already noted that, nine times out of ten, they carry bearish implications. They appear most often at or near an important topping out of the trend. Hence, it is reasonably safe to assume that prices when they finally break away from the formation will go down or, if they do go up will very soon turn around and come back down again. Therein lies one answer to the problem of what to do about a Broadening Formation.

In addition, the price action within the formation in many cases furnishes an *advance* indication of breakout direction. If the trend is going to break down from the Broadening area, the last rally within the area may fail to rise as high as its predecessor, thus breaking the sequence of ever higher tops within the pattern. And, alternatively, if the trend is going to emerge on the top side, the last reaction within the pattern may fail to depress prices as low as the preceding reaction. These "failures" within the pattern occur, as we have stated, in a majority of all Broadening Formations. But note that one cannot be sure of such a significant development (what we have referred to above as a failure, for lack of a better descriptive name) until prices go on and out the other side of the formation or, more precisely, have exceeded the last preceding move in that direction by a decisive margin (our 3% rule again).

A Typical Example

No doubt the foregoing paragraph sounds rather complicated. It will be easier to visualize the development of a "failure" signal if we cite an example using actual price figures. Easier yet, perhaps, if the reader will sketch out our example on a scrap of chart paper. Suppose stock **XYZ**, after advancing some thirty points on gradually increasing turnover, runs into heavy selling at 62 and reacts to 58. But there is still plenty of interest in the issue; it stops at 58 and then swings up to a new peak at 63. It "churns" there for a day or two and drops back again, this time to 56½ before it is halted by another burst of buying. Its third rally takes it up to 62 where it hesitates and falls back to 59 but is then picked up again and carried on to 65. (By this time, of course, a Broadening Formation has become evident on the chart.) At 65 there is a great show of trading, followed by another reaction which drops quotations quickly back to 60; support appears there momentarily and prices fluctuate for three or four days between 60 and 62 and then fall away again, finally to close at 56, with volume running high all through this phase. A fourth rally starts, but now the traders who bought in at 60 on the preceding down swing are frightened and looking for a chance to "get out even," and the advance is stifled at that level. Quotations start to slip and soon are down to 55, *below the previous pattern bottom*. When this occurs, the "failure" of the preceding rally is confirmed—its failure, that is, to rise above 65 and thus carry on the broadening movement. The decline below 56 by virtue of that failure may be regarded as a breakout.

If you followed the foregoing example closely you will have noted that there can be (and very often are) minor fluctuations *inside* the pattern which do not affect its outcome. Thus, the rise from 56½ to 65 really consisted of three moves, first from 56½ up to 62, then from 62 back to 59 and, finally, from 59 up to 65. The reaction from 62 had no significance so long as it stopped *above* 56½ and was succeeded by a new rise carrying beyond the previous pattern high which in this case had been 63.

The example just detailed is one of the commoner types in which the failure occurs on a rally and the breakout eventuates on the down side. But it

FIGURE 87.   Although this particular Major reversal formation appeared
on the charts over thirty-five years ago, it is so perfectly developed and on
such a large scale that it may well stand as our elementary model for an
orthodox Broadening Top.   This pattern in Air Reduction is discussed in detail on the following pages.   Note also the Symmetrical Triangle consolidation of July-August, and the examples of runaway, breakout and exhaustion
gaps (RG. BG and EG) which will be taken up in Chapter XII.

could have been converted into the opposite form if the last decline had stopped at 60 and then, instead of fluctuating for a few days between 60 and 62 and breaking down again, had pushed right back up and past 65. That action would have given us a failure on a decline and an up-side breakout. (The odds would be, however, that the final top was not far away.)

The Orthodox Broadening Top

There is one particular manifestation—a special case, as the mathematicians might say—of the Broadening price formation whose general nature we have discussed in the preceding paragraphs. This particular form appeared at the 1929 tops of many of the active and popular stocks of that day, but with less frequency at Bull Market highs since 1929, and rarely at high-volume tops preceding extensive Intermediate declines, as in 1933 and 1934. It is known to market technicians under the specific name of *Broadening Top* and although it conforms to our general descriptions for all symmetrical broadening price patterns, it has been so precisely defined, and so often cited in technical writings, that we may well take some time to examine it.

The orthodox Broadening Top has three peaks at successively higher levels and, between them, two bottoms with the second bottom lower than the first. The assumption has been that it is completed and in effect as an important reversal indication just as soon as the reaction from its third peak carries below the level of its second bottom.

Perhaps we can best see what this formation is like if we examine one of the classic patterns which developed in 1929. Our chart (opposite page) shows the daily market action (price and volume) of AIR REDUCTION from July 1 to December 31 of that year. We have numbered from 1 to 5 the significant turning points within the Broadening Top which ended that stock's Bull Market in October. A broadening price pattern was not detectable, of course, until prices had started to move up from the second Minor low (point 4); by then 3 had formed *above* 1, and 4 *below* 2. New highs at 5 (a and b), followed by the definite down-side breakout at B (nearly 6% under 4), completed the pattern and, according to the rules, signalized a *Major* reversal of trend. In this case there can be no doubt as to the importance of the reversal indications since, as our chart shows, the price of AIR REDUCTION dropped from above 220 on October 18 to below 80 on November 14, just four weeks later, and the final bottom was not seen until nearly three years later in 1932!

There are some fine points of this classic example which should be noted. First, a new high, i.e., a third and higher top, was made at 5a and the subsequent reaction was halted at 195, well above 4, and succeeded by renewed advance. This looked like one of the advance notices ("failures") to which we have referred on a preceding page, portending an up-side breakout. But the example before us will serve to emphasize the warning which we attached thereto

—that such an indication is not to be trusted until prices have decisively exceeded the previous top. At 5b AIR REDUCTION was traded briefly at 223, 2 points but less than 3% higher than 5a, and the day closed with quotations *below* 5a. The break on October 24 (to B) took prices more than 3% under the level of 4. Now occurred a development typical of Broadening Tops— a pull-back rally (to P) retracing about half of the ground lost between the last pattern top (5b) and the end of the initial breakout move (B). Such a recovery (and failure) will be attempted, according to our experience, in at least four out of five Broadening Top patterns, and may not fail until it has regained two thirds of the preceding decline although it usually peters out around or even below the half-way mark.

This, as we have said, is a classic example; there were many others at that time. The very fact that so many did evolve at the 1929 peak which was followed by history's most disastrous losses, probably accounts for the extremely bearish implications market technicians have ascribed to the Broadening Top formation. We regard it now with somewhat less awe; its measuring implications are probably no greater than those of a large, high-volume Head-and-

FIGURE 88. A small but perfect 1946 Broadening Top that formed at the end of a three-month chart pattern which also had over-all broadening (and, hence, bearish) aspects. The five critical points of reversal are numbered on the chart. The "breakout" was registered on August 27. The pull-back rally which followed immediately was strong but still held within normal bounds. Another interesting Broadening Top of 1946 appears in Figure 202.

FIGURE 89. When they appear as plain and as compact as this example, Broadening Tops on weekly charts carry very powerful reversal indications. The top of the fifth turn in this formation was capped on the daily chart by a Head-and-Shoulders, which was pictured in Figure 16. The dashed lines on the above chart are trendlines—to be discussed in Chapter XIV.

Shoulders, but it is a pattern characteristic of the last stages of a Primary up trend.

The insistence that the third top (our number 5), when followed by decline below the second bottom (our number 4), *completes* the reversal pattern may be regarded, in the light of experience, as setting too strict a limitation, since Broadening Formations do on occasion go on to make a fourth and higher top. Yet this rule may be, and usually is, justified by the fact that the over-all indications are undeniably bearish and, hence, one should not wait too long to get out. On the other hand, the requirement that there be a third top does seem to be justified on the score that major reversals are seldom completed until at least three attempts have been made to push prices on in the direction of the previous trend. This is the reason, of course, why pioneer technical students lumped together many formations under the classification "five-point reversals." The Broadening Top is a five-point reversal (vide: our numbers 1 to 5) and so, obviously, is a Head-and-Shoulders. A Broadening Top might, in fact, be called a Head-and-Shoulders with a high right shoulder and a down-sloping neckline.

Why No Broadening Bottoms?

All of the other types of reversal formations we have studied thus far can occur as either tops or bottoms. They can develop at the end of a decline to turn the trend up, or at the end of an advance to turn the trend down. But this does not seem to be true of the Broadening Formation. It has been assumed in the past that Broadening Bottoms must exist, but the writer has never found a good one in his examination of the charts of thousands of individual stocks over many years, and only one or two patterns which bore a resemblance to it in the charts of the averages. Apparently the circumstances which create Broadening Formations do not exist after a prolonged decline in prices. This would seem to bear out our earlier characterization of this sort of pattern as suggesting active, excited trading with much public (and, hence, not too well informed or managed) participation. Such conditions are naturally associated with the final phases of a Bull Market.

FIGURE 90. Broadening tendencies which appear on monthly charts, or very wide spread (with tops five or six months apart) like the above on weekly charts, should not be regarded as significant technical formations. Reversal points in a true Broadening Top should not be more than two months apart, as in Figure 89.

Right-Angled Broadening Formations

Price patterns of the "inverted triangle" shape having a horizontal top or bottom boundary occur about as often as the symmetrical type, which is to say, not nearly as often as true Triangles, Rectangles, etc. In recent years there have been very few of them. While the true Right-Angle Triangle with a horizontal top line and up-slanting bottom line is called an Ascending Triangle, just as its counterpart with a horizontal bottom boundary and a down-slanting top boundary is called a Descending Triangle, we cannot apply these terms to the inverted or broadening forms. Generally speaking, Right-Angled Broadening Formations carry bearish implications, regardless of which side is horizontal, in nearly the same degree as the symmetrical manifestations.

Obviously, however, they differ essentially from symmetrical formations in one respect: a horizontal side indicates either accumulation or distribution at a fixed price, depending of course on which side is horizontal. And it follows, logically, that any decisive break through that horizontal side has immediate forceful significance. Thus, if a broadening price pattern *with a flat top bound-ary* develops after a good advance and if prices finally burst *up* through that top line on high volume and close above it to a conclusive extent (roughly 3%), then it is safe to assume that the preceding up trend will be resumed and carried on for a worth-while move. This does happen, although it is rare. The odds favor the opposite; i.e., the eventual victory of the forces of distribution which created the horizontal top and a break away into an extensive decline.

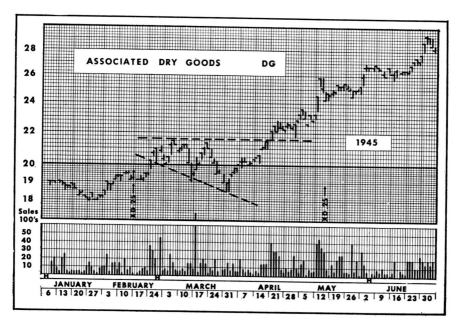

FIGURE 91. Three successive reactions in "DG" in February-March, 1945 made successively lower bottoms, but the intervening rallies came up to the same high (about 21¼), thus forming a Right-Angled Broadening formation with a horizontal top (supply) line. Penetration of this technically important top line on April 16 was a bullish signal. The flat-topped type of pattern does not necessarily portray a bearish situation.

Moreover, if an advance is to ensue from a flat-topped Broadening Formation, the chances are that the third reaction in the formation will be attended
by much diminished trading activity instead of the continued high or irregular
volume which is characteristic of bearish broadening movements, and that either
it or the fourth reaction will be halted and reversed *above* the low point of
the preceding.   This turns the formation into a *Consolidation Head-and-Shoulders,* a continuation-of-trend pattern which we shall take up in Chapter XI.
The message here for the trader owning a stock whose chart begins to develop
a Broadening Formation of this type is: Watch the third reaction.   If it carries below the second and volume does not fall off to a marked degree, sell out
on the next rally.   (You can always re-purchase the same stock if you wish
without much "loss of position" should prices finally and improbably recover
and push up through the top.)

Right-Angled Broadening Formations with horizontal lower boundaries (flat
bottoms) almost always break down.   Once prices have fallen below the lower
boundary line, there is frequently a pull-back rally to that line, either in a few
days or in two or three weeks, similar to the pull-backs that so often follow
the break down from a Head-and-Shoulders top.

FIGURE 92.   The 1946 top in Paramount Pictures, from which it fell to 46
a year later, was a Right-Angled Broadening formation with a horizontal
bottom line which was "cracked" the first week of June but not decisively
broken until June 20.   (This stock was later split 2-for-1.)

FIGURE 93. Another example of the flat-topped type of broadening price pattern which appeared near the end of 1945. "LS" went on up to 63 in 1946. Prices broke out of this formation with a breakout gap (G) and another breakout gap appeared on December 3. G-G marks an "Island." See Chapter XII for gaps.

Note that the third or fourth rally in a pattern which starts out as a flat-bottomed Broadening Formation may fail to carry prices as high as its predecessor in which case we have a Head-and-Shoulders to deal with. In other words, every Head-and-Shoulders begins as a Broadening Formation. And the statement of that relation takes us logically to our next type of reversal picture.

THE DIAMOND

The *Diamond* reversal formation might be described either as a more or less complex Head-and-Shoulders with a V-shaped neckline, or as a Broadening Formation which, after two or three "swings," suddenly reverts into a regular Triangle which is nearly always of the Symmetrical form. So far as the accompanying volume pattern is concerned the latter is possibly the better description. Its name derives obviously from its pictorial resemblance to the conventional diamond figure.

Although it is fairly conspicuous and easily detected when it appears on the

FIGURE 94. The 1946 Bull Market top in U. S. Steel was a three-month Diamond which might also be construed as an H & S.

FIGURE 95 (below). A Diamond (November) which broke out topside and thus functioned as consolidation rather than reversal.

charts, the Diamond is not a common pattern. Since its development requires fairly active markets, it rarely occurs at bottom reversals. It's "natural habitat" is Major tops and the high-volume tops which precede extensive Intermediate reactions. Many Multiple Head-and-Shoulders formations are border-line Diamond cases; i.e., they permit the drawing of slightly bent necklines. The reader is cautioned, however, against trying too hard to make Diamonds out of price patterns of the Head-and-Shoulders type. There is a temptation to do so because a V-shaped neckline may promise to give an earlier (and, hence, more profitable) breakout signal than the straight neckline of the Head-and-Shoulders, but it is much safer to stick to the latter unless the second half of the formation consists of a series of clean-cut, converging minor fluctuations which plainly demands definition by converging boundary lines, and unless activity shows some tendency to diminish during this period as it would in a Triangle.

The Diamond requires little further comment. Our illustrations will suffice

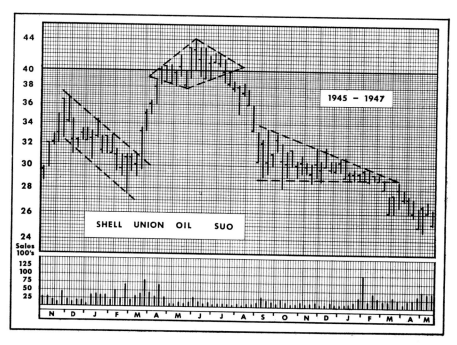

FIGURE 96. Diamond reversal formations are often easier to detect on weekly than on daily charts. Trace out the price swings and volume in this May-June, 1946 Diamond in Shell. Note also the remarkable Descending Triangle which developed from September, 1946 to February, 1947, and the March pull-back to its apex, another ideal place to sell short.

FIGURE 97. Hudson is another stock that ended its Bull Market in 1946 with a Major Diamond which could also be taken as a complex H & S. This formation was plain on the weekly chart but hard to see on the daily. Note how the Diamond gave a sell signal about 2 points higher than the H & S. The 14½-17½ area at the end of the year, when construed as a weak Rectangle, was barely fulfilled in February 1947.

to acquaint you with its typical details. It carries a minimum measuring implication which, having studied the Head-and-Shoulders and Triangle formulas, you can probably deduce for yourself. Prices should move *at least as far* from the breakout point as the greatest width in points of the pattern from its top (head) to bottom (V in neckline). This, it must be emphasized, is a *minimum* rule and subject only to the usual qualification that a reversal formation must have something to reverse. Generally, the new trend carries prices eventually well beyond the minimum measurement.

WEDGE FORMATIONS

All of the chart formations we have discussed up to this point can and do develop at changes in the *Major* trend of prices.   A few of them seldom occur at any other than a Major reversal.   We have now to consider three patterns which are ordinarily Minor or at most only Intermediate in their trend implications.   They are useful, nevertheless, in trading operations.   One of them, the *Wedge*, we have already alluded to (in Chapter VIII) as having some resemblance to the Triangles.

The Wedge is a chart formation in which the price fluctuations are confined within converging straight (or practically straight) lines, but differing from a Triangle in that both boundary lines either slope up or slope down.   In a Symmetrical Triangle the top border slants down while the bottom border slants up.   In Right-Angle Triangles one boundary slopes either up or down, but the other

FIGURE 98.   As U. S. Steel approached the top of its Secondary recovery in August, 1937, its price fluctuations tended to grow narrower, between upward sloping but converging boundaries, while volume diminished.   This pattern—a Wedge—carried a definitely bearish message.   The entire swing from July to the end of August was essentially a Rounding Top.   The three G's mark breakaway gaps (Chapter XII), the last (September 7) made as prices broke down through a support level (Chapter XIII).

is horizontal. In a Rising Wedge both boundary lines slant up from left to right, but since the two lines converge, the lower must, of course, project at a steeper angle than the upper. In a Falling Wedge the opposite is true.

Superficially, one might think that since an Ascending Triangle with one horizontal and one up line is a bullish picture, the Rising Wedge with both of its pattern lines up should be even more bullish. But such is not the case. Remember that the flat top of an Ascending Triangle signifies a supply of shares being distributed at a fixed price; when that supply has been absorbed (and the rising lower boundary line indicates that it will be absorbed) the pressure is off and prices will leap forward. In a Rising Wedge, on the other hand, there is no evident barrier of supply to be vaulted but rather a gradual petering out of investment interest. Prices advance but each new up wave is feebler than the last. Finally demand fails entirely and the trend reverses. Thus a Rising Wedge typifies a situation which is growing progressively *weaker* in the technical sense.

Of course, it might be said that any advance in prices, no matter what shape it may take on the chart, weakens the technical status of the market. Prospec-

FIGURE 99. An "ideal" Falling Wedge which developed in Loew's in 1936. Note volume trend therein, irregular but generally diminishing. July produced a small Flag (Chapter XI) and at the end of the year "LW" went into a Rectangle out of which prices "skyrocketed" to 75.

tive buyers are—or, at least, should be—more reluctant to pay high prices than low, and owners more willing to sell at high prices than at low; in other words any sort of rise tends to increase supply and diminish demand. (While theoretically true, the preceding statement must be qualified by the fact that rising prices actually attract rather than discourage public buying.) The difference between a Rising Wedge and what might be called a normal up trend channel (of which we shall have more to say later) is that the Wedge sets a sort of limit on the advance. Its converging boundary lines focus on a point near where the advance will halt and reaction set in.

We can state most of the essential facts about the up-pointed Wedge formation in a few short sentences. It can develop either as a sort of topping out pattern on a previously existing up trend, or start to form right at the bottom of a preceding down trend. It (the Wedge) normally takes more than three weeks to complete; a shorter pattern of this shape is nearly always better classified as a Pennant which we will discuss in the next chapter. Prices almost always fluctuate within the Wedge's confines for at least two thirds of the distance from the base (beginning of convergence) to the apex; in many cases they rise clear to the apex, and in some they actually go a short distance beyond, pushing on out at the top in a last-gasp rally before collapsing. Once prices break out of the Wedge down-side they usually waste little time before declining in earnest. The ensuing drop ordinarily retraces all of the ground gained within the Wedge itself, and sometimes more. Trading volume in a Wedge tends to follow the regular Triangle pattern, diminishing gradually as prices move up toward the apex of the Wedge.

THE FALLING WEDGE

Except for the fact that it is pointed down, the Falling Wedge appears in all respects like the Rising form we have just described. But the price trend which follows its completion differs in character. When prices break out of a Rising Wedge they usually fall away rapidly, but when they move out of a Falling Wedge they are more apt to drift sidewise or in a dull "saucering-around" movement before they begin to rise. The Rising Wedge may, therefore, call for quick action to secure profits, while with a Falling Wedge the trader ordinarily can take his time about making his commitment for the ensuing rise.

Both types should be well defined on the chart. Unless a trend pattern is quite compact with frequent fluctuations, and nicely bounded by lines which clearly converge to a point, and unless their up (or down) slant is marked, the Wedge construction must be considered doubtful. You will find border-line cases where one of the pattern lines so nearly approaches the horizontal in direction that it resembles a Right-Angle Triangle, and the latter would, of course, carry quite different implications for future trend development. It is difficult to lay down any hard and fast rules for distinguishing the two. If one bound-

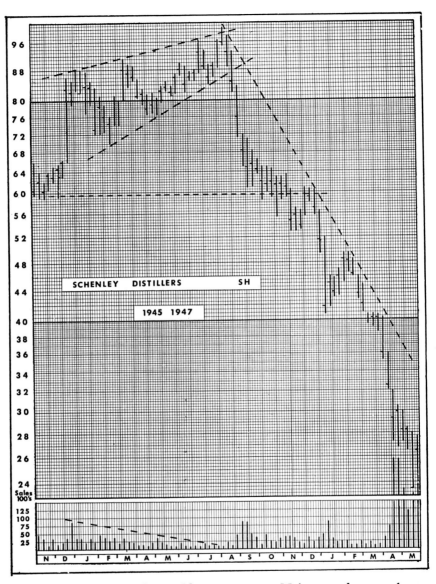

FIGURE 100. Wedges seldom appear at Major trend reversals, but Schenley's Bull high in 1946 was made at the end of an eight-month Rising Wedge, plain to see on its weekly chart. The dashed line at 60 marks a support level (see Chapter XIII) which served to stem the subsequent decline for nine weeks.

ary line is *nearly* horizontal, or if the daily *closing* prices tend to fall at about the same level, then the formation is safer construed as a Triangle. The reader need not let this problem worry him unduly as he will rarely be left in doubt for long after he has acquired a little experience with charts. One soon gets to recognize the characteristic "symptoms" of the different formations and make correct diagnoses almost instinctively.

WEDGES ON WEEKLY AND MONTHLY CHARTS

Most true Wedges are too short-lived (seldom longer than three months) to take on recognizable definition on a monthly chart, but they may be spotted occasionally on the weeklies. Long-continued, gradual down trends when plotted on arithmetic scale sometimes assume the wedge form. Thus, an entire Major Bear decline on any arithmetic monthly chart may appear like a giant Falling Wedge. This is due to the fact that the up and down fluctuations which compose the Major swing, while maintaining about the same extent in *percentage,* tend to shorten in terms of points (dollars) as prices move from higher to lower levels. Such major chart patterns are not, of course, the true Wedges we have discussed herein. When plotted on semi-logarithmic scale, these same moves would normally show a parallel or even slightly widening instead of converging channel.

RISING WEDGES COMMON IN BEAR MARKET RALLIES

As a final note, we might add that the Rising Wedge is a quite characteristic pattern for Bear Market rallies. It is so typical in fact that frequent appearance of Wedges at a time when, after an extensive decline, there is some question as to whether a new Bull trend is in the making, may be taken as evidence that the Primary trend is still down. When a Major Bear swing ends in a Head-and-Shoulders bottom, the last Rising Wedge will often appear as prices rally from the left shoulder to the neckline and just before they break down to the head (final low). A Rising Wedge on an arithmetically scaled weekly chart is almost invariably a Bear Market phenomenon, expressing as it does the diminishing vigor which is the normal property of any reaction against a prevailing Primary trend.

THE ONE-DAY REVERSAL

We referred in Chapter VI to a price pattern known as the *One-Day Reversal.* This particular technical reversal indication, when taken alone, can be accorded only temporary or strong Minor trend significance. True, it may appear at the very peak of a long advance, forming perhaps on the high day of the head in a Head-and-Shoulders pattern which will be followed by a long decline, but it can hardly be credited with forecasting that entire decline; all it really signalized was the turn in the "head" itself. A One-Day Reversal may

FIGURE 101. There are many interesting and technically significant features in this twelve-month daily chart record of "TWA." Note the extraordinary One-Day Reversal, December 3, which marked its Major top. Although the next four weeks produced a sort of poorly formed Descending Triangle, the Reversal Day was the only clear-cut and unmistakable signal to sell. When you come to page 174, turn back to this chart for its November Pennant. Its long Intermediate down trendline was tentatively broken in August, 1946 but without confirming volume (see Chapter XIV). Note that at no time during the decline did a "buy" pattern appear.

just as well occur, for example, at the beginning (the first peak) of a Symmetrical Triangle which only consolidates instead of reversing the previous up trend. Even so it serves, as you can see, to warn us of at least temporary exhaustion of bullish forces.

On the down side, a One-Day Reversal often appears in magnified and conspicuous form at the end of a panic sell-off, in which case it usually is referred to as a *Climax Day* or Selling Climax. This manifestation of it has special significance which we shall take up later. First, however, just what is a One-Day Reversal?

It is, to begin with, a day of unusually high volume, exceeding as a rule by a notable margin any trading turnover registered in any one market session for several months past. It comes after a fairly long and steady advance (or a similar decline), on which activity has been increasing gradually. Prices push right ahead from the opening gong as if nothing could stop them. Frequently even the opening sales are so far beyond the previous day's closing level as to leave a large *gap* on the chart. (We shall discuss gaps later.) The tape runs late, and before the advance (or decline) halts, prices have been carried as far in an hour or two as three or four days would ordinarily take them. But the halt does come finally, maybe at the end of the first hour or perhaps not until late in the day. Then quotations "churn," registering only fractional changes to and fro, with the tape still "fast" and often running late by spurts. Suddenly the trend reverses and prices move just as rapidly in the opposite direction. The session ends with a final burst of activity which puts the price at the close right back where it started the day. There has been an enormous amount of activity, and quotations may have traversed intra-day a range of more than five points, but the net change from the previous day at the end of trading is very small.

One-Day Reversals at tops appear quite often in the charts of individual stocks which are thin (relatively small floating supply of shares), which have had an active advance and have attracted a large public following. They develop rarely in the averages. Selling Climaxes (One-Day Reversals at bottoms), on the other hand, are found conspicuously in the averages at the end of many abnormal or panic declines.

One-Day Reversals, as we have already stated, do not carry Major trend implications. The nimble in-and-out trader can capitalize on them—maybe pick up several points if he has funds available and jumps in at the right moment. But, as a rule, the new trend (i.e., the trend at the close of the day) does not carry very far right away; prices usually "work" around in the nearby ranges for some time and build some sort of area pattern before they move away in a swing of Intermediate proportions. However, the One-Day Reversal, as a phenomenon which occurs frequently within or at the start of more pregnant technical formations, gives an important clue to *probable* trend developments.

In any event, it is an urgent warning to watch closely the chart in which it has appeared to see what pattern of price action may follow and be prepared for the worth-while move when it comes.

It is worth noting that the type of false move or shake-out which we described in Chapter VIII, as occurring at the apex end of a Symmetrical Triangle, often takes the form of a One-Day Reversal.

FIGURE 102.   The strong One-Day Reversal which marked Greyhound's 1946 Bull Market high.   Note climax volume.   A less conspicuous Reversal Day appeared on August 26.   It is suggested that the reader go back over all charts in preceding chapters; he will find many Reversal Days of greater or lesser consequence.   May gaps (G) were of measuring type—see Chapter XII.

THE SELLING CLIMAX

In the "bad old days" when stocks could be bought by putting up as little as 10% of their cost in cash, and there were no restrictions on short selling, professional operators could (and tradition says they often did) organize bear raids to shake out weakly margined holdings.   By selling short in quantity at a favorable moment when the "public" had gotten itself pretty well extended on the long side, they could break prices down.   Brokers then would send out calls for more margin from their "long" accounts, many of whom could not or would not put it up, with the result that their stocks were dumped on the market. That, in turn, produced further declines. The professionals could then step in, cover their shorts with a profit and secure a line of long stock for the next advance. Bear raids of this sort were effectively checked by the imposition of the SEC regulations, but margin calls and forced selling will, of course, always exist as a market factor so long as stocks can be bought on margin, and will come into play whenever prices drop extensively following a spree of public buying.

Most true Selling Climaxes, if not all, have been produced by distress selling of the type referred to in the preceding paragraph. They have come at the end of rapid and comprehensive declines which exhausted the margin reserves of many speculators and necessitated the dumping of their shares at whatever the market would bring. This process is progressive—feeding upon itself, so to speak—with each wave of forced sales jeopardizing another lot of margined accounts, until at last millions of shares are tossed overboard, willy nilly, in a final clean-up. Such is a Selling Climax in which the total turnover may exceed any single day's volume during the previous up swing. It is a harvest time for traders who, having avoided the bullish infection at the top of the market, have funds in reserve to pick up stocks available at panic prices.

Obviously, a clean-out day or Selling Climax radically reverses the technical condition of the market, for in its process shares have passed from weak hands into strong hands at very much lower prices. The ominous weight of potential selling that has been overhanging the market has been removed. And usually the panic has carried quotations (although only temporarily as a rule) well below even conservative values based on current business conditions.

A Selling Climax need not be completed, and the reversal of trend actually become evident, within a single day. We have classified it as a variety of One-Day Reversal but some of them have actually spread out over two days, with the decline exhausted and coming to a halt late on the first day, too near the end of the session to permit of much recovery. The next day sees an extensive rally right from the opening gong as it is immediately apparent then, if not late the preceding day, that there are no more distress offerings.

The all-time record for Selling Climaxes is held by October 29, 1929. Prices in terms of the Dow-Jones Industrial average opened that day practically at their high, 252.38, which was more than eight points below the previous day's closing level. Panic selling flooded the Exchange from the start and before it was over, the Industrial average had lost 40.05 points! From that low, 212.33, it rallied in the final two hours to 230.07 for a gain of nearly 18 points and went on up another 28 points the following day. This 1929 climax set the all-time record also for daily turnover: 16,410,000 shares were traded in those five hours, more than twice as many as in any one day during the entire preceding Bull Market. But the low level of October 29 was broken a week later and the bottom of that particular early phase of the 1929-1932 Bear Market was not reached until November 13. (We trust this brief mention of the market events of that period will not evoke distressing memories among too many of our readers.)

The panic of 1937 ended with a classic Selling Climax on October 19, another "Black Tuesday" in stock market annals. The Dow Industrials had closed at 125.73 the night before. Prices had already fallen without a rally of consequence from a high of 190 in mid-August and margin accounts were nearly all in precarious situation. The telephones had been worked overtime the preceding day by brokers demanding additional margin, most of which was not forthcoming. When the exchange opened on the 19th, quotations hit the toboggan under a flood of offerings. By 11:30 a.m., with the Industrial average

FIGURE 103. The "panic" selling of October 19, 1937 produced a conspicuous Climax Reversal Day in nearly all leading stocks as well as in the averages. This New York Central chart shows, beside the Selling Climax (S. C.), its Head-and-Shoulders recovery top of July-August and a consolidation Rectangle which ended as a Triangle in early October. "CN" made a final Bear Market low the following March at 10½. On a logarithmic price scale, its down trendline from August was not broken until June, 1938.

around 115, the selling was over and offerings disappeared. An hour later, prices were jumping a point between sales and the day closed at 126.85, recovering its entire loss. Volume on that climax was 7,290,000 shares, double that of any day at the top of the preceding Bull Market. An intra-day high of 141.22 was reached ten days later, but the panic low was subsequently broken on November 20, 1937, and that Bear Market finally ended at 98.95 (Dow-Jones Industrials' closing level) on March 31, 1938.

The foregoing were *general market* climaxes, a phenomenon which, of course, produces (or rather is produced by) simultaneous selling in practically every actively traded individual issue. A climax bottom, as a matter of fact, appears in an individual stock chart as a rule only as a concomitant of a general market clean-out, although there are cases where some particular and completely unexpected piece of bad news affects one certain company and causes panicky liquidation of its shares alone, terminating with a One-Day Reversal. The *top* Reversal Day, on the other hand, is normally a manifestation of an individual stock rather than of the general market average.

The two outstanding examples of Selling Climaxes which we have cited above, and numbers of others which have appeared at the conclusion of various panic sell-offs, obviously offered extraordinary opportunities for a quick turn to the trader who was smart (or lucky) enough to get in at the bottom. He could cash in a few days later with exceptional profits. Professional operators capitalize such opportunities. The problem is to recognize the climactic nature of the selling in time to seize the chance—and that isn't as easy as it may have sounded in our discussion. Just to emphasize the possibilities of error, there was a 30-point drop, followed by a 30-point recovery, on a turnover of nearly 13 million shares, on October 24, 1929, but the trader who didn't grab his profits within 48 hours never had another chance to get out even (in terms of the averages, that is).

But it isn't impossible to recognize a Selling Climax, if you have friends in the street to keep you informed on the condition of margin accounts and the amount of necessitous selling to be expected. The climax comes *after* a decline approaching panic proportions. The day usually opens with a substantial downside gap (opening prices considerably below the previous night's closing); offerings appear too great to be absorbed; prices collapse; the tape runs late; the market is exceptionally "broad" with nearly every listed stock crowding into the record. Then, some time after 11 a.m., perhaps not until afternoon, the selling appears to dry up; a few issues continue to decline while others begin to climb. Suddenly prices are jumping. That is the time to act. Buy a stock that has been thoroughly depressed but one which normally has at all times a good following (for example, U. S. Steel). Don't hang on too long; take a reasonable profit as soon as it is available and sell, in any event, whenever the recovery shows signs of bogging down.

FIGURE 104. The Selling Climax discussed on the preceding pages is typically a one-day phenomenon and on only one occasion (April, 1939) in the history of the past twenty years did a general market One-Day Reversal signalize the final low of a Primary Bear trend (although many individual stocks evinced a Selling Climax on their charts in March, 1938).

Occasionally a weekly chart will produce a formation which might be called a "One-Week Reversal," in some such conspicuous fashion as is shown above in "NC." In this instance, the subsequent rise proves that a Major change in its technical balance occurred in December, 1941. Curiously enough, no other obvious reversal pattern appeared on the weekly chart at this turn in the Primary trend of "NC." (Its daily chart showed an Ascending Triangle.)

But this example of a One-Week Reversal is not shown to give the idea that such phenomena carry important technical indications. On the contrary, most "reversal weeks" are followed by very disappointing moves.

Remember, a One-Day Reversal is not a dependable Major trend indicator. Selling Climaxes do not normally occur at the final bottoms of Bear Markets— weak holdings usually have been shaken out long before that stage is reached. Only one Primary down trend in all the record has, in fact, ended with the first panic phase, that being the five-month Bear Market of 1938-1939 which was followed by an equally short Bull Market.

*   *   *   *   *

One remaining reversal formation, the *Island* pattern, involves the whole subject of *gaps* which we have not yet had an appropriate occasion to discuss. Gaps will be taken up in detail in Chapter XII and we will defer the Island Reversal until then.

CHAPTER XI

CONSOLIDATION FORMATIONS

A N ARMY that has pushed forward too rapidly, penetrated far into enemy
territory, suffered casualties and out-run its supplies, must halt eventually,
perhaps retreat a bit to a more easily defended position and dig in, bring up re-
placements and establish a strong base from which later to launch a new attack.
In the military parlance with which we have all become more or less familiar
these past few years, that process is known as *consolidating* one's gains. Although it will not do to over-work the analogy, there is much in the action of
the stock market which may be compared to a military campaign. When a
stock pushes ahead (up or down) too fast, it reaches a point where the forces
that produced its move are exhausted. Then it either reverses its trend (in a
Major or Intermediate sense), reacts to a good support level, or *consolidates* its
position, in some sort of "sidewise" chart pattern composed of minor fluctuations, until it has caught up with itself, so to speak, and is ready to go on again.

We already have had occasion to refer to Consolidation Formations in our
study of Symmetrical Triangles and Rectangles. We saw how those two chart
formations might either reverse the previous trend or consolidate it in prepara-
tion for its continuation. We noted that about three out of four Symmetrical
Triangles will turn out to be consolidations rather than reversals—and Rectangles in about the same proportion. Even a flat-topped Broadening pattern,
constructed at the top of an Intermediate advance, may, despite its normally
bearish implications, be converted into a consolidation or continuation formation if its flat top is decisively penetrated on the up side.

A Dow Theory Line in the chart of one of the averages may be either a
Consolidation or Reversal formation, and is rather more likely to be the former
than the latter. A Dow Line is, of course, a sort of loose Rectangle. The
fact is that almost any sort of sidewise price pattern, such as is often termed a
"congestion" or trading area, provided trading volume tends to diminish during
its construction (and provided it does not show definite broadening tendencies),
usually functions as a Consolidation. But most areas of trend consolidation are
fairly well defined—take on a recognizable pattern.

FLAGS AND PENNANTS

We do not need to spend more time here on the Triangles and Rectangles;
they have been examined in both their reversal and consolidation manifestations

in previous chapters.   Our first two new formations, which are characteristic of Consolidation *only*, are the Flags and Pennants, and they are curiously related in certain respects, as we shall see, to Triangles, Rectangles and Wedges.

A *Flag* looks like a flag on the chart.   That is, it does if it appears in an up trend; the picture is naturally turned upside down in a down trend.   It might be described as a small, compact parallelogram of price fluctuations, or

FIGURE 105.   This is a typical and practically perfect Flag, constructed May 12 to June 2, 1945, in Martin-Parry.   Daily turn-over diminished to a low rate as prices settled down for exactly three weeks after their swift advance from 11 to 16½, but held up away from the lower boundary line during the third week, and then burst out top-side with high volume in another straight-line push from 15 to 21.   Study this chart again when you come to the Flag measuring formula on page 177.   The dashes at 12 indicate the upper range of an old resistance level (Chapter XIII).

tilted rectangle, which slopes back moderately against the prevailing trend.   Let us consider the up trend Flag first.   It usually forms after a rapid and fairly extensive advance which produces a nearly vertical, or at least quite steep, price track on the charts.   On such moves, volume normally shows a progressive increase until it reaches a high rate.   This volume (since every transaction signifies a sale as well as a purchase) is a warning, of course, that many holders of the stock are taking profits.   Eventually the pressure of profit-taking halts the mark-up.   Prices "churn" without further gain and then react two or three points on reduced turnover.   A new rally occurs but fails to equal the previous high or attain the previous top volume.   Another reaction carries quotations

FIGURE 106.   Another typical Flag of three weeks' duration, August 30 to September 18.   This National Gypsum chart overlaps that in Figure 49, showing the false move at the apex of the May-June Symmetrical Triangle. A buy signal was given when prices pushed up through the old apex level on August 23 with increased volume.   Most interesting is the second Symmetrical Triangle which formed in October-November, an almost exact replica of the first but with a down-side false move at its apex.   The sharp increase in volume on November 27 left no doubt as to its being a consolidation rather than reversal pattern.   "NG" went on up to 33.

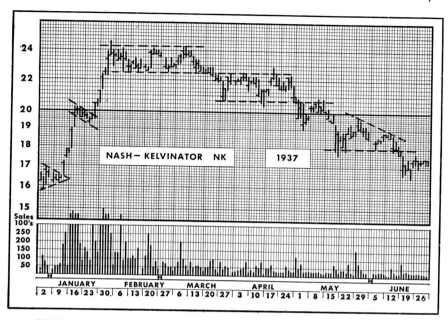

FIGURE 107.   Flags of the "half-mast" type appear most often in the later and most active stages of a Primary advance.   The above example (January) was the last consolidation formation before "NK's" 1937 Bull Market top.   Note the Rectangle reversal pattern in March and series of step-down patterns that followed.

slightly below the preceding bottom with further diminution of activity.   Then follows a series of similar minor fluctuations, each of whose tops and bottoms is successively a trifle lower than its predecessor, and with volume shrinking markedly and constantly as the pattern develops.   On the chart the initial, steep up-move followed by the compact, sidewise and slightly down-sloping price congestion area, which can be roughly bounded, top and bottom, by parallel lines, takes on the appearance of a mast (or halyard) with a flag flying from its peak.   Hence, of course, the name of the formation.

Sometimes each rally and set-back within the Flag takes three or four days, rarely more.   In other cases, prices will skip back and forth between the upper and lower Flag boundaries in a single day or two, in which event the pattern on the chart consists of an almost solid block of price range lines.   The wider the pattern (from top to bottom) the longer time naturally it should take for each swing within it to be completed.   This process of minor fluctuations may continue for only five days to a week if the Flag is narrow, or go on for as much as three weeks.   Daily turnover by that time usually will have shrunk to

FIGURE 108.   Sometimes a stock will make a long series of small consolidation patterns in its up trend, one following right on the heels of another as
successive groups of traders buy in while others take their profits on previous
purchases.   In this sequence of step-ups in Vanadium, the Flag pattern formed
in January, 1937 ran a few days over-long, but the volume breakout of
February 4 left no doubt that the trend was still up.   A final top was made
at 39½ in March.

This chart overlaps Figure 43 on page 85; you may find it interesting to
compare them.   Note strong buy signal given on December 14.   Refer to
this record again in connection with Support-Resistance studies in Chapter
XIII.

FIGURE 109. A Bull Flag in February and a Bear Flag in April, 1936, in Briggs. The top between was a Symmetrical Triangle. April 30 was a Reversal Day. Prices recovered to 64½ in November, 1936, making there a long-term Major Double Top with this March high. The support-resistance zone at 51-53, indicated by dashed line, was still effective in 1946! (See Chapter XIII.)

a relatively low ebb. Then suddenly prices will erupt with a new burst of activity from the end of the Flag and push straight up again in another advance which practically duplicates the original "mast" atop which the Flag was constructed.

We have spoken of the Flag pattern as being moderately down-slanting, but the very short and "solid" ones will frequently develop horizontally and look like small squares. (On rare occasions, a pattern of the Flag type in an up trend will even slope up a trifle.)

Flags form on steep down moves in much the same manner and with precisely the same implications as they do in up trends. Down Flags, of course, tend to slope up; i.e., they simply invert the picture presented by an up Flag. Trading volume diminishes during their formation and increases again as prices break down away from them.

FIGURE 110. The down-sloping, converging price formation of November 4-December 9 might be called either a short Wedge or a Pennant. Note small Flag in October; also runaway gaps November 4 and February 19, and breakout gap December 10.

THE PENNANT—A POINTED FLAG

The only important difference between a *Pennant* and a *Flag* is that the former is bounded by converging boundary lines rather than parallel. The normal Pennant, in other words, is a small, compact, sloping Triangle. It slants down when it appears in an up trend, and up in a down trend. It forms as a rule after a rapid advance (or decline), and trading volume shrinks notably during its construction. In fact, activity tends to diminish even more rapidly in a Pennant than in a Flag (which we naturally would expect on account of the progressively shorter fluctuations which compose it) and may drop almost to nothing before the Pennant is completed and prices break away from it in a new and rapid move.

The Pennant might also be described as a short, compact Wedge, characterized by marked diminution of activity. When, as is usual, it slants back against the preceding trend, its forecasting implications are similar to those of the Wedge in that prices break out of it in the direction opposite to its slant. But there are rarer minor variations of the Pennant, comparable with those sometimes found in the Flag, in which the price area is very short and "solid" and practically horizontal (like a Symmetrical Triangle) or in which the slope is actually slightly in the same direction as the preceding trend instead of against it. When prices move out of the last-named type they ordinarily do so not in a sudden straight-line breakaway but rather in an accelerating curve with volume increasing gradually instead of abruptly at the break. The whole pattern then resembles a curved horn which runs to a long, slender point. Don't let these variations worry you; there is nothing deceptive about their appearance; their kinship to the more common, normal form is quite apparent.

FIGURE 111. An example (in June, 1944) of the very brief and compact type of price "congestion" which can be classed as a Flag. The advance here started at 5 from a thirteen-month Symmetrical Triangle of which only the last two months appear above. The measuring implication (see page 177) of this tiny Flag was not fulfilled until after prices had undergone a sort of triangular consolidation in July.

FIGURE 112. Another example of the series of flag-type consolidations which may form in a rapid, third-phase Bull Market advance. Mullins went from 15 to above 39 in six months in 1936, dropped back to 31 and then rose again in March, 1937 to its previous high, making a Major Double Top. ("MNS" was split 2-for-1 in 1937.)

The July-August Flag ran for five weeks—too long to be trusted without additional technical evidence (see point 3 on next page). The danger in such prolonged formations is either that the breakout when it finally appears will fail to follow through, or that prices will keep right on drifting down. For the moment—on August 25—it looked as though this Flag had "gone stale," but when prices rose above the previous high on August 27, with a smart pick-up in volume, purchases were obviously safe.

THE MEASURING FORMULA

The same approximate measuring formula applies to the Pennant as to the Flag. They are both "half mast" patterns which ordinarily form after a fairly steady and rapid (steep) price movement. In applying the measuring rule, go back to the beginning of that immediately preceding move, to the point where it broke away from a previous Consolidation or Reversal formation (or through a significant trend line or resistance level, with which later chapters are concerned), a point recognizable as a rule by a quick spurt in activity, and measure from there to the Minor reversal level at which the Flag or Pennant started to form. Then measure the same distance from the point where prices break out of the Flag or Pennant, and in the same direction. The level thus arrived at is the minimum expectation of this type of Consolidation pattern. As a matter of fact, advances from Flags or Pennants in an up trend generally go farther (in terms of points or dollars) than the preceding move, while declines may not carry quite so far. Hence, the formula is best applied on a semi-logarithmic chart by measuring actual chart distance rather than by counting points. You can check this by referring to the examples illustrating this study.

RELIABILITY OF FLAGS AND PENNANTS

These pretty little patterns of consolidation are justly regarded as among the most dependable of chart formations, both as to directional and measuring indications. They do fail occasionally but almost never without giving warning before the pattern itself is completed. All that is necessary to guard against such failures is to apply strictly the tests as to authenticity of pattern which we already have incorporated in their description. These are:—

1. The consolidation (Flag or Pennant) should occur after a "straight-line" move.

2. Activity should diminish appreciably and constantly during the pattern's construction, and continue to decline until prices break away from it.

3. Prices should break away (in the expected direction) in not more than four weeks. A pattern of this type which extends beyond three weeks should be watched with suspicion.

The matter of practical trading on these particular formations will be taken up in the second section of this book, devoted to Tactics. But our test No. 2 deserves some further comment here. If a pattern begins to develop on the chart which, so far as the price picture alone is concerned, qualifies as a Flag or Pennant, but during which trading volume remains high or obviously irregular instead of diminishing, the outcome is more apt to be a quick reaction against, rather than continuation of, the previous trend. In other words, such high or irregular activity formations are characteristically *minor* reversal areas rather than true consolidations. Watch the volume half of your chart at all times.

FIGURE 113 (above). The vertical lines marked "M" show how the measuring formula is applied to a Flag pattern. Note that the first measurement is taken from the level where the mast leaves the previous "congestion" up to the peak of the Flag. This same distance is then measured up from the Flag breakout. In "WYO" the formula worked out exactly. Trading commitments should normally have been cashed in above 36 on this move. They might then have been re-instated when it became apparent by April 2 that a Rounding Bottom was completed (note volume) for a new advance.

FIGURE 114 (bottom of next page). A 1946 chart that delighted technicians. Contains a perfect "half-mast" pattern in January, with measuring gaps (G, G) above and below it; a down-side Flag in early February (check measurement); a fine Ascending Triangle at the bottom of this reaction, with a throw-back in April giving an ideal "buy spot."

WHERE THEY MAY BE EXPECTED

Flag and Pennant Consolidations are characteristic of fast moves. Naturally, therefore, they show up most frequently in the later, dynamic phase of Bull Markets, after the first accumulation and the more orderly early mark-up stages have passed. Hence, the appearance of these patterns may be taken as a warning that an advance is approaching its final weeks. The rapid phase of a Major Bear trend, on the other hand, is its second stage, often characterized by almost "vertical" panic declines. The Flags and Pennants which develop therein are usually short—completed in a matter of three or four days rather than weeks. In the late months of a Bear Market, formations which evolve on the charts in the Flag or Pennant similitude often will run too long (four weeks or more), begin to show an increase in volume on the rallies, and be succeeded by only dull and limited reactions.

In general, it may be said that these particular chart patterns are most common (and most dependable) in up trends. The appearance *after* a Major decline, of price pictures which at the start assume the down-trend Flag or Pennant form must be regarded with caution. Unless such developments hold strictly to the limitations we have stated above under the heading of "Reliability," do not trade on them.

FLAG PICTURES ON WEEKLY AND MONTHLY CHARTS

One of our requisites for a dependable Flag (or Pennant) was that it should not take more than four weeks to complete its pattern and break out in a new move. It stands to reason, therefore, that a true Flag cannot show up at all on

FIGURE 115. A Flag (end of November) which seemed for several weeks to have failed completely. However, prices rose quickly to 36¼ from their December 23 low, thus finally carrying through according to formula. Note flat-topped Broadening Formation which started the move.

a monthly chart and barely appears on a weekly chart. You will find price areas on long-range charts—patterns which have taken eight or ten weeks to as many months, and sometimes a year or two, in their construction—which assume the shape of a Flag, but do not expect them to function as Flags. Examined in detail on a daily chart, these same long areas almost always will be found to contain price formations having entirely different significance. Frequently what is really a Major *reversal* area following a long, rapid advance will look something like a Flag when it is condensed on a monthly chart. So, do not trust such pictures on long-range charts; do not take it for granted that they represent consolidation for a new rise; find out what the detailed *daily* plotting for the same period says.

Rectangular Consolidations an Early Phase Phenomenon

In contrast with Flags and Pennants which are typically last-stage Bull Market concomitants, consolidations of the Rectangle class are found more often in the earlier phases of Bull trend evolution. In Major Bear moves, Rectangles may develop in the first stage just *before* a panic decline, or in the last stage preceding a strictly limited final sell-off. The latter manifestation presumably betokens premature accumulation by interests who feel that prices have already gone low enough to suit their purposes. (They come out all right, of course, if they are able to hold on through the remainder of the Bear swing and long enough for the next Bull Market to put prices back up again to profitable levels.)

Head-and-Shoulders Consolidations

All our references to the Head-and-Shoulders formations up to this point (see Chapters VI and VII) have considered that pattern as typifying *reversal* of trend, and in its normal and common manifestation that is most definitely the Head-and-Shoulders function. But occasionally prices will go through a series of fluctuations which construct a sort of *inverted* Head-and-Shoulders picture which in turn leads to *continuation* of the previous trend.

There is no danger of confusing such continuation or consolidation formations with regular Head-and-Shoulders Reversals because, as we have said, they are inverted or abnormal with respect to the direction of the price trend prior to their appearance. In other words, one of these patterns which develops in a rising market will take the form of a Head-and-Shoulders Bottom. Those that appear in declines, assume the appearance of a Head-and-Shoulders Top. By the time these price formations are completed (left shoulder, head and right shoulder evident) there is no question as to their implications. But at the head stage, before the right shoulder is constructed, there may be—usually is—considerable doubt as to what is really going on.

The volume pattern in consolidations of this type does not follow the rule for reversal Head-and-Shoulders. In a down trend, for example, the consolidation formation resembles in its price contour a Head-and-Shoulders Top, but the attendant volume will diminish instead of increase on the left shoulder and head as well as on the right shoulder. The same holds true for the "bottom" patterns that develop as consolidation in an advancing market. Break-outs, however, resemble in all respects those arising from reversal formations.

Head-and-Shoulders Consolidations of the complex or multiple type very seldom appear on the charts. Theoretically, they might, of course, and should be as easy for the chart technician to handle as the simple forms.

The formula for determining the probable minimum price move (beyond the neckline) from a Head-and-Shoulders Reversal formation was discussed in Chapter VI. To anyone familiar with the vagaries of stock market trends and the endless variety of pictures which the charts can present, it is amazing how accurately that formula works out, how often the first consequential move away from a Head-and-Shoulders Top or Bottom will carry through to the point (or a little beyond) implied by the measurement of the formation. But, the same

FIGURE 116. Typical of the form which Head-and-Shoulders consolidation patterns may take, both as to price pattern and volume, was this development in Anaconda. Measuring formula for the small Flag in October should be applied from the point of breakout through the H & S neckline.

FIGURE 117. A 1945 H & S consolidation in which both of the shoulders and the head took a "saucer" form. Compare price and volume trends. Prices advanced to 31½ in July, came back again to 25½ in August, and then shot up to 40 in November.

formula applied to consolidation patterns of the Head-and-Shoulders form does not work out as well. Such patterns are usually quite "flat" and the ensuing move generally extends well beyond the measurement implied thereby, while in some cases it may not go quite as far. Consequently the Head-and-Shoulders formula cannot be applied to consolidation areas with assurance that it sets up a definite and dependable objective; one has to look in these cases to a variety of other chart indications as well, in order to appraise the probable proportions of the move to follow.

SCALLOPS—REPEATED SAUCERS

Our next chart picture differs from the consolidation formations previously discussed in that it does not constitute a more or less definite area of congestion or fluctuation to which one or more critical boundary lines can be affixed. We could, perhaps, take it up as well in a subsequent chapter under the general heading of normal trend action. Yet it is a pattern so characteristic of certain types of stocks and certain types of markets, and so nearly related to the principle of consolidation for further advance, that it may better be treated here.

When a stock in which there is a large number of shares outstanding and in which there is at all times a fairly active and "close" market emerges from a long-time bottom (as exemplified by the past history of Radio Corporation and

Socony Vacuum) it will often make a long Major advance in a series of "saucers." These successive patterns, each of which resembles in both price and volume action the reversal formation described in Chapter VII as a Rounding Bottom, are slightly up-tilted. That is, the rising end always carries price a little higher than the preceding top at the beginning of the saucer. The net gain accomplished by each saucering movement will vary from stock to stock but there seems to be a strong tendency for it to amount to about 10 to 15 percent of the price of the issue. The total reaction from the left-hand lip of each saucer to its bottom level is usually a little greater, from 20 to 30 percent. And the length (duration) of the saucers is normally five to seven weeks, rarely

FIGURE 118. Part of a genuine "scallop" up trend, typical except for the short duration and relatively small decline in the October saucer. The next scallop, which started in December, dropped prices back to 12½ in January and then carried them up to 18½ in February. A four-month saucer, from February, 1945 to June, preceded this chart. Note position traders found themselves in, who bought at 9 on the "new high on volume" in June.

FIGURE 119. Although the scalloping habit characteristically appears in low-priced issues, it is sometimes found in widely held, semi-investment stocks of medium price, such as "CWE."

less than three. Thus, over-all advance is slow but steady in much the same sense as the progress of the man who eventually got out of the deep well by climbing three steps for each two that he slipped back.

The charts of stocks which take this sort of course show a picture of strikingly similar and symmetrical rising scallops, one succeeding another with little or no pause between. Trading activity runs up to a peak at the latter stage of each scallop, as the previous high is approached and exceeded, then diminishes into dullness as prices curve down and flatten out at the bottom of the next saucer, and picks up again as prices curve up into their next rise.

The trading opportunities afforded by stocks of the saucering habit hardly require extended comment (although we shall set down some detailed specifications in the Tactics section of this book). The bottom level of each scallop is usually easy to detect by watching price trend and volume, and so is the topping out at the end. Yet it is curiously the fact that most "tape watchers" handle such stocks in the wrong way, becoming interested in them and buying when they show activity ("make a new high on volume") and neglecting them entirely when they are in the dull rounding-out stage of their trends.

(Many boardroom tape watchers scorn charts with unfortunate consequences to their capital in the long run. Genuinely expert tape readers—those who are able to show fairly consistent profits in their trades—are really extremely rare. When you do meet such an individual, you will find that he either in effect "carries charts in his head" or else takes a careful look at the record before he buys on a ticker showing of activity.)

As a stock with the scalloping habit finally works up in price to 15 or so, its pattern tends to become less regular; it begins to depart from the smooth, narrow, saucer-like curve of the lower levels.   Above 20 it is apt to break away entirely from the scallop sequence and produce from there on more rapid straight-line advances, interspersed with sharp reactions and standard types of consolidation formations, which are characteristic at all times of medium and higher priced issues.   (There are exceptions: some high priced preferred stocks for which there is always a market but whose trends depend almost entirely on the gradual changes in prevailing interest rates and supply of funds for investment, have a persistent scallop habit in their Primary up swings.)

We have named rather specific price levels (15 and 20) in the preceding paragraph, but price is not, of course, the sole factor determining the departure of a stock from a scallop trend.   The only safe assumption is that, once such a habit is detectable, it will be continued until the chart shows a definite divergence from it, and such divergence usually takes first the form of a greater than wonted advance arising at the end of one of the saucers.   Consequently, if you have previously taken a position in it at a favorable point (near the bottom of a scallop) you cannot be hurt when the stock finally alters its action.

Very low-priced issues may persist in a scalloping trend right up to their Major Bull tops and even attempt another saucer movement following what turns out to have been the final high, which attempt then fails, of course, to carry out the previous successively higher and higher pattern.   Such failures are not difficult to detect; the change from previous pattern appears before any appreciable damage is done to a properly assumed commitment.

Modern vs. Old-Style Markets

We have mentioned in our discussion of reversal formations that some of them have appeared less frequently in the charts of the past ten years than they did in prior years, and others more frequently.   The same is true of Consolidation formations.   Patterns of the compact, strictly defined sort such as Rectangles and Right-Angle Triangles are less common now.   Symmetrical Triangles are apt to be somewhat looser than they were in the twenties and early thirties—not as clean-cut and conspicuous on the charts.   Typical profit-taking patterns such as Flags and Pennants seem to be as common as ever, while "normal" trend pictures, including those formations associated with normal trend development (such as Head-and-Shoulders, Rounding Turns, etc.), are more common.

The reasons for these changes are fairly apparent.   SEC regulations, higher margin requirements, greater public sophistication, and a more conservative— we might better say more pessimistic—approach to the problems of investment and stock trading generally, all have played a part in this evolution.   SEC and Stock Exchange vigilance have done away with the flagrant pool manipulations designed to take advantage of the "lambs" of former years. There is even very little nowadays of the more "legitimate" sort of syndicate operation planned to facilitate large-scale accumulation or distribution.

It is still possible, of course, for "insiders" to hold back for a limited time, or to release prematurely, news announcements of good or bad portent with regard to the affairs of a particular corporation, in order to serve their personal strategic purposes. But the stock purchases and sales of officers, directors and principal owners are now too closely watched to permit of a great deal of "skull-duggery." (Nevertheless, the average investor had better still be a trifle skeptical as to the probability of any great advance in the market *following* publication of a good report.)

FIGURE 120. This chart shows the last five months of a broad, thirteen-month saucer-like consolidation in "IT" which followed its rapid run-up from 3 to 16 in late 1943 and early 1944. "IT" is an erratic actor and its volume is apt to be particularly deceptive in day-to-day movements. Major price patterns in it, however, are dependable. This final phase of its long consolidation (distribution and re-accumulation) took first the form of a Rectangle (with a premature breakout) and then an Ascending Triangle. Its 1945-46 Bull Market top was a massive Head-and-Shoulders.

FIGURE 121.   There are times when a consolidation pattern gives the only good technical signal that a reversal in an issue's Primary trend has actually taken place.   Although cases of a Major turn, particularly a bottom, without some sort of recognizable reversal formation on the chart are quite rare, they do occur.   This weekly chart of Flintkote illustrates such a phenomenon. A Bear Market low, from which it rose to 47 in 1946, was made at 8⅝ in December, 1941.   Without developing any important technical foundation on either daily or weekly chart, its first up-swing took it to 11⅞ the following April.   From that point it went into a six-month Symmetrical Triangle and then broke out topside at the three-quarters stage on increased volume. This action, plus the fact that it immediately thereafter burst up through an old and highly significant resistance level at 12, was sufficient to mark it as being in at least a strong Intermediate if not a full Primary up-trend.

The combination of technical developments illustrated in this chart—a large consolidation pattern forming just under a Major resistance and then a breakout upside from both—is something to watch for when it appears that a reversal from a Bear to Bull trend is due.

Resistance levels will be discussed in Chapter XIII.

Collusion between investment advisory services and trading pools has been effectually outlawed. (It is safe to say that it never did exist as flagrantly, even in the twenties, as many amateur traders seem to think.) The SEC (with the thorough co-operation of the Stock Exchange) polices the investment counsel profession thoroughly, constantly and most effectively. No well-established investment counsel can afford to indulge in deceptive or collusive practices even if the desire were there. Most of them go far beyond the most reasonable needs to safeguard themselves against any contacts which, however innocent or useful, might be viewed with suspicion.

The old-time "plunger" hasn't disappeared entirely but high margins and regulations preventing "bear raiding" have made present-day stock markets relatively difficult and unprofitable for him. The out-and-out boardroom gamblers still come in, although high margins have cramped them too. In recent years they have appeared in numbers only in the final stages of Bull Markets. Of course, their operations never did affect the charts much except to augment activity.

On the other hand higher taxes and greater regulation have most certainly not provided safer, closer or more stable markets for the small investor. Higher margins have not prevented panic collapses. If anything, markets have been "thinner" on the down side, more vulnerable to rapid and drastic decline, than they were prior to modern regulation. We still have the very same sort of Bull and Bear Markets, and much the same sort of market trend development, that we had fifty years ago. The surprising thing is not that a few types of chart patterns which were on occasion produced by unregulated trading are now less common, but that the great majority of technical phenomena have been practically unaffected. The chart student of 1907 would be quite at home with the charts of 1966.

CHAPTER XII

GAPS

A GAP in the language of the chart technician represents a price range at which (at the time it occurred) no shares changed hands. This is a useful concept to keep in mind, because it helps to explain some of their technical consequences.

Gaps on daily charts are produced when the *lowest* price at which a certain stock is traded on any one day is *higher* than the *highest* price at which it was traded on the preceding day. Or when the highest price of one day is lower than the lowest price of the preceding day. When the ranges of any two such days are plotted, they will not overlap or touch the same horizontal level on the chart. There will be a price gap between them. For a gap to develop on a weekly chart it is necessary that the lowest price recorded at any time in one week be higher than the highest recorded during any day of the preceding week. This can happen, of course, and does, but for obvious reasons not as often as daily gaps. Monthly chart gaps are rare in actively traded issues; their occurrence is confined almost entirely to those few instances where a panic decline commences just before the end of a month and continues through the first part of the succeeding month.

WHICH GAPS ARE SIGNIFICANT?

From the earliest days of stock charting, gaps attracted attention. These "holes" in the price trend graph were conspicuous. It was only natural that observers should attach importance to them, should try to assign some special significance to their occurrence. But the result was unfortunate, for there soon accumulated a welter of "rules" for their interpretation some of which have acquired an almost religious force and are cited by the superficial chart reader with little understanding as to why they work when they work (and, of course, as is always the case with any superstition, an utter disregard of those instances where they don't work). We refer to this situation as unfortunate not so much because the gap "rules" are wrong but rather because their blind acceptance has barred the way to a real understanding of a gap's implications and the establishment of a more logical basis for its uses in trading.

The most common superstition is that "a gap must be closed." Sometimes it is stated more cautiously in such words as: "If a gap isn't closed in three days, it will be closed in three weeks, and if it isn't closed in three weeks, it will be closed in three months, etc.—." There are numerous variations but they all add up to the belief that a gap must be closed, and that the trend is not to be trusted until the gap has been covered. It is the latter inference which leads to error.

CLOSING THE GAP

But first, what is meant by "closing" or "covering" a gap? Suppose a stock in an advancing trend moves up day after day, from 20 to 21, 22, 23, 24 and closes one night at the top of its range for that day, at 25. The next morning it opens at 26 and keeps right on moving up from there. This action leaves a 1-point gap, between 25 and 26, on the chart. Then suppose the rise continues to 28, halts there and is followed by a reaction in the course of which prices slip back to 27, 26 and finally to 25. The return move has carried prices back through the gap area (25-26); the gap has thereby been covered or closed. In brief, a gap is closed when a subsequent price trend comes back and retraces the range of the gap.

Must a gap be closed before prices move very far away from it? Certainly not! Will it be closed eventually? Probably yes. If it is not closed by the next Minor reaction, there is a chance it will be covered by the next Intermediate retracement, and if not then, pretty surely by the next great Major swing in the opposite trend. But that may be years later—hardly a matter of interest to the ordinary trader. The investor who bought Chesapeake and Ohio shares at 260 on October 21, 1929, counting on the closing of the gap which that issue had made on the preceding Friday, 2 points down from 266 to 264, had to wait nearly *seven years* to get out even! Not until it neared the top of the next Major Bull Market did CO attain an equivalent market value (65, since it was split 4-for-1 in 1930). In the meantime he saw his investment shrink in 1932 to less than a sixth of his purchase price. As a matter of fact there were hundreds of gaps made in the charts of the 1929-1930 markets which never have been covered in the 18 years since then and many of them, it is safe to say, never will be closed.

If you will think the matter over for a moment, you will see that the probabilities we have stated above for a gap's being closed apply just as well to a stock's returning to *any* price range at which it has once been traded, gap or no gap.

Another point: There are thousands of price gaps made in trading—some of them quite wide—which do not appear at all on the standard daily range charts because they are made *during* a single day and not between one day's closing and the next day's opening. Such *intra-day* gaps are ordinarily overlooked entirely; the gap theorists are oblivious of them, although their significance is often greater than that of many inter-day gaps. Practically every emphatic breakout move from a strictly defined Rectangle or Right-Angle Triangle is attended by a gap, but only those few show up on the charts that occur at the day's opening gong.

If we seem to have "protested too much" in the foregoing, it is only because we want our readers to study this topic with an open mind, free from preconceived notions as to any mystic qualities which gaps may possess. Turning to the other side of the picture, gaps—some gaps—have technical import. Some gaps are useful to the chart analyst in appraising trend possibilities. Let us see what we can make of them.

Ex-Dividend Gaps

First, however, we must eliminate from consideration the gaps that do *not* mean anything. An eighth-point gap obviously has no technical significance as it represents only the minimum permitted change in price. By the same token, a gap of a quarter of a point or even a half point in a high-priced stock such as Norfolk & Western (before the split) represents only a normal, in fact close, spread between successive bids. In brief, to carry interest for the chart technician, a gap must be wider than the usual changes in price which occur under normal or prevailing trading conditions. A second class of gaps which have no forecasting implications are those formed consistently and habitually by many "thin" issues in the medium and higher price brackets. You can spot them easily. If your chart of a certain issue shows numerous gaps as a regular thing, then no one of them is apt to mean anything special.

Finally, gaps which appear on the charts when a stock goes ex-dividend (whether the dividend be in cash, stock, rights or warrants) possess no trend implications. They are occasioned not by a change in the supply-demand relation which governs the trend but by a sudden and irreversible alteration in the actual book value of the issue.

Eliminating the technically meaningless types named above, we are left with the gaps which occur infrequently (and which are not occasioned by an ex-dividend change in value) in issues which are so closely and actively traded as ordinarily to produce "solid" charts. A one-point gap, for example, in the chart of New York Central would be an unusual event; it would demand attention; it would presumably have some forecasting significance.

Such gaps, for the purposes of our study, may be divided into four classes: common or area gaps, breakout gaps, continuation or runaway gaps and exhaustion gaps.

The Common or Area Gap

This type of gap gets its name from its tendency to occur within a trading area or price congestion pattern. All of the congestion formations which we have studied in the preceding chapters—both reversal and consolidation types— are attended by a diminution in trading turnover. The more strictly defined sorts—the Triangles and Rectangles—show this characteristic most conspicuously. Moreover, activity in these patterns tends to be concentrated pretty much at or near the top and bottom edges, their supply and demand lines, while the area in between is a sort of "no-man's land." It is easy to see, therefore, why gaps develop frequently within such areas. You will find numbers of good examples of pattern gaps in the charts illustrating Chapters VIII and IX.

Such pattern gaps are usually closed within a few days, and for obvious rea-

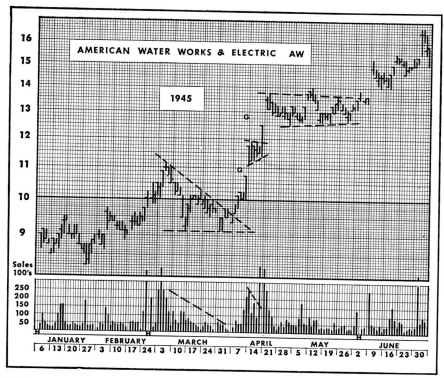

FIGURE 122. The April-June Rectangle on this 1945 chart of "AW" contained a number of significant pattern gaps. The two larger gaps marked "G" are of the continuation or runaway class. Note that prices closed at or near the top on each day that made a gap. See page 200. Neither of these was closed for two years.

Also of interest in this chart is the Descending Triangle which started to form in March but was never completed—a deceptive and discouraging picture until the April 7 gap was made.

The Flag of mid-April "measured" the move from 9½ to 14. The gaps measured the two halves of it, on either side of the Flag.

sons, before the congestion formation in which they have appeared is completed and prices break away from it. But not always. Sometimes a gap will develop in the *last* traverse of prices across the pattern area just before a breakout, and in such cases, it is not closed for a long time, nor is there any reason why it should be.

The forecasting significance of common or pattern gaps is practically nil. They have some use to the technician simply because they help him recognize an area pattern—that is, their appearance implies that a congestion formation is in process of construction. If, for example, a stock moves up from 10 to 20, drops back to 17, and then returns to 20 making a gap in the course of that rally, it is a fair assumption that further pattern development will take place between approximately 17 and 20. This is a convenient thing to know and may, on occasion, be turned to profit in short-term trading policy.

Pattern gaps are more apt to develop in consolidation than in reversal formations. Thus, the appearance of many gaps within an evolving Rectangle or Symmetrical Triangle reinforces the normal expectation that the pattern in question will turn out to be a consolidation rather than a reversal area.

Breakaway Gaps

The breakaway type of gap also appears in connection with a price congestion formation, but it develops at the *completion* of the formation in the move which breaks prices away. Any breakout through a *horizontal* pattern boundary, such as the top of an Ascending Triangle, is likely to be attended by a gap. In fact, it is safe to say that most of them are. And, if we consider what goes on in the market to create a flat-topped price formation, it is easy to see why breakaway gaps should be expected. An Ascending Triangle, for example, is produced by persistent demand for a stock meeting a large supply of it for sale at a fixed price. Suppose that supply is being distributed at 40. Other holders of the stock who may have intended originally to liquidate at $40\frac{1}{2}$ or 41 see quotations come up to 40 time after time, stop there and turn back. They tend, in consequence, either to join the crowd selling at 40, or else to figure that, once through 40, prices will go much higher; they may either lower or raise their selling price. The result is a "vacuum" on the books, a dearth of offerings in the price range immediately above the pattern. Hence, when the supply at 40 in our Ascending Triangle example is finally all absorbed, the next buyer of the stock finds none offered at $40\frac{1}{8}$ or $40\frac{1}{4}$; he has to bid up a point or more to get his shares, thus creating a breakaway gap.

As we remarked earlier in this chapter, gaps of this type actually occur on almost every decisive breakout from a horizontal congestion, although many of them do not show on the charts because they occur *during* a day and not between one day's close and the following day's opening. Breakaway gaps also develop at times when prices move out of other types of reversal or consolidation formation; they are not uncommon in connection with Head-and-Shoulders patterns, for instance, and they even occur on the penetration of trendlines which we shall discuss in a subsequent chapter.

What forecasting value can we ascribe to them? First, they serve to call attention to and emphasize the fact of a breakout. There can be little doubt

FIGURE 123. The large up gap made on July 5 in this chart was a typical breakaway gap, occurring as prices broke out of the Complex base for the July-August Secondary recovery. (Compare this chart with Figure 32 on page 75.) Another type of breakaway gap—through a trendline—occurred on August 26. That of September 7 was primarily due to the "ex-dividend," while that of September 18 was still another type of breakaway—through a support level.

The first gap marked, on April 26, must be classified as a runaway. It made a sort of "Island" of the whole April-June complex base.

FIGURE 124.   A potent breakaway gap which showed on Zenith's weekly chart when it broke out of a Head-and-Shoulders bottom in early 1942.   Note that high volume developed beyond the gap, suggesting that it would not be quickly closed.   The April reaction stopped short of it.   In fact, this gap had still not been closed in 1956, more than fourteen years later.

that a genuine breakout has eventuated when prices jump out of a pattern with a conspicuous gap. False moves are seldom attended by gaps. Second, they carry the suggestion that the buying demand (or selling pressure, as the case may be) that produced the gap is *stronger* than would be indicated by a gap-less breakout. Hence, it may be inferred that the ensuing move will carry prices farther or faster, or both. It does not do to make too much of this point; it is a logical inference and one which has been borne out in the majority of cases but it has its exceptions, may prove most disappointing on occasion. Nevertheless, *other things being equal*, of two stocks which emerged from Ascending Triangles at the same time we should choose to buy the one that gapped out over the one that pushed its way out by small fractional steps.

Except for that presumption of somewhat greater "steam" behind the move, the breakaway gap carries no particular measuring implication, nor any other forecasting significance. The next question is: Should we expect a breakaway gap to be closed within a relatively short time? Or, to put the question in more practical and pragmatic terms: Should we defer buying in the expectation that it will be closed before any worth-while move develops?

In order to give a fair answer to that question it is necessary to scrutinize closely the volume of transactions before *and after* the gap. If a great many

FIGURE 125. As a matter of interest, this monthly chart of Zenith Radio is reproduced for comparison with the weekly chart on the preceding page. The H & S bottom is easily seen.

sales were recorded at the take-off level from which prices jumped the gap, but relatively few as prices moved away from the far side of the gap, then there is a chance—perhaps about 50-50—that the next Minor reaction will carry prices back to the edge of the pattern of origin, thus filling the gap. On the other hand, if high volume developed at the *far* side of the gap, and a great many transactions took place there and as prices moved on away from the gap, then the chances are remote that any near-term throwback will close the gap. In such cases, a throw-back reaction is almost always stopped at the *outside* of the gap.

(One is constantly tempted in a work of this sort to employ the words "always" or "never" without qualification. Unfortunately, the authors have *never* been able to discover a rule of technics to which the market did not on rare occasion produce an exception. It is *always* necessary to be on guard against such exceptional developments. Many of them are caused by general market conditions which counteract the technical trend in individual issues. Keep an eye on the charts of the "averages" as well as the particular issues in which you are interested.)

Where breakaway gaps develop intra-day, the daily chart cannot, of course, indicate how the day's volume was distributed. In that event, it may be necessary to examine the ticker tape or ask your broker to refer to the published record of individual transactions to which most brokerage firms subscribe. Lacking any clear-cut volume clue, it is safest to figure that a breakaway gap will not be filled until long after the full move implied by the pattern of origin (usually a move of Intermediate extent in the Dow sense) has been carried out.

Continuation or Runaway Gaps

Less frequent in their appearance than either of the two forms we have discussed above, gaps of the continuation or runaway type are of far greater technical significance because they afford a rough indication of the probable extent of the move in which they occur. For that reason they have sometimes been called "measuring" gaps.

Both the common or pattern gap and the breakout gap develop in association with price formations of the area or congestion type, the former within the formation and the latter as prices move out of it. The runaway gap, on the other hand, as well as the exhaustion gap which we will take up later, are not associated with area patterns but occur in the course of rapid, straight-line advances or declines.

When a dynamic move starts from an area of accumulation, the upward trend of prices will seem often to gather "steam," to accelerate for a few days, perhaps a week or more, and then begin to lose momentum as supply increases when the very extent of the advance invites more and more profit taking. Trading volume jumps to a peak on the initial breakout, tapers off somewhat in the middle of the advance, and then leaps up again to a terrific turnover as the move is finally halted. In such moves—and in rapid declines of corresponding character—a wide gap is quite likely to appear at the time when the runaway is at its height, when quotations are moving most rapidly and easily with relation to the volume of transactions. That period comes normally at just about the halfway point between the breakout which inaugurated the move and the reversal day or congestion pattern which calls an end to it. Hence, a continua-

FIGURE 126. The early 1946 daily chart of Blaw-Knox contained a number of interesting technical features. Its spurt from 19 to 25 in December, 1945 was followed by a nine-week Rectangle consolidation, the end of which appears on the chart above. Prices erupted from this Rectangle on February 11 with a typical breakaway gap. Four days later another gap appeared on even greater volume and prices closed at the top of the day's range. This looked like a runaway gap, in which case continuation to 32 was implied according to the "rule" stated on page 201. (Note that the Rectangle "measurement" called for only 31.) On the following day, however, a One-Day Reversal, from 31 back to 30, appeared and the next session closed the February 15 gap, which now had to be re-labeled tentatively as an exhaustion gap (see page 202). Prices subsequently dropped back to the support of the nine-week Rectangle, rallied grudgingly along an established Intermediate up trendline, and broke that on April 24 to return again to the 25 support. In May another advance took "BK" up once more to 30 where it bumped against the previously broken trendline. That was its last effort; in late July the "valley" level at 25 was penetrated and a Major Double Top had been completed.

To return to the February 15 gap, this is fairly typical of many cases in which it is impossible to say whether continuation or exhaustion is being signaled until two or three days after the day the gap is made.

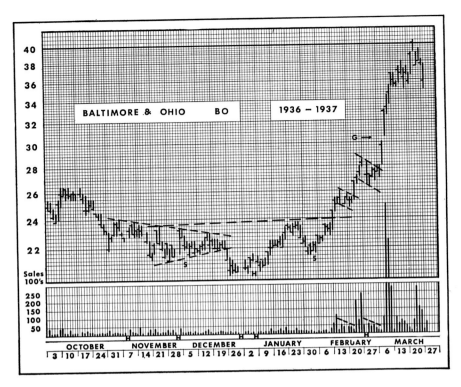

FIGURE 127.   A good example of runaway gap which performed according to rule.   After reacting from 26½ in late 1936, "BO" formed an H & S bottom (the left shoulder was a Triangle) and broke out of it on February 6, 1937.   A small Flag formed immediately thereafter, calling for 28.   At that level another Flag developed which signaled 30½ or better.   As prices reached this latter goal, however, a gap was made, on March 3, on extraordinary volume.   The next two days confirmed this to be a runaway or continuation gap.   As such, it implied further advance (measuring from the H & S neckline) to 37 plus.   "BO" made its Bull Market high at 40½ on March 17.

The measuring gap rule should be used for purposes of "getting out" rather than "getting in."   It does not guarantee that a move will continue to the implied limit but it does give assurance that the move is near an end when the rule has been fulfilled.

FIGURE 128 (bottom of next page).   Panic declines often produce large runaway gaps.   The September 7 gap in this chart, judged by its size, volume, subsequent action and the fact that it was made in "new low ground," marked it as of the measuring type.   Implied goal was 26 or below.   All other gaps in this chart were obviously of the "common" variety.

tion or runaway gap affords an approximate measurement of the move in which it develops.   Its inference is that *prices will go as much farther beyond the gap as they already have gone between* the beginning of the move and the gap, as measured directly (and vertically) on the chart.

Since there is a tendency for advances to run, in terms of points, beyond the price levels arithmetically implied by this rule, and for declines to be more strictly limited, the gap measuring rule works out particularly well when applied directly on semi-logarithmic scale charts.   On arithmetic charts, look for a trifle more on the up side and a trifle less on the down side.   (In any event, you will be wise to "bank" on something short of the theoretical goal.)

Runaway gaps are easy to find and identify in retrospect, but our task is to recognize them as such at the time they appear.   Of course, there is, obviously,

FIGURE 128.   See description at bottom of preceding page.

no danger of confusing them with pattern or breakout gaps. With those aside, any gap which shows up in a fast advance or decline *after* prices have moved well away from an area formation (or the penetration of an important trend line or break through a potent support or resistance level, which we shall discuss later) may be a runaway gap. What then becomes necessary is to distinguish it from our next type, the *exhaustion gap*. Usually, the price and volume action on the day following the gap furnishes the evidence required for a safe diagnosis.

Two or More Runaway Gaps

But it will be much easier to bring out the characteristics distinguishing runaway and exhaustion gaps when we take up the latter in detail. Before doing so, we must mention those cases where two, and rarely even three, gaps intervene in a fast move and are evidently all classifiable as of the continuation or runaway breed. It doesn't happen often, and is particularly unlikely to appear in the chart of a fairly large and active issue, but one of the thinner stocks in the midst of a "skyrocket" move may go skipping along for three or four days making gaps between each successive pair. The only question of practical importance that arises in such cases is: Where should the halfway measuring point be located? No quick and easy rule can be laid down, but studious inspection of the chart, especially of the volume trend, will usually afford an answer. Remember that half way in these fast moves tends to come at the stage where prices are moving most easily and rapidly with respect to number of transactions recorded (whence the tendency to gap). If there are *two* gaps, the halfway stage may very likely have been reached somewhere between them. Inspect your chart carefully and try to "average" the picture mentally; look for what appears to be the center of "thinness" and use that for your measuring level. But remember also that each successive gap brings the move inevitably nearer to exhaustion, so let your judgment lean to the conservative side; do not expect too much of the second or third gap.

Exhaustion Gaps

The breakout gap signalizes the start of a move; the runaway gap marks its rapid continuation at or near its halfway point; the exhaustion gap comes at the end. The first two of these are easily distinguished as to type by their location with respect to the preceding price pattern, but the last is not always immediately distinguishable from the second.

Exhaustion gaps, like runaway gaps, are associated with rapid, extensive advances or declines. We have described the runaway type as the sort that occurs in the midst of a move that accelerates to high velocity, then slows down again and finally stops as increasing resistance overcomes its momentum. Sometimes, however, "skyrocket" trends evidence no such gradual increase of resistance as they proceed, show no tendency to lose momentum, but rather continue to speed

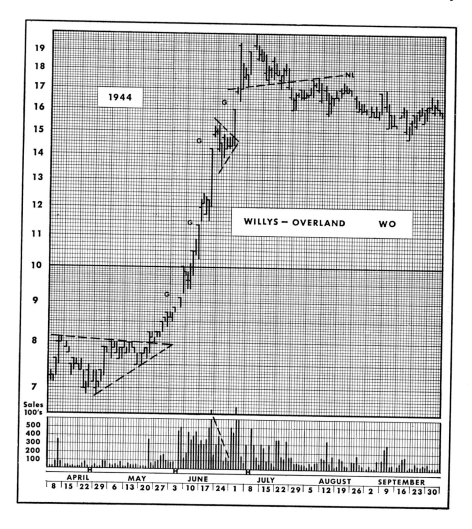

FIGURE 129. The "skyrocket" run-up of Willys-Overland in June 1944 was marked by a number of small gaps. The first two were too small to have much technical significance. The larger gap made June 16 was marked by the "stickiness" of prices on that day as exhaustion. A small Flag consolidation ensued. The June 27 gap also acted like an exhaustion gap in so far as price action was concerned, but volume had declined instead of climbing to a new peak. On June 28 prices jumped away again, so the June 27 gap was now marked as another runaway, with an implied objective of 18½ plus which had already been reached. Note the Head-and-Shoulders reversal which then formed and subsequent Intermediate reaction.

up until, suddenly, they hit a stone wall of supply (or, in the case of a decline, demand) and are brought to an abrupt end by a day of terrific trading volume. In such moves, a wide gap may appear at the very end, i.e. between the next to the last and the last day of the move.   This gets the name of exhaustion gap because the trend seems thereby to have exhausted itself in one final leaping spurt.

The best test of whether a gap formed in a rapid, straight-line advance or decline is of the continuation or exhaustion type comes on the day after the gap (more precisely, the day which makes the gap), although there are frequently other clues in the preceding chart picture.   If trading activity mounts to an extraordinary height during the session following the gap, and particularly if the previous trend in prices does not appear to be carried on along at a pace commensurate with that day's activity, the gap is probably of the exhaustion class. This interpretation is reinforced, in fact made a virtual certainty, if the day after the gap develops into a Reversal Day (as described in Chapter X) with the closing price registered back near the edge of the gap.

Evidence which may be derived from the chart anteceding the gap may be enumerated as follows.   If the trend has already carried out the full implications of the price formation or congestion area from which it emerged, exhaustion is more likely than continuation.   By the same token, if the reasonable measuring implications of the pattern of origin are still far short of attainment, the gap is probably of the continuation type.   An exhaustion gap is seldom the first gap in a runaway move; it is usually preceded by at least one continuation gap.   Thus, you may ordinarily assume (unless the contrary appears from other and more weighty indications) that the first gap in a rapid advance or decline is a continuation gap.   But each succeeding gap must be regarded with more and more suspicion, especially if it is wider than its predecessor.

We have referred to exhaustion gaps as *wide* gaps.   Width is of necessity relative in this study; it is impossible to lay down any exact rules to define wide or narrow.   Do not let this bother you too much.   Recognition of what constitutes an unusually wide gap for the particular stock you have under observation soon comes with a little charting experience.

Runaway gaps are usually not covered for a considerable length of time, not as a rule until the market stages a swing of Major or full Intermediate proportions in the opposite direction.   But exhaustion gaps are quickly closed, most often within two to five days, a fact which furnishes a final clue to distinguish exhaustion from continuation if it should still be needed at that stage.   (This, incidentally, upsets the common superstition that all gaps must be closed before the trend can be trusted to continue very far.   In the case of the runaway gap, it is not closed but the trend moves right along nevertheless, and often for a surprising distance.   In the case of the exhaustion gap, the closing of it actually contributes to the signal that the trend has run out.)

An exhaustion gap, taken by itself, should not be read as a sign of *Major* reversal, nor even necessarily of reversal at all. It calls "stop," but the halt is ordinarily followed by some sort of area pattern development which may, in turn, lead to either reversal or continuation of the move prior to the gap. However, in practically every case, enough of a minor reaction or delay ensues from the formation of an exhaustion gap, before a new trend is established, to warrant closing out commitments at once. (One can always re-enter if it subsequently appears that the previous trend is to be resumed.)

FIGURE 130. "SMC" is a thin stock whose daily chart is usually "full of holes" but this large gap which appeared on its weekly chart in September, 1946 evidently possessed technical significance. Treated as a runaway, and measuring from the eight-week congestion at 68, it called for a down-side objective of 44 or below, which was duly fulfilled.

FIGURE 131. A small Island in the right shoulder of the Head-and-Shoulders top that marked this issue's Major reversal. The Island served only to emphasize the chart's bearish implications.

FIGURE 132. Island "shake-outs" are not uncommon in thin stocks. Why they should develop as they do is hard to explain but their forecasting implications are obvious.

THE ISLAND REVERSAL

We mentioned (at the end of Chapter X) a reversal pattern—the Island—which was to be taken up under the general study of gaps. The Island pattern is not common and it is not in itself of Major significance, in the sense of denoting a long-term top or bottom, but it does as a rule send prices back for a complete retracement of the Minor move which preceded it.

An Island Reversal might be described as a compact trading range separated from the move which led to it (and which was usually fast) by an exhaustion gap, and from the move in the opposite direction which follows it (and which is also equally fast as a rule) by a breakaway gap. The trading range may consist of only a single day, in which event it normally develops as a One-Day Reversal, or it may be made up of from several days to a week or so of minor fluctuations within a compact price zone. It is characterized, as might be expected, by relatively high volume. The gaps at either end occur at approximately the same price level (they should overlap to some extent) so that the whole area stands out as an island on the chart, isolated by the gaps from the rest of the price path.

We have said that an Island does not of itself appear as a *Major* reversal formation, but Islands frequently develop within the larger patterns at turning points of Primary or important Intermediate consequence, as for example in the head of a dynamic Head-and-Shoulders top. By the same token, they appear occasionally at the extremes of the Minor swings which compose a Triangle or a Rectangle (in which event, of course, the gaps that set them off are really better classified as common or pattern gaps).

The reasons why Islands can and do develop—in other words, why gaps can and do repeat at the same price level—will be more apparent when we take up the general subject of support and resistance in a later chapter. Suffice it to repeat at this point that prices can move most rapidly and easily, either up or down, through a range where little or no stock changed hands in the past, where in other words previous owners have no "vested interest."

Sometimes the second gap—the breakaway that completes the Island—is closed a few days later by a quick pull-back or reaction. More often it is not. Rarely, the first gap—the exhaustion gap that starts the Island—is covered in a few days before the second gap appears, in which event the Island congestion takes on a sort of V-shape (if it is a top) and there is no clear "open water" across the chart horizontally between the Island and the trends preceding and following it. In any of these variations, however, the interpretation remains the same: the preceding Minor move should be practically retraced.

An Island pattern is not easy to trade on, unless it be for a short term "scalp," as obviously a good share of the retracement may already have been accomplished by the time the Island is charted and an order to buy or sell on its indications

FIGURE 133.   This Island reversal pattern at Bethlehem Steel's Major top in 1937 is a "classic," yet it was followed by a curious and disturbing abnormality in the strong rally that developed on March 30.   Those who sold out on the Island's signal around 95 on March 19 or 20 were startled, and if they had also sold short, justifiably alarmed when prices jumped up a week later, not only through the second gap level but well above it.   But eventually, as can be seen, everything worked out according to the original forecast.

This incident will serve to illustrate a general principle: When a clear-cut technical pattern of unquestionable significance has been completed on your charts, do not let some apparently contrary development that occurs shortly thereafter lead you to forget or neglect the previous plain signal.   Give such situations time to work out.

Figure 123 on page 195 shows the sequel to the above chart and, incidentally, another Island.   Compare the volume.

can be executed. Of course, if the entering gap is recognized as an exhaustion gap, the trader who is interested in the stock presumably will take action before the second gap forms and before the Island is in evidence. Perhaps, the greatest utility which Islands have for the chart analyst is that of calling attention to a situation, of putting him on the alert as to its potentialities.

GAPS IN THE AVERAGES

Gaps appear also in nearly all averages but, for obvious reasons, with rather less frequency than in the charts of individual issues. While it is not necessary for all of the stocks composing an average to make a gap simultaneously in order to produce a gap in the average figures, a majority of them must. As might therefore be expected, common or pattern gaps are particularly rare in average charts, but the breakaway and runaway types are not uncommon, although small as compared with the size of such gaps in single stocks. Exhaustion gaps, and in consequence Islands, again are rare. The conditions which create an

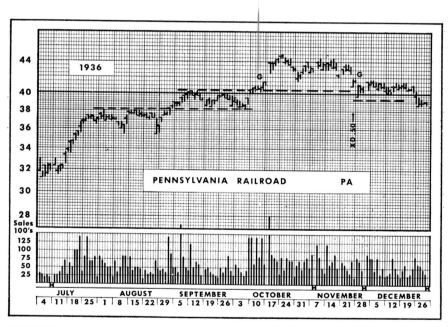

FIGURE 134. This looked like an Island in "PA" but the second gap was actually attributable to a 50 cent dividend which went ex on November 20, and had therefore to be discounted technically. Because of this dividend it was necessary to lower the support line at 40 (see Chapter XIII) by half a point. That support, therefore, was not violated in December and prices subsequently advanced to above 50 the following March.

exhaustion gap seldom develop in a sufficient number of individual issues at any one time to produce a counterpart in the averages.

The technical interpretation of gaps in averages is, in the main, the same as in single stocks. The authors have not found that an average gap possesses any peculiar potency or significance over and above that attributable to a gap in the chart of any actively and closely traded single issue.

The broader, and hence most representative, market indexes show the fewest and smallest gaps. On the other hand, the Dow-Jones Industrial average is quite volatile and a good gap producer.

(It is suggested that the reader review this chapter after he has finished studying the principles of Support and Resistance in Chapter XIII.)

CHAPTER XIII

SUPPORT AND RESISTANCE

THE phenomena which we shall study in this chapter are markedly different in kind from those discussed in preceding sections. We shall look now at the stock market from a new angle, and in so doing may find it possible to develop some very practical additional rules to guide us in selecting stocks for purchase or sale, in estimating their potential moves, in foreseeing where they are likely to "run into trouble." As a matter of fact, some experienced traders have built their "systems" almost entirely on the principles of what we here call support and resistance, paying no attention to the specific pictorial patterns of price and volume action we have been investigating in preceding pages.

But support and resistance phenomena are not by any means unrelated to the various patterns and formations previously studied. We have already had occasion to hint at a basic principle of support and resistance in our explanation of gaps and, as you read on, you will find that a number of the other patterns of price behavior are explained thereby, or at least become more readily understood.

The term *support* is commonly used in "the street." In one or more of its connotations, it must be fairly familiar to the reader. For example, we hear that such-and-such a crowd is supporting XYZ at 50, or is prepared to support the market by buying all stock offered on any 5-point concession. For the purposes of this chapter, we may define *support* as buying, actual or potential, sufficient in volume to halt a down trend in prices for an appreciable period. *Resistance* is the antithesis of support; it is selling, actual or potential, sufficient in volume to satisfy all bids and hence stop prices from going higher for a time. Support and resistance as thus defined are nearly but not quite synonymous with demand and supply, respectively.

A *support* level is a price level at which sufficient demand for a stock appears to halt a down trend temporarily at least, and possibly reverse it, i.e., start prices moving up again. A *resistance* zone, by the same token, is a price level at which sufficient supply of a stock is forthcoming to stop, and possibly turn back, its up trend. There is, theoretically and nearly always actually, a certain amount of supply and a certain amount of demand at any given price level. (The relative amount of each will vary according to circumstances and determine the trend.) But a support range represents a *concentration* of demand, and a resistance range represents a *concentration* of supply.

According to the foregoing definitions, you can see that the top boundary of a horizontal congestion pattern such as a Rectangle is a resistance level and its bottom edge a support level; the top line of an Ascending Triangle is unmistakably a resistance level, etc.   But we are more interested now in the reasons why support or resistance, as the case may be, can be *anticipated* to appear at certain price ranges.   Within reasonable limits, and with a certain few exceptions which we will examine later, it is quite possible to do this.   Expert chart readers are able frequently to make some amazingly accurate predictions as to where an advance will encounter resistance (supply) or where a declining trend will meet support.

The basis for such predictions—the elementary datum from which support and resistance theories are derived—is that turnover in any given issue tends to be concentrated at the several price levels where a large number of shares changed hands in times past.   Since any level at which a great volume of transactions takes place usually becomes a reversal point (Major, Intermediate or Minor) in that stock's trend, it follows naturally that reversal levels tend to "repeat."   But, here is the interesting and the important fact which, curiously enough, many casual chart observers appear never to grasp: these critical price levels constantly switch their roles from support to resistance and from resistance to support.   A former top, once it has been surpassed, becomes a bottom zone in a subsequent down trend; and an old bottom, once it has been penetrated, becomes a top zone in a later advancing phase.

Normal Trend Development

Perhaps we can make this plainer by citing a typical example of normal trend development.   Suppose a stock in a Bull trend moves up from 12 to 24 and there runs into a large volume of selling.   The result is a reaction which may take the form of a full Intermediate correction to, say, 18 or a series of minor fluctuations forming a consolidation pattern between, say, 24 and 21, the effect being the same in either case.   Following this correction or consolidation, a new advance gets under way and carries price on up to 30 before running again into supply in sufficient concentration to stifle the move.   Now another reaction is evidently due.   Again it may take the form of a sidewise consolidation pattern or an Intermediate correction.   If the latter, where will that corrective setback be reversed; where, in other words, will it meet support?   The answer is at 24, the level of the first top in the trend.   That is the level (below current quotations) where a large turnover had previously occurred.   Then it functioned as resistance, producing a halt or reversal in the first up-swing; now it functions as support, stemming and reversing at least in a minor sense the latest down-swing.

Why should this be?   It will be easier to suggest an answer to that question if we first go on with a similar example of typical action in a down trend.   This time suppose our stock makes a Major top and declines from, say, 70 to 50. There, at 50, a temporary selling climax occurs; there is a large turnover, prices rally, perhaps slip back for a "test" of 50, and then stage a good recovery to 60. At 60 buying peters out, the trend rounds over, turns down and accelerates in renewed decline which carries to a new low at 42.   Again a wave of buying comes in and a second recovery swing gets under way.   We can confidently expect that this recovery (from 42) will run into strong resistance at 50.   The price level which functioned as a *support* for the first phase of decline, now that it has been broken through down-side by the second phase, will reverse its role and function as *resistance* to the second recovery move.   The former bottom level will now become a top level.

Here we may ask again why this should be so, and now we can suggest an answer.   In the example of down-trend action cited in the preceding paragraph, our stock first dropped to 50, ran into considerable volume there, reversed its trend and rallied to 60 with activity dwindling on the rise.   A lot of shares changed hands at 50 and for every seller there was, of course, a buyer.   A few of those buyers may have been covering short positions and, having done so, had no further interest in the issue.   Others, short-term traders and professionals, may have purchased simply because they sensed a temporary bottom in the making and hoped to scalp a few points on the ensuing rally; presumably they (or at least some of them) took their profits and were out before prices broke very far on the next decline.   But a majority of those who acquired shares at 50, it is safe to say, did so because they thought the stock was cheap at that price, because they figured it had gone low enough.   Only a few months ago it was selling above 70; surely it was a bargain at 50—could be picked up and put away "for the long term."

THE EXPLANATION

Imagine yourself, for the moment, in the place of those new owners.   They see prices turn up, reach 55, 58, 60.   Their judgment appears to have been vindicated.   They hang on.   Then the rally peters out and prices start to drift off again, slipping to 57, 55, 52, finally 50.   They are mildly concerned but still convinced that the stock is a bargain at that price.   Probably there is momentary hesitation in the decline at 50 and then prices break on down. Briefly there is hope that the break is only a shake-out to be recovered quickly, but that hope vanishes as the down trend continues.   Now our new owners begin to worry.   Something has gone wrong.   When the stock gets down below 45, the former bargain doesn't look so good.   "Well, I guess I picked a lemon that time but I won't take a loss in it.   I'll just wait until it gets back up to 50 some day where I can get out even (except for expenses) and then they can have it."   (Does it sound familiar by any chance?)

Take the opposite side of the picture—the up trend process.   You, along with many others, bought **XYZ** at 12, carried it up to 24, decided that was plenty high for it and cashed in.   Thereupon **XYZ** reacted to 21 and you con-

FIGURE 135. Normal trend action. The last half of Jones & Laughlin's 1942-46 Bull Market and the first part of its subsequent Bear Market is plotted here on a weekly time scale. "JL's" rise from the end of 1941 to 1944 was slow, appearing on a monthly chart as a long Ascending Triangle, only the end of which shows above. Prices broke out top-side in mid-1944 and then went into a Head-and-Shoulders consolidation which was completed at the end of the year. Note first how the three reactions composing the H & S met support around 23, at the level of several tops formed in the preceding congestion area. This and subsequent support-resistance levels are marked on our chart by short, double, horizontal strokes.

Now note the top made at 27¼ in mid-1944. After prices had risen well above this (to 30¾ in January, 1945) the next reaction ended, i.e. was "supported," at 27¼. Another advance failed to lift prices decisively above the 30¾ top and they had to drop back to the level of the congestion around 29 before a new up move got going. This, however, pushed up to 33½, well above the former 30¾ top, so the latter then became the support for two reactionary weeks around the mid-year.

Why now was so much time spent, so much "work" done during mid-1945

(Continued at bottom of next page)

gratulate yourself on your astuteness. But then, unexpectedly, it turns around and rushes up to 30. Now you don't feel so smart; that was a better stock than you gave it credit for being. You wish you had it back. You will not pay more for it but if it comes back down to 24, the price at which you sold, you'll "reinstate your position."

Perhaps you yourself have never been in either of these situations. Perhaps your own reactions wouldn't, in such cases, have been the same as those we have indicated. But, if you have had a fair amount of experience in the market— have some knowledge of the psychology of the average "investor"—you know that the pictures we have described are typical.

At this point you may not be satisfied that we have succeeded in giving an adequate explanation for our basic principle of support and resistance levels. Remember, however, that the supply and demand balance in the market is nearly always a delicate thing. Only a moderate oversupply at any one price will suffice to stifle an advance; only a little extra demand concentrated at a certain level will stem a decline. And remember further that other traders are watching the tape—will be quick to sense any change in the situation, and quick to join the parade whenever a change in trend appears to be developing. Consequently, orders to buy or sell a few hundred shares may induce the transfer of several thousand.

Another point worth bearing in mind is that the traders and investors who

(Figure 135. Continued from bottom of preceding page)

under 33-34? We cannot see it on this chart but the previous monthly history shows that the bottoms of long congestion areas were made in this zone in late 1939 and late 1940. These old bottoms, representing support originally, were able to produce some supply (resistance) five years later. Once prices had worked through that supply, however, they were able to rise quickly to 44 and then their subsequent reaction found support just where you might have expected—at 33-34. Support had turned to resistance and then to support again.

We can skip over the next few swings which "followed the rules" and go on to the change in the picture which came with the first notable violation of a support level in 1946. Prices had pushed up the first of February nearly to 54, well out above the tops around 46 formed the previous November. The late February reaction should have "caught support" around 46—but it didn't; it crashed on down to the "round figure" 40. This was an ominous (although not necessarily "fatal") development. Thereafter a massive Symmetrical Triangle was formed and broke down-side in September.

The first panic decline in the Bear Market is no respecter of support levels. This one was no exception, although it is noteworthy that prices "bounced" several times from the important old 33-34 zone. By November the top triangle's measurement had been exactly fulfilled.

You should turn back to this record and study it again after you have read the next six or seven pages.

(because, as we have presumed, of their previous mistakes in either selling or buying prematurely) create support and resistance levels, are not necessarily ignorant or inexperienced. On the contrary, we must list them among the wiser and more alert of those who operate in the market. To make one more use of our previous theoretical example of typical down-trend action, those who bought at 50 were certainly smarter than those who bought at the top (70) or on the way down to 50, even though the latter price was broken later on. Giving them credit for somewhat superior judgment, it follows that they may be expected to appraise later developments pretty carefully and display something better than a wooden and stubborn determination to "get out even" when it comes to selling on a recovery move. Hence, in a marked Bear trend "overhanging supply," i.e., stock bought at higher levels by holders now waiting for a good chance to unload, will begin to come on the market *below* the theoretical resistance level. Wise owners will be willing to sacrifice a point or so to avoid getting caught in a worse loss.

By the same token, "sold-out Bulls" when a Major up trend is under way may be willing to pay a point or two more in order to replace the shares they had previously cashed in too soon. Thus it is characteristic of reactions in well-established (second phase) Bull Markets to drop back only to the very uppermost limits of a support range—and for recoveries in established Bear markets to reach only the lowest edges of resistance zones, or perhaps even fail of that by an appreciable margin. We shall have more of this sort of thing to point out later on, but first we must take up two other matters—how to estimate the potential importance of support and resistance zones, and how to locate more exactly the centers or axes of such zones.

ESTIMATING SUPPORT-RESISTANCE POTENTIAL

To go back to first principles, we have seen that the resistance which an upward move may meet at any given level depends on the quantity of stock overhanging there—the number of shares previously bought at that price by owners who now would like to get out without loss. Obviously then, *volume* is our first criterion in estimating the power of a resistance range. An old minor bottom level at which only four or five hundred shares changed hands cannot set up much resistance to a subsequent advance, but a selling climax bottom where several thousand shares were bought will provide a lot of potential supply after prices at some later date have dropped well below it and then attempt to rise up through it again.

A long Rectangle, or a Descending Triangle, has a number of bottoms at the same level. We can get a crude approximation of the amount of resistance there by summing up the volume of trading on all its bottoms, but then some discount must be taken for the shares which may have been bought at the bottom of the pattern in its early stages and then sold near the top before it was completed.   In brief, a single, sharp, high-volume bottom offers somewhat more resistance than a series of bottoms with the same volume spread out in time and with intervening rallies.

Another criterion is the extent of the subsequent decline.   Or, to put it another way, how far prices will have to climb before they encounter the old bottom zone whose resistance potential we are attempting to appraise.   Generally speaking, the greater the distance the greater the resistance.   Suppose PDQ sells off from 30 to 20, "churns" at that level for several days, rallies to 24 and then drifts back down to 19.   Investors who picked it up at 20 will not be greatly concerned at that stage.   If a rally now develops from 19, there will be little or no disappointed selling at 20.   Should prices dip to 18 before the rally starts, there may be some supply forthcoming at 20 but still not a formidable quantity.   From 17, resistance will become evident.   In brief, prices have to break far enough below the price at which a trader bought his stock to convince him that he made a bad investment and, hence, that he should sell when he gets a chance to do so without too great a loss.

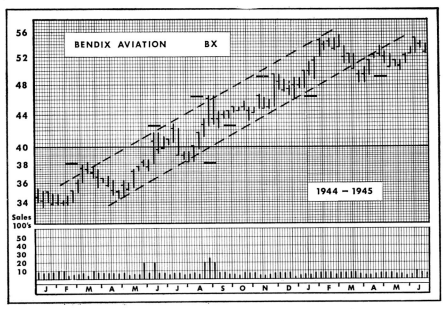

FIGURE 136.   Support-resistance levels in a long Intermediate up trend. The reader will need no guidance in applying the principles stated in this chapter to the Bendix weekly chart reproduced above.   Observe that when prices broke down in 1945 through a long trendline, their decline stopped nevertheless at the support set up by the previous November's top.

It is impossible to formulate any precise rule or equation to define how far a decline must proceed to set up resistance above it. However, do not look for much supply to come out of a bottom level in the low-middle price ranges (20 to 35) unless the trend later takes quotations more than 10% under it. This 10% rule cannot be applied to very low priced issues. A man may buy a stock at 5 and see it drop to 4 or 3½ with considerable equanimity despite the fact that he stands a loss of 30% at the latter figure. His "dollar" loss looks small and he still thinks it will be easy for his stock to get back up to 6 or 7; he is willing to wait.

FIGURE 137.   For Major support-resistance level study, monthly charts are most useful.   This one presents many points of interest.   Observe how important levels are formed and how, once formed, they appear again, and reverse their roles.   The price scale shows 1947 values with previous years adjusted for the splits of 1933 and 1946.

Another factor enters into and reinforces the "extent of decline" criterion. If our **PDQ** rallies as before from 20 to 24 and then drops rapidly to 12, not only will many of the old owners at 20 be thoroughly disgusted and glad to get out at that price, given an opportunity, but the new owners at 12 will also be pleased to take 20 (66⅔% profit) and quick to do so if they detect any signs of trouble there. New buyers at 18, needless to say, would not be quite so ready to sell at 20.

A third criterion for appraising the resistance potential at an old bottom level is the length of time that has elapsed since it was formed and the nature of general market developments in the interim. You will, no doubt, find it reasonable to suppose that an Intermediate bottom formed in the early stages of a Bear Market will offer relatively little resistance after prices have fallen far below it, have taken perhaps the better part of a year to make a Major base, and then have gradually climbed up to it again four or five years later. To some small extent this is true. A supply only a year or two old is apt to be more effective than one that is four or five years old, but the latter does not lose all of its potency by any means. In fact, it is often surprising how effective the resistance will be at a very old bottom zone, provided it has not been "attacked" in the interim and provided no changes have been made in the capitalization of the company which might obscure in the mind of the owner the original cost of his stock. Under the latter heading we would put split-ups and large stock dividends, or even an unusually generous cash "melon." We do not mean to imply that an investor is ever actually deceived as to the actual cost of his shares, no matter how they may have been split, or what dividend distribution has been made, but his disappointment (and desire to get out even) may be abated.

If, however, a resistance zone has once been attacked—if prices have come back up to it, hit it and then retreated—some of its power has obviously been removed. Some of its overhanging supply has been used up in repelling the first attack. The next advance, therefore, will have less stock to absorb at that level. Here again the volume chart may be looked to for some approximation of the amount of resistance consumed. In any event, it is an odds-on assumption that a third attack at a resistance level will succeed in penetrating it.

We have named three criteria—volume, distance away and time elapsed— to be used in assessing the amount of resistance to be expected at any given level. At this point it must be apparent to the reader (and perhaps disappointing) that his own judgment must play a large role in applying them. This cannot be helped. It is impossible to set up an exact mathematical formula for any of them.

But, after all, the problem is not too complicated. The general principles are simple enough and, we believe, easy to understand. We can look at the charted back history and see where in the last preceding down trend a bottom formed that may produce more or less resistance when the current advance reaches back up to its range. We have to estimate how much supply resides there, how many shares were bought originally at that price and are still held by owners who may welcome a chance to get out even.

The greatest danger in applying judgment to the measuring of these factors lies in under-estimating the amount of resistance to be expected. Guard against that error; it is safer always to over-estimate it. You may be bullishly disposed yourself; you may say, "Those fellows who were hung up there in this stock must realize that conditions have improved, and they will not be so anxious now to sell." Don't count on it. Remember that they have been "hung up" for a long time. Even if they are mildly bullish on the market in general, they may be so disappointed with this particular stock that they want to switch out

FIGURE 138. Particularly noteworthy in this monthly record is the resist-ance met in 1939, 1940, 1941, and even in 1944, at the bottom level (just above 26) of the three-month congestion of 1936. Also the appearance eight years later (!) in 1945 of resistance at the bottom level (28) of the high-volume top congestion of 1936-37. Prices were able to "skyrocket" when that resist-ance was finally overcome. You will find that several additional support-resistance lines might have been drawn on this chart. Note Major bottom formations of 1937-38 and 1942.

of it and try something else. (The stubborn and often costly refusal of the average American investor to "take a loss" operates even against timely switching.)

Everything we have said in the foregoing paragraphs about estimating potential resistance applies as well—but in a reverse direction, of course—to estimating potential support. The principles are precisely the same even though the underlying rationale may be less easy to grasp.

LOCATING PRECISE LEVELS

Our next problem to consider is how in practical day-to-day chart analysis we can locate as exactly as possible the limits of a support or resistance range, and in many cases the specific price figure representing the core or axis of such a range. In the theoretical examples we have made up so far to illustrate basic principles we have used plain even figures, but in actual trading the levels are seldom so nicely marked. Even the sharp and relatively patternless bottom of a minor recession may consist of a week of price fluctuations within a range of from 2 to 4 points. Perhaps the lowest day of that week's congestion will appear on the chart as a One-Day Reversal, or there will be two or three days which "spike" down below the general mass. Here again, although no mathematical rule can be laid down, it is easy to relate the price and volume patterns visually, and by simple inspection arrive at a near estimate of the figure at which supply in quantity is likely to be forthcoming. Look particularly at the closing levels of the days making up the bottom congestion and average them mentally; this figure is apt to be pretty close to the "center of gravity" of the entire resistance area.

Of course, some supply is likely to start coming in as soon as a subsequent advance reaches the bottom-most fraction of the resistance zone, and more and more will appear as the move pushes up into it. Sometimes it is possible to predict "to a hair" just how far prices will penetrate a resistance range by carefully comparing the vigor (volume of trading) on the advance with the volume registered at various levels in the original formation of the resistance. This takes experience but it is experience which you will find quite easy and not at all costly to gain. However, in most cases it is neither necessary nor particularly desirable to be so exacting.

Nearly every chart in this book shows some example of support and resistance phenomena and the reader should make it a point, when he has finished this chapter, to go back over them and study them all in detail. The practical application of the rules we have been discussing will be greatly clarified thereby. Equally instructive, if you can manage to obtain such a collection, is a study of the support and resistance levels appearing in the monthly charts of all actively traded stocks over a period of ten years or more. You will undoubtedly be amazed to see how tops, bottoms and sidewise congestions tend to form at the same approximate levels in successive Major swings, while prices move freely and rapidly, up or down, through the ranges between such levels. It is hardly necessary to dwell on the practical dollars-and-cents value of such information which may be derived from the chart history.

And that brings up a matter which we may as well pause to consider here—the kind of charts most useful for locating and appraising support and resistance levels. For near-term Minor moves, the daily chart is naturally the only source of information, and a daily chart record which extends back for a year or more may if necessary be used in the location of levels of Intermediate trend importance. The writers have found, however, that a daily chart does not give the perspective on the long range which one really needs to determine Major and Intermediate support and resistance zones. It is apt to overemphasize the potential of a recently set up Minor support (or resistance) zone and obscure the importance of a true Intermediate level. For true perspective a weekly chart, showing volume as well as price ranges, and covering at least the whole previous Major Bull and Bear cycle is most desirable. Lacking that, very good results can be obtained with a little study and experience from monthly charts.

To return to our study of support phenomena, we have had several occasions to refer in previous chapters to a "normal" trend. What we have had in mind might perhaps be better called an "ideal" trend, since like so many other so-called normal things, it represents a pattern from which the facts of experience frequently deviate. In stock trends, nevertheless, this normal or ideal appears as a fairly common pattern. If it be an up trend, it consists of a series of zig-zags, each "zig" carrying prices to a new high and each "zag" taking them back to

FIGURE 139. A monthly chart of Jewel Tea Co. with its Major support-resistance levels marked. Note reversal of roles.

the approximate top of the preceding "zig." To illustrate with figures: up to 10, back to 6, up to 15, back to 10, up to 20, back to 15, up to 26, back to 20, etc. Such a move is what technicians refer to as "self-correction" and regard as particularly sound and hence, likely to be continued. You can see that what it really represents is reaction to the nearest Minor support level following each step forward. If you become interested in an issue with such a trend pattern, the normal return to a support produces a good place to buy.

SIGNIFICANCE OF SUPPORT FAILURE

Sooner or later, however, a normal Minor wave pattern is bound to be broken up. This generally occurs in one of two ways (although there is an infinity of possible variations). In one, prices spurt away in an advance out of all proportion to the previous succession of up waves. Such a move is seldom

FIGURE 140. When prices broke down out of the large Descending Triangle which formed on Remington Rand's weekly chart in 1946, the decline might have halted, at least temporarily, around 37 at the level of the four-week congestion made in April, and should have "caught support" at 35-36, the level of the February top. Failure of the latter carried Major trend significance (see next page). Note later resistance at 40½.

followed by a reaction to the support now left far behind, but rather by the construction of some sort of area pattern—which may be either consolidation or reversal.

The other type of disruption appears when a reaction does *not* halt and reverse at the level of the previous Minor top but sifts on down through that zone, perhaps to the level of the preceding Minor bottom. This move has "broken its support" and any such action carries a distinct warning of a change in trend, a particularly emphatic warning if activity shows a tendency to increase as or after the support is violated. Note that we said *change* in trend rather than reversal, since the puncturing of a Minor support level may signify only a halt for sidewise consolidation. But it may also foretoken an impending reversal. Either of these is a change.

If you will now call to mind the picture of a typical Head-and-Shoulders top

FIGURE 141. York is a relatively thin stock which normally makes many small, technically meaningless gaps but its large, high-volume gap of October 8, 1945 demanded attention. It looked like a runaway gap and as such implied continuation to 26½ plus. But prices halted their advance at 24½ and went into a three-month Rectangle. An up-side breakout on January 10, 1946 carried out the minimum measurement of the Rectangle (and October gap); prices then reacted. See sequel in Figure 142, next page.

you will see that the decline from the head constitutes just such a break in Minor support since it comes down through the level of the top of the left shoulder, and you will recall that this decline is often the first intimation we have that something in the nature of a reversal formation is developing.

Thus even the violation of a nearby support level has a practical meaning in technical chart analysis. The breaking of a Minor support should always be regarded as the first step in the reversal of the Intermediate trend. (If it turns out to be consolidation only, there will be an opportunity later to re-enter an abandoned commitment if desired.) By the same token, the breaking of an *Intermediate* support range is frequently the first sign of a reversal in the *Major* trend. We do not believe it is necessary to expatiate further on this principle. Recommended trading tactics based thereon are discussed in the second part of this book; support and resistance levels are particularly useful as basing points for stop-loss orders which are there discussed.

FIGURE 142. The February reaction in Figure 141 met momentary support at 24; prices bounced far enough to close the February 7 gap and then broke down through the Rectangle top-line support—technically a distinct warning. Then a Symmetrical Triangle formed but the breakout came too near the apex, produced only a rally to the former high, and then an "end run" (see page 232). One did not need to wait for the Double Top signal on August 22 to forecast a decline of more than Minor consequence.

POPULAR MISCONCEPTIONS

The reader will understand, of course, that all we have said here about the breaking of supports applies as well, but in reverse direction, to the penetration of resistance levels. One more point may well be mentioned before we leave this subject. If you happen to have spent much time in boardrooms, you will have noticed that the concepts of support and resistance which are prevalent there are somewhat different from those outlined in this chapter. For example, if **X** has advanced to 62, reacted to 57, then pushed on to 68, many traders will speak of 57 as being the support level, presumably because that was the last price at which **X** was supported in sufficient strength to turn its trend from down to up. We, however, as you have seen, would name the vicinity of 62 as the support range. The distinction is important to grasp, and sometimes extremely important in practical results.

Admittedly, it does not come easy to think of a former top as denoting the level at which a later bottom should form or vice-versa; it would seem superficially to be much more logical to relate top to top and bottom to bottom. Moreover, it is perfectly true, to use our **X** example again, that some of the investors who wanted to buy it at 57 might not have succeeded in getting it before the second advance to 68 took it away, and that their buy orders might still stand at 57 or might be re-entered on any return to that price. Nevertheless, there is certainly no assurance that such is the case; there is no "vested interest" in **X** at 57 that will "automatically" bring in new buying. On the other hand, we have seen how there is a sort of vested interest set up at an old bottom which produces selling (resistance) and thereby creates a new top, and at an old top which produces buying (support) and thereby creates a new bottom.

The reader is urged to keep this concept well in mind. Any analytical study of the chart records will quickly show that it is much easier for prices to push up through a former top level than through the resistance set up at a previous volume bottom (and vice-versa, of course, with respect to declines). You will find that a little selling may come in at a former high but usually only enough to cause a brief halt rather than the more or less extensive reactions or consolidations which develop when the trend comes up against a real resistance zone.

THE ROUND FIGURES

There are certain other levels which may at times evidently produce considerable resistance or support without any reference to a previous "vested interest." We have in mind the "round" figures 20, 30, 50, 75, 100 etc. In setting a goal for taking profits when we buy a stock, it is natural for us to think in terms of such round prices. If a low-priced stock has advanced steadily from around 10, it is pretty certain on this account to meet with profit-taking **sales** at 20, *especially if that figure represents a new high for it for several years.* In fact, any time an issue gets out into new all-time high ground, where there is nothing in its chart history to indicate otherwise, it is a fairly safe bet that resistance will appear at the round figures. In old and actively traded stocks, such as U. S. Steel or New York Central, the round figures diminish in importance.

REPEATING HISTORICAL LEVELS

If, once they had been set up, important support and resistance levels always "worked," we should see Intermediate tops and bottoms form at exactly the same ranges year after year in one Bull and Bear cycle after another. As a matter of fact, there is a well-marked tendency for this to occur in old-line actively traded stock. In General Electric, for example, the 22-24, 34-35, 40-42 and 48-50 zones have been characterized by large turn-over (and, consequently, by many Intermediate reversals of trend) throughout the past thirty years. In New York Central, the 10-11, 15-16, 21-22, 31-32, 35-36 and 40-42 zones are similarly characterized. In Southern Pacific, there are historical support and resistance zones at 21-22, 28-30, 38-40 and 55-56. In U. S. Steel, 42-45, 55-58, 69-72, 78-80 and 93-96 are conspicuously marked as reversal ranges. And many other stocks might be cited.

Over long periods, however, such support and resistance levels do tend to be gradually modified, broadened or "blurred," and new ones created. One source of many important new supply zones is a Bear Market panic. For this is the one type of decline which can be counted on to pay no heed whatever to previous underlying support zones. Panics (which, as we have seen in our earlier study of Primary swings in connection with Dow Theory, typify the second phase of Bear Markets) once they get under way seem to sweep away all potential support in their calamitous plunges until they exhaust themselves in a general market selling climax. And that climax may or may not come at a level which bears a relation to some previously established support. To use U. S. Steel again as an example, the 1937 panic decline took the stock down through its 93-96 range, hesitated briefly at the 78-80 level, and then plunged through 69-72 and 55-58 to stop just above 50. In the 1946 panic, X again broke swiftly through 78-80 and 69-72 to halt at 66.

When there is a large turnover at a panic bottom in any given stock, that level acquires a strong "vested interest" for the future and will usually furnish conspicuous resistance to a subsequent advance (after another Bear Market decline has taken quotations below the panic level).

This discussion of panics brings us back to a consideration of support and resistance performance at other stages of the Primary trend—a matter on which we stated early in this chapter we should have more to say. Bearing in mind the relation of resistance to volume, it is easy to see why in a long drawn out, but otherwise typical, Bear swing in which trading interest diminishes to a very low ebb as the final low is approached, the next to the last Intermediate bottom may produce relatively little supply, and consequently only a small reaction, when the new up trend reaches its level.   Add to this the fact that many of the buyers in the last stages of a Major decline are deliberate scale-down investors who fully expect prices will go lower and, hence, are not easily shaken out.   The slow progress so often seen in the first part of a new Primary Bull Market is due not so much to overhead resistance as to lack of impatient public bidding.

FIGURE 143. We first discussed pull-backs in connection with the Head-and-Shoulders in Chapter VI (page 58) and refer to them again in this chapter (page 229) as support-resistance phenomena.   At least one pull-back to the neckline (after the breakout) occurs in the great majority of cases.   Many H & S formations produce two, the first within a few days after the breakout and before prices have gotten very far away and the second weeks later, some-times after the minimum measurement of the H & S has been fulfilled.   Good-year saw the unusual number of four pull-backs to its 1946 neckline—the first two weeks after the August breakout, another in October, a third in No-vember, and a fourth in February, 1947 which met the double resistance of the neckline and the down trendline (Chapter XIV) projected from the 1946 April head and August right shoulder.

The recovery trends which follow precipitous Bear Market panics usually exhaust themselves, for obvious reasons, long before they get back up to the last resistance level left behind in that Primary down swing (which is usually the bottom of the first Intermediate decline from the extreme top of the cycle), but they often meet supply at a lower resistance zone set up *in the preceding Bull Market.* Look way back on your charts, therefore, when sizing up the prospective advance in such situations.

A further thought along that line is: There is no law which requires an advancing trend to keep right on climbing until it reaches a distant overhead supply zone. It is true, as a corollary which we have already mentioned to our support and resistance theory, that prices can and do rise easily through a price range where no bottoms or congestion areas have formed in previous down trends, but if the first established resistance level is a long ways above, the advance may exhaust itself before it gets there. Heavy supply *may* come in for other reasons at a lower level. Think, then, of a distant resistance level as a maximum possibility rather than as a certain goal. However, between two stocks whose purchase you are considering, you should, of course, select the one which, other things being equal, has the "thinner" track overhead, can rise farther before it encounters a charted supply zone.

Pattern Resistance

We can revert now to some of the minor phenomena discussed in connection with reversal and consolidation patterns in earlier chapters. Take gaps, for instance. You will now see why it is easy and, hence, quite in order for a reaction which comes soon after a gap has been made to slip back and close that gap. There is no "vested interest" whatever in the range through which prices skipped to form the gap on the chart. You will also see why such a reaction may stop short and reverse as soon as it has closed the gap, *provided* there was a high-volume turnover in the price range immediately preceding the gap. Such is usually the case with a breakaway gap.

Any gap, for the same reason, is easy to close once a reaction starts prices moving back in that direction, if it is not too far away and if there are no intervening resistance levels to stop the reaction before it gets there. In the case of a runaway gap, however, there is no reason why a reaction should halt as soon as it has covered the gap range; on the contrary, it will probably continue on through the "thin" price track that preceded the gap.

Pull-backs and throw-backs—the quick return moves which we noted as developing so often shortly after a breakout from a Head-and-Shoulders or other area pattern—exemplify the principles of support and resistance. When prices break down, for example, out of a Descending Triangle, the horizontal lower boundary of the formation which was originally a demand line promptly reverses its role and becomes a resistance level. Any attempt to put prices back up through it, therefore, after a decisive breakout, is stopped by supply at or near the line. By the same token, the neckline of a Head-and-Shoulders Top, which was a demand line, becomes a resistance level after it has been broken. The top or supply line of a Rectangle becomes a support after prices have pushed above it on volume and by a decisive margin.

Earlier in this chapter, in our discussion of the three criteria for appraising the amount of resistance to be expected at a former bottom level, we named "distance away" as one of them and stated as a general rule that prices should

FIGURE 144. Several examples of the support "field" of the Symmetrical Triangle appear in this 1945 daily chart of "IT." Following the belated February 5 breakout from the first Triangle, prices returned on the 9th to the level of the mid-January top but then suffered a more extensive reaction which came down on February 26 to the Triangle's apex level. This was a critical juncture. The apex point itself is a strong support (or resistance) but its level becomes weaker as time passes. In this case an "end run" (see page 232) might have been developing. Stop-loss orders should always be entered under an apex level (see Chapter XXVII). Here the apex held, however, and prices went into another "coil," breaking out top-side on March 10. Their next reaction was supported, as was to be expected after an early breakout like this, at the top pattern line.

The price track from mid-March to the end of April fell into an Ascending Triangle pattern, the top boundary of which functioned as support in June but was broken in July. Refer back to Figure 120, page 187.

FIGURE 145. In this instance, a belated up-side breakout (August 10) from a Symmetrical Triangle failed quickly and the subsequent reaction, after holding for several days at the apex level, finally broke down for an "end run." Thereafter, note that the apex level turned into a resistance against recovery moves.

have gone at least 10% beyond that level in a medium priced stock before much resistance would be set up. This 10% away rule does not apply, however, in the case of a throw-back to a well-defined area formation, when it follows shortly after a breakout. All that is necessary to establish strong resistance to such moves at the pattern boundary is a conclusive breakout.

The Symmetrical Triangle has a different sort of support and resistance "field." You will recall that the first reversal point in the formation of a Symmetrical Triangle (a top if it forms on a rising trend or a bottom if on a decline) is normally accompanied by high trading volume, but that activity diminishes rapidly on succeeding fluctuations within its converging boundaries. Consequently, once prices have broken out of the Triangle and have proceeded well beyond the level of the pattern's first reversal point, that level, because of the volume of shares traded there, becomes a support (or resistance) against a subsequent reaction. But, if the breakout move does not carry beyond the Triangle's first reversal level by a clear margin, any throw-back will probably bring quotations back to the extended (sloping) pattern boundary, and if the reaction does not occur until the trend has worked out to or beyond the Triangle's apex, then the throw-back usually will not meet support (or resistance) until it has carried back to the level of the apex. The apex, in brief, represents the concentration level or *axis* of the Triangle's support and resistance.

The intersection of the two converging boundary lines of a Symmetrical

Triangle has sometimes been called a "cradle." The axis support (or resistance) is strongest near the cradle point and gets weaker as the axis line (apex level) is extended out to the right on the chart (i.e., as time passes). Thus, if a late breakout move fails to carry prices very far from the Triangle area and the trend then peters out, flattens and begins to react *after* the cradle point has been passed in terms of time, its action as it reaches the axis line must be closely watched. (A stop-loss order may be indicated here.) Should the axis support fail to hold, the reaction may plunge through and accelerate in a more extensive swing which has aptly been termed an "end run around the line."

Volume on Breaks Through Support

On those occasions when prices fail to retreat when they hit a resistance (or support) range but, after perhaps holding there for several days, push on through, there is nearly always a sudden acceleration and a marked pick-up in volume. This may be taken as confirmatory evidence of a decisive break and, consequently, an indication that the move will carry on. The reasons for this volume increase are obscure. Some say, "It takes volume to overcome resistance," which is true enough, but the volume usually comes *after* the resistance has been penetrated. Therefore, others say, "The volume is evidence that technicians see what has happened and are now jumping in." But that line of thought, in the authors' opinion, also has little to substantiate it. (We shall have more to say about the questionable influence of technicians on the trend later on.) Many of the arguments over volume change vs. price change savor of the old hen-or-egg riddle. In any event, causes for many technical phenomena such as this one may be left to the academicians, provided the practical implications are clear.

Support and Resistance in the Averages

As has been the case with nearly every other technical phenomenon we have studied, the principles of support and resistance apply, with suitable allowances, to averages as well as to individual stocks. Since an average reflects the combined charts of the majority of the issues which compose it, but with a minority of them frequently evincing quite divergent patterns, it follows naturally that support and resistance zones in the averages cannot be as sharply and narrowly construed. Minor tops and bottoms in the averages, particularly, are less dependable as resistance levels. Clearly defined and important Intermediate reversals, however, since they represent nearly always reversals in the entire market (practically all stocks) will normally produce strong resistance (or support as the case may be) in the subsequent average trend.

When the averages break down through a support level, but one or more stocks at the same time hold firm at or above their corresponding individual supports, there is a presumption that those particular stocks are in a stronger position than others to participate in the next recovery. The phrase "other things being equal" should be added, however, for there are qualifications to this presumption which must be considered. For instance, it may be that the stock which has resisted decline will, for that very reason, be less attractive to new buyers than one which broke drastically and is, therefore, now purchasable at a more "attractive" price.

Many of the claims made regarding future prospects for stocks which have, by one criterion or another, previously evinced "better-than-average" or "worse-than-average" market performance permit of argument either way. It is safest to treat all such relative performance indications as only one minor factor to be appraised in the over-all chart picture.

FIGURE 146. Here is a typical case of two pull-backs to an H & S neckline, the first immediately after the breakout and the second three weeks later. Note that the initial break-through "bounced" from the early April top support, and the late July decline met support at the general April-May congestion area. But what this chart illustrates particularly is how volume increases when a good support range is penetrated. Note the decided pickup on August 27, when the April-May area was left behind.

CHAPTER XIV

TRENDLINES AND CHANNELS

ONE of our basic tenets in this system of technical stock chart analysis—
indeed, a fact which any neophyte can quickly verify for himself by inspection of the market records for whatever period he chooses—is that *prices
move in trends*. The market in general and the many stocks which compose
it do not jump up and down in an altogether random fashion; on the contrary,
they show definite organization and pattern in their charted course.

Prices move in trends. These trends may be either up or down or sideways
(horizontal). They may be brief or of long duration. They may be classified
as Major (Primary), Intermediate (Secondary) or Minor according to the rules
of Dow Theory, or as horizontal Line formations. (The distinction between a
short Intermediate and an extended Minor trend is often more difficult to make
with individual stocks than it is with the averages, but it is not so important.)
But sooner or later trends change; they may change by reversing from up to
down or down to up, and they may also change direction without reversing as,
for example, from up to sideways and then perhaps to up again, or from a
moderate slope to a steep slope, and vice-versa.

Profits are made by capitalizing on up or down trends, by following them
until they are reversed. The investor's problem is to recognize a profitable
trend at the earliest possible stage of its development and then later to detect,
again as quickly as possible, its end and reversal. The reversal of any important
trend is usually characterized, as we have already seen, by the construction of
some sort of joint price and volume pattern—in brief, of a reversal formation.

THE TRENDLINE

All of the foregoing statements regarding trends have been expressed or implied in earlier chapters of this text. It is our purpose now to examine trends
as such more closely, to see how they may be plotted most effectively on the
charts, and determine to what extent they can be used to reinforce or supplement the technical forecasts derived from our other chart formation and support-resistance studies—sometimes to furnish even earlier forecasts or warnings
of change.

One of the first discoveries a new student is likely to make when he begins
to inspect stock charts with a critical eye is that nearly all Minor and most
Intermediate trends follow nearly straight lines. A few readers will, perhaps,

dismiss this as perfectly natural, something to be taken for granted. But the majority become increasingly amazed and excited as they delve deeper. Not only the smaller fluctuations but frequently also the great Primary swings of several years' duration appear on the charts as though their courses had been plotted with a straight-edge ruler. This phenomenon is, in truth, the most fascinating, impressive and mysterious of all that the stock charts exhibit.

If we actually apply a ruler to a number of charted price trends we quickly

FIGURE 147. A series of Intermediate trendlines drawn to illustrate the "basic" principle (see page 236) on a weekly chart of Atlantic Refining, extending from January, 1944 through August, 1947. Observe that each up trendline required two *distinct* bottom points to determine it, and each down trendline, two tops. In some cases the two determining points were formed only a few weeks apart, as in August and September, 1945. The bottom points that fixed the early 1946 up trendline, on the other hand, were months apart—February and June.

Many other experimental lines might have been drawn on this chart originally, including several up trends whose Intermediate authority was questionable because they were "too steep"—as in early 1944, late 1945 and early 1946. (See page 241.) Only final trendlines are shown here.

There are here also some interesting examples of pull-backs (after trendline penetration) which are discussd on page 252. Note July, 1944, April, 1945, September, 1945 and May, 1947.

discover that the line which most often is really straight in an up trend is a line connecting the lower extremes of the Minor recessions within those trends. In other words an advancing wave in the stock market is composed of a series of ripples and the bottoms of each of these ripples tend to form on, or very close to, an upward slanting straight line. The tops of the ripples are usually less even; sometimes they also can be defined by a straight line but more often they vary slightly in amplitude and so any line connecting their upper tips will be more or less crooked.

On a descending price trend the line most likely to be straight is the one that connects the *tops* of the Minor rallies within it, while the Minor bottoms may or may not fall along a straight edge.

These two lines—the one that slants up along the successive wave bottoms within a broad up move and the one that slants down across successive wave tops within a broad down move—are the basic trendlines.

It is unfortunate that a more distinctive name for them has never been devised than the threadbare word line which has so many other uses and connotations. A few analysts have called them "tangents," a term that has the advantage of novelty but, because it is a distinct perversion of the true meaning of the word tangent, even more confuses many readers. Perhaps "tangent" will eventually become established in this new sense. However, we shall be satisfied herein with the overworked "line," but can give it some distinctiveness in its present context by joining it to trend in the one word *trendline*.

Trendlines, you may have heard it said, "are made to be broken," but that is one of those exasperatingly sententious remarks which fail to clarify anything. Of course they are broken; they are all always broken ultimately and some very shortly after they are set up. The problem is to decide which breaks (i.e., penetrations by a price movement) are of important technical significance and which are of no practical consequence, requiring possibly only a minor correction in the drawing of the original trendline. There are no 100% certain, quick answers to this problem; the significance of some penetrations cannot be determined as soon as they appear but must await confirmatory indications from other chart developments. In a great majority of instances, however, an important break—one that requires a prompt review and possibly a revision of trading policy—is easy to recognize.

How Trendlines Are Drawn

But first, how are trendlines drawn? A straight line is mathematically determined by any two points along it. In order to draw a trendline, therefore, we require two determining points—two established top reversal points to fix a down trendline and two established bottom reversal points to fix an up trendline. The principle here is the same as the one we laid down in our specifications for drawing Triangle boundary lines in Chapter VIII. The fact is that boundary lines of Triangles and Rectangles, as well as necklines of Head-and-Shoulders formations, are simply special types of trendlines.

Suppose we start with a Major bottom point and describe how a series of up trendlines might develop therefrom. To make this first illustration simple, let us assume that the Bear Market bottom in our stock consisted of a Rectangle area between $6\frac{1}{2}$ and 8, and that the last move in this formation arose from the $6\frac{1}{2}$ level, broke through the pattern's top at 8, and proceeded to 9. From 9, prices reacted to 8 and then headed back up again. As soon as this last rally had gone far enough to leave the dip to 8 showing in the clear as a Minor bottom, we could draw our first up trendline because we then had two bottom points, the second (8) higher than the first ($6\frac{1}{2}$), to fix its slope. This would be a Minor up trendline. We would rule it in lightly on our chart in pencil and extend it on up and ahead for, perhaps, a week or more. (It will help you to visualize our example if you sketch it on a scrap of chart paper.)

To proceed, suppose prices push up to 10, then move sidewise for a few days, or dip slightly, until they have approached and touched once more our extended Minor trendline. Then they start to move up in a third advance but run into supply again without making much progress, quickly make a fourth contact with the trendline, hesitate and then break down through it. If prices now close clearly below the line and if, in addition, there has been some pick-up in trading volume evident on the penetration, we may conclude that our first Minor trend is completed, and that our stock either will build some sort of consolidation pattern before it stages another advance or will suffer a more extensive "correction" than any of the brief dips it registered during its first Minor up swing.

The whole Minor up trend we have described as an example in the foregoing paragraphs might well have run its course in two weeks and our first trendline would then have been very steep—too steep, obviously, to hold for any very long period of time. Now, let us assume that a series of downward fluctuations produces the more extensive correction which we have foreseen as one probability following the trendline break, and that this carries prices back to the support level set up at the top of the original Rectangle, i.e., at 8. (From our previous support-resistance studies, we would recognize this as a prime "buy spot.") Assuming that subsequent developments pursue a normal course, prices should not linger long at 8 but should start promptly on a new series of advancing fluctuations. As soon as this becomes evident and the new bottom at 8 is "in the clear," we can rule in a new trendline across the original base point at $6\frac{1}{2}$ and the new point at 8. This should be, and probably is, an *Intermediate* up trendline which will not be penetrated for several weeks, and maybe for several months, until the Intermediate advance tops out.

Then, if that Intermediate top takes the form of a Head-and-Shoulders reversal pattern, our Intermediate up trendline may be broken by the recession

from the top of the head to the neckline.   As a rule, however, the final advance
in a strong Intermediate move accelerates far enough away from the extended
trendline to leave room (to the right on the chart) for considerable pattern construction before the line is again touched and penetrated.   Hence, the actual
puncturing of the trendline is more apt to occur either on the decline from the
right shoulder to the neckline, or at about the same time as prices break down
through the neckline to complete the Head-and-Shoulders signal.   It is surprising to see how often the two lines, neckline and trendline, are broken
simultaneously.   In other instances, and there are many of them also, in which
the trendline is the first to be punctured, perhaps shortly after prices turn down
from the right shoulder, we do not have to wait for a neckline break but can
take action at once.   Here is one type of trendline indication which produces a
working signal a little earlier, and often at a much more favorable price level,
than is given by the completion of a reversal formation.

FIGURE 148.   This 1935-36 daily chart of Atchison illustrates how the latter
part of a long, strong Intermediate advance may accelerate away from its
trendline.   (Notice the action in late January and early February.)   Prices
dropped back to 66 in April, 1936 after this up trendline was broken
at the end of March.   Note also that at the point where the December, 1935
reaction met support, the trendline coincided with a Triangle apex level.
Such coincidences appear frequently in technical studies.

Arithmetic vs. Logarithmic Scale

By this time, the more mathematically inclined among our readers must have begun to ponder the difference between trendlines projected on the ordinary or arithmetic scale and on the logarithmic or ratio scale. A series of points which fall on a perfectly straight up-sloping line on arithmetic chart paper will when transferred to a semi-logarithmic sheet produce a curved line which rises sharply at first and then gradually rounds over. And points which fall on a straight line on a semi-logarithmic sheet will produce an accelerating curve on an arithmetic sheet, a line which slants up more and more steeply the farther it is projected.

As a matter of fact this variance is of little or no importance in defining Minor trends since they seldom run far enough for the dissimilar characteristics of the two types of scales to become effective. And the same holds true for average Intermediate moves of normal slope. But when it comes to very long and strong Intermediates, the divergence may become marked, may make a considerable difference in the time and level of ultimate trendline penetration. Therein lies one of the strongest reasons for using semi-logarithmic paper in charting stocks for technical analysis. But let us postpone further discussion of this point until we take up Major trends, and go on now with the Intermediate lines which are much the same on either type of scale. And, for the present, let us concentrate on Intermediate *up* trends. (Intermediate moves are emphasized rather than Minor for the obvious reason that the latter are of little practical importance in either trading or investing.)

To go back to first principles, and granting that price advances trend up in more or less straight lines, it follows that if we can find and draw the lines that accurately define those trends, they will serve two purposes, as follows:—

(1) When the trendline is broken (i.e., when prices drop down through it in decisive fashion) it signals that the advance has run out. It calls time for the Intermediate term trader to sell out that issue, and look for reinvestment opportunities elsewhere.

(2) When a small top reversal pattern forms on the chart of an issue well up and away from that issue's Intermediate up trendline, so that there apparently is room for the down-side implications of the reversal formations to be carried out *before* the trendline is violated, then the Intermediate trend trader may well decide to ignore the small reversal pattern. He can hold on so long as the trendline holds.

The advantages of the first named trendline function are obvious. Those of the second, though less obvious to the inexperienced, are equally important to the investor who has learned that it is an expensive practice to switch out of every holding as soon as it shows evidence of a minor setback, provided the chance of further Intermediate advance still exists.

To accomplish these purposes it is necessary, as we have said, to find and draw the line that accurately defines the Intermediate trend, and then to recognize when that line has been broken in decisive fashion. Our earlier quick review of how a trendline is constructed did not attempt thoroughly to cover these points.

FIGURE 149. Trendlines which defined the short-term swings in Crane Co. in 1945. Note that three bottoms formed on the first up line and that the third rally (late February) in this advance failed to reach a line drawn across the earlier tops parallel to the basic trendline. A failure of this sort frequently precedes a break in the trend. The same thing happened at the end of the second up trend in late May. "Failures" and the use of parallel or "return" lines will be discussed later in this chapter.

The down trend in March assumed Wedge form. Observe how the April 6 reaction met support at its previously penetrated top line. In June a rally met resistance at the previously broken up trendline. Such pull-backs are common. The small Complex Head-and-Shoulders in June was never completed, since prices did not break down out of it by the required margin.

TESTS OF AUTHORITY

Here are some of the tests which may be applied to judge the technical validity, the authority of an up trendline:—

a. The greater the number of bottoms that have developed at (or very near) a trendline in the course of a series of Minor up waves, the greater the importance of that line in the technical sense. With each successive "test" the significance of the line is increased. A first and tentative up trendline can be drawn as soon as two bottoms have formed, the second higher than the first, but if prices move back to that line a third time, make a third bottom there and start a renewed advance, then the validity of that line as a true definition of the trend has been *confirmed* by the action of the market. Should a fourth bottom later form on it and prices move up away from it again, its value as a trend criterion is very considerably enhanced, etc.

b. The length of the line, i.e., the longer it has held without being penetrated down-side by prices, the greater its technical significance. This principle, however, requires some qualification. If your trendline is drawn from two original bottoms which are very close together in time—say, less than a week apart—it is subject to error; it may be too steep or (more often) too flat. If the latter, prices may move away from it and stay high above it for a long time; they may then turn down and have declined well along in an Intermediate correction before the trendline thus drawn is reached. But if the trendline has been drawn from bottoms which are far enough apart to have developed as independent wave components of the trend you are trying to define, with a good rally and "open water" between them, then it is more apt to be the true trendline.

Greater weight should be given to the number of bottoms that have formed on a trendline (test *a*) than to its length alone (test *b*).

c. The angle of the trendline (to the horizontal) is also to some degree a criterion of its validity as a true delimiter of Intermediate trend. A very steep line can easily be broken by a brief sidewise consolidation move—as, for example, by a compact Flag forming on an advance of the "mast" type—only to have prices shoot up again in another extensive advance. Such steep lines are of little forecasting value to the technician. The flatter, more nearly horizontal the trendline, the more important it is technically and, in consequence, the greater the significance of any down-side break through it.

But steep, as applied to stock trends, is a relative term and one which, we must frankly confess, defies exact definition. Experience, which can only be gained by studying many charts and by actually building and working with them over a period of many months, brings an almost intuitive ability to distinguish between a trendline which is "too steep to hold" and one whose angle of rise is reasonable and should be maintained until such time as the trend is actually reversed from Intermediate up to Intermediate down. Trend slopes will vary from stock to stock according to their characteristic market habits. They will vary also according to the stage of the Primary cycle—tending to become somewhat steeper in its later phases. The more back chart history you have on any particular issue in which you are interested, the better able you will be to judge its present trend.

(The foregoing statement, we might remark, applies to the interpretation of most other technical patterns and phenomena as well as to trendlines.)

One clue to relative steepness is afforded to those who employ the TEKNI-PLAT semi-logarithmic chart sheet which has been used for most of the illustrations in this book. When projected on this scale, Intermediate up trends on the daily charts, in the great majority of issues selling in the 10 to 50 range, rise at an angle of approximately 30 degrees to the horizontal. Some will be a trifle flatter, some a trifle steeper, but it is surprising to see how often the trend-line falls very close to the 30-degree slope in stocks of average volatility and activity. Thin, highly speculative issues and heavy investment stocks offer exceptions, the former usually steeper and the latter flatter. The semi-logarith-mic scale has the virtue, of course, of reducing all movements regardless of

FIGURE 150.   Intermediate down and up trends in Commercial Solvents in 1946.   Note the increased volume on the March 30 penetration of the basic down trendline (and, at the same time, a breakout from a small H & S bot-tom).   The drop through the lower parallel at the end of February had no technical significance.   The up trendline from the March low was broken on June 14, simultaneously with a breakout from a Descending Triangle which, as it turned out, was the final Bull Market top.

price level to a ratio or percentage basis. On a straight arithmetic scale, the trendline will ordinarily be steeper on a stock trading in the 50 range, for example, than on an issue selling around 15.

On weekly charts employing the same price scale, the angle of Intermediate advance will, of course, be much steeper than on the daily plotting. Different scaling will produce different angles. It is pure happenstance that the TEKNI-PLAT sheet tends to produce the 30-degree ascending line.

VALIDITY OF PENETRATION

We have these three criteria then for appraising the authority or accuracy of an Intermediate up trendline: (a) the number of times it has been "tested" or contacted without breaking, (b) its length or duration and (c) its angle of ascent. Given a trendline which, by the application of one or more of these criteria (preferably by at least two of them) appears to be a reasonably accurate delimiter of the trend, our next problem is to determine when it has been finally and definitely broken.

Again we can set up three tests or criteria, two of which are practically identical with the rules laid down in earlier chapters for determining decisive breakouts from reversal or consolidation formations. The first is *extent of penetration*. To be decisive, prices must not only push through the line but close beyond it by a margin equal to about 3% of the stock's price. This does not need to be accomplished in a single day, although it often is. The 3% penetration may come as a result of two or three days of gradual decline.

The second is *volume of trading*. We saw how activity should always be expected to rise notably on a genuine up-side breakout from an area pattern, but need not increase to confirm a down-side break. We have seen how in many cases volume does not show much increase on the first day of down break from Descending Triangles, for example, but usually picks up rapidly as the decline proceeds. In our present discussion we are dealing with *up* trendlines and their penetration is, therefore, analogous to a down-side breakout. We should expect the same rules to apply and in general they do. Given a close beyond the line by a price margin of 3%, it is not necessary for volume to have expanded much at that point to confirm the validity of the penetration.

The fact is, however, that the breaking of an Intermediate up trendline much more often than not is attended by some visible intensification of trading activity. To that extent, then, an increase in volume may be regarded as confirmation of a decisive penetration. It is a particularly useful adjunct in borderline cases. If, for example, prices start to decline from a point somewhat above the trendline, move down through it on *conspicuously expanding* turnover, and close beyond it, say, only 2% of the price but at or near the bottom of the day's range, our 3% margin rule has not been satisfied but the lesser margin *plus* the volume action may be construed as decisive.

Beware, however, and do not be stampeded into a hasty commitment by the shake-out move which cracks down through a trendline with a great flurry of activity—perhaps several minutes of late tape—and then turns up again to close the day back above the trend or at least very close to it. This may very well be—in fact, usually is—a false move so far as that particular moment is con-

FIGURE 151. Valid trendline penetration and its normal consequences— reaction or consolidation—is illustrated on nearly every chart in this chapter and on many others throughout the book. The above weekly chart of Phillips Petroleum, however, is here reproduced to show an outstanding exception. The Intermediate up trendline projected from "P's" September 1936 low up across its early October and late November bottoms, was penetrated down-side decisively the third week of May, 1937. Moreover, a Multiple H & S top reversal pattern had been forming since February, with a critical neckline at 52. And the then current Bull Market had already run for four years; "P" had come all the way up from 2! Cover up the chart from July 1, 1937 on and you will agree that there was plenty of reason for any technician to sell at once without waiting for the 52 neckline to be broken. But this, as we have said, was one of the exceptions which occur to all technical patterns and rules. "P" turned right around and shot up to 64 before it was finished. Nevertheless, developments such as this carry a valuable warning. They very seldom appear unless the Major trend has almost run out; any further rise is dangerous to follow.

cerned. But watch the next few days' performance very closely; the technical situation is evidently critical else a shake-out could not have been easily staged.

The third test is also one that applies particularly to breaks which are borderline so far as margin of penetration is concerned. Suppose a stock which is quoted in the neighborhood of 40 declines through a well-established Intermediate up trendline and closes 1 or 1⅛ points below it—a margin which is only slightly less than our specified 3%—without much if any enlargement in trading volume. Suppose it fluctuates there for a day or two in a dull and narrow market and then starts to rally. If there is no pick-up in activity on this recovery move—if prices simply edge up feebly to the under side of the trendline and tend to "round over" there without being able to close clearly above it—then the situation is indeed critical and the slightest sign of renewed selling pressure may be taken as a signal that the up trend has been decisively broken.

Such a return move as we have described in the preceding paragraph is known as a throw-back or pull-back. We have previously described analogous developments which follow breakouts from Head-and-Shoulders and other patterns, and will have more to say about them in connection with trendlines later on.

The three tests we have been discussing, which help to establish the validity of a trendline penetration, cannot, unfortunately, be applied inflexibly and without a modicum of judgment. The majority of Intermediate trendlines can hardly be said to possess the precision of pattern boundary lines, and even in the latter some leeway must be allowed. There are exceptions, as we have taken occasion to remark several times before, to every technical rule of price action. But judgment in the establishing of significant trendlines and in interpreting their penetrations does come with experience.

Amendment of Trendlines

When a trendline is broken by a margin less than decisive and prices subsequently rally back up through it again, doubt naturally arises as to the continued authority of the original line. Should it be discarded, revised or allowed to stand as is?

Here again judgment and experience must be called into play but a few general principles are helpful in deciding. If the original trendlines depended on only two points, i.e., on the first two bottoms across which it was projected, and the indecisive penetration occurred when prices returned to it for the third time, the line had better be re-drawn across the original first and the new third bottoms. (Of course, you will not do this until prices have moved up from the third bottom point and it has become clearly established as a Minor bottom.) Or, you may find in such cases that a new line drawn across the *second* and third bottoms works better; if the first bottom was a Reversal Day with its closing level well above the low of its range, you may find that this new line, when extended back, strikes just about at that closing level.

If, on the other hand, the original trendline has been "tested" one or more times after it was drawn—if, that is, a third and perhaps a fourth bottom have formed on it without penetrating it and have thus "confirmed" it—then the subsequent indecisive penetration may be disregarded and the original line considered to be still in effect.

An intra-day break through an established trendline which, however, does not result in prices *closing* beyond the line, may be disregarded and the line left as is. In fact, as already has been suggested, the closing prices frequently make a better trendline than the extreme intra-day lows of successive bottoms, and this is most apt to be true with "thin" stock subject to erratic swings. A bit

FIGURE 152. Double trendlines (see next page) usually are not evident until after a trend has run for several months. In Paramount's accelerated phase of Intermediate up trend which began in October, 1945, the double nature of the basic trendline was not detectable until January, 1946. The inner (upper) line was broken again in April but the outer (lower) line was not decisively penetrated down-side until May, at the Bull Market top.

FIGURE 153. Trend channels in Bethlehem Steel in 1945. Prices burst out of the 92-98 horizontal channel (Rectangle) on the up side in January, 1946 and went on to 114. A short-turn trader might have sold around 94-96 in early November (because of the up trend break) and re-bought at 99 in January on the Rectangle breakout. See page 249 for channels.

of experimenting with different lines often pays. A thin, transparent ruler is especially useful for trendline study.

There is another type of price action that may require re-drawing a trendline. Sometimes after a line has been projected up across the first two Minor bottoms in an advancing trend, a third Minor bottom will form not on that line but well above it. In such cases, let the original line stand but draw in a new one across the second and third bottom points, and watch developments. If the rally from the third bottom peters out quickly and the new trendline as a consequence is soon broken, then the original trendline is probably the correct one. But, if the third bottom turns out to be a "strong" one and the new line stands up well for several weeks (and if it was not, patently, too steep to begin with), then the old line may be abandoned and the new one regarded as the better trend definer.

DOUBLE TRENDLINES AND TREND RANGES

In the course of your "cutting and trying" in an effort to fit a good line to an Intermediate up trend, you may find that *two parallel lines*, perhaps a point or so apart in a stock selling in the thirties, will define the true trend pattern much better than any single line that can be drawn. Sharp bottoms and shake-out thrusts in such cases will often fall along the outer or lower line while the

FIGURE 154.   A ten-month down trend, extraordinarily long and straight, which was nicely defined by double basic trendlines above the price channel, and also by a double set of return lines below it.   The Major top started with a strong One-Day Reversal on December 3, 1945, and worked out into a Descending Triangle which broke February 19, 1946.   The Symmetrical Triangle beginning to appear in September, 1946 also broke out down-side.

duller, more rounded reactions will stop at or near the upper or inner line. Or the two lines will mark off a *range* somewhere within which successive Minor down waves tend to halt and reverse.

Such double trendlines are really plentiful although the majority of chart technicians seem to be quite unaware of them. It pays to develop an eye for them—to watch constantly for trends to which they can be applied. They will clear up many situations in which attempts to find a single critical line lead only to frustration and finally giving up in disgust.

Trends which you find are best defined by double trendlines (or by a very broad trendline, if you prefer) cannot be regarded as ended until the outer, lower line has been decisively penetrated. In that connection, note what we said at the beginning of this topic: sharp, shake-out bottoms tend to fall on the outer line. The recoveries from such bottoms are usually just as sharp and prices, therefore, rally back above the upper, inner line quickly. Warning of an impending break in the trend is given when prices come down to the outer line steadily, rather than by the quick "shake" type of reaction, and then have difficulty rallying back through the inner line. Watch such developments closely. A breakdown may not follow; the situation may still be "saved," but the chances are that the trend is near its end.

TREND CHANNELS

At the start of this trend study we applied the term *basic trendline* to the line which slopes up across the wave bottoms in an advance, and to the line which slopes down across the wave tops in a decline. And we noted that the opposite reversal points, i.e., the wave crests in an advance and the wave troughs in a decline, were, as a rule, less clearly delimited. That is one of the reasons why all of our discussion up to this point has been devoted to basic trendlines. Another reason is, of course, that the technician's most urgent task is to determine when a trend has run out and for that purpose the basic line is all-important.

In a fair share of normal trends, however, the Minor waves are sufficiently regular to be defined at their other extremes by another line. That is, the *tops* of the rallies composing an Intermediate advance sometimes develop along a line which is approximately parallel to the basic trendline projected along their bottoms. This parallel might be called the *return line* since it marks the zone where reactions (return moves against the prevailing trend) originate. The area between basic trendline and return line is the *trend channel*.

Nicely defined trend channels appear most often in actively traded stocks of large outstanding issue—least often in the less popular and the relatively thin equities which receive only sporadic attention from investors. The value of the trend channel concept for the technical trader would hardly seem to require extended comment here; its tactical utilization is discussed in the second half of this book.

Its greatest utility, however, is not what usually appeals to the beginner when he first makes its acquaintance, viz., the determination of good profit-taking levels. Experienced technicians rather find it more helpful in a negative sense. Thus, once a trend channel appears to have become well established, any failure of a rally to reach the return line (top parallel of the channel in an Intermediate advance) is taken as a sign of deterioration in the trend. Further, the margin by which a rally fails to reach the return line (before turning down) frequently equals the margin by which the basic trendline is penetrated by the ensuing decline before a halt or throw-back in the latter occurs.

By the same token, given an established trend channel, when a reaction from the return line fails to carry prices all the way back to the basic trendline but bottoms out somewhere above it, the advance from that bottom will usually push up out of the channel on the top side (through the return line) by a margin approximately equal to the margin by which the reaction failed to reach the bottom of the channel (basic trendline).

Experimental Lines

Your experienced technician, in fact, is constantly drawing trendlines of all sorts—Minor, Intermediate and Major—on his charts. He will put them in at

FIGURE 155. Well-marked Intermediate basic trendlines and return lines in Southern Pacific, 1945. Note Flags within trend channels—an up Flag in June and a down Flag in August. The up trend channel which began August 22 ran until February, 1946.

FIGURE 156. Note that the extent by which prices failed to come down to their return line in late November measured the distance by which they advanced through and above the basic down trendline in early December. This rule is stated on the preceding page.

first very lightly penciled wherever he can find an excuse to draw one. Many will quickly prove to be of no significance and those he may erase. Others will "stand up"—will show evidence of technical authority—and those he will make heavier, or color as suggested later on. He will be constantly on the watch for double trendlines and will draw tentative return lines to mark off possible channels at every opportunity. As soon as he has what appears to be a basic up trendline projected from two bottoms, for example, he will go back to the top of the rally between those two bottoms and draw from that a parallel to the bottom trendline. If the next rally comes up to that parallel, stops there and turns down, he has a probable return line and channel established.

This practice of drawing in and experimenting with every trendline which the price action permits or suggests, is earnestly recommended to the reader of this book, particularly if the technical approach is new to him. It is the quickest way—in fact, the only way—of acquiring the experience we have stressed as essential to recognition, judgment and utilization of trendline implications in trading.

Perhaps we should add here one "don't" for the beginner. You will have noted that nowhere have we mentioned a line projected from a bottom to a top, or vice-versa. Trendlines are *always* drawn across two or more bottoms, *or* two or more tops. They should never be drawn to cross through the price track. (Prices may cross their extensions later, but this should not have happened at the time the lines are first drawn.) If you did not know better you

FIGURE 157. Six months of an up trend channel which actually started to form in December, 1943! It was broken down-side in August, 1945.

might, for example, put in a line from the top of the left shoulder to the top of the right shoulder of a Head-and-Shoulders formation, thus cutting through the head, but such a line would have no technical validity.

CONSEQUENCES OF TRENDLINE PENETRATION—THROW-BACKS

At the beginning of this chapter we mentioned the probable consequences of a break down through an Intermediate up trendline. To repeat, if an Intermediate up trendline has been constructed, has qualified as technically significant by the tests previously discussed, and has then been decisively broken, the inference is that that up trend is finished. And the consequences to be expected are either a full Intermediate recession or a period of consolidation (usually becoming a recognizable area formation). Technical indications of other sorts may be seen on the chart, which will suggest to you which of these two consequences is the more likely. In either event, the Intermediate trend trader will certainly look twice before attempting to find further profit in that particular situation at that time.

A more immediate but less important probable consequence of trendline penetration has also been mentioned—the *pull-back*. This deserves further discussion. Pull-backs that follow breakouts from reversal and consolidation formations have been described in our earlier studies of those price patterns. It is easy to understand why a rally which develops after prices break out through the lower boundary of a Rectangle, for example, will be stopped when it gets back to that boundary by the resistance (supply) now residing there. Support-resistance theory enables us to rationalize most of the throw-back moves which occur after prices have broken out of other types of reversal or consolidation areas.   The pull-backs which follow trendline penetrations cannot be thus rationalized; yet they occur much more frequently and they appear to be stopped much more exactly at the old trendline level than is the case with area formations.   Why should prices, after they have thrust down through a rising trendline, perhaps for several points, turn back up and ascend to or very near the old trendline, stop there and then go off in renewed decline?   The top of that pull-back rally may be two or three points above the original penetration level, since the trendline is sloping up all the time; nevertheless there it stops, falters, gives up.   No one knows why supply should overcome

FIGURE 158.   The down trend which started in June, 1946 in Nash-Kelvinator, signaled by the break of both its Intermediate and Major (MUT) up trendlines on July 15, made a nice channel until September.   An Intermediate down trendline, drawn across the June 17 and July 1 highs, held for the August rally.   The return line, drawn parallel to it across the June 20 low, held in late July but remained intact for only a few days at the end of August. The August rally in both price and volume pattern showed Bear Market characteristics.   Compare this chart with Figure 68 on page 118 and you will see that a Major Double Top was signaled on July 23.

FIGURE 159.   The decline which took Macy down through an Intermediate up trendline (IUT) in June, 1946, turned out to be also the drop from the head of a "flat-shouldered" H & S top, which was, in turn, part of a larger Complex.   The upper neckline was broken June 19 and the lower on July 16.   Note pull-backs to each.   F1, F2 and F3 are tentative fan lines (see page 257).   Prices were finally able to clear F3 in December, but by that time a Primary Bear Market had been signaled so the fan rule no longer applied.   Fans call the turn only on Secondary (corrective) moves.

demand, why resistance should be so plainly evident, at that particular point whose level is determined by *two* variants, the *slope* of the line and the *time* it is reached.

Of course, you cannot reasonably expect a pull-back rally to climb all the way back to a trendline that is ascending at a very steep angle, which may mean the attainment of a new high price for the entire Intermediate up trend; yet even that happens in more than just a few cases.   What can be counted on in the great majority of typical up trendlines (those which slant up at a normal or fairly flat angle) is that after the line has been broken a pull-back rally will develop, either in a few days or in the usual Minor wave tempo, and will carry prices back up to the projected trendline.

Throw-backs do not occur, it should be noted, when prices erupt through a *return* line, i.e., break out of the top-side of an up-trend channel.   Or, more correctly stated, the return line does not function as a support against a throw-back after prices have gone through it.   An unusually strong up-swing in a rising trend channel may carry beyond the top of the channel as defined by its return line, but the next reaction may go right back down through it without evidencing any hesitation at its level.

The throw-back is one of the mysteries in trendline price action to which we alluded at the outset. The technical analyst who studies trends and trendlines over any considerable period will discover many other even more mysterious phenomena which cannot find space in this treatise because no way has yet been found to put them to practical use in trading and investing. They are extraordinarily interesting in retrospect but are not subject to forecast.

INTERMEDIATE DOWN TRENDS

In all of the foregoing discussion of trends and trendlines we have concentrated on *up* trends; we have, in fact, had in mind specifically Intermediate advances in the direction of the Primary trend, i.e., within a Major Bull Market. Those particular trends are most apt to develop "normally," are most amenable to trendline definition. Intermediate *down* moves in a Major Bear Market may well be taken up next. Before we discuss the respects in which they differ from Primary advances, we should recall that the *basic trendline* on a down move is the line projected across the *tops* of the rallies within it. The trend channel will be to the left of that trendline and below it on the chart. The *return* line (if any) will define the *bottom* of the channel.

Intermediate (Bear Market) down trends are far less regular and uniform in their development than Bull Market advances. Their angles of decline are characteristically steeper and this is particularly true, of course, of the panic moves which are typical of the second phase of a Bear Market, as we saw in our discussion of Major trends in Chapter III. Moreover, prices have a tendency to drop away from any trendline which is drawn across the first two rally tops; in other words, to curve down or accelerate as the move proceeds. This shows plainly on an arithmetically scaled chart and, even more conspicuously on a semi-logarithmic sheet.

The *practical* results of this down-curving tendency are not so important in so far as it delays the penetration of the original trendline and, hence, the giving of a signal of trend change. The fact is that prices tend to thrash around for some time making a base at the bottom of one of these precipitous declines. In so doing they work out sidewise on the chart and the trend frequently does not turn up visibly until after the trendline has finally been reached and broken through on the up-side after all. Thus there is justification for drawing down trendlines and keeping them in view even though they may seem for some time simply to travel off into space with no apparent relevance to the actual trend of prices.

It naturally follows from the above that return lines on most Bear Market declines have little practical utility; they are more often than not very quickly broken down-side. Good channels are hard to find.

FIGURE 160.   A study in Bear Market trends.   "NWA" broke down from a Descending Triangle in January, 1946, simultaneously penetrating its Intermediate up trendline (IUT).   A tentative Major up trendline (MUT) had already been punctured.   "NWA" then went into a twenty-week Rectangle, broke down in June, pulled back to the Rectangle bottom line (RB) in August, and collapsed.   Note that a (tentative) third fan was never quite reached.

However—and this is of considerable practical importance—the very last Intermediate down swing in a Major Bear Market, i.e., the last Primary move which leads to the final long-term bottom, is usually cleaner, more regular, less precipitous—in other words, a more nearly normal trend of the sort we expect to find in most Intermediate advances in a Bull Market (except, of course, that it slants down instead of up). This interesting habit is, as we said, of practical importance. Knowing it, we have an additional and very useful clue to the end of a Bear Market.

When, after a Major Bear trend has proceeded for some time and distance and has experienced at least one panic sell-off, it then goes off in another but less active and more orderly decline and this decline develops and follows a good trendline, watch it closely. If this Intermediate holds to its steady and not too steep downward course—if its trendline is contacted several times by Minor rallies—if it produces a fairly consistent channel and prices do not "fall out of bed" down through its parallel return line, then the eventual up-side penetration of this trendline may well signal a *Major* turn, the inception of a new Bull Market.

CORRECTIVE TRENDS—THE FAN PRINCIPLE

In this study of Intermediate trendlines we have left to be taken up last the subject of Secondary or corrective trends. These are the Intermediate declines which interrupt the Primary advances in a Bull Market, and the intermediate recoveries which alternate with Primary declines in Bear Markets.

Intermediate reactions against the Major direction of the market take a variety of forms. Sometimes, as we have seen in our earlier study of chart patterns, they run out into consolidation formations—Triangles, Rectangles, etc. —in which the net price reaction is of minor consequence but time is consumed in backing and filling before the Primary trend can be resumed. In such cases, of course, there is no basis for drawing an Intermediate trendline, nor is one needed for any practical purpose.

At the other extreme, so to speak, we find corrective swings which develop as a more or less orderly straight-line return of moderate slope to the nearest good Intermediate support or resistance level, retracing perhaps a third to a half of the preceding Primary swing. These reactions produce good trendlines as a rule, and the eventual penetration of their trendlines is a good technical signal of reversal. Intermediate corrections clearly of this type, it may be added, are relatively rare.

A third form taken by Intermediate corrections is nearly as common as the first named above (consolidation pattern) and much more common on the charts than the second. In a Bull Market, it starts with a sharp reaction which proceeds for several days—perhaps for as much as two weeks—producing a steep Minor trendline. This line is broken up-side by a quick Minor rally after which prices slide off again in a duller and less precipitate trend. A second Minor trendline may now be drawn from the original high point across the top of the up-thrust that broke the first trend. This second trendline is broken by another partial recovery thrust and a third and still duller and flatter sell-off ensues. A third trendline can now be drawn from the original high across the top of the second up-thrust. The whole move by this time has taken roughly and irregularly a "saucering out" form. The three trendlines drawn from the original reversal point from which the corrective decline started, each at a flatter angle than its predecessor, are known as *fan lines*. And the rule is that when the *third* fan line is broken upside, the low of the Intermediate correction has been seen.

There are exceptions to this rule—as there are to every so-called rule of technical chart analysis. Rarely a correction of this type will go on to make another dip to a new low for the whole corrective move before prices really start to round up again. But the three-fan principle works in the great majority of cases. Moreover, it offers the trader an opportunity to take a position at a

FIGURE 161. A valid application of the three-fan principle. Note that prices, after they pushed up through F1 in March, fell back to it but did not re-penetrate it. When F2 was broken in late March, prices came back to it at the end of April but did not go below it. F3 was surmounted in May. This was a Bull Market reaction; "AS" made its final top above 64 in August. The March-May pattern might be called a weak Double Bottom.

point where he can logically employ a very close stop order and thus limit his loss to a trivial amount if the rule does not work out.

It is interesting to note that prices consistently throw back in these movements to the preceding fan line after each up thrust. The new Primary swing, once the low has been passed, usually starts slowly and carries out for a time the saucer picture.

The three-fan rule works just as well in calling the turn on Intermediate recoveries in a Bear Market, the majority of which take the rounding form which is adapted to its use.

Note, however, that the fan principle is normally applied only to corrective moves, i.e., to determine the end of Intermediate reactions in a Bull Market and of Intermediate recoveries in a Bear Market.

We shall take up Major trendlines in the following chapter but, before we leave this study of Intermediate trends, it will be well to state again that the practical application of trendlines in actual trading requires experience, and the good judgment to be attained only therefrom. Some technical analysts depend largely on trendline studies; a few attempt to use trendlines almost exclusively; but the majority have found that they are best employed as an adjunct to other technical data.

Technical analysis of a stock chart is something like putting together a jig-

FIGURE 162. Try the three-fan principle on this chart of the late 1944 Bull Market reaction (out of a Symmetrical Triangle) in "DH." F1 should be drawn from the August 30 high down across the September 12 closing. F2 is already marked on the chart but not labeled. F3 would extend from August 30 across the rally top of November 9. It was surmounted on increased volume November 21. The mid-September to November price pattern looked at first like a Descending Triangle *but* volume began to rise in October.

saw puzzle.   There are many items to be considered—among them volume, pattern and the measurements derived therefrom, support and resistance levels, trendlines, general market prospects—and all fitted into place to get the complete picture.

FIGURE 163.   Important trendlines developed by Texas Co. in the last half of the 1932-37 Bull Market.   A and B were Intermediate up trendlines.   C was a tentative IUT drawn from the October, 1936 low across the Minor reaction of late November, but obviously so steep that its penetration could hardly be figured to have important reversal significance.   The Major trend here, on an arithmetically scaled chart, would be a staight line through the September, 1935 low, and the June and September, 1936 lows, and would have been broken in September, 1937.   The line marked M, however, drawn through the June and September, 1936 lows was also broken in September, 1937, regardless of whether the scaling was logarithmic or arithmetic. (Questions involving Major trendlines will be discussed in more detail in Chapter XV.)

The July, 1937 pull-back to line B produced a Double Top which was completed with a down signal the second week of September, simultaneously with the penetration of line M.

Note large Ascending Triangle in 1936.

CHAPTER XV

MAJOR TRENDLINES

IN THE preceding chapter on Intermediate trendlines, mention was made of the distinctive effects produced by arithmetic and semi-logarithmic plotting, but it was noted that these differences were unimportant in connection with Minor trends or Intermediate trends of average duration. When we come to Major trends, however, we find the difference does become important.

If you will examine a large collection of arithmetically scaled monthly charts covering ten years or more of market history, you will quickly see that Bull trends in the great majority of actively traded, more or less speculative common stocks tend to *accelerate*. They start slowly and push up at a steeper and steeper angle as they approach a Major top. This up-curving path takes them farther and farther away from any straight trendline drawn from two bottom points in the first, slow-moving stage of advance. As a consequence, they top out and have gone down a long way in a recession which may be of Major consequence before their straight trendline is again touched.

Many of the stocks which show such typical *accelerating* curves in their advancing (Major) trends on arithmetic paper, produce *straight* trends on a logarithmic scale. As a consequence their logarithmic Major trendlines are broken more quickly, and usually at a higher price level, when at last their trends do top out and turn down. In the case of such stocks, then, the logarithmic scale gives a better trend signal.

But there are other stocks—mostly of the more substantial investment or semi-investment type—which tend to advance in straight arithmetic trends. Consolidated Edison, General Motors and Libbey-Owens-Ford Glass are examples. (The trends of these on logarithmic scale show a decelerating curve, of course.) Still a third class, made up largely of high-grade preferred stocks, produces a rounding over or decelerating Bull trendline even on the arithmetic scale. And, finally, there are a number of issues whose normal Bull Market trendlines fall somewhere between our first two types; that is, they curve up away from a straight path on the arithmetic scale, but curve over to the right (breaking through a straight line) on the logarithmic scale.

All of which, the reader at this point no doubt finds most discouraging. Some stocks do this and some stocks do that, and what help is there for us in such a mix-up? The answer lies in studying the past history of each issue in which you may be interested. Stocks—most of them at least—do not change their habits and their technical characteristics much from one Bull and Bear cycle to the next. An issue which, like General Motors, produces a straight-line Bull trend on an arithmetic chart in one Primary up swing is likely to repeat that performance in the next.

As a matter of interest, stocks do sometimes change, of course, over a long period of years. Companies which were regarded as extremely speculative when their shares were first listed may attain a more and more important and stable position in the general economy with the result that eventually their stock acquires a solid investment rating. Their Bull Market trends will then gradu-ally change from an up curve to a straight line and, finally, to a decelerating curve. Other old-established corporations may lose position and rating, shift from the investment type of trendline to the speculative. But it is true in general, nevertheless, that Major patterns do repeat.

If you are keeping your own set of monthly charts, you can choose which-ever scale you please. But most technical chart followers prefer to buy their long-range pictures ready made, thereby getting a much more extensive back history of many more issues than they could hope to chart themselves. Since the only comprehensive portfolios of monthly charts that are available at rea-sonable cost are arithmetically scaled, you will perforce have to make these serve all purposes.* You will find with a little experimentation that an archi-tect's French curve can be used to plot good Major up-trend lines on many of the issues whose normal Bull trends accelerate away from a straight line.

The tests for the technical significance of a Major trendline are substantially the same as those specified for Intermediate lines in the preceding chapter. A little more leeway must be allowed on penetrations—again a matter of judgment —but you are dealing with coarse data and long swings here and what you want from your monthly charts primarily is perspective on the broad picture.

One more point regarding the construction of Major Bull trendlines: the best lines—the most useful—are drawn, as a rule, not from the absolute low of the preceding Bear Market but starting rather from the next Intermediate bottom. The accumulation area at the beginning of a Bull Market is usually long drawn out in time and relatively flat. The first trendline that can be drawn from the extreme low point may, therefore, be too nearly horizontal to express the genuine Bull trend which starts with the mark-up phase. The sev-eral charts showing Major trendlines which illustrate this chapter will demon-strate the point. It applies as well, we might add, to many Intermediate moves which start from area formations. Take the Head-and-Shoulders pattern for example: the true Intermediate trendline usually starts from the right shoulder rather than from the head.

---

* Books of monthly charts including nearly all of the issues listed on the New York Stock Exchange are published by F. W. Stephens, 87 Nassau St., New York 38, N. Y. and by M. C. Horsey & Co., 37 Wall St., New York 5, N. Y. Monthly charts of about 500 stocks logarith-mically scaled are published by Securities Research Corp., 141 Milk St., Boston 9, Mass.

FIGURE 164   FIGURE 165

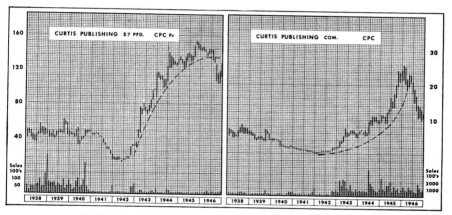

FIGURE 166   FIGURE 167

CONTRASTS IN BULL TRENDS

FIGURE 164.   The straight-line Bull Market trend of General Motors on an arithmetic monthly chart.   1941 low, 28⅝; 1946 high, 80⅜.

FIGURE 165.   The up-curving trend of a speculative motors stock, Hudson Motors.   Compare this with "GM."   1941 low, 2⅝; 1946 high, 34½.

FIGURE 166.   Typical de-curving Major Bull trend of a high-grade preferred stock.   This is Curtis Publishing $7 Preferred.   1942 low, 12; 1945 high, 154.

FIGURE 167.   The accelerating up trend of the common stock of the same publishing company.   1942 low, ⅜; 1946 high, 26.

FIGURE 168   FIGURE 169

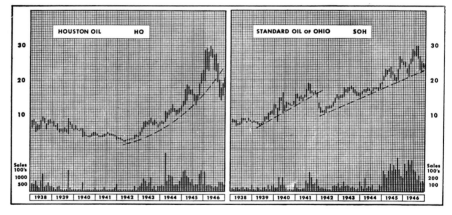

FIGURE 170   FIGURE 171

CONTRASTS IN BULL TRENDS

FIGURE 168.   A conservative investment type Utility stock makes a straight-line Major Bull trend.   This is Commonwealth Edison.   1942 low, 17⅜; 1946 high, 36⅛.   Leverage is an important factor in trends.

FIGURE 169.   The up-curving trend of a low-priced "junior" Utility, International Hydro-Electric A.   1942 low, ¼; 1946 high, 15½.

FIGURE 170.   A speculative Oil stock, Houston Oil.   1942 low, 2¼; 1946 high, 30.   Compare this picture with "SOH" in Figure 171.

FIGURE 171.   Straight-line up trends in an investment Oil, Standard Oil of Ohio.   1942 low, 10⅛; 1946 high, 30.   Note: trendline unbroken until 1948.

FIGURE 172   FIGURE 173

FIGURE 174   FIGURE 175

TYPICAL TRENDS

FIGURE 172. Steel stocks have the speculative or accelerating type of Primary up trend. Republic Steel. 1942 low, 13⅜; 1946 high, 40⅞.

FIGURE 173. The normal Major Bull trend of heavy industrial issues is up-curving. American Car & Foundry. 1942 low, 20; 1946 high, 72⅜.

FIGURE 174. A low-priced building stock, Celotex Corp. 1942 low 6⅛; 1946 high, 38⅛.

FIGURE 175. A highly speculative, low-priced issue, traded on the Curb Exchange, Claude Neon Lights. 1942 low, ⅛; 1946 high, 9.

FIGURE 176   FIGURE 177

TYPICAL BULL TRENDS

FIGURE 176. The Tobacco stocks follow the investment type of trend. This is Liggett & Myers. Note double trendline. 1942 low, 50½; 1946 high, 103½.

FIGURE 177. High-grade Food issues (this is Corn Products Refining) resemble the Tobaccos. 1940 low, 40¼; 1946 high, 75¾.

MAJOR DOWN TRENDS

From the technical analyst's point of view, it is to be regretted that few Bear Markets have produced Major trendlines of any practical significance on the charts of individual stocks. A notable exception was the long Bear Market of 1929-1932 which produced magnificently straight trendlines on the arithmetic plotting of a host of issues (as well as in the averages to which we shall refer later). But it is almost impossible to find other instances where a Bear trendline having any forecasting value could be drawn on either arithmetic or semi-logarithmic scale.

The *normal* Major Bear Market trend is not only much steeper than the normal Bull trend (because Bear Markets last on the average only about half as long as Bull Markets) but it is also accelerating or down-curving in its course. This feature is accentuated and, hence, particularly difficult to project effectively on the semi-logarithmic scale.

The net of it is that the technician cannot expect to obtain much if any help from his *Major* trendlines in determining the change from a Primary *down* to a Primary *up* swing. This should not be taken, however, as advice to draw no trendlines whatever on a Major down move, or to disregard entirely any trendlines which may develop with some appearance of authority. If you do

FIGURE 178. In the process of "pulling back" to a very steep up trendline, prices may easily go to a new high. Note the pull-back of August 1936 in this weekly chart of Westinghouse Electric. The second, less steep line turned out to be the true Major Bull trend. Note that the February-April price pattern in 1936 could not be considered a true Double Top reversal of Primary import because the recession between the two highs was only about 10% of the top's value (around 122). Figure 64 on page 110 shows on a daily chart the final top reversal formation which "WX" made in 1937.

A large Rectangle base was made on this weekly chart in April, May and June, 1937, but observe the poor volume which accompanied the breakout and rise from that formation—an extremely bearish indication for the Major trend. The "measurement" of the Rectangle was carried out by August, but that was all.

As is usually the case, it was impossible to draw a Major down trendline which had any forecasting value on this chart. The beautiful straight trendlines which appeared in the 1929-32 Primary Bear Market led many chart students to expect similar developments in every Bear Market, but the fact is that 1929-32 was unique in that respect.

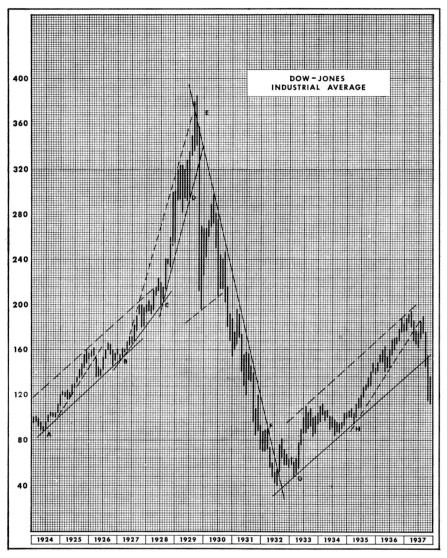

FIGURE 179. The 1929-32 Primary Bear Market was the only one in all stock market records which produced a straight line Major down trend. Trace also the support and resistance levels throughout this fourteen-year history of the Dow Industrials. Each rally in the great Bear move stopped at or near a previous bottom level. Each decline stopped near the level of a congestion in the 1924-29 Bull Market. See also level of 1937 top.

not expect too much of them, they may nevertheless afford some useful clue as to the way in which conditions are tending to change.

The student of stock market action who is not altogether concerned with dollars and cents results from his researches will find Bear Market trendlines a fascinating field of inquiry. They do some strange things. Even though they fail in the practical function of calling the actual Major turn, and go shooting off into space, they sometimes produce curious reactions (or, at least, appear to produce what would be otherwise inexplicable market action) when the real price trend catches up with them months or years later. But such effects, interesting as they may be, are in our present state of knowledge uncertain and unpredictable.

We must dismiss this rather unfruitful topic with the reminder that one clue to the end of a Primary Bear Market is afforded by the Intermediate trendline of its final phase which we cited in the preceding chapter.

Major Trend Channels

We run into another difficulty when we try to draw return lines and construct channels for Major trends on an arithmetic chart. Owing to the marked tendency for prices to fluctuate in ever wider swings (both Intermediate and Minor) as they work upward in a Primary Bull Market, their channel grows progressively broader. The return line does not run parallel to the basic trendline (assuming that we have a good basic trendline to begin with) but diverges from it. Occasionally a stock produces a clear-cut Major channel pattern, but the majority do not.

Semi-logarithmic scaling will in many cases correct for the widening channel effect in Bull trends, but then we run into the opposite tendency in Primary Bear Markets and for that neither type of scaling will compensate.

Trendlines in the Averages

Practically everything stated in the preceding chapter regarding Intermediate trendline development in individual stocks applies as well to the various averages. The broad averages or indexes, in fact, produce more regular trends and, in consequence, more exactly applicable trendlines. This may be due in part to the fact that most averages are composed of active, well-publicized and widely owned issues whose market action individually is "normal" in the technical sense. Another reason is that the process of averaging smooths out vagaries of component stocks, and the result thus more truly reflects the deep and relatively steady economic trends and tides.

In any event, it is a fact that such averages as the Dow-Jones Rails, Industrials and 65-Stock Composite, the New York *Times* 50 and the New York *Herald Tribune* 100-Stock Composite, and Standard & Poor's average of 90 stocks (the last two named being probably the most scientifically composed to typify the entire broad market) do propagate excellent trendlines on their charts.

The very accuracy of their trends, particularly their Intermediate moves, permits us to construe their trendlines more tightly. Less leeway need be allowed for doubtful penetrations. Thus, while we ask for a 3% penetration in the case of an individual stock of medium range, 2% is ample in the averages to give a dependable break signal.

We cannot trade in the averages. Our actual commitments must be made in individual stocks. But experienced traders know that it pays to heed the broad market trend. It is easier to swim with the tide than against it.

CHAPTER XVI

TECHNICAL ANALYSIS OF COMMODITY CHARTS

A LITTLE thought suggests that the variously interesting and significant patterns which we have examined in the foregoing chapters on stock charts should logically appear as well in the charts of any other equities and commodities that are freely, constantly and actively bought and sold on organized public exchanges. And this, in general, is true. The price trends of anything whose market value is determined solely (or to all practical purposes within very wide limits) by the free interplay of supply and demand will, when graphically projected, show the same pictorial phenomena of rise and fall, accumulation and distribution, congestion, consolidation and reversal that we have seen in stock market trends. Speculative aims and speculators' psychology are the same whether the goods dealt in be corporate shares or contracts for the future delivery of cotton bales.

It should be possible in theory, therefore, to apply our principles of technical analysis to any of the active commodity futures (wheat, corn, oats, cotton, wooltops, cocoa, hides, eggs, etc.) for which accurate daily price and volume data are published. It should be, that is, if proper allowance be made for the instrinsic differences between commodity future contracts and stocks and bonds.

In previous editions of this book traders who cast longing eyes on the big, quick profits apparently available in wheat, for example, were warned that commodity charts were "of very little help," as of 1947.

It was pointed out that successful technical analysis of commodity futures charts had been possible up to about 1941 or 1942. But that the domination of these markets thereafter by government regulations, loans and purchases—so completely subject to the changing (and often conflicting) policies and acts of the several governmental agencies concerned with grains and other commodities —had seriously distorted the normal evaluative machinery of the market. At that time radical reversals of trend could and did happen overnight without any warning so far as the action of the market could show. The ordinary and orderly fluctuations in supply-demand balance which create significant definite patterns for the technician to read, did not exist. And while fortunes were made (and lost) in wheat, corn and cotton futures during the World War II period, it is safe to say they were not made from the charts.

However, during the past five or six years the application of technical methods to commodity trading has been re-examined. Under today's conditions

271

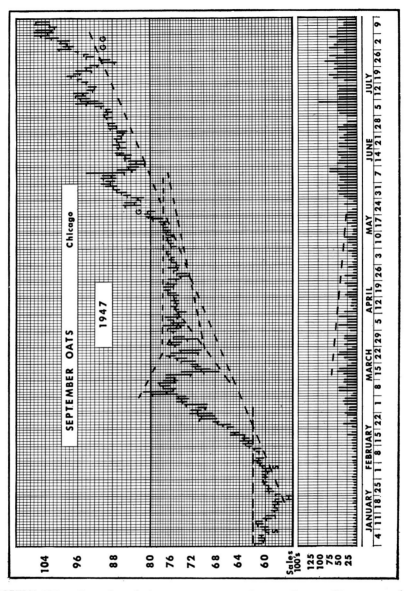

FIGURE 180.   Oats, for obvious reasons, traced more "normal" patterns than Wheat during the 1940s.   This chart contains an H & S bottom, a Symmetrical Triangle which merged into the Ascending form, a gap through a former top level and an interesting trendline.   The Island shake-out through the trendline was an extremely deceptive development.

(1956) it appears that charts can be a most valuable tool to the commodity trader. The effects of present government regulation have apparently resulted in "more orderly" markets without destroying their evaluative function. And allowing for the various essential differences between commodities and securities the basic technical methods can be applied.

It may be in order to discuss briefly some of the intrinsic differences between commodity futures and stocks referred to above, and some of the special traits of commodity charts. To begin with, the most important difference is that the contracts for future delivery which are the stock-in-trade of the commodity exchange, have a limited life. For example, the October cotton contract for any given year has a trading life of about eighteen months. It comes "on the board" as a "new issue," is traded in with volume increasing more or less steadily during that period, and then vanishes. Theoretically, it is a distinct and separate commodity from all other cotton deliveries. Practically, of course, it seldom gets far out of line with such other deliveries as are being bought and sold during the same period, or with the "cash" price of the physical cotton in warehouse. Nevertheless, it has this special quality of a limited independent life, as a consequence of which long-term support and resistances levels have no meaning whatever.

Secondly, a very large share of the transactions in commodity futures—as much as 80% certainly in normal times—represent commercial hedging rather than speculation. (It is in fact entered into to obviate risk, to avoid speculation.) Hence, even near-term support and resistance levels have relatively less potency than with stocks. Also, since hedging is to a considerable degree subject to seasonal factors, there are definite seasonal influences on the commodity price trends which the commodity speculator must keep in mind, even if only to weigh the meaning of their apparent absence at any given period.

A third difference is in the matter of volume. The interpretation of volume with respect to trading in stocks is relatively simple. But it is greatly complicated in commodities by the fact that there is, in theory, no limit to the number of contracts for a certain future delivery which may be sold in advance of that delivery date. In the case of any given stock, the number of shares outstanding is always known. As this is written, there are in the hands of stockholders 13,700,203 common shares of Consolidated Edison and that quantity has not varied for many years nor is it likely to change for several years to come. Every transaction in Consolidated Edison involves an actual transfer of one or more of those existing shares. In the case of commodity future contracts, however— say, September wheat—trading begins long before anyone knows how many bushels of wheat will exist to be delivered that coming September, and the open interest at some time during the life of the contract may exceed the potential supply many times over—and all quite legitimately.

One more important difference may be mentioned. Certain kinds of news

FIGURE 181. In contrast with the grains, the technical action of the Cotton futures markets has been fairly consistent with normal supply-demand functioning ever since prices rose well above government support levels. In this daily chart of the 1947 October delivery (New York Cotton Exchange) the reader will find a variety of familiar technical formations, including critical trendlines, a Head-and-Shoulders top that was never completed (no breakout), and support-resistance phenomena much the same as appear in stock charts. Double trendlines are not at all unusual in Cotton charts.

Volume of transactions in Cotton as well as grains, incidentally, is always reported a day late; i.e., Monday's volume is not published until Wednesday morning. This is a handicap to the technician who wishes to trade on the smaller fluctuations unless he has contacts with brokers' floor representatives who can keep him informed. For the more conservative trader who is interested only in the wider swings, the lag of a day in getting turnover figures does not matter.

—news about weather, drought, floods, etc., that affect the growing crop, if we are dealing with an agricultural commodity, can change the trend of the futures market immediately and drastically and are not in the present stage of our weather knowledge foreseeable. Analogous developments in the stock market are extremely rare.

Under what might be called normal market conditions, those chart patterns which reflect trend changes in most simple and logical fashion work just as well with commodities as with stocks. Among these we would list Head-and-Shoulders formations, Rounding Tops and Bottoms, basic trendlines. Trendlines, in fact, are somewhat better defined and more useful than in stocks. Other types of chart formations which are associated in stocks with short-term trading or with group distribution and accumulation, such as the Triangles, Rectangles, Flags, etc., appear less frequently in commodities and are far less reliable as to either direction or extent of ensuing move. Support and resistance levels, as we have already noted, are less potent in commodities than in stocks; sometimes they seem to work to perfection but just as often they don't. For similar reasons, gaps have relatively less technical significance.

It is not the purpose of this book to explain the operation of commodity futures markets, nor to offer instruction to those who wish to trade therein. This brief chapter is included only as a starter for readers who may want to pursue the study further. They should be advised that successful speculation in commodities requires far more specialized knowledge, demands more constant daily and hourly attention. The ordinary individual can hope to attain a fair degree of success in investing in securities by devoting only his spare moments to his charts, but he might better shun commodity speculation entirely unless he is prepared to make a career of it.

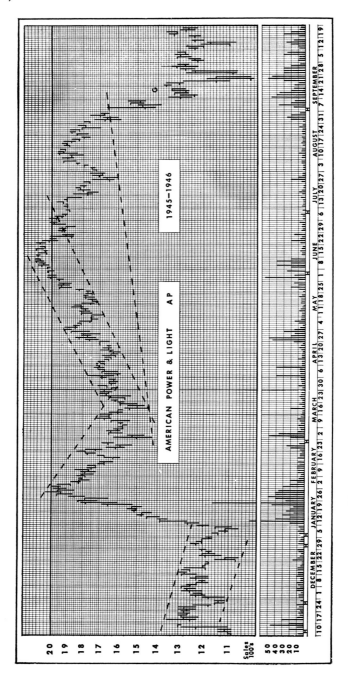

FIGURE 182. This 1946 Bull Market top was practically impossible to detect as such by reference to "AP's" chart alone, until after it had already lost 25% of its top value. Trendlines were helpful but no reversal pattern of obvious Major importance appeared until the August recovery move failed, thereby putting a brief right shoulder on a rather misshapen, but nevertheless recognizable, seven-month Head-and-Shoulders.

CHAPTER XVII

A SUMMARY AND SOME CONCLUDING COMMENTS

WE BEGAN our study of technical stock chart analysis in Chapter I with a discussion of the *philosophy* underlying the technical approach to the problems of trading and investing. We could ask that the reader turn back now and review those few pages to recapture a perspective on the subject which must have been dimmed by the many pages of more or less arduous reading that have intervened.

For it is easy, in a detailed study of the many and fascinating phenomena which stock charts exhibit, to lose sight of the fact that they are only the rather imperfect instruments by which we hope to gauge the relative strength of supply and demand, which in turn exclusively determines what way, how fast and how far a stock will go.

Remember that in this work it doesn't in the least matter what *creates* the supply and the demand. The fact of their existence and the balance between them are all that count. No man, no organization (and we mean this *verbatim et literatim*) can hope to know and accurately to appraise the infinity of factual data, mass moods, individual necessities, hopes, fears, estimates and guesses which, with the subtle alterations ever proceeding in the general economic framework, combine to generate supply and demand. But the summation of all these factors is reflected virtually instantaneously in the market.

The technical analyst's task then is to interpret the action of the market itself—to read the flux in supply and demand mirrored therein. For this task, charts are the most satisfactory tools thus far devised. Lest you become enrapt, however, with the mechanics of the chart—the minutiae of daily fluctuations—ask yourself constantly, "What does this action really mean in terms of supply and demand?"

Judgment is required, and perspective, and a constant reversion to first principles. A chart, as we have said and should never forget, is not a perfect tool; it is not a robot; it does not give all the answers quickly, easily and positively, in terms that anyone can read and translate at once into certain profit.

We have examined and tested exhaustively many technical theories, systems, indexes and devices which have not been discussed in this book, chiefly because they tend to short-circuit judgment, to seek the impossible by a purely mechanical approach to what is very far indeed from a purely mechanical problem. The methods of chart analysis which have been presented herein are those which

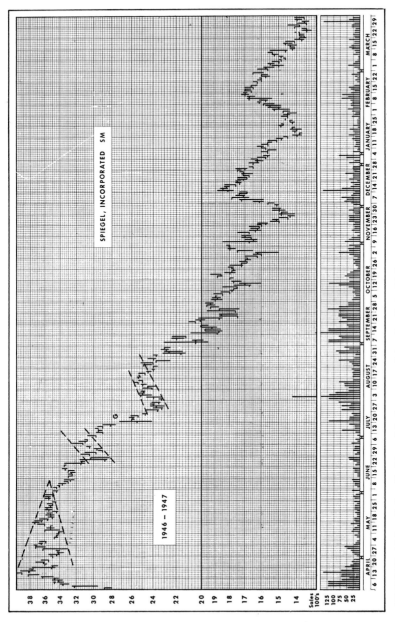

FIGURE 183.   Spiegel's Bear Market started in April 1946 from a Symmetrical Triangle which changed into a Descending Triangle.   Note the pull-back in June, and two Flags.   This history is carried on in Figure 184.

have proved most useful because they are relatively simple and, for the most part, easily rationalized; because they stick closely to first principles; because they are of a nature that does not lead us to expect too much of them; because they supplement each other and work well together.

Let us review these methods briefly. They fall roughly into four categories.

I. The **area patterns or formations** of price fluctuation which, with their concomitant volume, indicate an important change in the supply-demand balance. They can signify consolidation, a recuperation or gathering of strength for renewed drive in the *same direction* as the trend which preceded them. Or they can indicate reversal, the playing out of the force formerly prevailing and the victory of the opposing force, resulting in a new drive in the *reverse direction*. In either case, they may be described as periods during which energy is brewed or pressure built up to propel prices in a move (up or down) which can be turned to profit. Some of them provide an indication as to how far their pressure will push prices.

These chart formations, together with volume, furnish the technician with most of his "get in" and many of his "get out" signals.

Volume, which has not been discussed in this book as a feature apart from price action and which cannot, in fact, be utilized as a technical guide by itself, deserves some further comment. Remember that it is *relative,* that it tends naturally to run higher near the top of a Bull Market than near the bottom of a Bear Market. Volume "follows the trend"; i.e., it increases on rallies and decreases on reactions in an over-all up trend, and vice-versa. But use this rule judiciously; do not place too much dependence on the showing of a few days, and bear in mind that even in a Bear Market (except during panic moves) there is always a slight tendency for activity to pick up on rises. ("Prices can fall of their own weight, but it takes buying to put them up.")

A notable increase in activity, as compared with previous days or weeks, may signify either the beginning (breakout) or the end (climax) of a move, temporary or final. (More rarely it may signify a "shake-out.") Its meaning in any given case can be determined by its relation to the price pattern.

II. **Trend and trendline studies,** which supplement area patterns as a means of determining the general direction in which prices are moving and of detecting changes in direction. Although lacking in many cases the nice definition of area formations, they may frequently be used for "get in" and "get out" purposes in short-term trading, and they provide a defense against premature relinquishment of profitable long-term positions.

III. **Support and resistance levels** created by the previous trading and investing commitments of others. They may serve to indicate where it should pay to take a position, but their more important technical function is to show

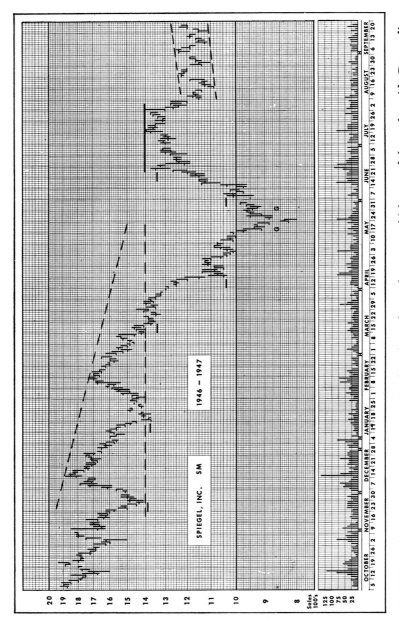

FIGURE 184. Overlapping Figure 183, this chart shows the move which ensued from the wide Descending Triangle of early 1947, culminating in a Reversal Day on May 19. Note various Minor and Intermediate resistance levels.

where a move is likely to slow down or end, at what level it should encounter a sudden and important increase in supply or demand as the case may be.

Before entering a trade, look both to the pattern of origin for an indication of the power behind the move and to the history of support-resistance for an indication as to whether it can proceed without difficulty for a profitable distance. Support-resistance studies are especially useful in providing "cash in" or "switch" signals.

IV. **Broad market background,** including the Dow Theory. Do not scorn this time-tested device for designating the (presumed) prevailing Major trend of the market. Its signals are "late" but, with all its faults (and one of these is the greatly augmented following it has acquired in recent years, resulting in a considerable artificial stimulation of activity at certain periods), it is still an invaluable adjunct to the technical trader's kit of tools.

The general characteristics of the various stages in the stock market's great Primary Bull and Bear cycles, which were discussed in our Dow Theory chapters, should never be lost to view. This brings us back to the idea of *perspective* which we emphasized as essential to successful technical analysis at the beginning of our summary. It is true that you cannot buy or sell "the market"; you can deal only in individual stocks. But that stock which does not to some degree follow the Major trend of the market as a whole is an extraordinary exception. More money has been lost by buying perfectly good stocks in the later and most exciting phases of a Bull Market and then selling them, perhaps from necessity in the discouraging conditions prevailing in a Bear Market than from all other causes combined!

So keep your perspective on the broad market picture. The basic economic tide is one of the most important elements in the supply-demand equation for each individual stock. It may pay to buck "the public" but it does not pay ever to buck the real underlying trend.

Major Bull and Bear Markets have recurred in fairly regular pattern throughout all recorded economic history and there is no reason to suppose that they will not continue to recur for as long as our present system exists. It is well to keep in mind that caution is in order whenever stock prices are at historically high levels, and that purchases will usually work out well eventually when they are at historically low levels.

Giving due weight to the long, rising secular trend of American industry and the ever declining value of the dollar, one might say that the stock market is nowadays in a "danger zone" whenever the Dow-Jones Industrial average, to use that popular index as a gauge, ranges above 250, and that it is in safe territory whenever it ranges below 150 (although it climbed to 381.17 in 1929 and went down to 41.22 in 1932, and reached 521.05 on April 6, 1956).*

* See note at end of chapter

If you publish your interest in your charts, you will be told that the chart analyst (like the Dow theorist) is always late—that he buys after prices have already started up, maybe not until long after the "wise boys" have completed their accumulation, and that he sells after the trend has unmistakably turned down. Partly true, as you have no doubt already discovered for yourself. But the secret of success lies not in buying at the very lowest possible price and selling at the absolute top. It is in the *avoidance of large losses*. (Small losses you will have to take occasionally.)

One of the most successful "operators" Wall Street has ever seen, a multi-millionaire and a nationally respected citizen today, is reputed to have said that never in his entire career had he succeeded in buying within five points of the bottoms or selling within five points of the top!

Before we leave this treatise on theory and proceed to the more practical matters of application and market tactics which are the province of the second part of this book, the reader will, we hope, forgive one more admonition. There is nothing in the science of technical analysis which requires one always to have a position in the market. There is nothing which dictates that something must happen every day. There are periods—sometimes long months—when the conservative trader's best policy is to stay out entirely. And there is nothing in technical analysis to compel the market to go ahead and complete in a few days a move which the charts have foretold; it will take its own good time. Patience is as much a virtue in stock trading as in any other human activity.

---

* Guideline figures suggested are based on 1948 when Mr. Edwards wrote this commentary. Obviously, in the 1970s these would need major upward adjustment.

TECHNICAL ANALYSIS
OF STOCK TRENDS

PART TWO

TRADING
TACTICS

MIDWORD

As a kind of foreword to the second part of this book we might mention a commentary, "On Understanding Science: An Historical Approach" by James Bryant Conant, president emeritus of Harvard University.

Dr. Conant points out that in school we learn that science is a systematic collection of facts, which are then classified in orderly array, broken down, analyzed, examined, synthesized and pondered; and then lo! a Great Principle emerges, pat, perfect, and ready for use in industry, medicine, or what-have-you.

He further points out that all of this is a mistaken point of view which is held by most laymen. That discovery takes form little by little, shrouded in questioning, and only gradually assumes the substance of a clear, precise, well-supported Theory. The neat tabulation of basic data, forming a series of proofs and checks, does not come at the start, but much later. In fact it may be the work of other men entirely, men who, being furnished with the conclusions, are then able to construct a complete integrated body of evidence. Theories of market action are not conceived in a flash of inspiration. They are built, step by step, out of the experience of traders and students, to explain the typical phenomena that appear over and over again through the years.

In market operations, the practical trader is not concerned with Theory *as such*. The neophyte's question, "What is the method?" probably means, actually, "What can I buy to make a lot of money easily, quickly?" If such a trader reads this book he may feel that there is "something in it." He may feel "It's worth a try" (a statement, incidentally, that reflects little credit on his own previous tries). And he may start out quite optimistically, without any understanding of Theory, without any experience in these methods, and without any basis for real confidence in the method.

In such cases the chances are great that he will not enjoy, immediately, the easy success he hopes for. His very inexperience in a new approach will result in mistakes and failures. But even with the most careful application of these methods in correctly entered commitments he may encounter a series of difficult market moves which may give him a succession of losses. Whereupon, having no solid confidence in what he is doing, he may sigh, put the book back on the shelf and say, "Just as I thought. It's no damn good."

Now if you were about to go into farming for the first time, you might be told (and it would be true) that the shade tobacco business offers spectacular profits. But you would not expect to gain these profits without investing capital, without studying how shade tobacco is grown, in what kinds of soils, in what localities, nor without some experience with the crop.

Furthermore you would need confidence—faith in the opportunity and also in the methods you were using. If your first season's crop were blighted (and these things do happen), you would naturally be disappointed. If it should happen that your second year's crop were destroyed by a hailstorm you would be hurt and understandably despondent. And if your third season's crop were to be a total loss due to drought, you would probably be very gloomy indeed (and who could blame you?). But you would *not* say, "There's nothing to it. It's no damn good."

You would know (if you had studied the industry and the approved cultural methods) that you were right regardless of any combination of unfavorable circumstances, and you would know that the ultimate rewards would justify your continuation no matter how hard the road, rather than a turn to some easier but less potentially profitable crop.

So it is with technical methods in the stock market. Anyone may encounter bad seasons. The *Major* turns inevitably will produce a succession of losses to Minor trend operators using the methods suggested in this book. And there will be times when a man who has no understanding of basic theory will be tempted to give up the method entirely and look for a "system" that will fit into the pattern of recent market action nicely, so that he can say, "If I had only averaged my trades . . . If I had followed the Dream Book . . . If I had taken Charlie's tip on **XYZ** . . . If I had done it *this* way or *that* way I would have come out with a neat profit."

It would be better, and safer, to understand at the start that no method that has ever been devised will unfailingly protect you against a loss, or sometimes even a painful succession of losses. You should realize that what we are looking for is the *probability* inherent in any situation. And just as you would be justified in expecting to draw a white bean from a bag which you *knew* contained 700 white beans and 300 black beans (even though you had just drawn out 10 black beans in succession!), so you are justified in continuing to follow the methods which over long periods seem most surely and most frequently to coincide with the mechanism of the market.

So this book should not be given a quick "once-over" and adopted straightway as a sure and easy road to riches. It should be read over and over, a number of times, and it should be consulted as a reference work. Furthermore, and most important, you will need the experience of your own successes and failures so that you will *know* that what you are doing is the only logical thing you *can* do under a given set of circumstances. In such a frame of mind you will have your portion of successes; and your failures, which you can take in stride as part of the business, will not ruin either your pocketbook or your morale.

In short, the problem stated and analyzed through this whole volume is not so much a matter of "systems" as it is a matter of philosophy. The end-result of your work in technical analysis is a deep understanding of what is going on in the competitive free auction, what is the mechanism of this auction, and what is the meaning of it all. And this philosophy does not grow on trees. It does not spring full-bodied from the sea-foam. It comes gradually from experience and from sincere, intelligent hard work.

The second section of this book, which follows, is concerned with tactics. Up to this point we have been studying the technical formations and their consequences. We should have a good general understanding of what is likely to happen after certain manifestations on the charts. Knowing that, however, we will still need a more definite set of guides as to *when* and *how* it is best to execute this or that sale.

This section is based on one man's experience and his analysis of thousands of specific cases. It takes up questions of method, of detail, and of application, and should provide you with a workable basis for your actual market operations. As time goes on you will very likely adopt refinements of your own, or modify some of the suggested methods according to your own experience. But the authors feel that the suggestions made here will enable you to use technical analysis in an intelligent and orderly way that should help to protect you from losses and increase your profits.

JOHN MAGEE

And, a postscript to these comments. With the publication of the 7th Printing of the Fifth Edition in early 1971 the basic trends and patterns of stocks continue to act very much in the same ways as they have over the past decades, to before the turn of the century. However, the never-easy path of the short term or "in-and-out" trader is considerably rougher and much more difficult, not because of changes in the technical behaviors of stocks, but on account of the increase in trading costs. During the Bear Market of 1969–1970 it became painfully evident that brokers were not able to cover their costs, and surcharges were added. It is likely that the combined expenses of commissions, transfer taxes, S.E.C. fee, odd lot fractions, and inevitable "execution losses" will tend to increase. So that as a matter of tactics it is less attractive than it once was to seize short term gains on Minor blow-offs; and more important to retain profitable positions, disregarding normal corrections and reactions, as long as the Major trend continues to look favorable.

CHAPTER XVIII

THE TACTICAL PROBLEM

I T IS possible (as many traders have discovered) to lose money in a Bull Market—and likewise to lose money trading short in a Bear Market. You may be perfectly correct in judging the Major trend; your long-term strategy, let us say, may be 100% right. But without tactics, without the ability to shape the details of the campaign on the field, it is not possible to put your knowledge to work to your best advantage.

There are several reasons why traders, especially inexperienced traders, so often do so poorly. At the time of buying a stock, if it should go up, they have no objectives, and no idea of what policy to use in deciding when to sell and take a profit. If it should go down they have no way of deciding when to sell and take a loss. Result: They often lose their profits; and their losses, instead of being nipped off quickly, run heavily against them. Also, there is this psychological handicap. The moment a stock is bought (or sold short), commissions and perhaps an odd-lot fraction are charged against the transaction. The trader knows that the moment he closes the trade there will be another set of charges. Also, since he is not likely to catch the extreme top of a rally or the extreme bottom of a reaction, he is bound, in most cases, to see the stock running perhaps several points against him after he has made his commitment. Even on a perfectly sound, wise trade, he may see a 10 or 15 percent paper loss (or even more), before the expected favorable move gets under way. Obviously, if he weakens and runs for cover without sufficient reason before the stock has made the profitable move he looked for, he is taking an unnecessary loss and forfeiting entirely his chance to register a gain.

The long-term investor who buys in near the bottom and remains in the market to a point near the top, and then liquidates and remains in cash or bonds until (perhaps several years later) there is another opportunity to buy in at the bottom, does not face the continual problem of when to buy and when to sell. This assumes that one can tell precisely when such a bottom has been reached, and that one can also tell when the trend has reached its ultimate top (and those are very broad assumptions indeed). The long-term investment problem for large gains over the Major trends is by no means as simple as it sounds when you say, "Buy them when they're low, and sell them near the top." However, such large gains have been made over the long pull, and they are very impressive.

This section of the book is concerned more particularly with the speculative purchase and sale of securities.

There are some basic differences between the "investment" point of view and the "speculative." It is a good thing to know these differences and make sure that you know exactly where you stand. Either viewpoint is tenable and workable, but you can create serious problems for yourself, and sustain heavy losses, if you confuse them.

One difference is that as a speculator you are dealing with stocks as such. A stock, to be sure, represents ownership in a company. But the stock is not

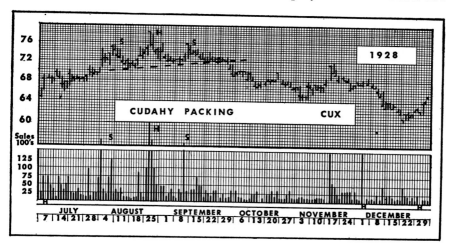

FIGURE 185. It is possible to lose money owning stocks in a Bull Market. Notice that this Major top formation did not occur in 1929, but in the summer of 1928. For more than a year after this, a majority of stocks and the averages continued the Bull Market advance. But Cudahy declined steadily, reaching a price below 50 well before the 1929 panic, and continued in its bearish course for over four years, ultimately selling at 20. Except for the somewhat unusual volume on the Head on August 21 this is a typical Head-and-Shoulders pattern with a perfect pull-back rally in mid November. It underscores what we have mentioned before; that a Head-and-Shoulders top in a stock, even when other stocks look strong, cannot safely be disregarded.

The Head-and-Shoulders pattern, either in its simple form or with multiple Heads or Shoulders is likely to occur at Major and Intermediate tops, and in reverse position at Major and Intermediate bottoms. It has the same general characteristics as to volume, duration, and breakout as the Rectangles, and the Ascending and Descending Triangles. In conservative stocks it tends to resemble the Rounding turns.

FIGURE 186.   What would you have done with Hudson Motors?   The great
panic move of October-November, 1929 carried the Dow-Jones Industrial
average down from its September all-time high of 386.10 to a November low
of 198.69.   A rally, bringing the average back to 294.07 in April, 1930, recovered 95 points or 51% of the ground lost, a perfectly normal correction.
    You can't trade in the averages.   But suppose you had bought HT after
the decline from its 1929 high of 93½, say at 56, in the belief that the 37
point drop had brought it into a "bargain" range.   On your daily chart you
would have seen the pattern shown above (which you will now recognize as
a Descending Triangle) taking shape in the early months of 1930.   Would
you have had a protective stop at 51?   Would you have sold at the market
the day after HT broke and closed below 54?   Or would you have hoped
for a rally, perhaps even bought more "bargains" at 50, at 48, at 40?   Would
you still have been holding onto your "good long-term investment" when HT
reached 25½ in June?   Would you *still* have been holding HT when it
reached its ultimate 1932 bottom at less than 3?   (See Figure 65.)

the same thing as the company. The securities of a strong company are often weak; and sometimes the securities of a very weak concern are exceedingly strong. It is important to realize that the company and the stock are not precisely identical. The technical method is concerned only with the value of the stock as perceived by those who buy, sell, or own it.

A second difference is in the matter of dividends. The "pure investor," who, by the way, is a very rare personage, is supposed to consider only the "income" or potential income from stocks; the return on his investment in cash dividends. But there are many cases of stocks which have maintained a steady dividend while losing as much as 75% or more of their capital value. There are other cases where stocks have made huge capital gains while paying only nominal dividends or none at all. If the dividend rate were as important as some investors consider it, the only research tool one would need would be a slide rule to determine the percentage yields of the various issues, and hence their "value." And on this basis stocks paying no dividends would have no value at all.

From the technical standpoint "Income," as separate from capital gains and losses, ceases to have any meaning. The amount realized in the sale of a stock, less the price paid and plus total dividends received, is the total gain. Whether the gain is made entirely in capital increase, or entirely in dividends, or in some combination of these, makes no difference. In the case of short sales the short seller must pay the dividends, but here again, this is simply one factor to be lumped with the capital gain or loss in determining the net result of the transaction.

There is a third source of confusion. Very often the "pure investor" will insist that he has no loss in the stock he paid $30 for, which is now selling at $22, because he has not sold it. Usually he will tell you that he has confidence in the company and that he will hold the stock until it recovers. Sometimes he will state emphatically that he never takes losses.

How such an investor would justify his position if he had bought Studebaker at over $40 in 1953 and still held Studebaker-Packard at around $5 in 1956, is hard to say. But for him the loss does not exist until it becomes a "realized" loss.

Actually his faith that eventually the stock will be again worth what he paid for it may be no more than a speculative hope; and a forlorn one at that.

Furthermore one may question whether his reasoning is always consistent. For example, suppose another stock this investor had bought at $30 was now selling at $45. Would he tell you that he did not consider a profit or loss until the stock was sold? Or would he be tempted to speak of the "profit" he had in this purchase?

It is all right to consider gains or losses either on the basis of "realized" or completed transactions, or on the basis of the market values "accrued" at a particular time. But it is not being honest with yourself to use one method to conceal your mistakes, and the other method to accentuate your successes. The confusion of these concepts is responsible for many financial tragedies.

As a trader using technical methods you will probably find the most realistic view is to consider your gains and losses "as accrued." In other words your gain or loss at a given time will be measured with reference to the closing price of the stock on that day.

Recapitulating, it is important (a) to avoid regarding a stock and the company it represents as identical or equivalent; (b) to avoid the conscious or unconscious attribution of "value" to a stock on the basis of dividend yield without regard to market prices; and (c) to avoid confusing "realized" and "accrued" gains or losses.*

The technical trader is not committed to a "buy and hold" policy. There are times when it is clearly advantageous to retain a position for many months, or for years. But there are also times when it will pay to get out of a stock, either with a profit, or with a loss. The successful technician will never, for emotional causes, remain in a situation which, on the evidence at hand is no longer tenable.

An experienced trader using technical methods can take advantage of the shorter Intermediate trends, and it can be shown that the possible net gains are larger than the entire net gains on the Major trend even after allowing for the greater costs in commissions and allowing for the greater income tax liability on short-term operations.

But it should be understood that any such additional profits are not easily won. They can be obtained only by continual alertness and adherence to systematic tactical methods. For the market, regarded as a gambling machine, compares very poorly with stud poker or roulette, and it is not possible to "beat the market" by the application of any simple mathematical system. If you doubt this it would be best to stop at this point and make a careful study of any such "system" that may appeal to you, checking it against a long record of actual market moves. Or ask yourself whether you have ever known anyone who followed such a system alone, as a guide to market operations, and was successful.

The technical analysis, on the other hand, is not a mathematical system, although it does, of course, involve mathematics. It is intended to search out the significance of market moves in the light of past experience in similar cases, by means of charts, with a full recognition of the fact that the market is a sensitive mechanism by which all of the opinions of all interested persons are

---

* Some of the most serious and dangerous "traps and pitfalls" of the market are tied up with difficulties of perception on the part of the investor, and consequent mis-evaluations and faulty identifications. For a particular study of these psychological problems see "The General Semantics of Wall Street" (by John Magee, 423 pages, illustrated).

reduced by a competitive democratic auction to a single figure representing the price of the security at any particular moment. The various formations and patterns we have studied are not meaningless or arbitrary. They signify changes in real values, the expectations, hopes, fears, developments in the industry, and all other factors that are known to anyone. It is not necessary that we know, in each case, what particular hopes, fears or developments are represented by a certain pattern. It is important that we recognize that pattern and understand what results may be expected to emerge from it.

The shorter term profits are, you might say, payment for service in the "smoothing out" of inequalities of trends, and for providing liquidity in the market. As compared to the long-term investor, you will be quicker to make commitments, and quicker to take either profits or (if necessary) losses. You will not concern yourself with maintaining "position" in a market on any particular stocks (although, as you will see, we will try to maintain a certain "total Composite Leverage" according to the state of the market, which accomplishes the same result). You will have smaller gains on each transaction than the longer-term investor, but you will have the advantage of being able frequently to step aside and review the entire situation before making a new commitment.

Most particularly, you will be protected against panic markets. There are times (and 1929 was by no means the only time), when the long-term investor stands to see a large part of his slowly accumulated gains wiped out in a few days. The short-term trader, in such catastrophes, will be taken out by his stop-loss orders, or his market orders, with only moderate losses, and will still have his capital largely intact to use in the new trend as it develops.

Finally, before we get on with the subject of tactics, the operations we are speaking of are those of the small and medium-size trader. The methods suggested here either for getting into a market or getting out of it will apply to the purchase or sale of odd lots, 100 shares, 200 shares, and sometimes up to lots of 1000 shares or more of a stock, depending on the activity and market for the particular issue. The same methods would not work for the trader who was dealing in ten-thousand-share blocks, since in such cases, his own purchases or sales would seriously affect the price of the stock. Such large scale operations are in a special field which is governed by the same basic trends and strategy, but which requires a different type of market tactics.

CHAPTER XIX

THE ALL-IMPORTANT DETAILS

IN THIS chapter and the one following, we take up a number of elementary suggestions which are intended largely for the benefit of those who have never kept charts before. Much of this will seem obvious and repetitive to the advanced student, although even he may find here some thoughts that will simplify his work. The beginner should read these chapters carefully and use them for later reference.

The details of how and when you keep the charts will not guarantee you profits. But if you fail to work out these details in such a way as to make your work easy as part of a regular systematic routine, you cannot expect to keep up your charts properly, or to make any profits either.

Charting and analyzing your charts is not a difficult process, nor will it take too much of your time if you have determined on a reasonable number of charts and if you have arranged for doing the work regularly, meaning every day without fail.

You will need a source of data—the day's market prices and volume. If you live in a big city, your evening paper will carry the complete list and you can plan to set aside a certain period before dinner, or after dinner, or during the evening. If you cannot allot such a period and keep it sacred against all other social or business obligations, then plan to do the charting in the morning. But set a definite time and let nothing interfere, *ever*, or you are lost.

In case you live in a place where there is no daily paper carrying the full data you need, you will have to arrange to get a paper in the morning, which will reach you by mail from the nearest city. We know of one chart trader who, faced with these conditions, has engaged a post-office box. He gets his Wall Street Journal by mail from New York, at about seven in the morning (considerably before the first regular mail delivery), and is thus able to bring his charts up to date and make his plans before the market opens at ten o'clock.

You should have a suitable place to work and keep your charts. If it is at home, in the dining room or living room, other members of the family should understand clearly that what you are doing is important. You should be able to shut the door and work without interruption. The light should be bright and as free from shadows as possible (it makes a big difference, especially if you are keeping a large number of charts). The ordinary desk lamp throws a reflected glare directly across the paper and into the eyes. It can be a strain if you are doing much of this close work. Better to have an overhead light, placed just a few inches in front of your head and a convenient distance above; and if this light can be a fluorescent fixture using two 40-watt lamps you will get almost perfect shadowless lighting. These suggestions apply, of course, in case you are not working by daylight.

Have plenty of room. A big desk top, a dining room table, with a large clear space for chart books, extra sheets, pencils, scratch paper, ruler, slide rule, and anything else you need. If your working surface is fairly low, say 28 or 29 inches from the floor, it will be less tiring than the usual 30-inch desk height.

Whether you are working in ink or in pencil, pick out the writing tool that is easiest for you to use. If you are using pencils try several different makes and degrees of hardness. Find one that is hard enough not to smudge too easily, and yet is not so hard that you have to bear down to make a clean black mark. The wrong kind of pencil can tire you and irritate you more than you realize. Also, have plenty of pencils, a dozen at least, well sharpened, so that as soon as one becomes a trifle dull and you are not getting a clean, fine line, you can simply lay it aside and continue at once with another fresh-sharpened pencil.

Keep your charts in loose-leaf books, with big enough rings to make turning the pages easy. Don't overcrowd the books. Get new books if a volume is too crowded. Finished charts may be kept in file folders. The only ones that need to be in the books are the current sheets and the sheets for the immediately preceding period. If possible use a seven-ring binder. Pages are easily torn loose from two- and three-ring binders, but seven rings will hold the pages safely and you will seldom have one tear out.

The charts you keep will become increasingly valuable to you as the chart history builds up. The old chart sheets will be very helpful to you for reference. Provide a file or space where they can be indexed and kept in chronological order; and also file folders for brokers' slips, dividend notices, corporation reports, clippings and articles, notes on your own methods, and analyses and special studies of the work you are doing.

In this connection you will, of course, keep a simple but complete record of each purchase, sale, dividend, etc., on stocks you have bought or sold. This record will make your work much easier when the time comes to figure out income taxes. It will also give you all the statistical information you need to judge the results of your trading operations.

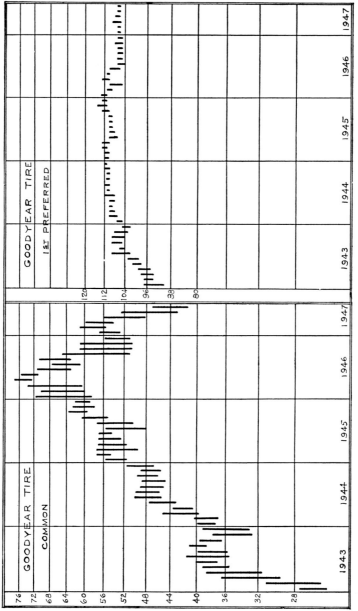

FIGURES 187 and 188.   Opportunity vs. Security.   Here (at left) is Goodyear Common, representing the resid-
ual interest in all profits after senior obligations have been met, compared (at right) with the Goodyear $5.00
Preferred which carries a high degree of assurance that the $5.00 dividend will be met, but no promise of fur-
ther participation in profits.   Monthly range of each stock for the same fifty-four month period is shown on a
ratio scale.   As the Common makes an advance of over 300%, the Preferred advances about 25%, leveling off
at a point which represents the maximum price investors are willing to pay for the sure $5.00 dividend.

CHAPTER XX

THE KIND OF STOCKS WE WANT

THE specifications of the *kind* of stock we want to chart are fairly simple, and they are few. We want a stock which will enable us to make a profit through trading operations. That means a stock whose price will move over a wide enough range to make trading worthwhile. There are those who are concerned mainly with safety of principal and the assurance of income from a stock. For them there are stocks which afford a very considerable degree of stability. You may (and probably will) want to keep a substantial part of your total capital in stocks of this type. They move in a narrow price range. They are extremely resistant to downside breaks in the market. They are also (and necessarily) unresponsive to fast upside moves in the market as a whole. These stocks are highly desirable for the conservative investor. However, they are not the most suitable issues for trading operations since their swings are small and commissions would tend to eat up the narrow trading profits that could be taken. Also, they do not make the sharp, clear, chart patterns of the more speculative issues, but move in rounding, sluggish undulations.

To amplify this comment and explain a bit what underlies what we are doing, let us assume a certain company has two issues of stock, a preferred and a common. Since (we will assume) the concern has a certain steady minimum profit which it has earned for years, sufficient to pay the preferred dividend, the continuance of these dividends seems practically assured. But the dividends on the preferred are fixed at, let us say, 6%. Now the common stock gets all that is left. In one year there may be 50 cents a share for the common stockholders. The next year there may be $2.00 a share or four times as much. In a case like this, if there were no other factors, you would expect the preferred stock to sell at a fairly steady price without much change, whereas the common stock is subject to a "leverage" and might shoot up to four times its former value. The more speculative issues represent either a business which is by its nature uncertain as to net profit from year to year, where the volume of business or the profit margin fluctuates widely, or one in which the majority of the "sure" net profit has been sheared off for the benefit of senior obligations. There are also other factors that affect the speculative swing of a stock, and as a result one issue may be very sensitive and another extremely conservative; and between them there would be all shades and degrees of sensitivity or risk. It is enough here to note briefly that the nature of the business itself does not always

account for the habits of the stock, since the other factors may be very important.   But most stocks have a fairly well-defined "swing" power, and you can
usually determine by past performance how a stock will behave in the future
as to the extent of its swings.

Incidentally, for short-term trading, we are thinking about the habits of the
stock which are only partly determined by the business it represents.   Purchase
of stock in one company which has a somewhat uncertain or fluctuating profit
record *may* be more conservative than purchase of a highly leveraged stock of
another company whose basic business is steadier and more conservative.   We
will take up the matter of determining these risk constants a little later.

One should also understand that the short sale of a stock does not imply
any feeling that the country is going to the dogs nor even that the concern represented is going to the dogs.   Such a sale merely indicates your belief that the
stock may be temporarily over-priced; that earnings or dividends may have been
abnormal in recent years and are likely to be reduced; or that for one reason or
another the stock of the company may be worth a bit less than it has been
worth.

For technical trading we want a fairly speculative stock, one which will
make sizable swings up in a bullish trend, and down in a bearish trend.   The
very factors which tend to make a stock safe and desirable to the investor may
make it entirely unsuitable for trading.   And with certain reservations, which
we will take up, the more speculative the stock the better it is for our purposes.

CHAPTER XXI

SELECTION OF STOCKS TO CHART

THE trader who operates on the statistical or "fundamental" basis, making his commitments on his analysis of earnings, dividends, corporate management, prospects for the industry, etc., will usually (of necessity) confine himself to a few stocks or a single group of stocks in the same field.

On the contrary, the technical trader, using daily charts, should have a large portfolio of issues. Since he is primarily interested in the technical chart patterns he will not try to make an exhaustive study of the background of each company. In fact, the characteristics of the stocks themselves, as they act in the market, are more important to him than what these companies make or what they are earning. This, as we have seen, is because, although the stocks represent ownership in the company, the capital structure, "leverage," and floating supply of the stock may (and very often does) mean fluctuations in the stock price that are not directly in proportion to changes in the affairs of the business.

You will also find many cases where the stock of a well-regarded, well-managed, long-established concern, whose latest earnings report shows increased profits, and with a long record of dividends paid, would not be a good buy at the market price. It may be overpriced and due for a serious depreciation. You will find other cases where a stock which apparently represents no great promise of either earnings or dividends, suddenly starts a series of spectacular moves upward, and is indicated clearly as a buy. Of course the answer, in each case, is that the records available apply to the past, not the future; and very often chart action will indicate the inside knowledge of those who are in possession of facts the public has not yet received.

To change our example to something more easily visualized: There are two houses for sale. One is a fine, well-built, modern home in an attractive part of town at, say, $20,000—and the other property, a somewhat shabby six-family tenement in a less attractive section, at the same price of $20,000. There is no question which is the "better" house. But in a case like this, the market for well-built single homes at this price may be poor, while the demand for apartments may be good. The six-family house may be the better investment.

And then again, we have the question of what is conservative and what is highly speculative. It is not always enough to judge from the type of business of the company itself. You may have a highly conservative concern, carrying on a stable volume of business, with a long record of successful operation. And yet, if there are bonds, debentures, preferred stocks and other senior obligations, the common stock may be subject to wide fluctuations. Also, if the issue is small or if a large part of it is closely held, you will have a "leverage" effect which results in wide swings in the stock.

Therefore, in choosing your stock to chart, you will want to consider the *kind of stock* and its character and habits in the market, rather than the business of the concern it represents. We will come back to this point and show you how you can shape up a list that will give you the kind of stocks you want for trading.

Meanwhile, the question "How Many Charts?" has been left hanging. One answer to this is that the more stocks you chart the more good opportunities you will have. Many stocks, even of active issues, will go through long periods when the chart tells nothing—when, indeed, there is nothing much to tell. In a period of stability the chart simply indicates that it *is* a period of stability, and the only possible trading activity would be purchases and sales at the bottoms and tops of its undulations. The charts are more informative when a change in the situation occurs; they will signal a change of trend as soon as (and usually before) the news back of the changed conditions has come out. If you have enough charts you will always have some stocks making decisive and clear-cut moves either up or down, at any time.

You should therefore keep as many charts as you can. Don't bite off more than you can chew, however. A man with only fifteen minutes to half an hour a day for this work might have to confine himself to 20 or 30 charts. It would be much better if he could have a hundred. And if he is in a position to give a major part of his time to the work, he could very well run as many as three hundred charts. A most important word of caution is indicated here. Do not start anything you can't finish. It is better to have too few at the beginning than too many. Then if you find that you can add others, you will be in a better position, from your experience, to pick out the ones you want to include. But if you start with too many charts, begin to run behind, and have to make up back charts over the week-end, you will not be getting the best use from your portfolio and it would be better to cut down at once.

From what we have already been over, you know that it is possible to chart anything that is sold in identical units in a free competitive market. This includes, of course, all kinds of commodities, bonds, debentures, when-issued contracts, etc., as well as stocks. You may have some special interest which will call for charting something outside the field of stocks. Well and good.

In general, however, you will want to chart active, listed stocks of well-established corporations. There is no reason an unlisted stock cannot be charted, but ordinarily the only figures you can obtain on it are the bid and offer prices. On these stocks you do not have a published statement of the volume of sales each day or any record of prices at which sales actually took place, and those are essential to the charting of daily technical action. Therefore, you will usually be charting stocks which are listed on some exchange. This is also an advantage since concerns listed on the larger exchanges are required to meet certain conditions, publish certain information, and comply with definite rules and practices.

In this book most of the examples have been taken from stocks listed on the New York Stock Exchange. There are over 1400 issues traded on the NYSE, and these stocks represent every type of security from the most conservative to the most speculative, from the cheapest to the most expensive, and they include every principal type of industry and business. It is convenient to choose stocks from this large list since the daily transactions of the NYSE are published in most leading newspapers, and the NYSE ticker is available at most brokers. However, there is no reason that stocks should not be chosen from the American Stock Exchange, or from any other exchange in this country, or for that matter in some other country. So far as the chart action is concerned, the patterns and their meanings will be the same.

FIGURES 189 and 190. Low-priced stocks move faster than high-priced stocks. Here are weekly charts of two rail stocks, charted on ratio scale over the same six-month period. Baltimore and Ohio during this time advanced from 12⅜ to 28⅞, a gain of 16½ points, while Union Pacific moved up from 109 to 137, a gain of 28 points. The advance in "UP," however, compared to its price, is much *less* than the advance in "BO." A thousand dollars used for outright purchase of UP would show you a capital increase of 25%. On the other hand, if you had put a thousand dollars into outright purchase of "BO," your increase would have been 133% or more than five times as much.

Bear in mind that low-priced stocks not only go *up* much faster, but also come *down* much faster than high-priced stocks. When you own a low-priced stock you cannot safely "put it away in the box and forget it." For security and stability you would do better to buy a few shares of a high-priced, gilt-edge security. But, for trading purposes you will want to strike a compromise between the rather sluggish "blue chips" and the extremely erratic "cats and dogs" in the lowest price bracket.

CHAPTER XXII

SELECTION OF STOCKS TO CHART—CONTINUED

IN CHOOSING your stocks you will probably look for the greatest diversity in the *kind* of industry. Since you are not specializing in the detailed study of a single group you will try to get stocks from as many different groups as possible. You will want to include mines and oils, rails and chemicals, liquors and amusements, airlines, utilities, etc. The reason for this is simply that very often many stocks in a particular industrial group will show the same or similar patterns as the entire industry is affected by certain major conditions. You will often find, for instance, that when Allis-Chalmers makes a Triangle, followed by a sharp upward move, Deere, Minneapolis-Moline, Harvester and Case will make similar Triangles, or possibly Rectangles or some other consolidation pattern, followed by a similar upward move. When Schenley is moving in a long down trend, you will very likely find that Distillers-Seagrams, National Distillers, Publicker and American Distilling are also moving in a long down trend.

Therefore, unless you plan to keep enough charts to include several stocks of *each* important group, it is best to pick your stocks to make up as widely diversified a list as possible. In this way, during times when certain groups are moving indecisively, or are inactive, you will have some representation in other groups which may be active. (Do not infer from this that all stocks of a group move together at all times. Individual concerns will frequently move according to special influences that bear on a single company. But where the major influence is some industry-wide condition, the group will move more or less as a unit.)

We therefore choose stocks representing a wide variety of groups or basic industries. But, suppose we are limited as to the number of charts, and we must choose one stock from a group; which stock to choose? Suppose, for instance, we must choose one stock from the rail group. As a matter of fact you would probably want more than one because this particular group is so important and so large. But for the moment, let us choose just one.

Should it be a high-priced stock or a low-priced stock? Let us examine that point first.

If you have access to the past records of stocks (in this case rail stocks), you will find that in general the lower-priced issues make much larger *percentage* moves than the higher-priced stocks. It is not unusual for a stock selling around 5 to make a rise of 100%, moving up to 10 sometimes within a few

303

weeks. On the other hand, you do not find 100% moves in days or weeks among the stocks selling at 100 or 200. The same industry-wide move which carries your $5 stock from 5 to 10 might carry your $100 stock from 100 to 140. Obviously, if you had put $1000 into outright purchase of the stock at 5, the move would have increased the value of your stock 100% or $1000. In the other case, if you had put the same amount into a stock at 100, the move to 140 (although many more points) would have increased your capital to only $1400. The gain in the lower-priced stock would be about two and one half times as great.

The authors have worked out and tabulated the percentage moves of large groups of stocks over long periods of time, and have set up a table which shows the *relative* average sensitivity of stocks at different price levels. This table pertains only to the price level of stocks; thus, the same stock which today sells at 5 and makes wide percentage swings, will not swing so widely when it has moved up to a price level of 20 to 30 (Appendix B).

Several questions may come to your mind at this point. Are not the commissions higher (relative to the price) on low-priced stocks than they are on higher-priced issues? Yes, they are, and you will find that below a certain price level this factor makes it difficult or impossible to make short and intermediate term trades in low-priced stocks. A table of average round-trip commissions and tax costs has been worked out by the authors (Chapter XXXI). This table will be helpful in quickly getting an approximate net on a theoretical or actual trade. The actual figures usually will be within a few cents or a dollar or so at most of the costs given in the table, on a round lot of 100 shares.

In selecting the price level of the stocks you prefer to trade in you cannot set too arbitrary a limit, since there are other factors to consider, and you may have to make some compromises on one score in order to get what you want in some other direction. Stocks from 20 to 30 are in a good trading price range. Very often you will find stocks in the 10 to 20 range which are so interesting you will want to chart them, and trade in them. You will find good situations in stocks selling at 30 to 40. Furthermore, you will understand of course that the stocks which are now selling at 10 may be selling next year at 40, or vice-versa. And since you cannot be changing your portfolio of charts all the time, you must not be too "choosy" in picking the price range of your stocks. However, you would not ordinarily pick out a stock that was selling far above the price range of most stocks of its group, say at 150 when several others in the same industry were selling at 15, 28 or 37. For the high-priced stock, as we have said, is likely to be sluggish as a trading medium. On the other hand, you would not take the very lowest-priced issues of the group, selling at say 4 or 2 when others were in the 10 to 30 brackets. You would not only be faced with erratic and tricky chart action, and much higher percentage costs for commissions; but you would not be able to operate on margin at all. There are limitations on the amount of margin on stocks at all levels. In the lower-priced issues these limits are more stringent. And in the lowest-priced stocks you are not permitted to trade on margin.

So when we consider the matter of price level alone, we find that there are these two factors. The higher the price of the stock the cheaper it is in commissions, and the more effectively we can use margin; but the more sluggish the action. The lower the price, the more expensive in commissions; and we have a curtailment of margin, but much more (perhaps too much) swing power.

Ordinarily you will get the greatest effective leverage at some point in the 20s, considering all these factors. And your trading can run down through the teens and up through the 40s. Above 40 and below 10, you will have to have strong reasons for trading. It would therefore be best to choose a majority of your stocks from the middle price range (10 to 40), plus only those special situations you are particularly interested in watching among the very low and very high brackets.

We were speaking, you recall, of rail stocks. From what we have just gone over, you will see that as ideal trading stocks we could eliminate such blue chips as Union Pacific and Norfolk & Western. And we could eliminate such thin or low-priced specialities as Cuba Railroad, 6% Pfd., Illinois Terminal, International Railways of Central America, etc., from our list of first-choice possibilities. (Bear in mind that conditions change and we might want to revise our selection in the future.) With this elimination we still have left the main body of important speculative rails. And while many of these are selling, at the time this is written (1956) somewhat above the suggested maximum of $40, we would not hold too strictly to an arbitrary limit, especially since these stocks have, on the whole, greater sensitivity than many other groups. In the sizable group of rails that have good trading characteristics are Baltimore and Ohio, Great Northern, Illinois Central, New York Central, Northern Pacific, Southern Pacific, and many others.

However, if you will go back to the long-time past record of these stocks you will find that even among stocks moving at nearly the same price levels today, there are widely different behavior patterns. You will find that some stocks respond to a severe market setback by reacting, let us say, 20%—that is, if they were selling at 30 they would move down to around 24. And you will find others that will respond to the same setback in the general market by a reaction of 50%—that is, if they were selling at 30 they would end up at around 15. And you will notice, if you examine the records, that the same stocks which make these relatively different reactions in one setback will make about the same moves, relative to each other, in other setbacks. Furthermore, the same ones which make only moderate corrections on declines will make only moderate advances on rises. And the ones that go down sharply on setbacks will also skyrocket on a bullish market. This has nothing to do with the phenomenon we discussed earlier by which we saw that cheap stocks move faster than expensive stocks. This is due to the habits of particular stocks and these habits seem to be quite stable over periods of many years. We find, for instance, that Missouri-Kansas-Texas, Pfd. A is a volatile and speculative issue. It makes larger percentage swings than most other stocks at its price level. And on the other hand we find that Canadian Pacific, selling for much less, has smaller percentage swings than most stocks at *its* price level. This fact may be obscured, since CP, being comparatively low-priced, may actually make larger swings than KT Pr. It is only when we have taken the price level into account that we can see what the individual habit of the stock really is. Knowing this we can project that habit to other price levels.

We are not too much interested, as we have said before, in stocks which do not ordinarily make substantial moves. We are very much interested in those which make the wider moves. We can compute the basic swing power of a stock, which we call the Sensitivity Index, and will outline the method for doing this (in Chapter XXIV).

So, you will have eliminated from your list stocks at the wrong price level and stocks without enough swing power (for you want to chart only those stocks in which you can trade profitably). Of the ones that are left you will eliminate others. You will find that some stocks which make wide price moves and apparently offer large opportunities for profit, may be very "thin." The charts will be spotty, filled with gaps, days of "no sale," and moves of several points on only a few hundred shares of business. These stocks are thin because of a small issue, because of ownership of a large block of shares by some corporation or by insiders, or for other reasons. They are difficult to trade in because they are hard to buy and hard to sell; you stand to lose heavily on the "spread" between bid and offer. It might be hard to liquidate even five hundred shares without driving the price down badly, to your loss, and sometimes you will see changes of one or two full points between sales of single hundreds. These you will want to eliminate, and if you do not know the habits before you choose your portfolio, you will probably find it worth while to drop any stocks that prove too thin, substituting new and more dependable choices.

After you have culled the list from all these angles (we are speaking of the rail group), you will find you have left a choice of a number of stocks, all of them selling in a price range that is attractive, all of them sufficiently active and responsive to market trends, and all of them available in sufficient supply to provide a good trading medium. The final choice of any one (or several) of these stocks is then a matter of personal preference. You may (in the case of the rails) want one road in the West, one in the South, one of the coal roads, or you may already have a special interest in certain particular rails.

After you pick out your rails, study the motors group, the amusements and so forth, until you have finally made up your selection of stocks to chart. Try to get as complete and balanced a representation of groups as the number of your charts will allow.

In this connection, if you are not planning to represent all groups, there are some groups that are more likely to provide good trading stocks than others. The foods and tobaccos, for example, are generally less responsive to market swings than the rails, liquors and airlines, which are very responsive. Do not worry too much, however, about exactly which stocks to choose. For even if you took the first fifty or hundred stocks in the listed issues, you would have among them at least 25 good trading stocks. You can start with almost any list, and as time goes on, you will drop some and add others, improving your portfolio and tailoring it to your own needs.

CHAPTER XXIII

THE MECHANICS OF BUILDING A CHART

YOU are now ready to start building your set of charts, which will in time, if faithfully kept, provide you with an invaluable working tool or "capital asset."

You have before you a supply of whatever type of chart paper you have decided to use, the binder or binders for the charts, pencils, triangle, ruler and the stock page of the daily newspaper. You will have these things arranged on a large, cleared, well-lighted working area; and you will be left free to work undisturbed. You have already chosen the list of stocks you intend to chart.

Fill out a chart form for each stock. In the upper left-hand corner put the dates covered by the 52 weeks or whatever period of time is to be covered by the chart sheet. It would be a good idea, right from the start, to divide your charts into four groups. All stocks from A to C inclusive might have chart sheets dated Jan.-Dec. 1957, for example (if you are using the full-year charting paper), followed on their completion by sheets dated Jan.-Dec. 1958. Then all stocks from D to I inclusive will be on charts dated Apr. 1957-Mar. 1958, and these will be followed on their completion by sheets dated Apr. 1958 -Mar. 1959. Similarly, a third group will include stocks from J through R, dated Jul. 1957-Jun. 1958, and a fourth group will include the remaining issues from S through Z, dated Oct. 1957-Sep. 1958. Thus, each three months a quarter of your charts will run out and call for new pages, and at no time will *all* your charts come to the ends of their sheets simultaneously. If the date on which you are starting a chart happens to fall in August, set up the sheet dated as for other stocks in its alphabetical group, leaving blank whatever months lie before the start of your chart. Then you will be on the right track from the beginning and will never have any confusion as to the dating of chart sheets.

Put the name of the company in the title space at the center of the top; put the dates covered by the sheet to the left, and the ticker symbol to the right. Then fill in the scale of prices on the vertical left margin. If you are using arithmetic paper you can simply write in the figures representing prices up and down from the center, letting the center come at or near the stock's market price at the time of starting the chart. With square-root paper or logarithmic (ratio) paper place the scale so that the center of the paper will be as near as possible to the present price. (Note: If you are using the *TEKNIPLAT* chart paper, which is a ratio paper, you will find a detailed outline of procedure in Appendix A, though if you are familiar with ratio scale you will have no difficulty in setting up the chart.)

From chart examples in this book you will see how charts may be titled, dated and scaled. You will also notice that on sheets especially printed for charting stock prices, each sixth vertical line is somewhat heavier than its neighbors; this represents a Saturday, on which you will have no entry since the market does not operate on Saturday. However, this slight break each week will not affect your trends and other technical indications materially; and serves to provide a space between the weeks, making it easier for the eye to pick out a particular day of the week quickly in charting. It is important to make your first entry on the correct vertical line for the day of the week so that the ending of the first week will come on a "Saturday" line. If a month should start on Monday, start your chart on the first line immediately to the right of the left border line. If the month should start on Thursday, begin three small spaces farther to the right so that Saturday falls on the first heavier line.

Finally, you will have a volume scale near the bottom of the chart, and a time scale along the very bottom showing the date of each Saturday over the period covered by the chart sheet.

There are four figures you must pick up for charting from the newspaper you are following. At first you will find it necessary to look back and forth several times, taking the high, low, closing price and day's volume separately. With practice, and by making a conscious effort to train your eyes and mind, you will find it possible to grasp the four figures in one single "grab," fixing them in your mind for the few seconds it takes to mark them in on the chart sheet. This knack, when you have mastered it, can cut down the time needed for charting 50% or more; it is well worth a bit of extra effort.

HOLIDAYS—EX-DIVIDEND DAYS

When a holiday occurs or when for any reason the market is closed, simply skip that day, leaving blank the space (vertical line) where you would have entered it. When there are no sales of a stock on a particular day, mark a small "o" in the volume scale. If you happen to be watching a particular situation in a stock closely you might want to indicate by a dotted line the approximate level between the closing bid and offer prices on the day no sale occurred. But there is no need to make this a regular procedure.

Ex-dividend dates can be indicated by an "x" along the bottom margin of the volume scale, and any data about dividends can then be written in on the extreme bottom margin; for example, "$.50 Unchanged Quarterly" or

"Payable in American funds, $1.00." Or the amount of the dividend may be written in vertically right on the face of the chart on the line representing the ex-dividend date. Stock dividends and rights should be entered in the same way and their market value indicated. When stocks go ex-dividend, especially if the dividend is a large one, there may be a price gap which can sometimes appear to change or spoil a technical chart pattern. An ex-dividend gap is not a significant gap in the technical sense, and if it is no larger than the amount of the dividend (or rights or other benefit), it may be disregarded. The newspaper tabulation of stock prices takes this into account. For example, if a stock goes ex-dividend 50 cents and closes ⅜ of a point lower than the previous day, the paper will report the stock "plus ⅛" not "minus ⅜."

In the case of ex-dividend gaps you may, if you wish, extend the price range of the stock by a dotted line equal to the amount of the dividend; and you should on the day of ex-dividend or similar distribution, move down stop-order levels, limit orders, trendlines, etc. Very often the stock will continue in the (adjusted) pattern or trend even though its *level* has been changed on the ex-dividend day.

Stock split-ups or other changes in capitalization cause extra work in charting. Where the split is two-for-one or four-for-one, there is no problem because the entire scale from that point on is simply changed to the new price by halving or quartering each horizontal line's previous value. You re-scale the chart and continue. The chart may, and probably will, become more active as to volume (because of the larger number of shares outstanding) and may develop "coarser texture" in its patterns from this point on, but it will respect the (adjusted) resistance and support levels, trends, etc., previously established. Where a split-up is not two-for-one or four-for-one but some odd figure such as three-for-one or four-for-seven, you will usually have to start a new sheet, plotting the chart at the new prices and then extending it back a few weeks by dividing the previous prices by 3 or by 4/7, and plotting them on the new scale.

You may find it convenient to mark on your charts special information on certain companies—purchases of subsidiaries, reduction of bond issues, earnings or other important data—although in this work we do not concentrate on these "fundamental" matters, but on the chart itself.

When the Chart Goes Off the Paper

When one of your stocks which has been selling in the neighborhood of 20 moves up close to 40 and appears likely to rise through 40, it will be well to re-scale the center of the chart at 40. For a time you can chart the stock on both scales simultaneously, so that if it should proceed up through the 40 level, you will have a few weeks of the chart in centered position all ready to continue. If, on the other hand, the stock recedes to 35 or so, the new auxiliary chart may be dropped for the time being. Naturally, when such a situation exists, where you are carrying the same stock on two scales simultaneously, the next following chart sheet will be scaled to continue only the chart on which the price trend is nearer the center of the paper.

THE CHART RECORD OF TRANSACTIONS

It would be possible to give a good deal of space to the interesting study of "Paper Accounts" in which theoretical trades are marked and recorded on the charts, without actually making commitments in real cash. Detailed suggestions for this work were outlined and it was planned to include a chapter on the subject, but then the authors decided that very few readers would be willing to carry out the detailed study, records and analysis which, to be of any value, would require as much work as actual trading.

However, it should be pointed out that anyone who contemplates further research or original work in Technical Analysis, or who intends to make his career in the stock market, will need a great many more cases for tabulation than his own actual trades will supply. He will need hundreds of situations in order to strike an average so that he can say "This particular idea seems to work out in 75% of the cases," or "That plan does not provide, on the average, enough gain to justify the risk and the costs of taxes, commissions, etc."

The important thing about theoretical trading is that the buying or selling points should be clearly marked on the chart *before* the expected move has occurred, and theoretical orders should be assumed to have been executed exactly as they would have been in a broker's office, with proper deduction made from the final gross gain (or additions to the loss) to cover broker's commissions, odd-lot fractions, dividends or rights received, and (in case of short sales) dividends or rights paid. It does not pay to cheat at solitaire, and the only possible value of such "paper trading" is a record of experience that represents exactly what would have happened in an actual account.

By recording every promising situation and the action to be taken, as it unfolds, an analyst will maintain an alertness to possible opportunities for actual trading. He will be ready to seize opportunities as they appear, and he will acquire confidence as he sees his own predictions materializing. If he keeps a careful and honest record of his theoretical trades, and tabulates all of these on the completion of each series of charts, he will have a yardstick for studying his own improvement, and the comparison between his theoretical work and his actual results. Furthermore, he will have source material for almost any type of advanced research he may want to delve into.

For the beginner (although these words will fall mostly on deaf ears), it will pay to make all trades "on paper" for a number of months before venturing any actual capital in the market. If good opportunities for profit occur, there is no need to feel that this or that situation is the last good chance the market will offer. The market will be there next month and next year; there will be other opportunities just as good. Meanwhile, it is possible to appraise a situation, indicate what you would like to do, and study what subsequently happens. If only more novices had the patience to experiment in this way for a time before risking their money, they could avoid many of the pitfalls and traps that so often lead to losses and discouragement.

SUPPLEMENTARY MEMORANDA ON THE CHART

There are several special marks to go on the chart which should be mentioned. We have already spoken of keeping (on the chart itself) a record of possible buys and sells, and of theoretical trades—when bought, when sold, time of holding, net gain or loss after commissions and after dividends, etc. You should also record any *actual* purchases or sales, noting the number of shares, price, broker (if you carry more than one account), etc. This record can be kept near the top of the sheet, perhaps in blue if long and red if short, extending from the date of original commitment to the date of closing out.

On starting a new (continuation) chart sheet, transfer to its left margin any notes as to actual or theoretical commitments that are still open, stop orders, etc. Also it would be a good idea to mark all the sheets covering a certain 52-week period with an identifying series number or letter ("A," "B," etc.) in the upper left corner. This would make it easy to re-file charts in their proper chronological folder after they have been taken out for study.

In the left-hand margin, at the proper price levels, mark the highest closing price of the previous sheet with a dotted blue line. Also mark the lowest closing price of the previous page with a dotted red line. These levels give you important high and low points, violation of which often means important further moves in the same direction. They also give you the "range" of the stock in the preceding 52-week period, which is essential in figuring its velocity, or what we call the *sensitivity* of the stock during that period. We will use this range in making the longer-term Sensitivity Index which is a factor in determining Composite Leverage ratios.

One last point on chart mechanics: The longer you keep a record of a stock the more useful your chart will be. Do not make unnecessary changes in your chart portfolio but add and drop stocks only gradually and when you feel certain the change will improve the group. When you first start a new chart, mark it "New," showing that it is an addition to your portfolio. Then you will not waste time later on looking for a previous sheet on that stock. Also a new chart may well have to be carried along for a number of weeks or even months before you have enough definite chart formation to enable you to trade in it. If it seems desirable to make a commitment in a stock you do not now chart, it would be best to run back a chart for at least three months from your files of the financial pages which we hope you cherish and keep to meet just this need.

FIGURES 191 and 192.   Some stocks move faster than others.   We have
already noticed that low-priced stocks have much larger percentage moves
than high-priced issues.   But even between two stocks which may, at a particular time, be selling at the same price, there are enormous differences in
their habits.   Furthermore, these habits change very little from year to year.

Here we have a weekly chart of Corn Products Refining Co., covering an
eighteen-month period in the years 1945 and 1946.   Also a chart of Schenley
Distillers for the same period.   The *average* price between the high and low
on these charts is about 64½, the same for both stocks.

However, during this period we see "CFG" moving between a low of 58½,
and a high of 71, a range of 12½ points, while at the same time "SH" has
moved between 28½ and 100, a range of 71½.   A thousand dollars put into
outright purchase of "CFG" at its extreme low would have grown to $1,210
at its extreme high, whereas the same amount used for outright purchase of
"SH" at *its* low would have grown to $3,510.   Your gain of $2,510 in "SH"
would be more than ten times the gain of $210 in "CFG" and this without
using margin.

It is not likely, of course, that you would actually purchase either stock
at the extreme low, nor sell at the extreme high.   The point we are bringing
out here is that there are enormous differences in the swing habits of stocks.

Individual stocks have their characteristic habits, and so do some entire
industries.   In general the food stocks, of which "CFG" is one, are stable and
slow-moving.   On the other hand, liquor stocks make wide moves on any
general advance or decline of the market.   At this time "CFG" had a Sensitivity Index of .58, whereas Schenley's was 2.05.   In the future as in the
past we may expect wider swings in "SH" than in "CFG."

CHAPTER XXIV

THE PROBABLE MOVES OF YOUR STOCKS

AT FIRST glance all stocks appear to move helter-skelter without rhyme or reason, all over the lot. All stocks go up at times, and all go down at times—not always at the same time. But we already have seen that in these rises and falls, stocks do follow trends, make various typical patterns, and behave in a not completely disorderly manner.

It is also true that each stock has its own habits and characteristics, which are more or less stable from year to year. Certain stocks normally respond to a bullish phase of the market with a very large upsurge, while others, perhaps in the same price class, will make only moderate moves. You will find that the same stocks which make wide *upward* swings are also the ones which make large *declines* in Bear Markets, whereas the ones that make less spectacular up-moves are more resistant to downside breaks in the market. In Chapter XLI you will find in a discussion of Composite Leverage that there are stocks which ordinarily move many, many times as fast as others. We do not know, for example, whether a year from now Glenn Martin will be moving up or down, but we *do* know, and it is one of the most dependable things we know, that whichever way Glenn Martin is going it will be covering ground much faster than American Tel. and Tel. These differences of habit, of course, are due to the size of issue, floating supply, nature of business and leverage in the capital structure, matters we have touched on briefly before. As a matter of fact we are not especially concerned with *why* the differences exist. We are interested mainly in what the differences are, and how we can determine them.

This is important. Stocks which habitually move in a narrow range, although excellent for investment purposes where stability and income are the chief desiderata, are not good trading stocks. A fairly high degree of sensitivity, with wide percentage moves, is necessary in order to make possible profitable commitments that will cover commissions and leave a net gain. In order to be in a position to make a profit you should see the probability of at least a 15% move in your stock.

How then are you going to tell which stocks are most sensitive and potentially most profitable?

If it is possible to obtain the record of a certain stock for a number of years back and compare the percentage moves it has made with the percentage

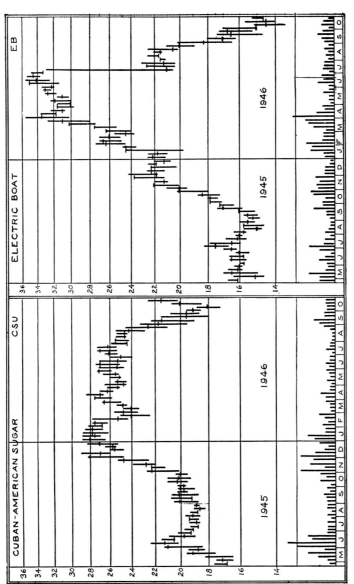

FIGURES 193 and 194. Another example of the difference in swings between stocks. In this case also the stocks show the same average price between the high and low of the period, and both stocks are plotted for the same eighteen months in 1945 and 1946. Although in a lower price range, and although the disparity in their Sensitivity Indexes is less, there is a considerable difference in their actions. Cuban-American Sugar, a food stock, shows a range of 76% from its low of 16½ to its high of 29, whereas Electric Boat, a shipbuilding concern, advances more than 140%.

moves of the market as a whole, you can obtain a fair picture of that stock's habits. You will not be able to say, at any particular moment, "This stock is now going to move up 25%," but you can say, with a good deal of confidence, "If the market as a whole makes an advance of 10% this stock will probably advance about 25%." Or, conversely, of course, "If the market goes down 10%, this stock will very likely go down at least 25%."

Many methods have been used for measuring and checking these percentage-move habits, differing only in detail. Indexes on several hundred important stocks listed on the New York Stock Exchange have been computed by the authors (see Sensitivity Indexes, Appendix C).

The Indexes are relative. They show that stocks with a high Sensitivity Index will move much faster in either Bull Markets or Bear Markets than stocks with low Indexes, and about how much faster, relative to the other stocks.

In order to compute the Sensitivity Indexes, the range of each stock from high closing to low closing, on each sheet of the chart, is marked with a dotted blue (top) and red (bottom) line in the left-hand margin of the next chart sheet for that particular stock. At the end of each series of chart sheets, this price range for each stock in the period covered by the chart sheet just finished is measured from top (blue) line to red (bottom) line, and these ranges, expressed in eighths of an inch, are added together and divided by the total number of stocks charted. This gives you an *average range* for the period, representing the composite or average movement of the entire group of stocks. An arbitrary "normal" average range is permanently selected (on the basis of the average range for a number of series of charts for several years),[*] and as each series of new charts is completed this "normal" average range is divided by the average range for the new series, to arrive at a decimal fraction which represents the reciprocal of the market movement for the period. (Thus a period of wide market activity would show a small decimal, less than 1, such as .65, whereas a period of dull and inactive markets would result in a larger figure, such as 1.49.) We will call this (just to give it a handy name for future reference) the Market Reciprocal for this period or series of charts.

Now the price range, expressed in eighths of an inch, for each stock in turn, is divided by the range corresponding to the "normal" or average range for a stock at that price (see Range-for-Price table, Appendix B), and this fraction is multiplied by the Market Reciprocal. The resulting figure is the fractional Sensitivity Index covering the action of this particular stock for this particular market period. In order to obtain the over-all or long-term Sensitivity Index for a stock, we simply add the fractional indexes for each period together and divide by the number of periods. As new chart sheets are completed we add the new fractions and compute the new index. A single fractional index

---

[*] Theoretically, the "normal" average range should be adjusted continuously at the close of each period. Practically, there is no need for such refinement.

is, as you might expect, unreliable and rather meaningless as regards the future. The second, third, and fourth series fractions will revise and "smooth" the Index. As time goes on and new series are added, these Sensitivity Indexes will settle down to fairly constant figures; corrections, if any, will be slight, as new series are added. And these Indexes are very reliable in forecasting the probable future sensitivity of each stock.

The measuring of price ranges in eighths of an inch, in order to get figures representing percentage moves, implies of course that you are using a ratio chart paper. With other types of paper you would have to compute the percentage price range for each period from the high and low closing prices on your charts.

We have outlined this method in some detail so that you can, if you wish, compute your own Sensitivity Indexes. Or, if you are using the table of Indexes from Appendix C, you will be able to revise these and keep them up to date as gradual changes in the habits of the stocks take place; and also you can figure other stocks, not included, on a uniform basis with those for which we show Indexes. It is not necessary that your stocks all be from the New York Stock Exchange. Using this method you can include others from other exchanges, averaging them all together and treating your entire portfolio as a group in determining your Market Reciprocals.

In the Sensitivity Index table you will find that sensitivity runs from over 2.00 (which we would speak of as 200%) in the case of highly speculative issues, down to .20 (20% that is) or less on ultraconservative investment stocks. Roughly you may consider that stocks with S.I. of 50% or less are extremely conservative, 50% to 100% moderately conservative, 100% to 150% speculative, and anything over 150% highly speculative.

CHAPTER XXV
TWO TOUCHY QUESTIONS

THIS chapter is directed largely to the new trader, to the man who has followed other plans, and to the investor type who is now, for the first time, taking up the technical trading of stocks for the shorter term.

The first question here is the use of margin. There are many people who, knowing of the disastrous margin calls of 1929 and the staggering way losses can be multiplied against one in a margined account during a sharp break in the market, take the attitude that the use of margin is intrinsically bad, dangerous, foolish and unsound. They will tell you that they are willing to risk their own money but they never speculate on borrowed funds. They will tell you that by buying securities outright they are safe against any kind of break in the market.

There is something to this line of argument, although very often you will find that the arguer has not really thought the case through all the way. If he had he might realize that in buying outright stocks which are sensitive or highly leveraged, he is accomplishing almost exactly the same thing as someone else who buys more conservative stocks on a margin basis. Very often, despite his feeling that outright purchase is more conservative than margin buying, he is at heart a speculator. He is not really interested only in dividends and a stable investment. Rather, he is looking for "something with appreciation opportunity." And because he is not facing the issue squarely, he may fall into expensive errors.

To be thoroughly consistent here, a man who shuns the risks inherent in margin trading should shun the risks of leverage. He should avoid risk, forget "opportunity for appreciation," and confine himself to sound, income-producing stocks of a sort that will not fluctuate widely.

If we are looking for stability we do not want excessive fluctuation. And there are securities that provide stability. In this work, however, we are looking for "swing power." We want the highest degree of fluctuation we can handle safely. We can secure this by buying outright a stock that is normally subject to fairly broad swings; that is, a stock with a high Sensitivity Index. We can get the same effect by trading in a stock of more conservative habits, but increasing the Composite Leverage by using margin. (The method of computing and comparing Composite Leverages in various situations is covered in Chapter XLI.)

Let us assume, for example, that we will buy 100 shares of a rather speculative stock which we will call **UVW** on an outright basis. It has a Sensitivity Index of 1.50, and now sells (let us say) at 20. At the same time we buy a somewhat less speculative stock, **XYZ**, also selling at 20; but in this case we buy on 70% margin, putting up only three quarters of the value of the stock. In a general advance affecting both of these stocks, the probabilities would favor a somewhat greater percentage move in **UVW** than in **XYZ**. If such a general rise should bring **UVW** to 30, we might expect **XYZ** to rise to a lesser degree, say to 28. Now the advance of 10 points on the $2000 invested in outright purchase of **UVW** will represent a gain of $1000, or 50%. The advance of **XYZ** to 28 on the $1400 invested at 70% margin will mean a gain of $800, or 57%. In other words we have, by the use of margin, increased the effective leverage of **XYZ**; made it, in fact, slightly more speculative than **UVW**.

The effect of margin is simply to accentuate or increase the sensitivity of a situation. It is a mechanism for assuming more risks and, therefore, more opportunities for faster gains. Assuming you are willing to assume risk (as you must be if you intend to make speculative commitments), it is simply a matter of knowing approximately what risks you are taking and whether you can afford to take them. The danger in margin lies in cases where the customer grossly over-extends himself, taking on a risk far beyond his ability to protect himself. This will not happen if he sets a reasonable limit to his total leverage.

The margin transaction is simply a matter of buying (or selling short) more stock than you have money to pay for in full. The purchase of a home on a mortgage is essentially a margin transaction. The financing of business operations, using borrowed money for part of the capital, is the same. The buying of anything where the purchaser puts up part of the capital and borrows the rest, using the value of the purchased property as security for the loan, is exactly similar to the trading of stocks on margin. In each case any change in the value of the property will cause a larger net change in the value of the *margin* capital. Thus, if a man buys a home for $10,000, paying $5,000 cash, and later sells it for $15,000 (an increase of 50% in the value of his property), he will benefit to the extent of $5,000 profit, or 100% on his invested capital.

The question of margin calls, and being "wiped out" on margin transactions, will seldom if ever come up if you protect yourself properly by maintaining stops at all times or by closing out the transaction when it has violated certain predetermined danger points. Needless to say, if you have allowed a trade to go so bad that it has reached the minimum margin maintenance range, the best thing is to take your loss and forget it; not try to meet the margin call. But again—this need not ever happen.

As we will see in discussions of sensitivity and leverages, stop levels, etc., there are certain limits which can be fairly well defined, beyond which you cannot safely venture. If you could buy stock on a 10% margin as you could at one time, you might have visions of highballing a thousand dollars up to a million in one Bull Market. But that is not a reasonable hope, and it is not safe to risk your capital on a 10% margin, since in many cases your perfectly logical purchase would sag enough to wipe you out entirely before going ahead to the normal advance you expected. In judging how much margin you can or should use, within the limits of margin trading laid down by law, you must take into account the method of trading you are using, the amount of adverse fluctuation you must expect in the normal operation of your method, the nature of the stock you are dealing with, that is, its Sensitivity Index and Normal Range-for-Price at the time you make the original commitment. Under present conditions with an original margin of 70% required, or even if this should be reduced to 50%, you may properly use the full limit of your margin *except* on the most highly speculative or thin issues and on very low-priced stocks, which are not now marginable anyway under the SEC rules.

Short Selling

The other touchy question is that of short sales. A majority of traders avoid the short side of the market. Six out of seven you meet who have bought or sold stocks will tell you that they would never sell a stock short under any conditions, at any time. In fact, short selling is limited, very largely, to a comparatively small number of professionals.

Now, if you have studied long-term charts (weekly and monthly), and the daily charts in this book, you will recognize several facts about the action of markets. Most stocks go *up* most of the time. There are almost always more advances than declines in the list of most active stocks published each day. Stocks, in general, advance about two thirds of the time, and go down only about one third of the time.

Furthermore, most of the news releases, rumors, and comments in the press relating to stocks and corporation affairs have to do with the brighter side of industry. It is only natural that executives, public relations men, and the reporters themselves, should be interested in forward-looking developments, new processes, expansion of facilities, increased earnings, and the like; and that such items should prove more newsworthy than less optimistic reports.

These various factors may explain why "the public" is always bullish. The public is always hoping and expecting stocks to go up *all the time*. If stocks are rising and in a bullish phase, the public expects them to go still higher. If stocks have declined sharply, the public will argue that they are now better buys than before and must surely go up soon. But it is *up, up, UP*, always up, in the mind of the public.

And yet examination of the long-term charts, covering the action of the averages over many years, will show you that through these long periods the levels rise and fall about the same amount.*

This being the case, it must follow that stocks come down as far as they go up, and since they go up about two thirds of the time, they must come down much faster than they go up. This you will find is true. The angles of decline in the averages and also in individual stocks are usually steeper in Bear Market moves than the advances are in Bull Market moves. A corollary to this is that profits *can be made faster on the down side* of the market than on the up side.

Such profits are made by *selling short.* It is important if you are a trader that you understand the meaning of a short sale. When you sell a stock short, you borrow that stock from someone who owns it and then you turn around and sell it to someone else, agreeing with the original owner to replace his shares at some unspecified time in the future. All of the detail of this transaction is, of course, handled by your broker. Shares of most stocks of large outstanding issue are available for loan at all times in the hands of brokers, and your own broker has access to them. The mechanics of this borrowing and sale are interesting; you may wish to get from your broker the whole story of how these operations are carried out. For all practical purposes, however, all you need to do is tell your broker what you wish to sell and leave the rest to him. He will advise you if, by any chance, the stock you have selected for short sale is not available for loan. Another practical point, although of minor consequence, is that a slight additional tax is assessed against short sales.

It is important also, if you are a trader, that you accept opportunities to sell short as readily as you buy long stock. Unfortunately, there are psychological barriers to short selling. There are, for example, the unintelligent and entirely irrelevant slogans about "selling America short." There is the feeling on the part of many who are poorly informed that short selling is the somewhat unethical trick of the manipulator. Others have the impression that in selling short one is hoping to profit by the misfortunes of others at times of disaster and panic. It is not the purpose of this book to persuade anyone to sell stocks short any more than it is our purpose to advise anyone who shouldn't to speculate on the long side of the market. But so many questions are constantly raised even by fairly sophisticated investors about the ethics as well as the practical procedure of short selling that we may perhaps be pardoned for saying a few more words in its defense.

_____

* This principle probably still holds even after the extension of the Dow Industrial Average into new all-time high ground since late in 1954.

In spite of the long-term "secular trend" and the history of these recent years in the average it seems safe to assume that there will continue to be Major general declines in the future as there have in the past. As a matter of fact a number of important stocks have been in Major down-trends throughout the past few years of Bull Market: Celanese, for example, Kresge, Lorillard, Schenley and Studebaker-Packard.

All of the popular ideas about short selling mentioned in the preceding paragraph may be branded as so much nonsense. There is nothing more reprehensible about selling short than buying long. Each is a speculation in relative values. The truth is that money is a commodity, just as much as a share of stock. There is no moral or practical difference between borrowing money to buy stock because you believe that the latter will go up in value in terms of the former, and borrowing stock in order to "buy" money because you believe the latter is going to go up in value in terms of the former. In each case you are obligated eventually to repay the loan whether it be money or stock. In each case you are taking a risk on the basis of your considered forecast as to the future trend of *relative* values.

There are, in fact, many common business practices which are more or less analogous to selling stocks short. For example, every time the publisher of a magazine accepts cash in advance for a subscription he is making something like a short sale. His ultimate profit or loss will depend on what the magazines he will eventually supply have cost him by the time the subscription runs out.

When you sell stocks short, you (or rather your broker) receives the proceeds of the sale at once but you are obligated to turn back an equal number of the same shares at some future date to the man from whom the stock certificates were borrowed. Consequently, sooner or later, you have to go into the market again and buy those shares. When you buy them, you (or rather your broker) returns the shares to the original lender thus discharging your obligation. If the cost of your purchase was less than the proceeds of the earlier sale, the difference is your profit. If it costs you more to buy in the shares—or as it is termed, cover your short—then the difference represents a loss. Of course, you do not enter into a short-side transaction unless you expect the price of the stock to go down and, hence, show you a profit.

One of the little appreciated results of a large volume of short selling is actually to strengthen the market. Every short seller is a potential buyer. Most short sellers are glad to cover and take their profits on a relatively minor decline. Consequently, if there is a big short interest at any given time in a particular issue, that means that there are many people waiting to buy that stock when it goes down. This situation tends to "cushion" bad breaks. Some astute operators will actually buy a stock when they learn that there is a very large short interest in it (that is, that a great many shares of it have been sold short and not yet covered) because they realize that competition among the short sellers to buy the stock whenever it has a small decline may result in a very fast and profitable short-covering rally. Any stock is stronger, technically, if there is a good-sized short interest in it.

There is one further objection raised against short selling. It will be pointed out that when you buy long stock your loss, if worse comes to worst, can be no more than the total amount you paid for it. But in the case of a short sale, the price of your stock could, theoretically, rise against you to 50, 100, 1,000, 10,000 dollars a share; in other words, could rise without limit. This argument sounds much more alarming than it really is. Certainly there is no occasion to lose sleep over it. Stocks do not go up without limit all of a sudden. It is just as easy to set a stop on the loss you are willing to take on a short-side transaction as it is on a long purchase. Such situations as the famous 1901 corner in Northern Pacific are not likely ever to occur again under present regulations.

The authors realize that nothing they can say, and probably no amount of cold-blooded analysis on the part of the reader himself, will remove entirely the trepidation which most non-professional traders experience when they sell short. The mental hazards will always be slightly greater than in buying long. Nevertheless, from every practical angle, a short sale is exactly the same thing (although in a reverse direction) as a long purchase, with no greater risk, with actually somewhat greater chance of a quick profit, and differing only in details of execution.

A commitment in commodity futures contracts whether long or short, though quite different in theory, has some similarities to a short sale of stock. In making a contract no actual sale takes place, and no loan of either cash or the commodity is involved. Such a contract is simply a binding legal agreement to accept delivery or to deliver a certain commodity at a certain price at a certain time. In this respect it is *different* from a short sale of stock. It is also different in that it must be closed out on or before a definite date. But the purchase or sale of a commodity contract is similar to a stock short sale in that: (a) It is necessarily a margin transaction, and (b) it creates an "open" or incompleted transaction which must eventually be liquidated.

A short sale of stock must *always* and necessarily be a margin transaction. Thus, if you buy 100 shares of stock outright at 20, it can sink to 15 and you cannot be called for more margin. You have lost $500 but the stock is still yours. If you sell you get back $1,500 disregarding commissions. On the other hand, if you sell a stock short at 20, putting up a margin of 100%, and the stock rises to 25, you will also have lost $500. The broker under certain conditions, such as the 100% margin requirements in effect a few years ago, might call on you for $500 additional margin. Or, if the transaction were to be closed out at that point, you would receive back $1,500 less commissions, the same as in the long transaction. In the case of this short sale, had the price dropped to 15 your profit would have been $500.

On short-term moves, the effect of short selling is exactly the same as the buying of long stock, but in the opposite direction. You simply apply the same methods here in reverse, during a Bear Market, that you would use in a Bull Market. As we have already seen, the various technical indications that point to upward moves in a bullish phase have their counterparts in downside signals during a bearish phase.

Execution of short sales cannot be made at any time and at any price you wish. A short sale must be made on a *rising* market. You are not permitted to sell a stock short on the New York Stock Exchange during a market break when each regular sale is at a lower price than the one before it. However, this need not bother you much since ordinarily you would make such a sale on the rally as it reached your price, and this would naturally fill the requirement of a rising market. Your broker can give you in detail the special rules and regulations that apply to short sales, including the rather complicated rules governing short sales of odd lots. It will pay you to study these so that you can place your orders correctly when the proper time comes to make such sales.

CHAPTER XXVI

ROUND LOTS OR ODD LOTS?

ONE of the minor tactical questions bound to plague you is whether to trade in round lots of 100 shares or odd lots (less than 100 shares in active stocks).

There are several brokers who specialize in odd lot transactions, though your odd-lot orders will be placed through your regular broker who, in turn, deals with the odd-lot brokers. Your broker can get you without charge a copy of one of the books published by odd-lot specialists on the operation of the odd-lot market. It is worth study and will require study. Many brokerage houses hold seminars to review these rules and refresh their own customers' men in regard to odd lots.

In general, the rule is that on any odd-lot purchase or sale of a stock selling under 40, the odd-lot broker receives an extra eighth over and above the commission you pay your broker; and on any stock at 40 or more, a quarter point. And the odd-lot transactions are based on round-lot transactions as they appear on the tape. If you purchase a stock at a limit price of 25¼, a round lot must actually sell on the tape at 25⅛ which makes your purchase effective at 25¼. Similarly, if you sell "at the market" and the next round lot sale is 25⅞, you will receive 25¾.

In cases where a stock is inactive and quoted with a wide spread the odd-lot trader might gain some advantage. If the stock was offered at 28 but bid at only 26, an odd-lot market order to buy would be executed at 26⅛ if the next regular transaction was an order to *sell* at the market. However, a limit order to buy 100 shares at 26⅛ would get the same price, so the advantage is somewhat of an illusion. What seems more to the point is that the odd-lot trader is not continually forcing himself to buy more of a stock than he is really justified in buying, simply to "make up a round lot."

There is this advantage to trading in odd lots, and there are others by which you may benefit on overnight gaps even where you have specified a limit price. The main question is whether the gains outweigh the cost of ⅛ point on each transaction (that means ⅛ point on the purchase and another ⅛ point on the sale—a total cost of ¼ on the round trip in a stock selling under 40). And this seemingly insignificant extra cost can mount up to serious expense, especially on low-priced stocks when they are actively traded for the short term.

You will find that the cost of odd-lot trading is proportionately less on higher priced issues. A quarter of a point is not a great factor when you are dealing with a stock selling at 50 or 60. In such cases you will be expecting a profit of perhaps 8 to 10 points, and the advantage of trading in odd lots is worth the small cost. On the other hand, the extra expense of $\frac{1}{8}$ point each way on stocks selling around 4 or 5 would be ruinous. The round trip cost would be $\frac{1}{4}$ point against an expected profit of perhaps a point or less, and this is too heavy a load to carry.

It is hardly possible to set a definite rule and limit on this. But we could say that, in general, stocks selling below 20 should be bought where possible in round lots, while stocks selling above 20 can be traded just as well in odd lots as in round lots (perhaps better). Certainly no stock selling at 10 or less should be bought or sold on a short-term trading basis in odd lots.

STOP ORDERS

WE ARE going to take up two kinds of stop orders, or rather, two entirely different uses of the mechanism of stop orders.

First let us look at the protective stop order. At best it is not a happy subject. Stop orders of this type are like fire extinguishers. The occasions when they are put into operation are not times of rejoicing. Stop orders are used for emergency rescue when things get so bad that there seems no reasonable hope for a situation.

Wherever you set your protective stop it is likely to be touched off at what seems to be the worst possible moment. You will set it at a safe distance under a certain bottom. The stock will break through, catch your stop, and then proceed to build a new bottom at this level, for the next rise, or to rally at once and make new highs. No matter. You had your reasons for setting the stop. The stock did not act the way it should have. The situation is not working out according to Hoyle, certainly not the way you hoped it would. Better to be out of it, even at a loss, rather than face a period of uncertainty and worry. If the stock has started to act badly you cannot tell how much worse it is going to behave. If you fail to set a stop you may go on day after day hoping for a rally that never comes, while your stock sinks lower and lower, and eventually you may find (as millions *have* found) that what started to be a small reaction and an annoying but trivial loss, has turned out to be a ruinous catastrophe. Stop orders cannot always be placed. In certain cases in active stocks the exchange may restrict the use of stop orders.

The question is where and when to set the stop, realizing that there is no perfect and absolutely satisfactory rule. If the stop is too close, you will of course take unnecessary losses; you will lose your holdings of stocks that eventually forge ahead and complete the profitable rise you hoped for. If stops are too wide (too far away) you will take larger losses than necessary in those cases where your stock definitely has broken out of pattern.

Now it will be obvious that the setting of stop orders depends on the price of the stock and its habits. You would not place your stop level at the same percentage distance under a bottom in a conservative, high-priced stock like AT when it is selling at 80, that you would to protect a speculative issue like PTC at a time when it is selling at 8.

The higher priced stocks, as we already have seen, make smaller percentage moves. Conversely, the lower priced stocks make wider percentage moves. Therefore the lower priced stocks should have more leeway for their gyrations.

We will need a wider stop for them than we will for the less volatile "blue chips."

Similarly, we can take our Sensitivity Indexes to give us a picture of the individual habits of the stock. Although two stocks may be selling at the same price at a given moment, you would expect a stock like GFO to make wider swings than a stock such as CFG; therefore you will set your stops on GFO wider than on CFG.

We must take these factors into account and work out some sort of simple rule-of-thumb that we can follow. Let us arbitrarily assume an imaginary stock of "average" habits and a price of 25. Let us further assume that we will be satisfied, in this particular case, with stop protection 5% below the last established Minor bottom.

For a stock of the same sensitivity selling at 5, we would need about half again as much stop leeway (on a percentage basis). That is, the stop would be placed 7½% below the last bottom. We arrive at this by taking the normal expected range of an average stock at price 25, which is represented by the index figure 15.5 (see Table of Normal Range-for-Price, Appendix B), and comparing it with the Normal Range of a stock selling at 5, which is 24. These are merely relative indexes and mean only that the stock selling at 5 will normally move about 24% while the stock selling at 25 is making a move of about 15.5%. We multiply the basic stop distance of 5% by the fraction $\frac{24}{15.5}$, and we get approximately 7½%.

In exactly the same way we introduce the relative sensitivity of the stock, using the Sensitivity Index. If this index should be 1.33 we multiply the stop distance again by this figure and get 10%. In the case of a stock having a sensitivity of 2.00 at this same price, our stop distance would be 15%. If the sensitivity of the stock were only .66, we would get 5%.

In any case the stop distance, expressed as a percentage, is obtained by dividing the Normal Range for the Price by 15.5, then multiplying by the Sensitivity Index, and multiplying this result by 5%. (This operation can be done most easily and quickly with a slide rule.)

All of the foregoing may seem needlessly complicated to the average reader. We realize that many will not care to take the time and trouble to work out an exact, scientific stop level for each of their occasional commitments. However, the method of determining where stops should be placed in a systematic and consistent way has been given in some detail here, so that the principles involved will be perfectly clear, and so that you can change or adapt the various factors if you feel your experience justifies changes.

For most ordinary purposes a simplified table of stop distances will be sufficient. This table, which follows, gives you the approximate stop distance you would get by the method outlined above, for stocks in various price classifications and of various degrees of sensitivity.

TABLE OF STOP DISTANCES

(Expressed in Percent of the Price of the Stock)

Price	Conservative Sensitivity under .75	Median Sensitivity .75 to 1.25	Speculative Sensitivity Over 1.25
Over 100	5%	5%	5%
40 to 100	5%	5%	6%
20 to 40	5%	5%	8%
10 to 20	5%	6%	10%
5 to 10	5%*	7%	12%
Under 5	5%*	10%	15%

* Note: Ordinarily stocks in these price ranges would not be in the conservative group.

The stop level should be marked on your chart as a horizontal line as soon as an actual or theoretical transaction has been entered into, and it should be maintained until the transaction is closed, or until *progressive* stops (which we will explain in a moment) have been started in order to close it out. In the case of purchases, the stop level ordinarily will be at the indicated distance below the last previous Minor bottom. In the case of short sales it ordinarily would be at the indicated distance above the last Minor top.

To determine the position of this stop level simply figure what the percentage distance would amount to at the price of the stock. If you are dealing with a stock selling at 30 and the stop distance comes out 10%, then allow three points under your last Minor bottom.

To make this even easier, if you are using the *TEKNIPLAT* paper, you will see that it is possible to divide each of the two cycles making up a chart sheet into five spaces. If the center of the paper were numbered 10, then these spaces would be from 10 to 12, 12 to 14, 14 to 16, 16 to 18, and 18 to 20. Each of these "jumps" is made up of sixteen of the smallest vertical spaces. In the lowest section it will take about four of these small spaces to make 5%. It will take five in the second position, six in the third position, seven in the fourth and eight in the top position. You will soon learn to count out an approximate stop interval of 15% or 8% or 12% at any price level, without a moment's hesitation.

In no case would we ever set a protective stop level at less than a 5% interval, even for the most conservative, high-priced stocks.

These questions remain: "What constitutes a Minor bottom? What makes an established Minor top? How do we know how to choose the Basing Point from which to measure off our stop level interval?" What constitutes a bottom or a top will be taken up in the next chapter. For the present let us accept the proposition that we will determine the correct Basing Point and that we will always, always set our stop level at the moment we make the commitment.

It is understood, of course, that protective stops under long stock are *never* moved down, nor are protective stops over shorts ever moved up. As soon as the stock has moved in the right direction far enough to establish a new Basing Point the stop level is moved up (on longs) or down (on shorts), using the same rules for determining the new stop level as were used in fixing the original level.

The Progressive Stop

There is another use of the stop which is properly considered here. This is the progressive stop, used to close out a stock that has made a profitable move, or in some cases where a stock has given a danger signal before either completing a profitable move or violating a previous Minor bottom.

You will find that on many moves the stock will progress in the primary direction for several days, and then may develop exceptional volume. Often this occurs just as the stock reaches an important trendline or pattern border or resistance area. This heavy volume means one of two things. Usually it means that the Minor move has come to an end, that this is the top of the rise for the moment. Occasionally, however, the volume may signal the start of a breakaway move that may run up several (and perhaps many) points, almost vertically. (The reverse situation, of course, may develop on downside moves.)

If, noticing the heavy volume following a good rise, and assuming that this day marks the end of the move, you sell the stock at the market or at a limit, you are going to be dreadfully disappointed if this should be one of those rare cases where the stock opens next day on an upside gap and continues three, five or twenty points up in the following days. On the other hand, experience will have shown you that it will not pay to expect that sort of move very often. You will know that nine times out of ten you will be better off out of the stock.

Very well. After such a day when volume is exceptionally high (provided this is not the first day of breakout into new high ground beyond the last previous Minor top), cancel your protective stop and set a stop order for the day only, just ⅛ point under the closing price. For example, you have bought a stock at 21. It goes up on moderate volume, smashes through the old Minor top one day at 23 on very heavy volume, the next day continues to 23¾ on moderate volume, the third day advances on moderate volume to 24¼, and finally the fourth day makes a rise to 25 on much heavier volume than it has shown on any day of the rise except the day it broke through 23. The morning after this close at 25 you will notice the volume signal. You will cancel your protective stop, which may be at 18, and you will place a stop order, for the day only, to sell on stop at 24⅞. In most cases this will mean that your stock will be stopped out on the first sale of the day. And you may get a slightly lower price than you would get with a straight market order. On the other hand, after a day of high volume activity, you are not likely to be left in a thin market; there should be bids enough, near the top, to get you out at or near your stop price.

Meanwhile you are protected against losing the stock if there should be a continued move in the right direction. Suppose the opening the morning after you set your stop at 24⅞ should be on a gap at 25¼ and that prices then move up further, closing at 26. (On "runaway" moves of this sort the closing for the day during the move is likely to be at the top.) You will then set your stop, again for a single day only, at 25⅞. If the stock then opens at 26⅜ and moves up to 28 you will set another day stop at 27⅞, which, let us assume, is caught at the opening the following day at 27⅝. In this example you risked only ⅛ point on the first day, and eventually netted an extra gain of 2⅝ points. This, it should be pointed out, is all *net* gain, since your commissions are approximately the same in either case.

A progressive stop of this sort can be indicated on the chart by any mark you choose to use; for example, a band of short diagonal lines. When a stock moves for several days in a runaway move, you may repeat this mark each day, indicating a close stop ⅛ point under the close for each successive day until finally one of these stops is caught. In the case of short sales a buy stop is used in precisely the same way as the selling stop we have discussed, to follow the stock down on a sharp runaway dive.*

This use of stop orders is indicated wherever a stock has reached its reasonable objective on high volume, or where it has exceeded its objective and is moving out of the trend channel in free air, so to speak, and in some cases where a stock has failed to reach its objective.

If your stock, for instance, is rising in a trend channel, and about halfway between the lower and upper trendlines suddenly develops great volume, then a progressive close stop will protect you against the threatened failure of the move. Extreme volume in such a case, before there has been a breakout to a new high above the last Minor high, is definitely a warning and a threat. This would be especially true if there were also a gap or a One-day Reversal at this point.

The one day on which a close stop would *not* be applied after heavy volume had appeared would be the day the stock made a new high, running entirely through the previous Minor top and closing above it. This action generally

---

* In the case of a stock which has presumably completed its profitable move and has given a Minor top signal by volume, you may place a close (⅛ point) stop the first day. If the stock moves up next day, without abnormal volume, you may leave the stop at this same point each day until another "blowoff" or top signal appears; that is, until you see another day of heavy volume, a gap, or a One-Day Reversal, and then move the stop up to ⅛ point below the close of that day. This method often works out somewhat better than the continuously progressive close stop.

means the move is not yet completed. However, should the move continue higher and *again* show heavy volume, even if it is the very next day, we would then protect with a close, progressive stop.

In this chapter, as throughout the book, the expression "heavy volume" means heavy only with respect to the recent volume of sale in the stock you are watching. A thousand shares may be significantly heavy volume in some thin issues, whereas 10,000 shares would be no more than a normal turnover in more actively traded stocks. The volume chart itself will show, by a marked peak, when a day of abnormally heavy volume occurs.

It should be understood that the progressive stops we have been discussing are intended to take short-term gains, or to close out an exceptionally profitable runaway move terminating in an Intermediate climax. While the extreme conditions that call for this type of operation are by no means rare, they are not the usual, everyday action of the market. In the case of ordinary Minor tops, even when they are fairly apparent on the basis of trend channels, volume peak, and other indications, many traders and investors will prefer to wait out the expected reaction rather than pay additional commissions and lose a position that is still presumably in a favorable Major trend.

In short, the progressive stop is a device which may be very useful on occasion, but it is intended to cope with a special and somewhat unusual move.

The protective stops, on the other hand, offer the average trader, the man who is not able to spend his entire time studying the market, or who has not had long experience, a device by which he can limit his possible loss. He will be protected from his own unwillingness to close out the bad holding, and so, he will avoid the ruinous condition of becoming frozen into a hopeless situation. Since he will be taken out automatically, regardless of whether he has an ultimate gain or loss, he will have the capital to use in better-looking issues and will not have to worry about the prospects of recovery in his stock after it has gone many points against him.

However, if one has sufficient knowledge and sufficient determination to get out as soon as the trend has shown convincing evidence of a turn, there is less need for the stop orders. It is possible for such a person to operate successfully without them; and there are some advantages in doing this, since a stop order will occasionally be caught by a false move or an extended dull reaction. There are also advantages in not using stop orders for the experienced technician who is looking toward a possible long-term gain and who is willing to wait out a Secondary reaction. But it is a thousand times better for the man who is not sure of his methods to be stopped out early, than to be left holding a stock bought at, say 60, when it has declined to 20—or to 5!

CHAPTER XXVIII

WHAT IS A BOTTOM—WHAT IS A TOP?

IN THIS chapter we are not talking about what makes a *Major* top or bottom, nor what makes an *Intermediate* top or bottom. We are speaking of the *Minor* tops and bottoms that give us important hooks on which to hang our technical operations. Stop-order levels, trendlines, objectives, supports and resistances, are determined by these Minor tops and bottoms. They are of prime importance to us as traders.

Usually these Minor tops and bottoms are well marked and perfectly clear. Often they are not. Sometimes it is not possible to say definitely that this or that place is or is not a top or bottom. But it is possible to set certain standards, practical working rules, that will help us in marking these points; and these rules will not fail us too often.

A good rule for setting stop levels is to consider that a bottom has been made when the stock has moved "three days away" from the day marking the suspected low of the bottom. If a stock reacts for some days and finally makes a low at 24, with the high for that day at 25, then we will not have an established bottom until we have had *three days* in which the stock sells at no lower than 25 ⅛. The entire price range for three full days must be entirely above the top price for the day making the low. This is the "three days away" rule, and it would apply in reverse in declining markets, where the range for three days must be entirely below the entire range of the day making the high.

This gives a rule for setting an original stop order. It also gives a rule for changing the stop order. As soon as the stock has moved three days away from a new bottom, we move the stop order to a position below that bottom (we have already explained, in Chapter XXVII how we determine the distance this stop level should be below the bottom).

Protective stops for *long* stocks can move only *up*. A stop level once established is never to be moved down except when the stock goes ex-dividend or ex-rights; then the stop may be dropped the amount of the dividend or rights. Similarly, protective stops for short sales are to be moved only down, and may not be raised. (In the case of ex-dividends and ex-rights, the short-sale stop would be dropped the amount of the dividend or rights.)

There are certain situations where it is difficult to determine bottoms and tops; where indeed, it seems as though a consolidation or correction had been made without any significant move in the Secondary direction. In such cases

FIGURE 195. Advance of a protective stop order in a long commitment. The daily chart of American Cable and Radio in the summer of 1945 made a Rounded Bottom, part of a long period of consolidation following the advance which ended in July, 1944. A breakout on heavy volume occurred September 12, and purchases were then possible on any minor recessions.

The first protective stop would immediately be placed 6% below the previous Minor bottom of August 21, using the table given in Chapter XXVII. This would put the stop level at 9⅞. On September 19 and 20 we would have two days of market action entirely "away" from the September 17 Minor bottom, and on September 28, a third day. We would then move the stop up to 6% under the September 17 bottom, or to 10⅝. The next move would come after the new high closing of October 11, which is more than 3% higher than the October 1 Minor peak. The stop would now be placed at 11⅞. On November 2 a new high close was registered more than 3% over the October 15 Minor peak; the stop would be raised to 12¾. On November 15 another high closing topped by over 3% the Minor peak made on November 7. The stop would be moved up again; this time to 13½. November 29 made the third day the entire price range was "three days away" from the November 26 bottom, and the stop was upped to 13¾. The closing on December 5 gave us a 3% advance over the November 17 high and again we moved the stop, raising it to 14⅞. Finally, on January 3, 1946, this stop was caught as shown on the chart.

In a Bear Market, protective stops would be moved *down* in exactly the same manner to protect a short sale.

(as contrasted to the obvious situation where the stock moves up or down in series of well-marked steps and reactions, like a staircase) you will need all your judgment and experience to determine where the Minor *Basing Points* actually occur.

BASING POINTS

Let us call the levels which determine where stops should be placed *Basing Points*. In a Bull Market move, we will consider the bottom of each Minor reaction as a Basing Point from which we will figure our stop-order level as soon as the stock has moved up to "three days away." We will also use each Minor top as a Basing Point in a Bull move. In a Bear Market we will consider the tops of each rally and also each Minor Bottom as Basing Points for the protective stops, in the same way.

Where a stock makes a substantial move in the Primary direction, say a move of 15% or more, and then moves back at least 40% of the distance covered from the previous Basing Point to the end of the Primary move, that surely gives us a Basing Point as soon as the stock again starts off in the Primary direction. However, if the stock reacts less than 40%, perhaps even marks time at the same level for a week or more, that should also be considered a Basing Point as soon as the move in the Primary direction is continued (provided the volume indications are right).

The daily volume, as we have seen, is like the trained nurse's clinical thermometer; it tells a great deal about what is happening in a stock, more than the superficial symptoms of price alone. There are three times at which you may look for exceptionally heavy volume: (a) On the day of breakout from a pattern or a period of inaction, especially if the breakout is on the upside; (b) on the day on which the stock goes into new ground in the Primary or Intermediate direction, that is, goes above the last Minor top in a Bull Market, or below the last Minor bottom in a Bear Market, and (c) the day on which the Minor move is completed or nearly completed, that is, the new Minor top in a Bull Market and the Minor bottom in a Bear Market. To this we might add that extra heavy volume on any *other* day during a move in the Primary direction is likely to indicate that the move is at an end and will not complete the hoped-for advance or decline.

Now, after a Minor top has occurred, the stock now being in new high ground, and the top having been made on very heavy volume, we may look for the corrective move. Ordinarily that would be a decline of several days, a week, sometimes longer. Occasionally the correction, as we said a few paragraphs back, will take the form of a horizontal hesitation lasting a week or more without any particular corrective move in the downward direction. Where there is a downward correction, it is likely to come down to or near the top of the last previous Minor high (support). Also, and often at the same time, the corrective move will carry down to the basic trendline drawn through two or more previous Minor bottoms; or to the "parallel" to a trend-line drawn through the last two or more previous Minor tops. If the correc-tive move is horizontal, it is likely to run out until it meets one of these lines.

In any case, the thing to watch for is the decline of volume. If the trading shrinks, perhaps irregularly, but on the whole steadily, for some days after a new top has been made, during which time the stock either reacts or at any rate makes no progress in the Primary direction, then you are justified in con-sidering this as a Minor correction. If the stock now continues the Primary move and gets to a point that is "three days away," you can consider the bot-tom (that is, the point you draw your trendline through; not necessarily the extreme low point in the case of horizontal moves) as a new Basing Point.

Where a stock is starting what appears to be a new move, a breakout from a period of vacillating moves, it is sometimes hard to say precisely what point should be considered the bottom. There may be several small and indecisive moves on low volume preceding the real breakout. In such a case we would consider the appearance of high volume as the breakout signal, and set our Basing Point at the low point immediately preceding this signal. There will usually be such a point on one of the low volume days in the three or four days just before the breakout.

All that has been said about Basing Points in a Bull Market would also be true in reverse in a Bear Market, except that heavy volume does not always accompany a downside breakout.

Now there comes the difficult and distressing situation where the stock, hav-ing made a long runaway move (let us assume it is an upward move), starts out, apparently, to make a Flag, and is bought after a sufficient correction of 40% with a decline of volume; and then continues to go down steadily, with-out any rallies and without any clear volume indications. This is an unusual situation but it does happen on both the up side and the down side, from time to time. In the case we have just mentioned, we would look for support levels (consolidation patterns, multiple tops, etc.) formed on the way *down* in the previous trend, and lying below the level at which we purchased the stock. We would use these supports as Basing Points rather than hold a stop under the extreme bottom of the vertical move.

In many cases of this type you will not be able to find adequate Basing Points. Therefore, it seems unwise to try to get in on corrections after long runaway moves except (a) where the stock has risen well above good support that can serve as a Basing Point, or (b) where the stock is completely above all prices for several years and is moving "in the clear." (The reverse, of course: In Bear Markets the stock should have fallen below a strong resistance area, or must be in new low ground for the past several months before you con-sider a short sale.) And in any case of this sort where you are thinking of a trade in a stock that appears to be making consolidation after a fast, long, vertical move, you *must* have pronounced and conspicuous drying up of volume throughout the formation of the Flag or Pennant correction.

There is one more word of caution needed here as regards trading in an Intermediate trend. A series of moves in a trend will often take place in very regular form. There may be a good trendline, and the reactions may be about 40% to 50% and may come back to the previous Minor tops. The volume on the corrections may shrink, with increasing volume on the new tops. It is easy to start trading on such a "staircase" in the expectation that the moves will continue regular and consistent. But trends do not go on forever. Any Minor top may be the last. The importance of finding your Basing Points is to enable you to get out, at best on any closing violation of one of these points, and at worst on your protective stop order. The volume may again come to your aid in this question of when to stop trading on a trend. Although you look for high volume on the tops, you will be exceedingly suspicious of volume that is *much* higher than that on any of the preceding Minor tops. (Or bottoms in a Bear Market.) The final, or the next-to-final "blow-off" of a trend will usually show more volume than any of the minor blow-offs along the way; and when you see such climactic volume you should prepare to retire into your shell and wait for a full correction of the entire series of moves making up the Intermediate trend. Later, weeks later, or perhaps months later, you may find the stock has corrected 40% or more of the whole Intermediate move and is resting quietly with very little activity. Then is the time to watch it for new opportunities and a new trend in the Primary direction.

CHAPTER XXIX

TRENDLINES IN ACTION

FROM what has already been said in Part One of this book, you will be familiar with the characteristic straight-line trends of stocks, and the numerous exceptions and deviations that come into the picture from time to time. We know that stocks often move in parallel trends, sometimes for months, occasionally even for years. We also know that they may, and do, break out of trend or change the direction of their trends without notice.

Most of the pattern formations we have studied can be considered as manifestations of trend action, that is, as continuations or reversals of a trend.

Thus, a Symmetrical Triangle is simply the meeting of two trends. During the formation of the Triangle the stock is following both trends in a narrowing pattern until finally the dominant trend asserts itself. An Ascending Triangle is following an upward trend but has encountered a resistance level at the top. A Head-and-Shoulders shows the end of an upward trend and the beginning of a downward trend. A Rectangle is a parallel trend channel running in a horizontal direction. And so on.

We can project a parallel trend, and in the case of stocks which happen to continue moving in that trend, we can buy and sell at almost the precise points of contact with the trendline. Unfortunately, long and perfect straight-line trends of this sort are the exception rather than the rule. For actual trading purposes we will project our trends more or less continuously on the basis of *the most recently established data.*

Let us therefore, from the standpoint of tactics, consider the trends as they are indicated by the successive Minor tops and Minor bottoms. For illustration of this, and as a guide to what we are leading up to, we will consider simplified, ideal situations (see diagram examples).

To avoid confusion, we will mark the top trendline in blue and the bottom trendline in red. This can be done on daily charts easily, by using colored pencils. We will refer to the upper trendline as the Blue Trend, and the lower trendline as the Red Trend. From time to time we will also want to draw a line parallel to a Blue Trend across the bottom of the trend so as to include a segment of the trend channel between two tops within parallel lines. This we will call the Blue Parallel, and we will mark it with a dotted or broken blue

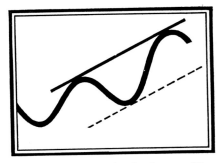

DIAGRAM 3 (Left).   Here is a rising trend showing the basic trendline across two bottoms, which we call the Red Trendline, and its parallel (indicated by a broken line) through the top of the intervening peak.   The parallel suggests the approximate objective of the next move if the stock continues in trend.

DIAGRAM 4 (Right).   The same rising trend with the return line, which we call the Blue Trendline, drawn through two tops.   Broken line represents its parallel through the intervening bottom.   This Blue Parallel is useful in determining a buying point, especially in trends of rapidly changing form when the stock may not react to its *basic* trendline.

 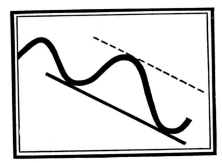

DIAGRAM 5 (Left).   This is a declining trend showing the basic trendline across two tops, which we call the Blue Trendline, and its parallel (indicated by a broken line) through the bottom of the intervening decline.   The parallel suggests the approximate objective of the next move if the stock continues in trend.

DIAGRAM 6 (Right).   The same declining trend with the return line, which we call the Red Trendline, drawn through two bottoms.   Broken line represents its parallel through the intervening top.   This Red Parallel is useful in determining a point at which to make short sales, especially in trends of rapidly changing form when the stock may not rally to its *basic* trendline.

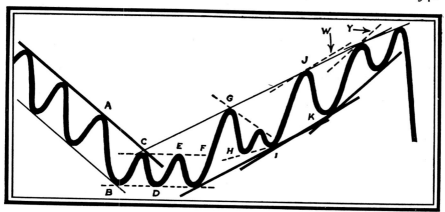

DIAGRAM 7. Simplified diagram of a stock chart showing trend action. Basic trendlines are marked with heavy lines; return lines are marked lightly.

At the start the stock declines in a parallel trend channel. Blue Trendline is basic here. A short sale on a rally to the Red Parallel at point A will find its objective on the Blue Parallel at B. Another short sale on the Red Parallel at C would be followed by failure to reach the objective. Chances are good, however, that increased volume would develop at the double bottom and give warning to get out of short commitments. The upside penetration of the basic Blue Trendline at E, alone, is not sufficient reason to reverse position and go long. Trendlines set up during formation of the Rectangle would be marked in the regular way, but are indicated here by broken lines to emphasize the pattern. Another short sale, if tried on the sixth point of contact with the Rectangle at F, would be stopped out on the breakout.

The trend is now rising although we cannot yet draw a basic (Red) trendline. The first buy would be made on a 40-50% correction of the breakout move from the Rectangle, or on a return to the top (support) level at H.

A trendline would be drawn to the first bottom established in the Triangle. This is not shown as it would ultimately be replaced by the line shown through the outermost point in the Triangle. We have indicated by broken lines the trendlines set up during the formation of the pattern.

The objective of the breakout move from the Triangle would be the Red Parallel to our now rising basic trendline. This objective is reached at J. A return line (Blue) would be drawn from the first reversal top of the Triangle at G through the top of the breakout move at J, and the parallel to this through point I would indicate about where to make the next purchase. As a matter of fact the stock does not actually get back to that point; in practice the purchase would probably be made at K on the basis of a 40-50% correction, or on a reaction to the support level G.

The subsequent upward move would not carry through to the Red Parallel marked W. However, the alarm would probably be sounded clearly by a day of heavy volume, a One-Day Reversal, or a gap. Since the trend is now obviously convergent no further purchases would be considered. The next move fails to make much headway and falls far short of the objective set by the Red Parallel marked Y. Soon after, the Wedge breaks out downside.

line. Conversely, we may wish to draw a parallel to the Red Trend so as to include the segment of the trend channel between two bottoms; and this dotted red line we will call the Red Parallel.

Since ordinarily a top will be formed after a bottom and a bottom after a top, we will expect to draw alternately, a Blue Trendline and then a Red Trend line, these lines being drawn as soon as the new top or bottom is established. (In some cases a light pencil line may be drawn to indicate suspected tops or bottoms, until developments confirm their validity.)

We have already taken up the important and rather difficult question of determining the Minor tops and bottoms. Very often these points will be clear and obvious. Sometimes they will be obscure, and you will be able to draw trendlines with confidence in such cases only after considerable experience covering many types of action. The most difficult times to determine Minor trends are during reversals, especially where these are of the rounded and irregular types. However, in these cases (of reversal), we will not depend so much on the trendlines to determine buying and selling points.

So long as a stock persists in a parallel trend channel it is perfectly clear that you should buy near the bottom of the channel and sell near the top. From the geometry of the situation (see examples), you will see at a glance that it is not likely to be profitable to sell short in an upward-moving trend (since the reactions are necessarily smaller than the advances), nor to buy long stock in a downward-moving trend.

Therefore a trend must show that it is presumably an up trend before you are justified in buying long stock. And you must have what is presumably a down trend to justify a short sale.

You will notice from the simplified examples shown here that pattern formations indicate trends. The breaking of a Rectangle on the upside results in an upward slope to the Blue Trend. The move up out of an Ascending Triangle confirms the rising Red Trend and creates a rising Blue Trend. The down-side breaking of a Head-and-Shoulders neckline confirms a descending Blue Trend and sets up a descending Red Trend. And so on.

From studies of these patterns and various trend actions, we arrive at a compact set of trading rules based on these Red and Blue trendlines. These rules are summarized below:

Buying Long Stock

Preparatory Buying Signals (indicating that a buying opportunity may be in the making). Penetration of Blue Trend to a new high closing (in most cases). (The simple breaking of a descending Blue Trendline where no other pattern or indication is present is not sufficiently conclusive evidence of reversal to justify commitments.)

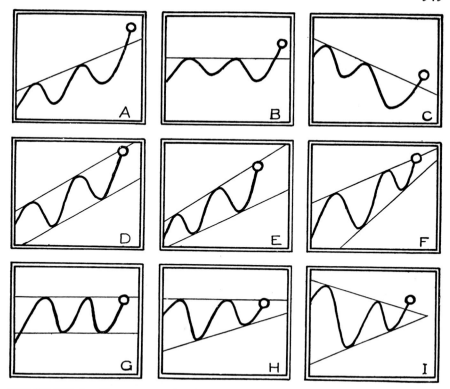

DIAGRAM 8. Preparatory Buying Signals Shown by Trend Action.

A. Penetration of an ascending Blue Trendline.

B. Penetration of a horizontal Blue Trendline.

C. The penetration of a descending Blue Trendline without other technical indications is *not* conclusive evidence of a change in trend, and does *not* justify long commitments.

D. Contact with the Blue Trendline of an ascending parallel trend pattern.

E. Contact with the Blue Trendline of an ascending divergent trend pattern.

F. In this case, contact with the Blue Trendline does *not* suggest a buy on the next reaction, since the trend appears to be converging; a Possible Wedge in the making, with bearish implications.

G. Contact with the Blue Trendline of a Rectangle at its fifth point of reversal.

H. Contact with the Blue Trendline of an Ascending Triangle.

I. Penetration *on volume* of descending Blue Trendline when Red Trendline is ascending (Symmetrical Triangle).

In rising trends the Blue Trendline is a return line; and purchases will be made on reactions to a line parallel to the *new* Blue Trendline established at the top of the signal move and drawn through the intervening bottom. Note that in the case of decisive breakouts from patterns such as Rectangles and Triangles, a purchase may also be made on the basis of a computed 40-50% correction of the breakout move, or on a return to support.

Contact with the ascending Blue Trend if Red Trend is also ascending, provided the trends do not converge (parallel or divergent trend channel).

Contact with horizontal Blue Trend if Red Trend is also horizontal or ascending (Rectangle, Ascending Triangle).

Penetration of descending Blue Trend on volume if Red Trend is ascending (Symmetrical Triangle).

Execution of Buys (after preparatory buying signal).

In case the previous Blue Trend has been ascending, draw the Blue Parallel and buy at or near this line.

In case the previous Blue Trend has been horizontal or descending (that is to say, emerging from Rectangles, Triangles, and various reversal patterns) buy on a reaction of 40 to 45 percent of the distance from the last previous Minor bottom to the extreme top of the most recent move.

SELLING LONG STOCKS

Immediately on execution of the buy order determine the stop level (see chapter on Stop Orders), and place your protective stop. Penetration of this stop level will automatically close out your transaction. The stop level may be moved up according to the "three days away" rule, but may never be moved down (except to adjust for ex-dividend or ex-rights). If the stock closes below a previous Minor bottom (thus setting up a descending Red Trend), sell on close *progressive stops.*

If the stock advances on moderate volume and then develops unusually high volume on any day during the advance before either the Blue Trend is broken (with a close above that trendline) or before the stock has made a new high closing over the last Minor top, close out the transaction on close progressive stops.

If the stock develops high volume on the day on which it either tops and closes above the Blue Trend or makes a new high closing over the previous Minor top, hold it. If heavy volume again occurs on the following day or any subsequent day, however, sell on close progressive stops.

You will find that in many cases the heavy volume signal will develop (sometimes with also a One-Day Reversal or an exhaustion gap) on or near the Red Parallel. You will watch especially for this volume indication as a sign of a good profit-taking point. If the volume signal does not show up, your selling objective is this Red Parallel, at a limit or on close progressive stops. In case there is no such volume signal at the top of the move and the move does not reach the Blue Trend nor make a new high, you are very likely running into a Triangle situation. In that case you will have to wait for a breakout one way or the other. Meanwhile maintain your stop protection underneath.

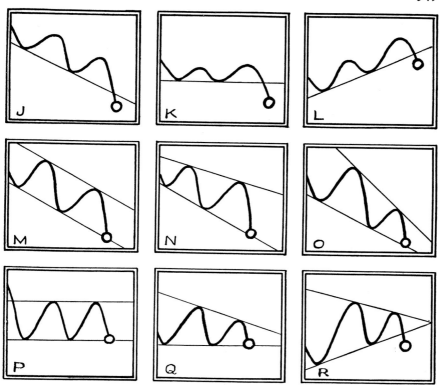

DIAGRAM 9. Preparatory Signals for Short Sales Shown by Trend Action.
J. Penetration of a descending Red Trendline.
K. Penetration of a horizontal Red Trendline.
L. The penetration of an ascending Red Trendline without other technical indications is *not* conclusive evidence of a change in trend, and does *not* justify short commitments.
M. Contact with the Red Trendline of a descending parallel trend channel.
N. Contact with the Red Trendline of a descending divergent trend pattern.
O. In this case, contact with the Red Trendline does *not* suggest a short sale on the next rally, since the trend appears to be converging; a possible Wedge in the making, with bullish implications.
P. Contact with the Red Trendline of a Rectangle at its fifth point of reversal.
Q. Contact with the Red Trendline of a Descending Triangle.
R. Penetration of ascending Red Trendline (with or without volume) when Blue Trendline is descending (Symmetrical Triangle).

In descending trends the Red Trendline is a return line; and short sales will be made on rallies to a line parallel to the *new* Red Trendline established at the bottom of the signal move and drawn through the intervening peak. Note that in the case of decisive breakouts from patterns such as Rectangles and Triangles, a short sale might also be made on the basis of a computed 40-50% correction of the breakout move, or on a return to resistance.

SELLING STOCK SHORT

Preparatory Selling Signals (indicating that an opportunity for short sales may be in the making).

Penetration of Red Trend to a new low closing (in most cases). (The simple breaking of an ascending Red Trendline where *no other* pattern or indication is present is not sufficiently conclusive evidence of reversal to justify commitments.)

Contact with descending Red Trend if Blue Trend is also descending, provided the trends do not converge (parallel or divergent trend channel).

Contact with horizontal Red Trend if Blue Trend is also horizontal or descending (Rectangle, Descending Triangle).

Penetration of ascending Red Trend (with or without volume increase) if Blue Trend is descending (Symmetrical Triangle).

Execution of Short Sales (after preparatory selling signal).

In case the previous Red Trend has been descending, draw the Red Parallel and sell at or near this line.

In case the previous Red Trend has been horizontal or ascending (that is to say emerging from Rectangles, Triangles, and various reversal patterns), sell on a rally of 40 to 45 percent of the distance from the last previous Minor top to the extreme bottom of the most recent move.

COVERING SHORT SALES

Immediately on execution of the Short Sale determine the stop level (see chapter on Stop Orders), and place your protective stop. Penetration of this stop level will automatically close out your transaction. The stop level may be moved down according to the "three days away" rule, but may never be moved up.

If the stock closes above a previous Minor top (thus setting up an ascending Blue Trend), buy to cover on close progressive stops.

If the stock declines on moderate volume and then develops unusually high volume on any day during the decline before either the Red Trend is broken (with a close below that trendline), or before the stock has made a new low closing under the last Minor bottom, close out the transaction on close progressive stops.

If the stock develops high volume on the day on which it either breaks and closes below the Red Trend or makes a new low closing under the previous Minor bottom, hold it short. If heavy volume again occurs on the following day or any subsequent day, however, buy to cover on close progressive stops.

You will find that in many cases the heavy volume signal will develop (sometimes with also a One-Day Reversal or an exhaustion gap) on or near the Blue Parallel. You will watch especially for this volume indication as a sign of a good profit-taking point. If the volume signal does not show up, your buying objective is the Blue Parallel, at a limit or on close progressive stops. In case there is no such volume signal at the bottom of the move and the move does not reach the Red Trend nor make a new low, you are very likely running into a Triangle situation. In that case you will have to wait for a breakout one way or the other, meanwhile maintaining your stop protection overhead.

ADDITIONAL SUGGESTIONS

When a level is reached which appears to be either a Minor bottom on a reaction or a Minor top on a rally, and when the stock continues to stall and remain at this point, moving in a very narrow range for three weeks or more without giving any signal either by way of price change or volume action as to its next move, it is wise to assume that this congestion is definitely a key area, should be considered a Minor top or bottom, and protective stops adjusted to it as a Basing Point, instead of the previously established top or bottom, as against the possibility that the move out of this area, when it comes, *may* be in the wrong direction.

After a series of moves in a trend, with each move in the Primary direction marked by heavier volume than the retreats or corrective moves against the trend, you are likely to have a move in the Primary direction which is marked by *extraordinary* volume; that is to say, by much larger volume than the normal increase for a Primary move. On such a move, after taking your profits on previous commitments, you would ordinarily begin to plan the next commitment on the correction. But in this particular case, noting the extreme volume, you would cancel any immediate plans for further commitments in the Primary direction.

The reason for this is that such *climactic* volume normally indicates the final "blow-off" of the Intermediate trend, to be followed either by a reversal, or at least by a period of stagnation, or formation of consolidation patterns, or intermediate correction. In such a case it is not safe to make any further commitments on this trend pending further developments and the positive reassertion of the trend.

If you can examine daily charts of various stocks, covering long and important trends, you will find that the series of Minor moves making up the Intermediate trend are likely to culminate in a Minor move marked by tremendous volume. This is more true of tops than bottoms, although at the end of the panic phase of a Bear Market we very often see climactic volume. The climax indicates, on the one hand, the sale of large amounts of stock by strong investors to weak traders, near the top; on the other hand, the liquidation of holdings by weak traders near the bottom, into the hands of strong investors who will hold them for the next Major move.

One of the most common errors, and one of the easiest to fall into, is to mistake a climactic top or bottom for a normal confirmation or preparatory signal for a new commitment in line with the preceding trend.

It is similar in nature to the error often made by novices in the market of buying on the Minor tops (becoming dazzled with the rapid price advance and the great volume of activity). However, in the case of these final "blow-off" moves the volume is greater and the adverse portent far more serious.

General Outline of Policy for Trading in the Major Trend

A. Always trade in the direction of the Major or Primary Dow trend as it is indicated at the time.

B. If the two component averages of the Dow theory (Industrials and Rails) are not in agreement, trade in the direction of the last established Primary trend but only in the component which is still following that trend.

C. If you have access to charts of group averages covering groups of businesses in the same or related lines, trade in the Primary direction when the trend of the group corresponds.

D. Trade in any particular stock when its own individual chart indicates a trend in the same direction as the Primary trend, and when the technical picture has indicated a probable move in that direction.

Make all new commitments on the reactions or rallies following the signaling move in the Primary direction, except in the case of Primary reversals from Bull Market to Bear Market, when short sales may be made at the market immediately following the reversal.

Exception: After an extended move or a series of moves in the Primary direction when signs of exhaustion and reversal appear in individual charts, commitments in the opposite direction may be made with objectives limited to a correction of the preceding Intermediate move in the Primary direction.

CHAPTER XXX
USE OF SUPPORT AND RESISTANCE

WE KNOW that after many breakouts from well-defined reversal and consolidation patterns we get a short counter-move back to the edge of the pattern, and that the checking of this move at that point is an example of support or resistance as the case may be. Also, we should be familiar by now with the tendency of stocks to move up or down in a series of zig-zag steps. If the move is upward, the reaction after each advance tends to stop at the level of the preceding peak. If the move is downward, the rally after each decline tends to stop at the level of the preceding bottom. This is again a matter of support and resistance, and provides the basis for buying on reactions or selling on rallies.

It has also been pointed out that Intermediate Secondary moves will frequently stop at or close to the previous Intermediate top or bottom.

It is necessary to evaluate the importance of these phenomena of support and resistance and apply them in market practice, for they are among the most important tools we have. Unfortunately it is not easy to reduce this particular subject to a neat formula or body of rules. Here you will depend very largely on experience and observation. You will have to be alert in spotting the levels where resistance or support is likely to be encountered, and some judgment is needed in balancing the various factors that will affect the situation.

For example, there is a stock which has broken up out of a well-defined Rectangle of considerable duration. Should the heavy volume of the breakout move give way to a dull reaction, you will look for an opportunity to buy this stock at a point a little above the top level of the Rectangle. It will probably not penetrate very far below that level and, indeed, will often fail to react *all* the way to the support. If the stock should then advance to a new high, and once more decline on low volume, you may look for another buying point at about the level of the peak reached on the original breakout. Another advance may be followed by reaction to the second peak, and this process may be repeated a number of times, each reaction carrying back to the level of the preceding high.

Now we all know that this sort of thing does not continue indefinitely. When the stock first breaks out, moving from, say, 15 to 19, we may buy rather confidently on the reaction to 17, if that is the support level. If we did not buy on this move, we may buy with considerable assurance on the reaction

349

to support after the next advance. This advance might have carried the price to 21 and our buying point would, of course, be at the previous peak of 19. However, as the stock moves up to 25, 30, 40, it must be clear that we are approaching a real top; that although we cannot say where that top will be reached, we can be sure that it is becoming increasingly tempting to long-time holders of this stock to sell and take their substantial gains. The series of steps is bound to come to an end. To be sure, the Major course of the stock and of the market may continue up for months or years, but after a series of sharp rises, we may reasonably expect a reversal and a rather substantial Intermediate decline before the upward move is continued.

Therefore, we must regard each successive step of advance with increasing suspicion, and it is a fair rule that after a stock has made three such moves in the Primary direction, it is time to look for an Intermediate correction, or at least an important period of consolidation.

Thus we have the rough shape of a rule. Buy on the reaction to support after the first breakout. Buy on the reaction to the first Minor peak after the next move. But do not buy on the reaction to the second Minor peak.

Let us say, then, that we have been successful in two short-term moves, buying on the reaction to support and selling on the climax after a new top has been made. But we have decided not to attempt a third such trade. What, then, may we expect next? We may see a period of consolidation, we may see the beginning of an Intermediate decline, or we may see the stock actually go right on moving up. No matter. We will wait for the Intermediate reaction. We will wait until the stock makes a very substantial decline, and this may take many weeks. Then, if the Major trend has not reversed itself, we will again look for a buying opportunity at (or somewhat above) the *Intermediate* support which will usually be the top level of the advance *preceding* the one just completed. For this is the level from which the next Primary advance is likely to proceed, and is a good buying point.

Of course we find the same situation in Bear Markets. A breakout is likely to be followed by one, two, three or more steps of decline, with intervening rallies to Minor resistance. Sooner or later (and we would count on no more than three such steps in a series) we will get a turn and an Intermediate recovery. We will then wait for this rally, which may itself be made up of several Minor steps, to reach or approach closely the preceding Intermediate bottom at which point we may look for substantial resistance. Here is the place again to put out shorts.

Questions will come to your mind. One of them, and one of the most important is: How do we decide when an expected support or resistance has failed us, and at what point do we then abandon our position?

It will be clear that this question can be a very painful one. Let us suppose you have seen a stock rise to 25 and have placed an order to buy it at

23½ on the basis of expected support at 23, the level of a previous **Minor peak.**
The order is executed during a dull reaction. The next day the stock **slips**
down to 22½, on perhaps only two or three sales. The next day it continues
down to 21½, still on low volume. And during the next week it goes down
steadily, without much volume, nearly every sale being at a lower price as
though no new bids were being received, and as though no substantial number
of bids were standing on the book at any point. A decline of this sort can
eventually assume the magnitude of an Intermediate reaction. The move may
carry down to 15 before it turns. Obviously this was not what you expected,
and you should be out of the stock.

The painful part of these drifting moves is that you do not want to sell
your stock (which you bought at 23½) on just a slight move down, say to
22¾, since the probability is strong that it will shoot up at any moment to new
high levels. And yet, at some point during a continued decline, you must
decide, "This has gone through the support; I should sell and take a small loss
now, rather than risk a more serious loss." And the most painful part of all is
that sometimes, the moment you have sold and taken your loss, the stock will
come to life and complete what would have been an extremely profitable move.

You might just as well prepare yourself for this sort of disappointment; for
it will happen to you. But to avoid nights of pacing the floor and days of
worry, you should decide, *at the time you make the original commitment,* just
how much leeway you are prepared to give the stock. Then you will not be
tempted to put off a decision from day to day if things are not going the way
you hoped.

In the case of purchases or short sales, made against Minor peaks or bottoms
as the case may be, you might set up the following rule. Measuring from the
extreme high of the previous (supporting) Minor top, or the extreme low of
the previous (resisting) Minor bottom, set a stop, using the method we have
outlined in Chapter XXVII. This would often be the intra-day high or low,
not necessarily the closing price. Penetration to that extent should be presumptive evidence that your expected support or resistance is not going to
function.

Where you are buying against Major or Intermediate support, or selling
short against Major or Intermediate resistance, you can allow a little more
leeway for penetration. In such cases, examine the support or resistance area,
and estimate visually its core or axis; in other words, try to gauge the "center
of gravity" of this area, the point which is most nearly the mean price of sales
occurring there, taking into account the volume, since the important thing is
to determine the approximate price level at which a great many shares changed
hands. Having determined this point, set your stop beyond it, according to
the methods specified in Chapter XXVII.

Up to this point we have concerned ourselves (reversing the usual order) with how to get out of situations which have gone bad. We have said nothing about where, precisely, to get in, nor where, precisely, to take profits.

In the matter of getting in, i.e., making the original commitment, you will feel, perhaps, that there is a conflict between acting on support or resistance, and acting on either trendline action or a computed reaction of 40 to 50 percent after a previous move. At times there is such conflict and it is not possible to state any exact rule which will reconcile these three different trading indications. However, in a great number of cases you will be delighted to observe that a reaction of about 45 percent will bring your stock to the trendline, and will also bring it near to the support or resistance level. After a move to a new Minor top, a stock may be expected to react (a) about 40 to 50 percent of that move, (b) to the basic trendline, and (c) to the previous supporting Minor top. Your purchase, then, will be based on a consideration of all three factors. If you have bought "early," on the basis of one factor alone, you may expect the stock to react a bit further without spoiling the triple indications to the extent of catching your stop. It would be best to make your purchases on the basis of whichever factor indicates the smallest reaction, and to place your stop beyond the greatest reaction indicated by any of the three. Ordinarily there will not be too much difference between these three points. As usual, the method applies in reverse to short sales.

Where you are buying after an Intermediate decline, or selling after an Intermediate rally, you will lean somewhat more heavily on support and resistance than on either a computed percentage for the Secondary move or a trendline. You will, of course, examine the history of the stock, preferably on weekly or monthly charts first, to see its Major trend, to locate important support or resistance areas, and to estimate roughly the extent of the corrective move the termination of which you are trying to gauge. You will then check this data in the more detailed picture you can get from your daily charts. As the Intermediate corrective move approaches within 4 or 5 percent of the support or resistance level, you may come to a day of extremely heavy volume; and this day may also be a One-Day Reversal. If so, your commitment should be made at once, protected of course by a stop. Otherwise, you may make your commitment whenever the chart begins to hesitate or flatten out, or, lacking other indications, when it has come to within 3 percent of the support or resistance.

Now in this case, your problem in taking profits is a bit more difficult than in the case of Minor moves. You are expecting a reversal of the Intermediate corrective move and the establishment of a new Intermediate trend in the Primary direction. You are at a point where the course of the market is uncertain. You must realize that prices may stay at the support (or resistance) level, forming a Line or Rectangle, and finally penetrate that level, establishing reversal of the Major trend. Or they may be stopped and turned at the support or resistance level, only to make a small move away and then return for another, and possibly successful, attempt at penetration.   Or (and this is what you hope, of course) a continuation of the Major trend may develop, with a sharp move on increased volume in the favorable direction, to be followed, perhaps by a Minor corrective move, and another thrust in the Primary direction; perhaps a new series of Minor moves carrying the entire Primary trend into new ground.

Taking these cases one by one, if the stock remains at the support or resistance level for many days or for several weeks, and then penetrates that level, closing at a price that is clearly through it, get out at once.   If the stock makes a small move in the right direction and returns to the support or resistance, prepare to get out if there is a definite penetration.   If, however, the move is in the right direction, watch for volume indications, and prepare to set close stops to take your profits as soon as heavy volume appears (except on a day of breakout).   Of course, once such a signal has appeared, you are then justified in continuing to make new commitments on the following Minor correction, and the one following that, for you are again moving in the Major trend.

There is one other situation that should be mentioned here.   Up to this point we have assumed that all of your commitments have been made to take advantage of a move in the direction of the Major trend.   Let us suppose, however, that a move which has carried a stock up to new high levels in a series of Minor steps, proceeds to form and then breaks out of a reversal pattern. We must now look for a Secondary move of Intermediate extent.   We may sell short on the rally to the Minor resistance, and, if the move continues down, we may make a second and even (more cautiously) a third commitment against successive Minor bottoms.   But, in this case, we will be looking for the decline to end somewhere in the vicinity of the last previous Intermediate top which is now a support level.   Similarly, following a recognized reversal pattern and upward breakout on volume during a Bear Market, we may expect an Intermediate rally which can be used for trading up to the previous Intermediate bottom where strong resistance is likely to show up.   A skillful trader can turn these Secondary moves into profits during periods when it is not possible to trade along the indicated Primary trend; but it should be remembered that ordinarily such moves cannot be expected to go as far as will those in the Primary direction.

We might close this chapter by reminding you again that, while support and resistance action in the Minor trend is shown clearly in daily charts, the Intermediate and Major supports and resistances are most easily recognized on weekly or monthly charts.

CHAPTER XXXI

NOT ALL IN ONE BASKET

DIVERSIFICATION is important because technical patterns do not always carry out their original promise. If all your capital is tied up in one stock, or in a few stocks of the same group or line of business, you may be hurt by a false move affecting only your holdings, even though the rest of the market may continue to hold firm or even to move farther along the Primary trend. By diversifying you are protected by the law of averages against *all* of your holdings going the wrong way, except of course, in the case of some reversal that affects the entire market or a large segment of it.

Intelligent diversification calls for study of the costs of buying and selling stocks, especially in small quantities. You might wish to have a portfolio of stocks representing the entire Dow-Jones averages, or a selection that includes at least one stock of every major group. But if your capital is limited, this might mean buying only a half-dozen shares of each stock, and the minimum commission charges would make this an expensive operation, entirely too costly for short-term trading. The short-term trader must always think of these costs. They are more important to him than to the long-term investor who may intend to hold the same stock for many months or years. To you as a trader, a quarter point or a half point may mount up to serious proportions when it is multiplied through a number of transactions.

Commissions are charged on each purchase of stock and on each sale, according to schedules worked out from formulas that are set by the stock exchanges. In addition there is a transfer tax which is charged to the seller (but not to the purchaser) of stock, based on the par value of the stock. Brokerage rates may be changed from time to time. Your broker can give you a schedule of current commissions and other costs of trading such as transfer taxes and the S.E.C. fee.

Your broker can give you a schedule showing commission and tax costs, and in case there are any important changes in the rates you should study them to see what effect they will have on your costs of trading in stocks at various prices. The following table, based on the latest rates at the time of publication, will give you an approximate guide as to the cost of trading round lots of stocks at various price levels. Allowance is made for commissions and also for stock transfer tax.

Costs of Buying and Selling 100-Share Lots (Round Trip)

(Approximate: Estimated as of new commission rates effective March 30, 1959)

Stock selling below			$ 5.00 a share, figure	¼	point round-trip costs.
"	"	at $ 5.00 to 10.00 " "	"	⅜	" " " "
"	"	" 10.00 " 15.00 " "	"	½	" " " "
"	"	" 15.00 " 25.00 " "	"	⅝	" " " "
"	"	" 25.00 " 40.00 " "	"	¾	" " " "
"	"	over 40.00 " "	"	1	" " " "

You will find that your round-trip costs are a higher percentage of the capital invested in low-priced stocks than in high-priced stocks. Also, that the percentage costs will be higher on a smaller number of shares than on a round lot, and increasing as the number of shares decreases. Also, that the percentage costs rise as the total amount of capital used is less.

Involved in this question of costs is the matter of the ⅛ or ¼ point "odd-lot fraction" which is charged on every purchase and every sale of less than a round lot of stock. (Ordinarily this means on any lot of less than 100 shares, though there are certain stocks, classified as "inactive," where the round lot or unit of trading is 10 shares.)

Since these commissions, taxes, and odd-lot fractions can become serious factors in active trading it will be helpful to have a table here, showing how under the present rates you can invest your capital at reasonably low cost. It is necessary to decide more or less arbitrarily what "low cost" will mean, since costs of trading will run from around 1% on round lots of high-priced stocks to 20% or more on the lowest-priced. A practical figure might be 5%, and we will consider that any round-trip transaction that results in a total gross cost of 5% or less can be classified as "low cost."

If you are investing your capital in units of approximately	Trade in stocks priced as indicated (For round-trip gross costs of 5% or less)	
	Round Lots	Odd Lots
$ 500	—	60 and over
750	—	25 " "
1000	8 and over	20 " "
1500 or more	8 " "	16 " "

A good general rule for low-cost trading might be stated: *Do not trade in less than 100-share lots in stocks selling at 15 or less: do not place less than $500 in any single transaction.*

If your capital is, say, $1000 or $2000, you might do well to divide it into units of about $500 each and confine your trading to odd lots of stocks selling at 40 or higher. With larger capital you could use larger trading units and extend the range of your trading into somewhat lower priced stocks. In any case it is important to diversify your holdings. By dividing your capital and using it in such a way as to avoid unnecessary penalties in high costs, you will have greater protection against freak moves and sudden changes that might affect a single stock very seriously.

On the other hand, if you have sufficient capital to secure plenty of diversification (8 or 10 stocks should be a maximum for an active trading account), you can increase the size of the trading units. The whole question here is as to the *minimum* amounts to be invested in a single commitment, and if these amounts were doubled or tripled it would not increase costs, but would, in many cases, reduce them.

Under the commission rates as of May, 1958 the total Round Trip costs (commissions, odd-lot fractions, transfer tax, etc. on the purchase and sale) of $1000 worth of a stock will amount to approximately $44. This figure runs fairly constant for stocks at various prices; in some cases the costs may run a dollar so less. Where the unit of trading is more than $1000, the percentage of cost will be somewhat reduced.

May 1st, 1975 Competitive Commissions Approved

The long-discussed question of fixed commission rates was presumably resolved by the opening up of flexible commission rates for member brokers, permitting a customer to seek the most favorable rate for him. This would depend, of course, on the size of the account, and on the customer's need for special services from the broker, the commission rate to be determined by negotiation.

CHAPTER XXXII

MEASURING IMPLICATIONS IN TECHNICAL CHART PATTERNS

IF YOU show one of your charts to a friend and tell him it looks bullish he will reply immediately, "How far do you think it will go?" This is an automatic response; you can count on it.

The question is a good one. How far is this expected move likely to go? You don't know. Nobody knows. Very often you can say, with a fair degree of assurance, "This stock which has just made such-and-such an advance, is likely to react to around such-and-such a price." *That* you can estimate fairly closely seven or eight times out of ten, by referring to the basic trendline, the parallel projection of the top trendline, the 5/11 reaction (45%) rule, or the support level.

These rules work out fairly well as applied to reactions in a Bull trend, and similarly we can estimate rallies in a Bear trend. Not so with the move in the direction of the trend itself. A bullish move may and often does overrun the upper trendline by running up as far again as the move to the trendline. A bearish move may exceed the down trend, dropping apparently without limit. (That is one reason we have protective stops—to prevent disaster in case the trend suddenly reverses itself.) And that is why we prefer the use of close progressive stops as a method of taking profits, rather than using limit orders placed at a trendline, resistance level, or at some other definite point. Very often, to be sure, a stock *will* check its advance at one of these indicated points, but the cases where a move carries beyond its objectives are fairly common, and in such cases no one can make even a reasonable guess as to what limit the stock will reach on the move.

This follows because the move itself is an unreasonable one. It is an example of public participation, the surge of uncontrolled speculation (and very often it is the final surge of that particular trend).

In exactly the same way, and often more violently, the uncontrolled falling out of trend in a downward move is an example of panic, and being completely beyond reason it follows no rule and knows no pre-determined limits.

There are, however, certain patterns and certain situations where we can make some estimate of the probable extent of a move in the Primary direction —usually an estimate of its minimum extent. In these cases we have a guide to help us in making the decision as to whether the situation offers enough potential gain to be worth the risks involved. Also, the indicated measurement gives us at least a hint of about where we might reasonably begin to look for the volume which will indicate the top.

For example: A decisive breakout from a Symmetrical Triangle is likely to carry *at least* as far as the height of the Triangle measured along its first reaction. This is a conservative measurement. The move may go much farther. In fact, the trend implications of the Triangle would suggest a continuation equal to the move preceding the Triangle and leading into it, for if the trend continues valid, the move should run up to the upper limit of the channel. In the case of a reversal we would also use the height of the first reaction as a minimum measure.

With Right Angle Triangles, we also can take the long side (formed by the first reaction) as a rough measure of the minimum expected move.

And with Rectangles, the minimum we may reasonably expect after a breakout is a distance equal to the height of the Rectangle.

The Head-and-Shoulders pattern carries a good measuring stick. The height of the formation from the extreme top of the head down to the point directly beneath where the neckline crosses, represents the minimum probable move from the neckline down. Again, this is a matter of trend channels, and most emphatically this is only a minimum move. Some Head-and-Shoulder patterns, representing an implied move of no more than three or four points, have marked the start of a decline eventually running to hundreds of points.

The rather unusual breakout which takes the form of an almost vertical "mast" running up (or down) many points before arriving at a stopping point where some consolidation pattern is made carries with it a most explicit measuring rule, and one which works out with amazing accuracy. The Flag or Pennant consolidation will occur at the halfway point—"The Flag flies at half mast." The spectacular move leading up to the Flag very likely will be duplicated by another rise, at least equal to the first, in the near future. Following this rise there may be another consolidation and other rises, or there may not. After two surges of this sort it is best to stand back and let someone else carry the ball. If you keep enough charts, and for a long enough time, you will see many perfect examples of this beautiful formation. You will also see some imperfect examples, some failures. And because the move is so spectacularly profitable when it works out, you will be tempted to buy on every consolidation pattern formed after a sharp rise. It would be best to wait until the example is clear—a nearly vertical, almost unbelievable rise, followed by several days of congestion with practically no volume. If the congestion continues or sags off for more than about three weeks, sell the stock; it is probably not the real thing.

Needless to say, this same pattern appears in reverse in down trends and can be traded on accordingly.

The questions relating to the measuring attributes of gaps have been

reviewed in detail in Chapter XII. The only type of gap which carries substantial implications as to the extent of the move to follow is the runaway or
continuation gap. The appearance of such a gap during a rapid price move
is likely to mark approximately the halfway point; and two or more such
gaps can be weighed, in connection with volume and total extent of the move,
to estimate the probable mid-point of the move, and thus to predict probable
ultimate objective.

Measuring properties have been ascribed to other patterns and occasionally
work out according to plan. In general, however, the best measuring devices
are your trendlines, support and resistance levels, and the all-important signals
of increased volume.

CHAPTER XXXIII

TACTICAL REVIEW OF CHART ACTION

THE DOW THEORY

THE record shows that an investor who had bought a representative group of stocks on every Major Bull Market signal according to the Dow Theory as outlined in Chapters III, IV, and V, and had sold all his stocks on every Major Bear Market signal, since the start of the Dow Averages, would have come out very well indeed over the years (see table, Page 43). Although this tabulation does not take short sales into account it would be perfectly consistent to add that a representative group of stocks might be sold short on every Major Bear Market signal and covered at the next Bull Market signal. And if the figures for such short sales, based on the level of the Industrial Average, were included, the total profits on these theoretical transactions, both long and short, would be enormous.

We believe that this record carries some weighty implications which have a bearing on the operations of every trader and investor. We will comment on these shortly.

But before doing so, it should be pointed out that few, if any, investors have actually followed the long-time Dow signals, buying or selling 100% on every Major signal.

In the first place, to do so would require a long market lifetime, and would presuppose that the investor had accepted the Dow Theory in its classic form in toto from the start, and that he had never wavered, never altered the definitions nor his method of trading, and that he had never withdrawn any of his capital during the entire period.

In the second place, we would have to assume that our ideal investor had an extraordinary degree of courage on the one hand, in order to stand firm in periods during which the Major trend appeared to be making dangerous threats against his position; and an extraordinary degree of patience on the other hand, in order to wait out the many months of stagnation when the trend seemed to be getting nowhere at all.

And in the third place, we would have to make the assumption that the group of stocks actually bought or sold, did really represent a fair cross-section of the average in that they would make about the same moves as the average itself. As a matter of fact, if the group were well diversified the chances are good that its moves might approximate those of the averages.

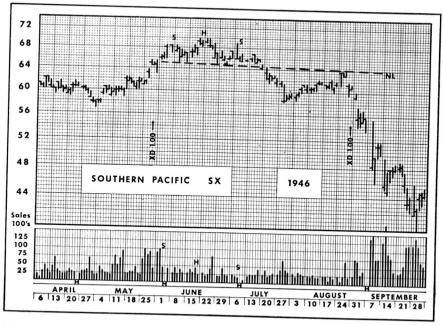

FIGURE 196. Head-and-Shoulders top. The Bull Market that carried Southern Pacific from 8 to 70 in the years 1941-1946, culminated in June, 1946 with this formation. Notice the heavy volume on the left shoulder, lower volume on the head, and small volume on the right shoulder. The breakout signal, which was decisive on July 15, served notice on holders of long commitments to sell at the market the next day (at about 63) instead of waiting for the protective stop, which would have been set at 61, to be caught. Volume eventually developed at the bottom of the breakout move at around 58½, which move incidentally, carried out the *minimum* measure of the Head-and-Shoulders prediction.

From this point, however, a weak rally on low volume started, and continued up for four weeks. The weakness of this picture would justify a short sale on a rally of 40 to 50% of the move from the left shoulder to the bottom, or on a return to the neckline; say at 63. The rally actually extended to the neckline at 64, broke away on a gap with volume, and continued down in a move that led, in the next three months, to prices below 40, and later even lower.

An extraordinary feature of Head-and-Shoulders tops is the frequency with which a comparatively small formation, such as the one shown here, will herald a Major move, changing the course of the stock for months or even years to come. Not *all* patterns of this type will lead to such big moves as this; but *no* Head-and-Shoulders should be regarded lightly, *ever*.

But it is taking a lot for granted to suppose that an investor could meet all these conditions over a period of years, which he would have to do in order to operate strictly as a "Dow Theory" trader. It is not seriously suggested that anybody try to follow any such plan literally.

The important implications of which we spoke are these: If the record of the averages shows that on these Major signals it is possible to take substantial theoretical profits over the long term, and if the averages are composed of the prices of individual stocks, then the probabilities favor buying or selling a majority of stocks in line with the Major trend of the averages. The evidence shows that Major trends normally continue for months or years. The line of "most probable gain," therefore, is the line of the Major trend.

On this basis we would be on safe ground to say that when a trend of sufficient importance to have given a Major signal in the averages is under way, there will be a *greater likelihood* of finding profitable situations among individual stocks moving in that trend than among those moving in the reverse trend.

It is suggested that you read this preceding paragraph again, carefully. It means that we do not try to sell stocks "at the top" in a Bull Market. We do not try to "pick up bargains at the bottom" in a Bear Market. We do not deliberately buck the kind of trend that history shows is likely to continue for an undetermined and possibly long time.

What we have said here is stated with a little different emphasis than in previous editions of this book. You will notice we have not said that you will *never* sell a stock short during a Major Bull Market, nor buy a stock in a Bear Market. There will be, and often are, cases of stocks which are moving against the Major trend, and which, on the basis of their individual technical behavior, may justify a commitment against the trend of the averages.

But we feel such trades should be made cautiously and with a full realization that the majority of stocks are moving in a contrary manner. Such trades might be made, for example, in particular cases as indicated by the charts of the stocks involved, as partial hedges to reduce over-all risk. For example, if a Bull Market had persisted for several years and was still presumably in effect, but certain stocks had broken badly and showed individual weakness, a trader might continue to hold three quarters of his capital in good long positions, but might make a limited number of short sales in the weaker stocks. If, then, the Bull Market continued, he might eventually have to close out the shorts for losses, which could be regarded as the reasonable cost of "insurance." On the other hand, if the general weakness became greater and eventually reversed the Major trend, then the short sales would cushion the depreciation of the longs up to the time of the reversal signal.

By using an Evaluative Index* instead of or in addition to the averages,

* See Chapter XXXVII.

it is possible to say, "The market appears to be about 60% bullish," or "55% bullish," instead of merely bullish or bearish. This takes account of the fact that some markets are more bullish or more bearish than others; and it enables the investor to "roll with the punch" instead of having to take an all-out position one way or the other.

It should be noted, however, that while he may take such a partial position against the (presumed) Major trend, he will continue to use the bulk of his capital in situations which accord with the main trend. He will never risk the larger part of his assets in opposition to the trend, and he will make any countermoves with a clear understanding that they are of the nature of insurance and serve this purpose even though they ultimately may be closed out as small losses.

Summarizing all these implications of the Dow Theory: Do not make a majority of your commitments against the Major trend. During periods of potential reversal gradually reduce your long holdings, and make short sales to a limited amount in weak stocks; but do not attempt to anticipate either a Major top or Major bottom in the Averages by making an all-out commitment counter to the main trend.

HEAD-AND-SHOULDERS TOP

(A) *If you are long of the stock.* Should a breakout down through the neckline occur, with a closing at least 3% below the neckline, next morning place a stop $\frac{1}{8}$ point below the last close. Continue to place such "close stops" if not caught the first day, $\frac{1}{8}$ point under each day's close until one is caught.

(B) Short sales may be made after a breakout, on a recovery of 40% of the distance from the top of the right shoulder to the bottom of the breakout move, or on a recovery to a line drawn down across the top of the head and right shoulder or on a pull-back to the neckline; *whichever point is reached first.* If the breakout move continues down another day, or for several days, the 40% recovery would be based on the entire move from the top of the right shoulder to the lowest point reached.

HEAD-AND-SHOULDERS BOTTOM

(A) *If you are short of the stock.* Should a breakout *on increased volume* occur, penetrating the neckline and closing at least 3% above it, place a stop next morning to cover at $\frac{1}{8}$ point higher than the close. If such a stop is not caught, continue each day to place a stop $\frac{1}{8}$ point higher than the previous day's close until one is caught.

(B) New purchases may be made after a breakout, on a reaction of 40% of the distance from the bottom of the right shoulder to the top of the breakout move (which reaction must be on decreasing volume), or on a

FIGURE 197. Head-and-Shoulders bottom in Braniff Airways, 1945. Strictly speaking, a continuation Head-and-Shoulders after a Secondary correction in the Bull Market. A Major bottom, reversing a long Bear Market, would normally take much longer to form.

Here we see heavy volume on the left shoulder, somewhat less on the head, and very little on the right shoulder, with a sharp increase, as required, on the breakout move of September 21. The breakout was followed by a throwback to the neckline on diminishing volume, providing a good opportunity for purchases at 23. The upward move was resumed and again there was a reaction to the neckline support. A second reaction of this sort is not unusual. The closing at 22¾ on October 19, below the previous Minor bottom, and on increased volume, was mildly disturbing. But in view of the strength of the pattern and breakout we would not have sold the stock, and the protective stop at 21⅞ was not even threatened. On October 25 the advance was resumed with a breakaway gap and continued up to 29½, where the move was signed off with a One-Day Reversal and exhaustion gap.

Notice that on reaching 29½ "BNF" went into a consolidation pattern for over three weeks, making an Ascending Triangle, before leaping to 37½. Notice also (we might as well get all we can out of these examples) that the Ascending Triangle takes shape at approximately the half-way point of the whole advance. We are already familiar with this tendency of stocks in fast moves to form "half-way" patterns.

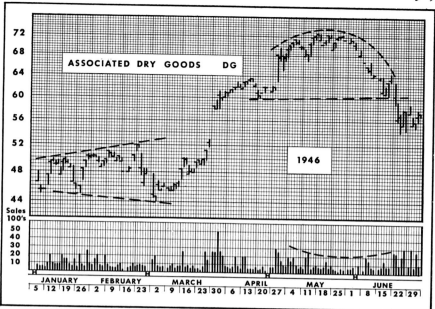

FIGURE 198. Associated Dry Goods winds up its Bull Market trend with a Rounding Top. This is a daily chart for the first six months of 1946.

The advance in "DG" from 4 to above 72 in just 3½ years, when seen on monthly charts, is a smooth, accelerating curve which emerged from a long bottom formation that had lasted five years from 1938 through 1942.

As we enter the final six months leading up to the ultimate peak, note first the action during January and February. "DG" had just completed a fast run-up in the last quarter of 1945 and was about due for a consolidation or a Secondary correction. On reaching 48 it turned back to 45, advanced to 50½, to 51, and finally to 52, and then reacted to 44 at the end of February. Had the move on January 22 gone a little lower and closed below the January 3 low, and *then* been followed by an even lower closing on February 26, we would have had to consider this January-February pattern a completed Broadening Top, a definite reversal signal. However, the pattern was not perfect and therefore not valid; but the erratic price action shows incipient weakness.

It is not unusual in these last stages when public participation is running high for the climactic advances to be spectacular and fast. And that is what we see here. A five-point breakaway gap occurred on March 25, followed by an advance which petered off at 63½, reacted and then ran up to over 68.

From here on the move advanced slowly, with suggestions of a convergent trend and a succession of "heads" and "shoulders," and volume dropping off as the top was reached. The drop on June 4 to below the May 7 Minor bottom on increased volume would complete the Rounding Top and call for immediate sale if we were still long; and the penetration of the "neckline" on June 18 was a conclusive break.

FIGURE 199. Greyhound: a Rounding Bottom in 1945. A continuation pattern after the May run-up to over 29 and reaction to support at 24, the 1944 high.

In July volume ran fairly high on downside days, drying up as we entered August. August 10 showed a spurt of volume on the upside, then more dullness.

The various small moves through August and September would not give us any basis for trading operations. The move to a new high in the pattern on August 31 suggested an up-turn, and again on September 19-20 we see another little push up to the 26 level. Still not conclusive, however.

The move which got under way in the week ending October 13 is more definite. This decisive move with good volume carries right out of the "bowl" in an almost vertical ascent. Not a big move, but a clear indication of the probable trend. We would look for a point to buy G on a correction of 40-50% of the entire move up from the bottom or on a return to near the support level around 26. The purchase would probably be made around 26½. Notice the drying up of volume on this reaction.

The advance from here to 30, marking an entirely new Bull Market high, came almost immediately. On November 3, with very heavy volume for a Saturday, G closed at 30, and since this volume was not on the day of breakout we would have closed out the transaction on a close stop at 29⅞ on Monday (unless we had elected to wait out the next Minor reaction for a further advance).

Two weeks later, on the basis of the reaction to good support, we would have bought G again at about 29 (you cannot figure on getting the extreme low price on any reaction). The following advance carried up to 34¼ in two days. At that point profits could have been taken or the stock held for the longer term. G, it might be noted, continued up eventually to 54.

reaction to a line drawn across the bottom of the head and the right shoulder or on a throw-back to the neckline; whichever is reached first. As in the case of the top formation, this 40% reaction is figured on the entire distance of the breakout move if it should continue up for several days.

COMPLEX OR MULTIPLE HEAD-AND-SHOULDERS

The same tactical suggestions apply to these as to the simple Head-and-Shoulders. Definitions and special features of these formations are covered in Chapter VII.

ROUNDING TOPS AND BOTTOMS

It is difficult to set precise rules for trading on these gradual changes of trend. In the case of Rounding Tops, if one is long of the stock, the general appearance of a rounding formation, extending over a period of several weeks, leveling off from the rise and then turning down, very likely with a tapering off of volume nearing the top of the rise and a pick up of volume as the turn starts down, would suggest getting out of the stock at the market as soon as the picture looks suspiciously definite. A short sale of a Rounding Top could be very profitable; but no exact rule could be stated except that in the absence of fixed Basing Points one would want to be very certain that the formation was unmistakably a Rounding Top; it would want to be well formed and following a long rise, and extending over a period of some weeks in its formation. It would also want to be protected with a stop above the top of the curve, as explained in the chapter on stops.

You would not be likely to be short of a stock on a Rounding Bottom. The long and gradual rounding appearance with dull volume, followed by a sudden revival on greatly increased volume would be signal enough to cover if you should find yourself in this uncomfortable position. Purchases would be justified in a stock whose chart showed a rounded bottom or saucer, after the first spasm of activity following a long, dull period of dormancy. You would buy, according to the rules we have given for purchases on reactions, not on the breakout, but on the reaction following it, which would almost surely come.

SYMMETRICAL TRIANGLES

(A) *If you already have a position in the stock.* During the formation of a Symmetrical Triangle, you may be unable to make any change in your holdings. Let us say you have bought the stock on a reaction after a bullish move. The next upsurge fails to make a new high and gives no sufficient volume signal to cause you to sell out. The next reaction fails to carry below the

FIGURE 200.   Symmetrical Triangle in Allied Stores, a consolidation in the
1946 decline.   Notice heavy volume as "LS" crashed to the first reversal point
of the pattern on September 10, and the drying up of volume during the
successive swings of the Triangle.   In Point-and-Figure charts this type of
pattern is known as a Pendulum Swing, since it does seem to come to rest like
a pendulum.   Often volume will pick up somewhat at each reversal point,
but a valid Triangle must show some over-all decrease of volume.

If, by some unhappy chance, you were then long of "LS" you should have
had your protective stop at 33⅛, 8% below the bottom reached at 36.   However, the move down out of the Triangle on Friday and Saturday, October 4
and 5, although on slight volume, was a true breakout (remember that *down-
side* breakouts do not require volume confirmation) and you would have been
justified in selling your long commitment at the market on Monday.   You
would have received about 38½.   To justify a *short sale*, however, the breakout would have had to close at least 3% outside the Triangle.   The return
to the border of the pattern at 40 was interesting and you will notice that
volume increased characteristically as the decline really got under way on
October 9 and 10.

No question about the validity of this breakout.   Short sales were in order
on a return to the border of the Triangle, or a 40-50% correction of the
breakout move, say at 38½ to 39.   The rally carried to the apex of the
Triangle, then broke away fast for the decline to 33 where, on October 30, a
Selling Climax and One-Day Reversal occurred—a signal to take profits.

Notice the small Head-and-Shoulders in August.   This was a continuation
pattern marking the top of the rally before the September-November crack-up.

previous one. You are "locked" into the Triangle, and you cannot safely sell since the Triangle that has formed may eventually break out in the original direction and show you a good profit (in fact the odds favor that it *will* break out in that direction). In case of a breakout move (which of course must be on increased volume on the up side), you can close it out for a profit (according to rules for trading we have already given), and immediately mark it as a re-buy on the next reaction.

If the breakout is down (whether or not on increased volume), with a closing outside the Triangle, you should protect yourself with a close ($\frac{1}{8}$ point) stop the next day, and continue to set such close progressive stops under each day's close until it is sold.

If you are short of the stock the same rules in reverse would apply, except that the breakout in the right direction (down) would require no volume confirmation, and the adverse breakout (up) would need such increased volume.

(B) *If you do not have a position in the stock.* Stay away from any stocks making Symmetrical Triangles until a clear and definite breakout close has been made. After such a breakout, if on the up side, buy on the next reaction if the Major trend is up, or if on the down side, sell short on the next rally if the Major trend is down. Rules for making such commitments have already been given.

Note: Avoid breakouts from Symmetrical Triangles of the type which have continued to narrow until the breakout point comes far out toward the apex. The most reliable breakouts occur about two thirds along the Triangle.

RIGHT-ANGLE TRIANGLES

The same rules would apply to Right-Angle Triangles as to Symmetrical Triangles (see the chapters on Triangles). Early breakouts are more dependable here, as in the case of Symmetrical Triangles. Volume confirmation is more important on upside breakouts from Ascending Triangles and is not strictly required on downside breakouts from Descending Triangles. Commitments already made are retained until the breakout and then closed out in the same way as any transaction that shows a gain.

Since the Ascending and Descending Triangles carry a directional forecasting implication that the Symmetrical Triangles do not have, it is possible to make new commitments or reactions *within* an Ascending Triangle or rallies within a descending one. However, since the flat horizontal side of one of these Triangles represents a supply or demand area of unknown magnitude, and since therefore such a Triangle can be (and sometimes is) turned back before the horizontal line has been decisively penetrated, it might be better policy to note such formations in the making, and wait until the decisive breakout before making the new commitment.

FIGURE 201.   An Ascending Triangle.   "CMR," after emerging from the doldrums in 1943, forged up to about 12 early in 1945.   The first eight months of the year on a monthly chart show an Ascending Triangle with top at 12¼.   On daily charts, however, we see the more detailed aspects of this large pattern.   For instance, the final reaction of the whole (monthly) formation in August became here a Symmetrical Triangle.   The breakout from this pattern carried out the minimum measuring requirements, bringing the price again to the 12¼ top, from which point there was a reaction which was stopped cold at 11, the apex of the Triangle.   A purchase on the reaction after the powerful breakout from the Triangle, say around 11½, would have been closed out on progressive stops, starting September 28 when "CMR" reached 14, the sale being consummated October 2 at 14⅞, a highly profitable move.

Profit-taking of this sort would largely explain the stopping of the rise and the formation of a consolidation pattern which turned out to be the Ascending Triangle with top at 16¼, lasting eight weeks.   Notice the November 7 volume when the price went through the 16¼ level but failed to close outside the pattern; and the volume on November 30 when a clean, decisive breakout move closed at 17.   This move ran to 20 and purchases would have been made at 18 or less on the reaction.   The next wave took "CMR" to its ultimate Bull Market top at 24 in January.   On the ratio scale the top of the Ascending Triangle was exactly half-way between the September bottom at 11, and the extreme high of 24.   This type of half-way consolidation is typical of Flags and Pennants, and this is a very similar case.

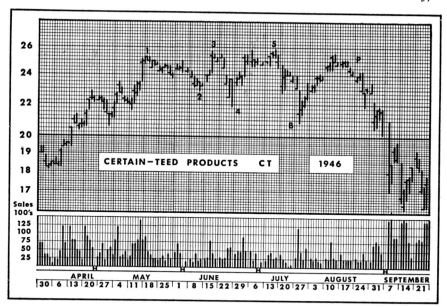

FIGURE 202. A Broadening Top. This somewhat rare but beautiful and highly dependable formation developed as Certain-teed made its Bull Market peak in 1946. A quick glance at the volume scale in this daily chart shows the high volume on the final stages of the advance, the dullness during development of the top pattern, and the increased volume after the breakout.

As we all know by now (or go back to Chapter X and review the specifications), a Broadening Top is a five point reversal, differing from the Head-and-Shoulders, Triangles, Rectangles, etc. in that each reversal must be at a new high or low for the pattern. It is, if you wish, a sort of reversed Triangle with its apex to the left, the swings becoming continually wider.

In the second week of May "CT" (the symbol has since been changed to "CRT") made a new Bull Market high at 25¼ (marked "1"). The reaction carried back to support at the previous Minor peak (point "2") and the following week "CT" advanced to another new high at "3," closing ⅛ point above the previous top.

Another week had brought "CT" down to point "4" with a closing at 22½, three quarters of a point below point "2." This in itself is not sufficient reason for making short commitments. Three weeks later "CT" closed at 25⅝, another new high, at point "5." Finally the stock dropped to 21½ on July 23, and at this point (marked "B") the pattern was completed. Notice the tendency of volume to rise at each reversal point of the pattern.

Long holdings would be sold at the market the day after the breakout. But short sellers should wait for a correction of 40 to 50% of the move from point "5" to point "B." If shorts were put out at 23 we would not worry if the stock advanced for a time, as it did, without making a new high. The downside move in "CT" went quickly to 15½, and within 12 months to 11½.

FIGURE 203.   Rectangles in Remington Rand.   This is part of a long Bull Market rise that carried "RR" from under 10 to above 50 in the period from 1942 to 1946.   The last three years of this advance were almost continuous as seen on monthly charts, without any extensive reactions.   When we put the chart on a daily basis such as this section covering the end of 1944 and the early months of 1945, right in the middle of the advance, we see that the rise was not actually continuous but was built up of steps in an ascending "staircase" of accumulation patterns.   Each sharp advance on increased volume is followed by a period of dullness and slight recession.

A picture of this type suggests the methodical campaign of buyers who intended to purchase large blocks of the stock for large long-term advances without creating a "sky-rocket" market by their own buying operations. Presumably each advance was checked by the temporary distribution of part of the stock held by such buyers, and re-accumulation started on reactions.

In October and November there is a well-marked Rectangle between 20¾ and 22.   A purchase could have been made at or near the bottom limit, say at 21, on the fifth reversal on November 14.   The move out of pattern in the week of December 2 did not carry 3% out of pattern, but about two weeks later a move got under way that qualified as a valid breakout, with volume confirmation as required on upside moves.   Notice the volume increase and One-Day Reversal on December 20 as this move neared its top.   Purchases would have been made at about 22½ on the basis of a normal correction, and you would have expected support at the 22 level.   This support was respected but the move did not advance beyond 23¾, made this same top three times in a period of two weeks, and returned again to 22¼.

There was no question about the breakout on January 25.   Extent and volume were decisive.   Notice the gap and One-Day Reversal on the following day as this Minor move reached its end.

In mid March, as you will see, "RR" plunged down from its high of 27, but the decline was stopped in its tracks at the top level of the January Rectangle, a good support shelf.   Never again during the Bull Market did "RR" even threaten this level, since it moved up in April and continued its long march to the 1946 top.

Broadening Tops

Presumably you would not be long of a Broadening Top. The early reversals in the pattern would have taken you out of the stock, if you follow the tactical rules based on trendlines, as previously outlined, long before completion of the pattern. Neither would you be tempted to buy into such a pattern, since the trend indications would be clearly against a move.

On the other hand, a Broadening Top, after its completion, offers excellent opportunities for a short sale. After downside penetration and close below the fourth point of reversal in the pattern, you are justified in selling short on a rally of about 40% of the distance covered from the extreme top (fifth point of reversal), and the lowest point reached on the breakout move. The stop, of course, would be placed at the proper distance above the fifth reversal, that is, the extreme top of the pattern.

Rectangles

(A) *If you already have a commitment in the stock.* The early moves of a Rectangle may provide no volume signals to permit you to get out. And there will, of course, be no "breakout" moves during the formation of a Rectangle that will allow you to take a profit. However, as soon as the character of the Rectangle is well established (and that will require at least four reversals to set up a clear top and bottom), you may trade on the tops and bottoms, that is, sell at or near the top; or buy at or near the bottom. Since, as in the case of Symmetrical Triangles, there is a definite presumption in such formations that they are more likely to lead to continuation moves than to reversals, this would mean that you would probably pass up your first opportunity to get out (on the fifth reversal), and would indeed probably decide to "ride along" in the expectation of a continuation of the original move, which will be the "right" direction for your commitment. In the case of a breakout in the right direction, you would dispose of your commitment according to the rules for trading already stated. If in the wrong direction, use the close (⅛ point) progressive stops, the same as with the Triangles.

(B) *If you are not committed in the stock.* Trades can be made within the Rectangle on the fifth and subsequent reversals. Since there is the slight probability that the move will eventually continue in the same direction as the preceding move leading up or down to the Rectangle, it might be best to wait until the sixth reversal for new commitments, which would set your interests in the same direction as a continuation. And of course short sales can be made after any downside breakout close from a Rectangle; or purchases after an upside breakout close with increased volume. Both the short sales and the long purchases would be made on the corrective move following the breakout.

FIGURE 204.   A Double Bottom in Paramount Pictures.   Double Tops and
Double Bottoms are not so common as many traders like to think.   They
require considerable time to develop and must conform to specifications as to
price range and time, and also (on upside breakouts from Double Bottoms) as
to volume.   They are easier to spot on weekly charts than on dailies.

This is a weekly chart of "PX" from September 1941 through March 1943.
A bottom was made on climactic volume at 11¾ during the "Pearl Harbor
panic" move.   Then came a rise lasting eight weeks which brought "PX"
back to 15⅝—a rise, incidentally, on feeble volume strongly suggesting the
possibility of another crack-up to even lower levels.   This rise, you will
notice, was a considerable one, amounting to 35% of the price at the December low.

The downward move, however, which lasted to mid-April, was on low volume and ended precisely at the December low of 11¾.   (Note: It is not
necessary that moves of this sort end at exactly the same level; the second
bottom could have been a bit higher or lower without spoiling the pattern.)

The second week in July shows the first sign of a possible reversal, when
the price advanced on increased volume, but it did not close above 15⅝; and
was therefore not a breakout.   Two weeks later, on heavy volume, "PX" had
moved up to 16½, closing the week at 16.   This is a true breakout, and
purchases would have been in order on reactions from this point on.

The move continued up for three years to an ultimate top at 85.

FIGURE 205. A Right-Angled Broadening Formation in Associated Dry Goods. A beautiful example of a breakout through multiple tops, followed by an important move. This is, however, a pattern that is more fun to observe in retrospect than to follow as an active trader. The stock had moved up from an important bottom around 4 established in 1938, 1940 and 1942. At the time of this chart in 1945, "DG" was starting the accelerating climb that eventually ended with the 1946 Rounding Top at over 70. (See Figure 198.)

If you had been holding the stock you would have been watching for a substantial corrective move after the advance from 12 to 20. In late February and the first week of March, "DG" went into new Bull Market high ground, reacted to support around 19-19½, and then advanced again in the week of March 17, failing in this move to make a new high. Ten days later "DG" had reacted to 18½, closing below the previous Minor bottom. An inexperienced observer might, at this point, have commented "Double Top" and planned to sell "DG" at once or even to make a short sale. However, the pattern was not large enough in duration nor extent of price movement to qualify as a Double Top, nor did it conform to any other recognizable pattern of reversal. Nor was the volume as high as one would expect on an important top.

The rally in early April carried through to a decisive breakout of more than 3% in the move which reached 22⅞ on April 18. This move was a clear penetration of the multiple top, and confirmed the up-trend. If you still held your long stock you would now rest easier, and in any case you would have looked for a chance to buy on a reaction after the breakout. If you had tried to buy at the 21½ support level you would have been left behind, but if you had put your order in a little higher, say at 22, you would have had a nice profit on the advance to 25⅞ where you would have sold on close stop at 25¾.

FIGURE 206. A Diamond pattern in American Can. The daily chart covers the period from December, 1946 through May, 1947, inclusive. For background on this situation keep in mind that "AC" made its Bull Market peak in October, 1945 when it reached 112. The tendency of high-grade, high-priced stocks to top out early at the end of a Bull Market has already been noted. The first decline carried nearly to 90 and was followed by a rally to 106. The stock then dropped to below 80 and a second rally brought us to the situation we see here.

You will notice at once that the moves have a gradual "rounding" appearance, due to the fact that at this price conservative stocks do not make large percentage moves. If charted on a scale having larger vertical intervals the patterns would look very much like those in more speculative stocks.

The first part of the pattern is similar to a Broadening Top. The first Minor peak at 96 is followed by a reaction to 92. The second peak carries even higher, to 98; and the reaction this time goes down to 91¼. A third rally takes "AC" to 99. So far, we have the five reversal points of a Broadening Top, needing only a close below 91¼ to confirm the bearish indications. However, the next decline fails to break out of the pattern and for several weeks we have a *narrowing* picture like a Symmetrical Triangle.

Eventually the stock makes a clean breakout to 89, which is the signal to get out of longs and to consider short sales on the next rally. As a matter of fact, the three-week rally which then started never made an upside penetration of the resistance level at 94, the level of the apex of the converging lines bounding the latter part of the Diamond.

American Can did not make a spectacular move down from this point, which is not surprising considering the markdown that had already taken place in "AC," and considering the habits and price of the stock and the general condition of the market. It did not, however, again rise to the level shown here, and in fact retreated to the 80 level.

To review the nature of the Diamond. It is not too common a pattern. It is somewhat like a Complex Head-and-Shoulders with a bent neckline. It resembles at the start a Broadening Top, and its latter phase narrows like a Symmetrical Triangle.

Double Tops and Bottoms

Double and multiple tops or bottoms are not valid unless they conform to the requirements for such formations. The chapter on these patterns should be read carefully in this connection.

(A) *If you are long of a stock.* On penetration and close at a price lower than the extreme bottom of the pattern between the multiple tops, dispose of the stock on close (⅛ point) progressive stops.

(B) *If you are short of a stock.* On penetration of the highest point of the inverted bowl or rise between the bottoms, with a close above that point, close out the short sale on close stops.

(C) *If you are not committed in the stock.* Consider a penetration and close beyond the limit of the correction between the tops (or bottoms) as a signal of reversal, and make new commitments on rallies or reactions.

Right-Angled Broadening Formations

The handling of these on breakouts through the horizontal side would be similar to what has been said about Multiple Tops and Bottoms, and Right-Angle Triangles.

The Diamond

If you are sure that what you have is a valid Diamond pattern, the rules for trading will be the same as those we have already covered in connection with breakouts from Symmetrical Triangles. As in the case of such Triangles, new commitments should wait for a definite breakout; and commitments already in force would have to remain until such a breakout had occurred, either declaring a reversal, or indicating a probable continuation of the original trend.

Wedges

There is no need to set forth detailed rules for policy within a Wedge and during its formation, since the general principles taken up in connection with trendlines, support and resistance would take you out of such a situation at the first opportunity after the convergent nature of the pattern became clear. At the very worst, your stops (which we hope you maintain faithfully in all situations) will take you out before the consequences become serious.

Regarding new purchases (from a Falling Wedge breakout) or short sales (from a Rising Wedge), the same volume characteristics would be expected: notably increased volume on an upside breakout from a Falling Wedge; less pronounced volume action on the first stages of breakout from a Rising Wedge. New commitments, in line with the implications of the breakout, may be placed on rallies or reactions after a clear breakout closing occurs, carrying beyond the trendlines forming the Wedge.

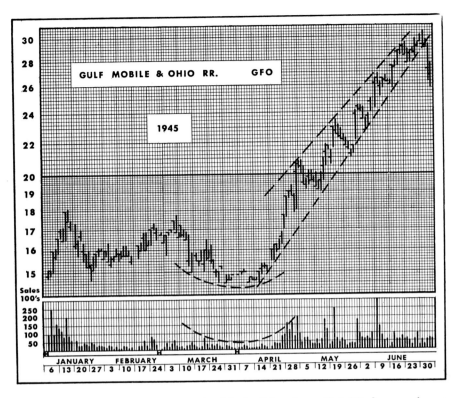

FIGURE 207. Gulf, Mobile and Ohio builds a beautiful Wedge, as shown on this daily chart for the first half of 1945. This was the move which terminated the spectacular rise of "GFO," its final Bull Market top.

Immediately after the downside breakdown from the Wedge, "GFO" came down to 18¾, and from this Intermediate low which was reached in August, rallied into a long Rectangle between 23¾ and 26¾ from which it eventually broke down in a series of crashes that found it, in May, 1947, selling for 6⅛!

It is rather hard, with a formation of this sort, to say at what precise point the convergency of the trends is established. The breakout move late in April was, of course, normal; the stock was a buy on the next reaction. The following advance in May which reached 23½ did not carry out a parallel trend channel, and we saw a tendency to converge as prices retreated on the reaction. The next three advances all repeated and confirmed the Wedge picture, and at the top we see a sort of "bunching up" as prices make little or no headway. The chances are that an alert trader would have taken profits on long commitments after the high volume appeared at the top of the Minor move ending June 4 and 5. In any case he would have maintained a protective stop at all times to take him out if and when a downside breakout occurred.

ONE-DAY REVERSALS

One-Day Reversals are not technical patterns suitable for trading in the same sense as the important reversal and consolidation pictures we have examined. They are mainly useful as a gauge in helping to find the precise top or bottom of a Minor move in order to protect profits on commitments previously made. The One-Day Reversal, the exhaustion gap, and the day of exceptionally heavy volume following several days of movement in a minor trend, are strong indications that the move may have run out. Any of these three signals is worth watching for; any two of them together carry more weight than one alone; and the appearance of all three carries very strong implications of a Minor top or bottom.

So far as trading on movements signaled by One-Day Reversals, this type of trading would lie almost in the field of gambling, or at least trading for quick small profits on short moves. It would not be the same kind of trading at all that we have been studying in the greater part of this book. The indications and some suggestions for trading on those one-day moves are covered in the discussion of them in Chapter X.

FLAGS AND PENNANTS

In many cases the total decline of a Flag in an up trend will bring the price back to a point where the stock may be bought according to our regular trading tactics, that is, the decline may carry down to the basic (Red) trendline, to the Blue Parallel, or make a 40-50% correction of the rising "mast" preceding the Flag. If the "mast" move is the first such move out of a level or only moderately rising trend, and if the Major trend of the market is bullish, we would be justified in buying at the first opportunity, which would be on the Blue Parallel. In such a case we would expect, and ordinarily get, some further reaction, but it is important to get in early because sometimes the reaction is very brief, and does not meet either of the other requirements for the correction. It is most important in a situation like this that the volume drop off sharply. *Volume must decrease and remain slight.* Any increase of volume during the formation of the Flag should be viewed as casting suspicion on the entire pattern; except, of course, the increasing volume that characteristically attends the start of the breakout drive. This drive is usually so virile that we would be safe in placing a close (⅛ point) stop under the close of any day during formation of a Flag or Pennant that showed notably increased volume. So that if the volume indicated failure of the pattern, we would be taken out at once; but if the breakout was under way, we would probably be left in, since the stock would ordinarily move up then without a reaction, very often making a breakaway gap.

FIGURE 208.   A Pennant in Martin-Parry.   This type of pattern is fairly
common in fast moving markets.   The extraordinary point about Flags and
Pennants (and sometimes other consolidation patterns in fast moves) is their
tendency to form almost exactly half-way between bottom and top.

Just before this move, "MRT" had built a Rectangle between 10 and 12
lasting seven months, which followed the 1944 rise from around 4 to 12.   The
May breakout on heavy volume carried "MRT" right to the top of the Pennant without any adequate reaction.   Note the increase of volume at the
top of that rise.   For three weeks prices drifted off with a drying-up of
volume that is clearly shown in the chart.   The pattern did not correct the
entire first phase, but found support at the Minor peak at 14½.

Suddenly, on high volume, the move was resumed and this time went right
up to 24¾.   The chances are that traders who were still long of their original
stock or who had bought in around 15 on the Pennant, would have sold
after the high volume of June 6 when "MRT" reached 19⅞.

In downward movements, when the Major trend of the market is bearish, the same suggestions would apply, with one difference. The final high day of the Flag type of rally may be on high volume; and of course may also show the exhaustion gap or One-Day Reversal. If a short sale has been made into such a day showing high volume, gap, or One-Day Reversal, a stop order placed above the peak of the Flag will protect you should the advance be resumed unexpectedly.

In either the up-moving or down-moving manifestations of this type of action, there may be Flags having horizontal tops and bottoms, which are, of course, Rectangles. If the drying-up of volume and other aspects of the picture, including the sharp upward or downward move preceding it, suggest a Flag-type consolidation, you would be justified in making a commitment on the sixth reversal point, or for that matter at almost any point in the pattern (since you cannot expect this pattern to continue very long).

Flags and Pennants which do continue too long (over three weeks) are open to question. Stops should then be set, at the usual computed distance above or below their extreme tops or bottoms (as the case may be). The fairly frequent appearance of flag-like formations which eventually fail is unfortunate, since it is particularly hard to give up hoping with this kind of pattern, and it is necessary to set the three-week time limit to prevent the stock from drifting all the way back to previously established stop levels. On the other hand, breakout moves from these patterns, when completed normally, are among the fastest and most profitable forms of market action.

The question remains what to do in the case of stocks you may be holding as they go into Flag or Pennant formation. Obviously, they should be held, if you are long and the move leading to the Flag is up; or short positions should be retained if the move is down. However, this would not happen ordinarily if you had followed the trading rules strictly. In most cases your signals calling for close (⅛ point) progressive stops would have appeared during the formation of the "mast." You would have been taken out of the picture somewhere along the way, possibly at the extreme top of the mast (though ordinarily you could not count on being so fortunate).

If, however, no signal should appear, and you still are holding a position as the Flag starts to make its appearance, by all means *hold* your position. The odds favor a continuation of the original move.

Now if you have been holding the stock long (in a Bull Market) and have seen it break out and start leaping to new highs, say from 20 to 32, and you have been stopped out at 30, and then you see the price advance halt and during the next several days retreat with the rather high previous volume drying up to practically nothing (it must be a drastic drying-up and no mistake about it), then you are justified in buying right back in again, even at a higher price than you received only a few days before.

FIGURE 209. This daily chart of Lehigh Valley R. R. through late 1945 and early 1946 shows a variety of gaps. At this particular time LV was completing a Secondary corrective move before making one more (and as it turned out, a final) effort to exceed the 1945 top just above 17. This long-term situation could be used for a discussion of Double Tops, since the bottom of the intervening move was violated in the summer of 1946 and the stock continued a downward course to below the 5 level.

Not all gaps are significant; for example, the first gap shown, on October 3, when the stock was moving in a narrow range on low volume. The gap on Saturday, November 3, however, is important, since the Saturday volume (when doubled) is high. The move failed to qualify by a 3% new high closing as a true breakout, but the implications of the move were bullish and might well have justified purchases on Minor reactions. The low volume gaps on these reactions were of no particular interest.

It is not until the third week of January that we see another gap that looks like a real breakaway. On January 14, with high volume, "LV" moved up and out in a rush that took it to 15⅞ on January 16, closing at 15½. The second appearance of volume here would have suggested application of progressive stops, and long trades would have been closed out at 15⅜.

New purchases could have been made on the reaction at 14½. A second advance accompanied by a breakaway gap developed on January 23. If we consider the second gap (of January 24) a runaway or measuring gap we would estimate the probable top of this move at around 17¾. However, when a third gap appeared on January 28 with a One-Day Reversal and climactic volume, it would be clear that this move was about finished, and progressive stops would be used to close out longs at 16¾.

Note the attempt to rally after the sharp drop, and the One-Day Island formed by two gaps as "LV" fails to hold at the 15 level.

GAPS

If you are long of a stock which is in a well-marked pattern formation, or in an area of dull movement within fairly narrow limits, and the stock suddenly breaks out on the up side with high volume and a gap, that is a bullish indication. You will hold the stock until signs of exhaustion appear as the rise continues, or reappearance of high volume, or another gap or One-Day Reversal. Then, particularly if two or all three of these indications show up at the same time, you can protect your commitment with close progressive stops. You will have to consider whether a second gap should be considered an exhaustion gap or a continuation gap, depending on the volume and the speed of the rise, as discussed in the chapters on gaps and their measuring implications.

Ordinarily, after a breakaway gap, regardless of whether you sell on the next Minor top, you would consider the move bullish, and would prepare to make a purchase on the next reaction.

Now if you are long of a stock and during the course of a sharp rise, it develops a gap after several days of the move, you must make your decision as to whether or not it is a continuation (runaway) gap. If so, you would prepare to hold the stock for a further rise approximately equal to the rise up to the gap; and you would watch the approach to the ultimate objective indicated very closely, so that on the appearance then of reversal signals you could protect your holding with close stops.

If you are satisfied that a gap following a good rise is actually an exhaustion gap, then you should protect your stock with a close progressive stop at once.

In Bear Markets, you would apply these same rules in reverse to your short sales, remembering that a downside breakaway is not necessarily accompanied by the high volume you expect on an upside breakaway.

Where you are long or short of a stock which is moving in a pattern formation, and the stock then makes a breakaway gap in the adverse direction, the commitment should be closed out immediately at the market, or on close progressive stops.

SUPPORT AND RESISTANCE

When you are long of a stock, you do not want to see it violate any Minor bottoms previously made. Neither do you want to see it violate any of the preceding Minor tops which it has surpassed. Therefore, your stop orders will be placed at a computed distance, as explained in the chapter on stop orders, using both the Minor bottoms and the Minor tops as Basing Points. Normally the Minor bottom most recently formed will be at the approximate level of the preceding Minor top, so that often these Basing Points will coincide. Ordinarily, therefore, in a rising trend we look to the most recently formed

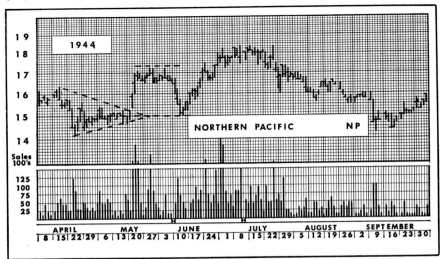

FIGURE 210. This daily chart in Northern Pacific covering six months during 1944, shows several examples of support and resistance. The entire chart covers only part of the series of consolidations that took place in 1943 and 1944 preceding the 1945-46 advance that carried beyond 38.

Support and resistance phenomena appear, of course, on many, in fact on most of the charts in this book, and you will find them on the charts you set up for yourself. There is nothing unique or even unusual about the support-resistance action in "NP."

Starting at the left in April, after the downside move on volume to 14¼, notice the recovery to 15⅝ where the move stops at the resistance level of the preceding two weeks. After the formation of the Symmetrical Triangle there is a breakaway move with a gap which runs right on up to above 17 where a small Rectangle is built during the next three weeks. The stock ultimately breaks down from this pattern on considerable volume. It is doubtful whether one would want to trade on this as a normal reaction after the breakout from the Triangle on account of the downside volume and the implications of the Rectangle.

However, note how the reaction stops cold at the 15 line, the apex level of the Triangle, and then moves right on up. Rather surprisingly, there is only a three-day hesitation at the bottom of the Rectangle, but a little set-back occurs at the top of that pattern.

The July top might be classed as a Head-and-Shoulders or Complex or Rounding Top; in fact it is almost a Rectangle, and after the downside breakout, prices hesitate at the level of the top of the May Rectangle, continue down, find temporary support again at the April support shelf around 16, and ultimately wind up a bit under 15. Although "NP" actually did penetrate and close slightly below the apex of the Triangle, the violation was barely 3%, and it is interesting to note that this September bottom was the lowest point reached. From here the stock started its climb to the 38 level which was reached in December 1945.

Minor bottom. When the stock has for three days made a price range which is entirely above the entire range of the day marking this bottom, you may move up your stop protection to a place indicated by this new Basing Point.

The same procedure will apply in Bear Markets; the "three-day" rule being used to confirm Basing Points established by Minor peaks and also by the preceding Minor bottoms. But ordinarily it will be sufficient to use the Minor peaks as the Basing Points.

Intermediate tops and bottoms are used in determining the probable objectives of Intermediate moves, since previous tops constitute support under Intermediate reactions, and previous bottoms indicate resistance over Intermediate rallies.

Multiple Tops are support levels. Multiple Bottoms are resistance levels. The neckline of a Head-and-Shoulders pattern is a support or resistance level as the case may be. The apex of a Symmetrical Triangle is a strong support and resistance point which may show its effect again on a subsequent move. Any congestion or area at a certain price level or within narrow price limits may provide support or resistance when a stock again moves to that price or range.

TRENDLINES

We have already gone into the methods of following trends in stocks, and the use of the top and bottom trendlines (basic and return lines) as indicators of bullish and bearish opportunities, and as price determinants for executing purchases or short sales.

There remains the tactical problem of the stock in which you are committed, which is acting badly, but which has neither broken out of a recognized pattern nor violated an established Minor peak. This is not a common situation but it can present a very difficult problem when it does come up. Let us say the Major trend is bullish, and a certain stock which has been moving up irregularly in a parallel trend channel confirms its up trend by a long, more or less continuous advance and calls for repurchase on the next reaction. You buy on the reaction and the stock continues down; that is, the reaction continues with prices sagging for days and weeks, without any rallies, consolidations or corrections that are sufficiently well-defined to serve as Basing Points for stop orders.

In the absence of clear indications during the reaction, and also during the preceding large upward move, your stop would be placed at a computed distance *below the top of the preceding rise.* And if the reaction continues down until *that* level is reached, you will have sustained an abnormally large loss.

In a case like this you should examine the trendlines making up the long advance in the trend channel. The points of contact with the basic trendline can serve as a fair emergency substitute for Minor bottoms. Your stop level should therefore (in the absence of more definite Basing Points) be placed at the

FIGURE 211.   Trendlines in American Steel Foundries.   This daily chart shows the tendency of trendlines to develop along straight channels.   We have already pointed out that these channels are frequently easier to see in retrospect than during their formation, that stocks move in perfect channels only occasionally, and that all channels come to an end, frequently without warning.   In this case the long trend channel does give a warning of reversal.

In 1946, "FJ" had declined from 48 to a support level at 30.   From here it rallied for three months in a trend channel that brought us to the February top at 37.   The next decline broke the previous trend and volume developed at the bottom of this break.   If you will follow the entire chart you will notice that volume nearly always shows an increase at the points of reversal, which are also usually points of contact with the trend channel. Notice also the way the corrective rallies tend to stop at or near the previous Minor bottoms in the downward trend, and how reactions tend to stop at the previous Minor tops in the upward trend.

Trading on this situation would have been profitable.   The Secondary intermediate rally up to February approached the resistance level marked by a 1946 bottom around 40, and a correction of the drop from 48 to 30 would indicate short sales around 37 (which objective was just barely reached). Such sales, if made, would have been covered after the first drop (week of March 1) around 33¼.   New shorts at 34½ would have been closed in the week of March 15 at about 31½.   Shorts made on the rally of the March 22 week around 33 would be covered in the week of April 19 at 30.   If shorted again, the same week at 31, the sale would have been covered after the climactic bottom in the week of May 24; and the combination, here, of great volume and a One-Day Reversal would have warned against further shorts.

The rising channel, being a Secondary, presumably of limited extent, would not offer any great inducement to long-side trading in the absence of other good reasons.

computed distance below the last point at which the stock made contact with the bottom trendline and moved decisively up away from it. If penetration and close below this point occurs without catching the stop, sell on close progressive stops.

The reverse of this rule would apply to the same type of situation in a Bear Market, where stops for short sales would be placed at the computed distance above the point at which the stock made contact with and fell away from the upper trendline.

The changes of angularity and direction in Intermediate trendlines are helpful in showing the gradual turning of a Major trend.

CHAPTER XXXIV

A QUICK SUMMATION OF TACTICAL METHODS

THERE are three types of tactical operations: (1) Getting into new commitments; (2) getting out of commitments which have moved as expected and show a profit, and (3) getting out of commitments which have not moved as expected, whether the transaction shows a profit or a loss.

The principles of taking profits, based on trends, resistance and support levels, measuring implications of patterns, and most especially on the daily technical and volume action of the stock, already have been covered. These profit-taking operations seldom present very difficult problems, since the picture has developed normally and in the way you hoped and expected it would. The "stepping off" point is usually easy to determine.

The more difficult problems arise in making new commitments correctly, and in the very important defensive operations of getting out of losing commitments with the least possible loss.

It should be emphasized that a stock which has ceased to act in a bullish manner and which should therefore be sold, is not necessarily a short sale on the next rally. In other words, the signal that shows weakness or failure of a move in one trend is not always a signal to make new commitments on the opposite side of the market. More often than not, in fact, it is nothing of the kind.

We know that certain moves, such as adverse breakouts from Symmetrical Triangles or Rectangles, advise us simultaneously to get out of commitments in what is now clearly the "wrong" direction and to make new commitments in the "right" direction. The simple failure of a trendline, however, where the stock merely penetrates an old Minor bottom without completing a Head-and-Shoulders or other reversal pattern, although reason enough to get out of commitments which are showing losses, is not sufficiently conclusive, by itself, to justify reversing policy and making *new* commitments in the opposite direction. Therefore we separate the two types of signals as follows:

Get out of present commitments
> On adverse breakout from Head-and-Shoulders formation.
> On adverse breakout from Symmetrical Triangle.
> On adverse breakout from Rectangle.
> On establishment of new Minor low or new Minor high in adverse direction.

On adverse breakout from Diamond.

On adverse breakout from Wedge.

On One-Day Reversal if marked by heavy volume or a gap.

On adverse breakout from Flag or Pennant.

On clear penetration of any resistance or support level in the adverse direction.

On an adverse breakaway gap.

On the appearance of an Island after a move in the favorable direction.

On penetration of basic trendline in the absence of pattern or other favorable criteria.

Note: It is understood that all breakouts must *close* in the breakout area. A closing 3% beyond the support, trend or pattern is sufficient to give the danger signal. All take-outs are performed by the use of ⅛ point progressive stops.

Make New Commitments

In line with the Major Dow trend, or to a limited amount in counter-trend moves as insurance to reduce over-all risk.

On breakout from Head-and-Shoulders pattern.

On breakout from Symmetrical Triangle provided it is not working into the final third of its length toward the apex.

On breakout from Right-Angle Triangle.

On breakout from Rectangle, or (possibly) on points of contact, beginning with the sixth reversal.

On breakout from a Broadening Top.

On breakout from Double or Multiple Top or Bottom. (By this is meant breakout through the bottom of the valley between tops, or upside penetration of the "dome" between bottoms.)

On breakout by penetration through the Double or Multiple tops or bottoms of such a formation.

On breakout from Diamond.

On breakout from Wedge, or (possibly) commitments within the Wedge in the last third of its length as it approaches its apex.

On Flags and Pennants, after sufficient secondary or corrective move by the pattern, or (possibly) within the pattern, provided that volume and all other indications tend strongly to confirm the pattern.

On clear penetration of a well-defined support or resistance area.

On breakaway gap (possibly).

After formation of an important and well-defined Island following a considerable move.

On contact with, or penetration of, the "favorable" trendline if both

trendlines are moving in the Major trend direction. (Blue top trendline in a Bull Market, Red bottom trendline in a Bear Market.)

Note: Breakouts and penetrations must show a closing in the breakout area
and must conform to volume requirements. Breakout closings should
conform to the 3% rule.

New commitments (marked "possibly") may be made in certain cases
within some patterns: Rectangles, Wedges, Flags and Pennants. Exceptional care should be used in such cases.

It is extremely difficult to catch breakaway gaps and we would not
recommend this as a general practice.

All commitments except those just noted are made on the next following reaction or rally, to rules previously stated.

All commitments are protected by stops from the moment they are
made. Stops are moved, as conditions justify moving them, but always
in the favorable direction, never in the adverse direction.

CHAPTER XXXV

EFFECT OF TECHNICAL TRADING ON MARKET ACTION

THE question often is asked whether the very fact that traders are studying methods and patterns tends to *create* those very patterns and trends—in other words, whether the technical method sets up, to some extent, an artificial market in which the market action is merely the reflection of chart action instead of the reverse.

This does not seem to be true. The charts we make today seem to follow the old patterns; the presumption is very strong that markets have followed these patterns long before there were any technicians to chart them. The differences mentioned briefly in Part One, due to changed margin requirements, restraint of manipulative practices, etc., seem to have changed these habits, if at all, only in degree and not in their fundamental nature.

The market is big, too big for any person, corporation or combine to control as a speculative unit. Its operation is extremely free, and extremely democratic in the sense that it represents the integration of the hopes and fears of many *kinds* of buyers and sellers. Not all are short-term traders. There are investors, industrialists, employees of corporations, those who buy to keep, those who buy to sell years later—all grades and types of buyers and sellers.

And not all short-term traders are technicians by any manner of means. There are those who trade on fundamentals for the short term; those who rely on tips, hunches, on reading the stars, on personal knowledge of the company. They are all part of the competitive market, they are all using methods different from yours—and sometimes they will be right and you will be wrong.

The technician using the various tools of technical analysis—Dow theory, point-and-figure charts, oscillators, scale order systems, and monthly, weekly, and daily charts—is in the minority. The cold attempt to analyze a situation on the basis of the market record alone does not appeal to many people. Technical analysis leaves out the warmth and human interest of the boardroom, the fascinating rumors of fat extra dividends to come, the whispered information on new patents, and the thrilling study of the quarterly earnings reports.

It is the influence of all these rumors, facts and statistics that causes men to buy and sell their stocks. It is their actions that build the familiar chart patterns. You are not interested in *why* they are doing what they are doing. So far as your trading is concerned you are interested only in the results of their actions.

The habits and evaluative methods of people are deeply ingrained. The same kinds of events produce the same kinds of emotional responses, and hence the same kinds of market action. These characteristic approaches are extremely durable. It is not quite true that "you can't change human nature," but it is true that it is very difficult to change the perceptive habits of a lifetime. And since the "orthodox" investors greatly outnumber the technicians we may confidently assume that technical trading will have little or no effect on the typical behavior of free markets.

CHAPTER XXXVI

"THE SAME OLD PATTERNS"

TO THE newcomer the market appears as filled with wonders and mysteries as the landscape of Mars will no doubt appear to the first space travelers to effect a landing there. There are strange rumblings, apparently unexplainable upheavals, weird growths. An unknown stock will suddenly emerge from a morass of debt and deficit, and proceed to soar to great heights. An old and trusted issue will paradoxically sag and droop although apparently rooted in the soil of economic stability. All will seem peaceful and secure; and suddenly the ground opens up and swallows values in a sensational market break.

Such a newcomer, perhaps not realizing that what appears unusual and alarming is only the normal fluctuation and adjustment that goes on continually in the market according to the changing evaluations of thousands of investors, will feel frightened, insecure, and indecisive. He may scurry from boardroom to boardroom, personally or on the telephone, scan the financial pages, talk with friends, accumulate a mass of conflicting information; and end up shutting his eyes and making a blind stab in the hope that he may come up with the right answer.

Some there are who never, even after years of contact with the market, achieve a tranquil and assured approach.

But it is possible to learn something about the basic nature of stock trends. It is possible to know, within reasonable limits, about what might be expected in certain situations. And it is also possible to find ways of coping with these situations, including the exceptional cases that persist in doing the unexpected. To repeat: it is possible to deal successfully with the unexpected and with that which cannot be precisely predicted.

To put it another way, it is possible to be wrong part of the time, and still to be successful on balance. And to do this it is only necessary to have a background of experience sufficient to know what will usually happen under particular conditions, about how often the unexpected will occur, and how to deal with the unexpected when it does happen. These are the same general problems that would confront the space traveler, the chemist, the physician, or almost anyone else in his daily affairs.

There are men who have observed the market long enough and carefully

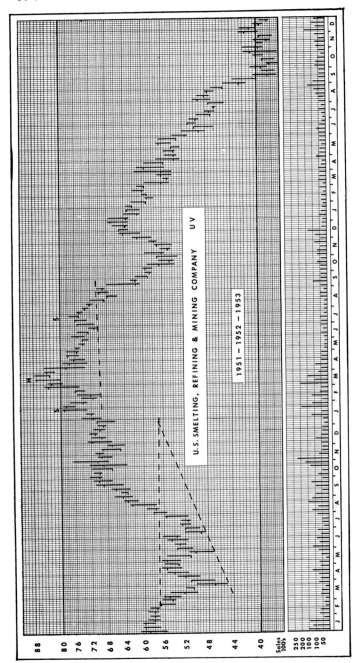

U.S. SMELTING, REFINING & MINING COMPANY   UV

1951 – 1952 – 1953

FIGURE 212. A 1952 Major Head-and-Shoulders top in U. S. Smelting, Ref. & Mining. This stock had moved up from a bottom at 33 in 1950 to the peak at nearly 88 shown here. The decline carried down to 37. This chart shows the typical high volume on the left shoulder. The volume at the head is a little higher than in the "ideal" pattern. Light volume on the right shoulder is a definite warning. Notice the pullback rally to the neckline in the last week of August. Also the Secondary recovery in November and December. There also appears at the left side of this chart in 1951 a beautiful example of an Ascending Triangle, indicating the resumption of the previous interrupted advance.

enough to discover that there are not quite so many unexpected events as the newcomer might be led to believe.

The charts in this book are, in the main, the same as used for examples in the first edition in 1947. Some of them show situations from 1928 and 1929, others from the 1930s and the 1940s. The reader can hardly overlook the similarities that occur in various stocks at different times during corresponding phases of their trends or turning points.

We have said that these same patterns, trends, and support-resistance phenomena repeat themselves over and over again; and that they may be observed by anyone in his own current charts for any period of time, in any normally active stocks, and on any exchange or market.

By way of demonstration there have been included in this chapter of the Fifth Edition a number of typical technical examples, similar to those already discussed, but taken from the period 1947-1966. It would be possible to include ten times the number of good examples, for almost every situation that has been previously illustrated has appeared again and again in recent years.

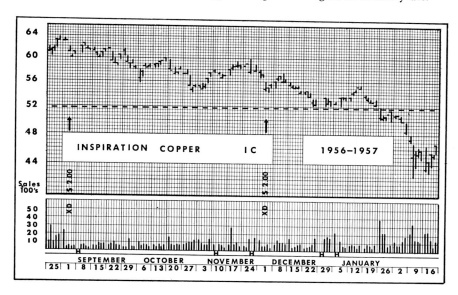

FIGURE 213. Down trends seldom show the perfect and regular trendlines we often see in up trends. But in spite of the irregular, ragged rallies and spotty volume action, the basic principles are about the same as for advances. Notice that in this six month period Inspiration Copper had no rally which carried above the top of a preceding rally. A well-marked down trend of this sort must be presumed to continue until there is a marked change in the pattern and volume action. Notice the volume on the day "IC" broke the historically important 52 level; and subsequent action.

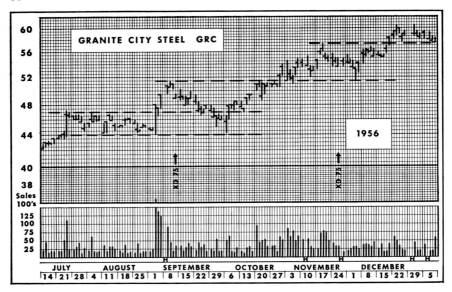

FIGURE 214. Part of the Major advance in Granite City Steel. Here we see the familiar phenomena of support and resistance in almost every move through the period shown.

The August-September Rectangle held for six weeks between the top limit of 47 which was reached on three occasions, and the bottom at 44. Like most Rectangles, it was marked by heavy volume at the start on July 19, and gradually declining volume as the pattern progressed. The breakout move on August 29 was on enormous volume.

After this breakout there was a typical Flag-like reaction on sharply diminished volume; and while this move penetrated the top border of the Rectangle the penetration was not decisive or significant; and the lower border was never violated. Now see how volume appears on October 15 as the old high is reached, and again at the top of the move on November 14. The decline returns to the level of the September high on a low-volume reaction. It is interesting how on five occasions in this chart the 52 level served as a support or resistance point; twice as resistance on the way up, and three times after the new October high, as support.

On the next rise we see almost the same type of advance. In this case the support-resistance level is about 57. Notice the approach to the critical level, the backing away, the aggressive move into new high ground (in mid-December), and the recession to the support at 57.

Advances of this sort seem to represent the flow and ebb of the Minor moves during a Major trend when there are no great "news developments" to change the normal progress of the trend. Where there are frequent and important changes in the market or in news affecting the industry we may see long consolidations or Secondary reactions. But the Major trend is durable. We must not assume a Major reversal prematurely.

FIGURE 215. During the same period that Granite City Steel was making the series of steps upward, as shown on the opposite page, Masonite was doing almost the same thing in reverse.

To have continued to hope for a change in trend with a stock which was acting as "MNC" did through the latter part of 1956 would have required an unusual amount of optimism or innocence about the habits of stocks. Actually, of course, there would be good reason for optimism if the stock had been sold short early in the trend.

This is almost a perfect counterpart to the "GRC" chart. We have not only a series of declines with rallies which fail to establish even Minor highs above the previous tops; but we are also able to draw a trendline which has a number of points of contact on the way down, which is somewhat unusual in a down-trending situation.

Notice the tendency of rallies to stop short at the level of previous bottoms in a series of support-resistance levels. We see such action at 44, at 41, at 38, and at 36.

We would certainly not consider the breaking of the trendline on the up side in late December as evidence of a reversal. Such a break after a trend of this sort probably means no more than a Secondary recovery. To be of greater significance it would certainly call for some volume showing, which was utterly lacking here; and before we would consider the stock again strong enough to buy there would have to be some sort of reversal pattern. A faltering rally back to around 40 would, in fact, suggest the advisability of further short sales.

FIGURE 216. Very often you will hear the question, "But how can you tell whether a technical formation or a breakout is valid?" In many cases, and in a great majority of upside patterns the volume gives such a decisive answer that all doubts are removed. Not always is the volume confirmation as clear as in this chart of Delaware, Lackawanna & Western, but this is typical of a good many breakouts in up trends. You will see that the volume was generally light during the Rectangle, in which we see five plainly marked tops and bottoms.

On Thursday, November 4 the volume increased sharply as the price moved up to the top of the Rectangle and closed at that point. The following day, Friday, we see good volume again with a close beyond the top border. From this point on the move is obviously upward.

There was no indication of reversal at any time after the breakout. A top was reached in March at 25½.

This was an especially vigorous move as it came out of the Rectangle. Normally we would look for Minor set-backs such as the series of reactions in "GRC," Figure 214. And if these had occurred it would in no way have weakened the bullish pattern.

FIGURE 217. This situation, somewhat similar to "DL" on the page opposite, presents a little complication. The problem would have been whether to sell or continue to hold "LA" after the late October break down through the bottom of the Rectangle. There was no important volume on this drift move, and on only one day did the price close barely 3% below the bottom of the pattern. A holder of the stock might well have sold it, might even have executed a short sale.

Suppose now, that you had actually sold the stock short. Observe the volume and the price action on Thursday, November 4 and Friday, November 5. Notice the volume and the price on the following Monday and Tuesday as it reacted slightly. Then see the quick pick-up in volume as the price advanced on Wednesday, the week and a half of dull consolidation, and the larger volume on the move up on Friday. Surely by the middle of the first week of December, if not before, you would have seen the danger signals and closed out your short.

Such a turnabout does not need to be a tragedy nor even a discouragement. Some easily-discouraged traders would be so concerned about the small loss realized on their unsuccessful short sale that they would not be ready to seize the opportunity to reverse position and buy the stock long after the strong up signals. This move carried to 26¾ in March, 1955.

FIGURE 218.   Bottoms normally take longer to complete than tops.   That is one reason we have shown this chart of Fansteel on a weekly basis so that a year and a half of the action can be shown.

The pattern shown at the left is a consolidation formed after a rise from the 1953-1954 multiple bottoms around 21.   The top of the Ascending Triangle corresponds roughly with the April, 1953 peak.

Of course, at the time this Triangle started, in early 1955, it was not possible to identify it as such.   Particularly since the February high ran a little higher than the horizontal tops that eventually formed.

However, during the seven months that preceded the first breakout move it became increasingly clear that each rally to the neighborhood of 32½ was followed by a reaction on low volume, and that these reactions were forming a series of rising bottoms.

In the first week of September we see a clean penetration upside; and from here on the advances and declines fit into the typical pattern of a Major advance.   Notice the breakaway gap in November, and the low volume throughout the December-January-February reaction.

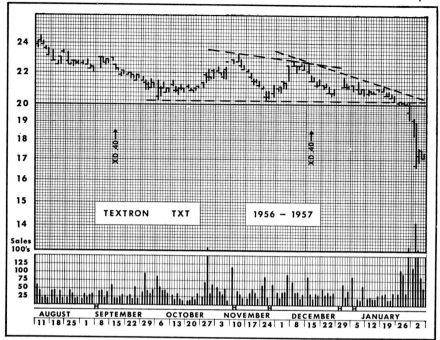

FIGURE 219. Here, in a daily chart we see once again the dramatic sequel to a Descending Triangle. Here is the typical series of declining tops on rather low volume, with retreats between the rallies to a horizontal line.

Notice that the important support here was violated with heavy volume on Friday, January 25. Although the degree of penetration was not great, in view of the generally bearish action to this point, we would sell at once. A Descending Triangle has bearish implications even before the breakout.

There was no substantial pull-back after the breakout. Since it is not possible to count on such a recovery after a break through support, it is safest to sell long holdings immediately or to place a very close stop on them as soon as a close outside the pattern occurs (in this case, outside the pattern as adjusted for ex-dividend).

Notice the pick-up of volume as the price drops into a tailspin at the end of January. Heavy volume is not necessarily a feature of important downside moves, but it may and often does accompany them and when it does it simply underscores the significance of the move.

Question: Does Textron look like a "bargain" to you at the end of January on this chart? Would you be tempted to buy this stock because "it can't go down any more," or because it is "due for a rally," or because it is "selling below its true value"?

Suppose that "TXT" did have a technical rally, which seems quite likely after the move shown. How far would you look for it to go? Would you expect it to penetrate the 20 level in the near future? Would you call this a bullish situation at the end of January, 1957?

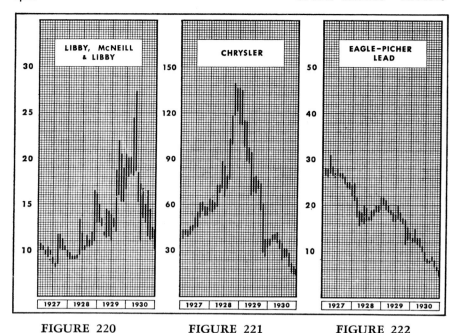

FIGURE 220   FIGURE 221   FIGURE 222

FIGURE 223   FIGURE 224   FIGURE 225

NOT ALL THE SAME

Although a majority of stocks will participate in a big market trend they will not all move at the same time nor to the same degree. Some will move quite independently and contrary to the average.

There was a "boom" in the 1920s. And there was a panic in October, 1929. But these are inadequate statements, half-truths if you will, and can be very misleading if they are swallowed whole. A technician, following the individual behavior of stocks would have been able, through a balanced and diversified portfolio, to protect himself against irreparable loss.

The facts are that of 676 stocks we have studied through the period 1924-1935 only 184 made a Bull Market top in August-September-October, 1929 and suffered Major declines in October and November of that year. 262 stocks were actually in Major down trends *before* the year 1929. 181 other stocks made their Bull Market tops in the first nine months of the year and were already moving down before the end of the summer. 5 stocks did not start their decline until *after* 1929. And 44 stocks continued to make new highs after 1929. Here, on the opposite page, top, are three stocks showing very different trends during the years 1927-1930.

FIGURE 220. Libby, McNeill & Libby showed no serious effects at the time of the October, 1929 panic; went on to new highs in March and April, 1930.

FIGURE 221. Chrysler, one of the great market leaders, made its Bull Market top in 1928, more than a year before the panic, and had already lost 60% of its value *before* October, 1929.

FIGURE 222. Eagle-Picher Lead never enjoyed any Bull Market at all. Aside from an unimpressive rally in 1928 it was in a down trend all the way.

The examples given are not rare exceptions. There are many others involving important stocks which did not follow the pattern set by the averages. This variety of behavior is typical of the market. It is to be seen today. They are *not* "all the same"; and each stock must be studied individually. Here, in the group at the bottom, opposite page, are a few examples showing disparate action during the years 1953-1956. There are hundreds of others that would illustrate the point equally well.

FIGURE 223. West Indies Sugar broke out of its "scalloping" pattern in late 1956 to make its own Bull Market at a time when action in the averages was apathetic and generally weak.

FIGURE 224. Although the averages continued to make new highs through the spring of 1956, Westinghouse Electric made its top and went into a Major decline more than a year earlier.

FIGURE 225. Here is a companion piece to Eagle-Picher's chart of more than twenty-five years ago, shown above it. Kresge, like a number of other "blue chips" did not participate in the Bull Market moves of 1953-1956.

These six charts were adapted from "Graphic Stocks" (F. W. Stephens, New York). The 1927-1930 charts are from a Special Edition covering nearly 700 stocks through the period 1924-1935. The 1953-1956 charts are from a later edition of "Graphic Stocks."

FIGURE 226.   A beautiful top formation in Northrop Aircraft, 1954-1955. The move which ended here at 39¾ in January, 1955 emerged from a bottom in 1953 at 6¼.

The Descending Triangle is marked by rather unusual volume at the peaks of rallies in February and March.   Otherwise it is typical of this sort of reversal pattern.   As so frequently happens there was a pull-back effort after the March 14 breakout; but this rally lasted only two days.

You will notice that the volume on the breakout and throughout the downside move was not so spectacularly heavy; not nearly as heavy in fact as that on the Minor rallies within the Triangle.   However, as pointed out previously, we do not need nor expect so much volume on a decline as we look for in an advance.

Volume did not develop until the end of the first stage of the decline.   It is quite usual for heavy volume to show up at the end of a Minor move whether on the up side or the down side.

Notice the Flag formed on the subsequent rally in mid-April.   The measuring implications of this Flag were approximately carried out a month later.

During the following year and a half "NOC" never reached 31 again.

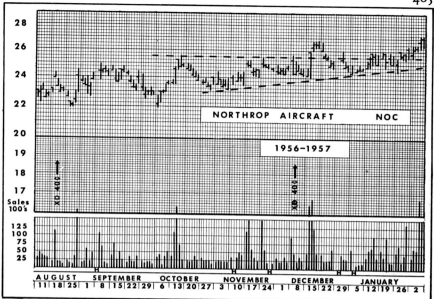

FIGURE 227. Bearing in mind the 1954-1955 chart of Northrop on the facing page, we now turn to the action in this same stock in the latter part of 1956 and the beginning of 1957. The question, of course, is whether the Major down trend is still in effect or whether an important upturn has taken place.

As usual it is the volume that must be watched and studied. Notice the Minor peak on August 14, then the very heavy volume on August 24. See how the activity dries up during September, but resumes briskly as a new Minor top is established in October. Observe the drying-up of volume on declines and the activity on rallies to the 25½ level, which, by the middle of December has become the horizontal top of an Ascending Triangle.

There was no question about the validity of the breakout move on December 10; and the subsequent reaction in the next two weeks confirmed this by the lack of activity on the decline. And again, in early February, we see volume pick up notably as a new high is registered.

At the time this is written it is not possible to say whether or not "NOC" will continue this upward course and eventually smash the "31 barrier." But we feel there will be no doubt in the reader's mind that at the beginning of February, Northrop was presumably moving in an up trend, and must be presumed to be in that trend until a definite change in its market action has taken place. It seems quite probable that if "NOC" should advance to the 30-31 level there is likely to be a period of consolidation with the formation of an area pattern before a successful advance above 31 is accomplished.

As a sidelight on this chart it might be mentioned here that during the period of advance shown above many aircraft stocks were moving lower.

FIGURE 228.   The 1954-1955 advance in Chicago, Milwaukee, St. Paul &
Pacific is an object lesson in Bull Market technics.   Where would such a
trend (of which there are many similar cases) leave the man who sells just
"because he has a good profit," say at 15, or who feels "17 is too high a price."

A MAGNIFICENT UP TREND IN ST. PAUL

FIGURE 228. Here is a chart that is worth considerable study, since it exemplifies a great many features of the "ideal" up trend. In this full year of advance there is no point at which even a tyro technician could find reasonable cause for anxiety or justification for selling the stock. And we should not overlook the tax advantages of long-term gains.

Here, in August and September, we have a perfect example of the Symmetrical Triangle as a consolidation. The volume is typically heavy at the start of the pattern and shrinks to almost nothing as it progresses. The breakout volume is decisive.

The reaction after the breakout, also on lower volume as it should be, runs right back to the apex, the "cradle point" which is nearly always a strong support on such a reaction.

Now follow the action from here. The two days of higher volume in the early November rally represent the penetration of the previous Minor top, and the end of the rally, respectively. The reaction comes back to the previous top.

The December rally is marked by heavier volume when the November top is exceeded; and again to a lesser degree, at the end of the move. Once more there is a reaction; this time to the November top.

A fast move near the end of December repeats the same price and volume action; and is followed by a typical low-volume reaction to the early December top. (This is becoming monotonous. But it is important. You are seeing here a long-term demonstration of bullish technical action.)

Next we have the January breakout. How far would you expect its Minor reaction to go? Would you be surprised if it found support at the level of the three little tops formed early in the month at 17½?

The following advance drives through the 20 level, and in a series of small fluctuations forms an Ascending Triangle.

By the end of February another new high has been established. Can you estimate where to look for support on the reaction?

And now we see the formation of the second Ascending Triangle (notice the relatively low volume), which is broken on the up side in a burst of trading activity toward the end of April. The next reaction comes back to the support of the former tops as you would expect.

Once again an Ascending Triangle is formed, and you will see how the volume dries up throughout this pattern, coming to life emphatically on the breakout on Wednesday, June 8.

Many students on first seeing this chart remark, "Well, the trend wasn't broken until Tuesday, June 21." Actually, of course, no break occurred on that day. The stock simply went ex-dividend $1.50, which as you will see if you adjust the price by that amount, merely brings it back to the support at the top level of the April-May Ascending Triangle.

It is inconceivable that any such regular series of bullish patterns could appear throughout a full year of trading in a stock "by accident." This is part of the normal mechanism of the market, representing the judgments, opinions, fears, hopes, and trading tactics of thousands of traders and investors. However, it should be added that it is not often that one sees such a long and "perfect" Major advance as this. Normally there are interruptions, distortions, or Secondary reactions from time to time.

FIGURE 229.   Does it require the Second Sight to perceive that this is a
bearish stock?   If you were keeping a chart on Westinghouse Electric & Mfg.
wouldn't you have recognized, long before the end of the period shown above,
that the trend was down, not up?

It is one of the great delusions of the market that the stock we own must
be "good."   As prices decline, the price-dividend ratio, based of course, on
past history, will improve.   And the price-earnings ratio likewise will look
continually better.   Investors will begin to speak of "averaging their cost"
by putting more money into a tumbling stock (instead of looking for something that is going their way).   They will talk endlessly about improved
outlook, new products, a forward-looking management.   They will prove to
you that it is selling "below its true value," whatever that may mean.   They
will bend every effort to establishing that what is going on before their eyes
is not true; that the very weak-looking stock is actually strong; that the
American public is making a great mistake and is misjudging this stock;
that the tape is wrong because they *must* be right.

But values in the market are determined democratically and by-and-large
probably represent the best composite appraisal you can find.   A move like
this is not meaningless; nor is it possible today to attribute it to the machina-
tions of a few manipulators.   In the chart we are seeing the reflection of a
collective evaluation which cannot lightly be disregarded.   Westinghouse
reached 50⅞ in November, 1956.

CHAPTER XXXVII

BALANCED AND DIVERSIFIED

THE average investor wants a clear-cut, simple, easy answer to his question, "What do you think of the market?" To him it must be at all times either a Bull Market or a Bear Market. If, in answer to his insistent demand you reply with the question, "What particular stocks are you interested in?" he will avoid that issue and say, "Oh, I mean *in general.*"

And if you will examine the pages of any magazine or newspaper carrying a great deal of financial advertising you will find that many advisers and advisory services make a great point of giving "unhedged" opinions as to the future course of the market, and these opinions are most frequently couched in terms of what "the market as a whole" is going to do.

Now, there is just enough truth in the common belief that "they all move together," to make this an exceedingly dangerous assumption. It is true, for example, that we can set up *definitions* of what we feel constitutes a Bull Market or a Bear Market, such as the Dow Theory, and if a given set of conditions meets the rules we have laid down (our definitions, that is), then we can say accurately, "according to my premises this is now a Bull Market (or a Bear Market, as the case may be). It is also true that over the years, if we had treated the Dow Industrial Average *as if* it were a stock, and had theoretically bought it and sold it according to classic Dow Theory, we would have done very well.

It is also true that in the great inflationary and deflationary movements, which reflect the changes in the relative values of dollars to equities, there is a tendency for the majority of stocks to move with the tide.

And it is furthermore true that in the day-to-day movements of stock prices it appears that most stocks "move up" or "move down" together.

But we should never lose sight of the fact that the Averages themselves are abstractions, not railroads, manufacturing companies, airlines, etc. If the Averages move, it is because the individual stocks making up the averages have moved. And while it is true that during a time when the Averages are advancing, a majority of stocks are also advancing, it is not quite possible to reverse this and make it absolute by saying that *because* the Averages are advancing, therefore *all* stocks *must* advance. If we carried this to its logical conclusion we would arrive at the point (which some have arrived at) where the fact that a stock has not advanced, but has declined in a Bull Market, is considered sufficient to make the stock attractive for purchase on the basis that it must "catch up" with the others.

If we examine the facts, that is the long-term records of what stocks have actually done, we find that there are periods when most stocks go up in value and other times when most of them go down.   We find, sometimes, that laggard stocks will eventually join the procession in an upward trend.

But this does not always happen.   And it can be extremely uncomfortable to have bought stocks in a presumably bullish market, because they are "behind the market," or because "they are all going to go up," and then wait for months as we watch other stocks climbing to new highs while our own securities continue to languish or decline further.

From what you already know of the market you will surely agree that it is not a wise policy to put all your capital into buying stocks in what is clearly a Bear Market in the Averages and in most stocks.   And you will agree, too, that it is not a safe thing to sell stocks short to the limit of your resources in a skyrocketing Bull Market.

If you have to be 100% on one side or the other, it is much better to go with the trend.   In that way you will be in line with the probabilities as shown by a majority of stocks, and by the Averages.

But you should realize that "going with the trend" is not always as easy as it sounds.   We can set up definitions, as we have, of what constitutes the Major trend.   Then the question is whether you have the patience and the courage to maintain a position in line with these definitions through months of uncertainty and possible adverse moves.   During turning periods it is often hard to make the decision to buy or sell.

And most especially, there is the difficulty of knowing what to buy or what to sell, and when.

For the simple patterns and signals of the Averages do not tell the whole story.   There is a certain usefulness in regarding "the market as a whole" in studying Dow Theory; just so long as we keep in mind that the Averages we are studying are generalities (high-order abstractions), and the rules for determining their trend apply to these generalities and not necessarily to each and every stock listed on the Stock Exchange.

In many cases, for example, a group of stocks will "top out" and start an important bearish trend while other groups of stocks are continuing to make new highs.   This occurred in 1946, when we saw a large number of stocks topping out in January and February, and others continuing strong until the end of May.

We think of 1929 as the year "the market" made its great peak, and crashed in October to start the series of breaks that continued into 1932. There is some truth in this; but it is not the whole truth.   There were some important stocks that made their highs long before the 1929 top. Chrysler, for example, made its high in October, *1928,* and had dropped from 140 to 60 *before* the panic of 1929. There were stocks which never enjoyed a Bull Market at all in the whole period from 1924 to 1929. By actual count of nearly 700 listed stocks, 262 issues made their Bull Market highs before 1929, 181 topped in 1929, but before August of that year. There were several stocks which did not have their first downside break until *after* 1929. 44 stocks went into new Bull Market high ground after 1929 and before mid-1932. Only 184 of the 676 stocks studied made their Bull Market highs in August, September or October of 1929 and crashed in October and November.

In other words, only 27% of the stocks acted the way everybody "knows" *all* stocks acted.

It is all right to accept the "general" trend as a useful device so long as we know it is a device only, and not a picture of the detailed reality. We have to face the problem which continually confronts every student of the market; how to protect ourselves from uncertainties in interpretation of the Averages, and how to protect ourselves against stocks which are not moving with the majority.

The problem can be met, first of all, by not taking an unreasonable amount of risk at any time (See Chapter XL).

It can also be met by using an Evaluative Index instead of switching from all-out bullish to all-out bearish. By this we mean using an indicator that will show not merely whether it is a Bull Market or a Bear Market, but "how bullish" or "how bearish" it seems at a given time.

At first glance this may seem not too different a conception from that of classic Dow Theory. The same technical methods apply. Also, during a strongly bullish market, an Evaluative Index will show the trend, as will the Averages. But with this difference; that the Evaluative Index will also indicate approximately the *degree* of strength. As the market begins to develop weak spots, as did the market in 1928 and 1929, the *degree of bullishness* will gradually decline.

Before considering the use of this Index, let us outline what it is and how it may be constructed. You will understand it is not a precise tool; it gives only an approximate picture of the state of the market; it gives no positive signals; and in the final analysis it is a reflection of the judgment and opinion of the person who is maintaining it.

Suppose you are keeping daily charts of 100 stocks. At the end of each week you can mark these along the bottom of the chart with a small "plus" or "minus," indicating your opinion as to whether each particular stock is moving in a bullish Major trend, or is bearish. In some cases you will find it hard to make a decision. This is not too important, however, since these cases will not be numerous, and in the majority of stocks you will normally be able

DIAGRAM 10.   The Evaluative Index shows the percentage of stocks that appear in bullish or bearish Major trends.   In 1961 this Index conflicted with "stock averages," suggesting a possible Major turn.

to mark them "plus" or "minus" on the basis of their obvious action. If you now total the "plus" stocks and also the "minus" stocks, including those in which you have had to make a tentative decision, you will have two figures totaling the number of your charts. If 75 of these are "plus," you can say that the market looks 75% bullish to you. If next week the percentage is higher, say 80%, it indicates a stronger or more bullish condition. If it is lower, say 70%, it shows that on balance there are fewer of your stocks that look strong, hence the market is presumably weaker.

As we have said before, if the Averages are making new highs you will expect (and find) that the Evaluative Index will range well above 50%. In an obvious Bear Market, the Index will stand considerably lower than 50%.

But notice that we do not speak, here, of "signals." There is no point at which we need to say "Sell everything." Neither is there a point at which we can say "Buy now," in an all-out sense. The Index will float and adjust itself continually to the shifting conditions.

It must be clear that a market in which only 53% of a large group of representative stocks are moving bullishly is not as strong as one in which 80% of these stocks are acting bullish.

Therefore you would be justified in making larger commitments on the long side in this second case.

You would still have the problem of *selection* of the individual stocks to buy. But you would be justified in making larger total commitments, or in assuming total greater risk (see again Chapter XL), than in a market that was barely qualifying as a Bull Market.

By bringing the total of one's investment program into line with this Index, it is possible to "roll with the punch"; and one would almost automatically be withdrawn from a deteriorating market before things became too dangerous. Furthermore, this would be accomplished without the need for torturing decisions as to whether to "sell now" or "wait a while."

There is a further extension of this method. If an investor were to follow the Evaluative Index only by increasing or decreasing his long commitments with the rise and fall of the Index, he might be better off than if he had only the two alternatives of complete optimism or complete pessimism. But in this case he would still be pointed always in one direction, and would stand to lose to some degree on his long commitments if the market did eventually reverse and go into a panic move.

The extension of the method is to proportion capital, or a certain portion of capital, between the long side and the short side of the market. Assuming that your interpretation of your own charts is reasonably correct in a majority of cases, you can, at any particular time, select several stronger-than-average stocks; and similarly, several weaker-than-average issues.

With the Index standing in the vicinity of 50% (as it did for a number of months in mid-1956) you can then select several strong stocks to buy, and several candidates for short sale, making commitments that will approximately balance your total risk.   In the case of an upward surge that sweeps all before it, you will, of course, accrue losses on the short sales, and may eventually have to reverse your classification of them from "minus" to "plus," closing them out for a loss.   But in such a case, the gains on your good long positions will more than offset the loss, assuming your choices were well made; and the loss realized can be absorbed as "insurance," the price you have paid to be in a protected position.

On the other hand, should the market collapse suddenly (as it did, for example, at the time of President Eisenhower's illness in 1955), the accrual of loss in the long positions will be offset by accrual of gains in the short positions. And if the decline should continue to a point calling for sale of the long stock, the losses here could be considered the price of the "insurance" protection to the shorts provided by the longs.

It is also quite possible, in a more normal market, that both the long positions and the short positions will show gains.

What we are proposing is a systematic and continuous arbitrage or hedge. As the Evaluative Index advances, the proportion of short positions would gradually be reduced, and the long positions increased.   As the Index declines, the reverse would happen.

This method is essentially conservative.   Those who have always feared the short sale as a purely speculative gamble, might well re-examine short selling from the standpoint of using the short sale as a regular part of their investment program as counterbalance to the long holdings.

The result to be looked for in this conservative "balanced and diversified" program is primarily protection of capital.   By its very nature it eliminates the possibility of "plunging" for spectacular profits.

But it also provides the mechanism by which the technical method can stand on its merits, largely independent of the "changes and chances" of the market.   It makes it possible to eliminate a large part of the anxiety and uncertainty that so many traders and investors carry every day and often late into the night.

CHAPTER XXXVIII

TRIAL AND ERROR

YOU will not expect to turn in a perfect record from the start. You may indeed do poorly. That is one of the reasons we have suggested using only a safe amount of your capital, allowing enough leeway so that if you should misread and misdirect your campaigns, or if you should encounter an Intermediate setback in the trend or a Major turn, you will be able to get back on course, undismayed, and richer in experience.

Your records of actual transactions (and notes on theoretical transactions) will help you. As time goes on you will discover new trading refinements. Try these methods against your previous chart records. See whether your improvements work out consistently to your advantage. In that way you can test new details of method without risking actual capital until you have checked the operation thoroughly.

In one actual case a trader who had shown a rather poor record of performance through a fast-moving Bear phase of the market, rechecked thirty of his actual trades made during that period in the light of new methods he had subsequently developed. Where the original record showed a loss at the rate of about 40% per year on the capital for the time it was tied up, the changes he introduced, applied to the same situations, would have resulted in a profit at the annual rate of 156%. Such a result, while not conclusive, would strongly suggest trying out the new method on all similar situations in the future, and if the performance continued to show this advantage, to adopt it as a permanent policy. It is only by continual checking and testing that you can learn to pick up more of the profitable opportunities and protect yourself better against the unexpected reversals.

If you follow the suggestions of this book, those already given, and those in the following chapters, you will proceed slowly and cautiously, not risking all your capital on a single move in a single stock. Errors and plain bad luck, when they hurt you, will not hurt you too seriously. You will be prepared for false moves, wrong interpretations, and complete reversals of expected developments.

If you have worked thoughtfully and serenely, without permitting your emotions to rule your judgment, the law of averages will bring you continually greater success. You are not gambling blindly in this work; you are intelligently using past experience as a guide—and it is a dependable guide. Your operations are part of the competitive workings of a free market; your purchase and sales are part of the process of interpreting the trend, checking runaway inflations and crashes, and determining the value of the American industrial plant.

The market will continue to go up and down in the future as it has in the past. Your technical knowledge will save you from "buying at the top" in the final climactic blow-off, and it will save you from selling everything in a fit of depression and disgust when the bottom is being established. In your studies of past market action you have a strong shield and buckler against the sudden thrusts that surprise and often defeat the novice trader.

CHAPTER XXXIX

HOW MUCH CAPITAL TO USE IN TRADING

UP TO this point we have been talking mostly in terms of points and percentages. Little has been said about dollars. From here on we are going to turn the spotlight on the questions revolving around money, capital, the dollars you will actually be using in your operations. For, just as an understanding of the technical signals and patterns alone will not guarantee your profits without a tactical method of application, so your tactics alone will not insure you profits until you have tailored your method to fit your pocketbook, and until you have a systematic control of your trading in terms of dollars and cents.

At the start of your charting operations you will be using no capital. You will be making no trades either actual or theoretical. Any commitment you might make during the first four or five weeks on a new chart would be no more than gambling on a hunch.

It will take about two months of thankless charting before you have any clear picture of how any of your stocks are acting technically. From then on your chart history will become more valuable each week.

Your first trades probably will be theoretical ones. You will want to get the feel of the charts and learn to apply the methods you have studied. Eventually you will want to make an actual transaction.

Then the question will come up, "How much of my capital shall I use for trading purposes?"

That will depend on your circumstances and how much of your time and effort you plan to put into stock trading, and also on your experience in the market. If you have been buying and selling stocks for a number of years you will naturally continue along the same lines, simply applying the new techniques to your operations.

On the other hand, if stock trading is entirely a new field for you, or if it is only a minor hobby or sideline, it would pay to make haste slowly. Some writers have pointed out that it usually takes about two years to gain enough practical experience to operate safely in the market, that during the two-year apprenticeship period many traders come in, gradually lose their capital, and retire permanently from the field, leaving their money behind them. Therefore, no matter how confident you may be or how anxious to get in and start pitching, it would be safest to do most of your experimenting on the theoretical basis, and to use only a small amount of your actual capital, so that, after say two years, if you have shown some actual profits, consistently and regularly, even though small, you will be much better prepared to use more of your capital wisely and safely. And conversely, if during that time you have made repeated mistakes and have registered many unnecessary losses, you will be able to correct your methods and continue on a sounder basis, without having lost your main capital reserve.

In no case do you want to risk everything you can scrape together on the theory that here is the quick way to make easy money. That simply is not true, and the chances are overwhelmingly against you if you go ahead under any such plan.

Better to figure out how much you can spare, how much you could afford to spend for experience, considering that the amount you start with is in the same category as money you might use for taking a special course of instruction, or for improving property you hope to sell. Or, to take another example, it would be similar to the salary you might lose in accepting a lower-paid position in a new kind of work that eventually should be worth more than your present job.

In other words you will not depend, from the start, on *any* returns from the capital you use in trading. You will plan your own budget outside of these funds, even if that calls for trimming your budget to make that possible. Then you can go ahead and follow your trading method free from any pressure to take unnecessary risks, free from the need to sell stock prematurely to meet obligations, and free from heckling fears and worries.

You can start operations with as little as $500. Better to have $1,000 or several thousand. It makes little difference, so long as you have worked out what you can *afford* to use during the apprenticeship period, and as long as you are sure you will have capital to continue your operation as you develop ability. The important thing at the start is not how many dollars you can make, but what percentage of increase per year you can average with the capital you are using.

If you approach the serious business of trading in this frame of mind, you will not be afraid to take losses when it is necessary (and there are times when that is the only wise course to adopt), you will not be straining to make an unreasonable or impossible profit (with the usual disastrous results), and you will be able calmly to build your trading policy in the sure conviction that the market will still be there next year, that opportunities will still be waiting for you, and that the basic procedures you are developing are more valuable than any "lucky break" you might pull out of thin air or a boardroom rumor.

CHAPTER XL

APPLICATION OF CAPITAL IN PRACTICE

LET us now restate a number of things we have already investigated and on which (let's hope) we are thoroughly agreed.

1. Major trends ordinarily run for long periods of time, covering a tremendous number of points in total advance or decline.
2. Almost unbelievable profits could be made by one who could buy stocks at the extreme bottom of a Bear Market and sell at the extreme top of the following Bull Market; or sell short at the extreme peak of a Bull Market and cover at the extreme bottom of the following Bear Market.
3. It is not possible to accomplish either of these desirable results.
4. It is possible to avoid becoming trapped in purchases made at or near the extreme Bull Market top so that losses become dangerous or ruinous in a Major reversal. It is also possible, of course, to avoid such losses through ill-advised short sales near the extreme bottom of a Bear Market.
5. It is possible to make profits by trading in line with the Major trend, and in some cases by trading on the Intermediate corrections to the Major trend, or, occasionally, on the individual behavior of a stock which is moving contrary to the Major trend.
6. The greatest and most dependable profits may be made along the Major trend during the principal period of advance (or decline in the case of short sales), but not during the earliest phases when the movement first gets under way, nor during the rounding off or reversal phenomena near the end of the movement.

Therefore, in order to get the greatest benefits from following the Major trends, one would want to have a relatively small equity in the market at the very start of the move and very little at or near the termination of the move, but a very substantial interest during the mid-portion when the advance or decline was making the greatest headway.

The writer has felt it should be possible to express this relation between the amount of capital tied up and the state of the Major trend in a neat and definite equation. But inasmuch as the idea of a Major trend is, itself, a matter of definition, and since, as we have already pointed out, the trend is an abstraction from the individual movements of many stocks, it does not seem possible to arrive at any such easy solution to the problem of how much capital to use at a given time.

Nor is it necessary to have a definite and exact answer. As we have already seen, it is possible to set up an Evaluative Index which will give an approximate answer good enough for all practical purposes so far as weighing the "strength" of the trend at a particular time.

There are, however, some other questions. Most importantly, there is the question of how much total *risk* you are assuming. Since some stocks are very conservative and others are very speculative, it is not enough to determine what part of your capital should be applied in a market trend. The proportion of your total capital used is not necessarily the whole measure of your participation. The price level of a stock will affect its habits (low-priced stocks make bigger percentage moves than high-priced stocks). The amount of margin you are using will have an effect on the degree of risk.

There is some substance to this plan (otherwise we would not be taking the time to discuss it here at all), but there is a serious question whether the decision as to the amount of capital to be used at any specified time can ever be reduced to a simple mathematical operation.

Let us suppose you are convinced that this is a Bull Market in a phase of such potency that you would be justified in using 80 percent of your capital. But you will immediately realize, from what has been said in earlier chapters, that if this money is put into a high-priced stock, say American Telephone & Telegraph, it will not give you as much likelihood of either profit (if you are right) or loss (if you are wrong), as it would if put into a lower-priced stock such as American Radiator. In the same way, your money put into a stock having a low Sensitivity Index, that is, a conservative stock such as Detroit Edison, will not give you as much likelihood for either profit or loss as a stock of high Sensitivity Index, that is, a speculative stock such as Lockheed. These factors, quite as much as the amount of actual dollars, affect your status, and are factors in answering the question, "Am I out on a limb and, if so, how far out?"

To make this perfectly clear, we could take 80 percent of our capital, say $8,000 out of $10,000, and put this amount into the market by purchasing United States Steel 7% Preferred, outright. A great rise in the general market might bring us an increase in value of a few points, perhaps 4 or 5 percent. And conversely, a great decline might depress the issue by about the same amount. An example of going to the other extreme might be to purchase $8,000 worth of options on a low priced, extremely speculative stock, in which the probable result within 90 days would be either a profit of several hundred percent, or a total loss of the $8,000.

Obviously, we could vary our status during the progress of the market either by increasing or decreasing the amount of the total commitment, or by changing the nature of the account, switching part of the total into more or less speculative stocks, higher or lower priced stocks, and also by varying the amount of margin used.

In the following chapter we will show how the principal factors affecting a given sum of capital used (namely: sensitivity, price and margin) can be combined into one figure, which we are going to call the Composite Leverage Index.

It is perfectly true that you must vary your Composite Leverage so as to take advantage of the fast-moving central portions of important moves, using a lower Composite Leverage at the beginning of such moves, and during the tapering-off or turning periods near the end.

However, it is one thing to express the Composite Leverage accurately, and another thing to write a formula for applying specific degrees of leverage at particular times. The method suggested at the very beginning of this chapter has some value, but owing to the Secondary reactions and the difficulty of determining Major Trends in individual stocks, it is not possible to make this into the neat, pat rule we were looking for.

It must be a matter of experience, or intuition based on experience. You will not permit your Composite Leverage factor to run out to a dangerous point on the limb. Neither will you allow it to become so low during times of good market opportunity that you are not getting full benefits from the move.

We can keep the general shape of a Major swing in our minds as we consider this. Bull Markets normally rise through a series of irregular advances and declines, starting with a moderate upward trend, and gradually accelerating as the market approaches its ultimate top. Bear Markets are likely to move fastest at the start, and taper off gradually toward the end. Bear Markets are steeper than Bull Markets. These considerations will help us to judge the times when the market will offer the best opportunities, the times when our Composite Leverage should be increased.

There are other factors, even harder to pin down in simple figures. We would at times make switches of our holdings for reasons that had no direct relation to the factors making up the Composite Leverage Index of the stocks. We know, for example, that high-grade issues, the active market leaders and perhaps some stocks of a more conservative nature, will tend to start their moves in a Bull Market fairly early, and to continue their advance at a fairly steady pace. Eventually they will reach their tops and make a reversal pattern. They will decline from this point, probably at a steeper average angle than the ascent. Low priced and low grade issues, on the other hand, tend to be slow in getting started, will remain dormant during the early phases of a Bull Market, and will then suddenly and spectacularly skyrocket in a series of moves that brings them to their ultimate top. However, this top is likely to be reached at a later point (perhaps months later) than the point at which many of the more conservative stocks topped out. The speculative group will then drop very fast and will return to the dead levels of inaction before the conservative group has finished its more leisurely Major decline.

This means that you will do well to concentrate your Bull Market trading in the early stages, in the higher grade stocks; and in the later stages, in the lower grade stocks. In a Bear Market you would perhaps be able to make short sales successfully in high grade stocks even while some of the "cats and dogs" were still completing their final run-up; but you would be watching for the opportunity to cover those shorts and go short of the low grade stocks as soon as their reversal was signaled.

The next chapter will go into the Composite Leverage Index. It should be a useful gauge for you in your market operations, and a protection against overtrading. But do not expect that you can use it mechanically as an index against the market to answer all your questions involving the nature and size of your commitments. For in gauging the condition of the Major trend at any time, your own experience and judgment must be the final arbiters.

PUT AND CALL OPTIONS

Options of various sorts have a long history in commercial markets. Nearly 2000 years ago the merchants who operated in the Mediterranean region used "to arrive" agreements which amounted to option contracts, as insurance to reduce the risks of storm and piracy. Modern commodity futures contracts resemble stock options in their dual nature of serving either as trading media or as insurance devices. Options are also widely used in real estate transactions and in various other applications.

For many years stock options were traded only on the basis of individual agreement between a buyer or a writer, and an opposite number, directly or through a broker or dealer. The customer and the writer can decide what stock (any stock) will be optioned, at what exercise or striking price, for what period of time, and at what premium. A classic treatise on this type of "unlisted" options is the definitive book by Herbert Filer, the founder of the oldest and largest of the group of option dealers, "Understanding Put and Call Options."[1]

In 1973 a new method of handling option contracts was inaugurated by the Chicago Board Options Exchange and later the American Stock Exchange, in which call options on a selected list of actively traded stocks are offered with standard expiration dates (like commodity contracts) and at definite exercise prices, the premium depending on the bids and offers of buyers and writers. An excellent guide to this rapidly expanding market is Nicholas R. Bokron's book, "How to Use Put and Call Options."[2]

---

1. Published by John Magee. At your bookseller, or $5.00 postpaid in U.S.
2. Published by John Magee, Inc. At your bookseller, or $10.00 postpaid in U S

CHAPTER XLI

A DISCUSSION OF COMPOSITE LEVERAGE

AS WE suggested in the preceding chapter, there is some relation between the state or stage of a Major Market and its potentialities for profit. There are many mechanical plans and systems for coping with the problem; but we do not believe it can be fully solved by mechanical means alone. We mentioned one plan by which the commitments were governed according to the consensus of trends in an entire portfolio of charts. There are other plans which depend on pyramiding the commitment as the trend proceeds; and still others which are based on averaging costs by increasing the commitment working against the trend; that is, by buying on a scale down at progressively lower levels in a Bear Market, and selling on a scale up in Bull Markets.

None of the plans, taken by themselves alone are adequate to answer the questions of when to buy and when to sell. The primary purpose of this book is to study the technical phenomena of individual stocks. If we can learn from the charts at what points to buy and under what conditions to sell, we have acquired the basic machinery for successful trading. On the other hand, obviously, if your buying and selling are at points which more often than not result in net losses, then it makes no difference how you divide up your capital or apply it in the market, for it will be bound to shrink until eventually it has all disappeared.

The first problem, then, is to learn to use the technical tools, patterns, trends, supports, resistances, etc. Then we can consider how much money we will risk and in what way.

We have already seen that it makes a difference, sometimes a great difference, how we apply our capital. The various factors of price level, sensitivity and margin, enter into the concept we are going to call the Composite Leverage Index. In the latter part of this chapter we will give a definition of this. Meanwhile, we have said enough so you will understand what we are driving at if we use the term in connection with your market commitments.

You realize, of course, that you do not want to be so conservative that you will rule out practically all opportunities for making gains. If you decide never to oppose the Primary trend you will have to be inactive during long Secondary trends, and may be left waiting, sometimes for weeks on end, for a continuation of the Primary move. Naturally, you will pass up all weak signals and convergent trends, and shun new commitments after very active blow-offs or panic climaxes. You could, no doubt, carry your refinement of caution so far that your percentage of success, instead of being a mere 60, 70 or 80 per-cent, might approach 90; you might actually be right 95 percent of the time in your decisions. But this extreme conservatism would also mean that you would trade only in the very finest possible situations, when every factor was clean-cut and favorable. You would not have such opportunities very often. The result might be a profit, but too small a profit to justify all the work and study you would be putting into your charts. For you can obtain 2% return, or 3% or even 4% on your capital without very much study and without much risk, and you must expect a much higher rate of return if your efforts are to be worth while.

In order to put your charts to work, you have to avail yourself of the higher leveraged stocks, stocks which carry more opportunity for gain and, hence, more risk of loss. You have to accept, deliberately, a greater risk than the man who is content to buy a "safe" security, put it in the box and forget it.

By maintaining your Composite Leverage at or near some constant level which your experience and judgment tells you is safe for the particular state of the market, you will be protected against over-caution. More important, if you maintain this Composite Leverage in your operations, you will be protected against unconsciously over-trading. This is a fault more common than ex-treme caution, and can be a dangerous enemy even when your percentage of theoretical trading gains is high. When you select a definite Composite Lever-age and adhere to it in your trading commitments, changing it as necessary to meet changed conditions, you will be forced to restrain your enthusiasm within safe limits, and you will be continually aware of the risks you are taking.

OVER-TRADING—AND A PARADOX

This leads to another point. A series of identical percentage gains and losses on your capital does not give you a series of equal gains and losses in dollars and cents. This is a serious problem, worth understanding. For a trader who is greatly over-extended is intensifying this problem (which exists in any case, but which does not need to cause him too much worry if he has planned his program).

You can understand the paradoxical statement that percentage gains and losses are not equal if you take the extreme case, first, of a man who in every business venture he enters risks his entire capital with the expectation of either a 100% gain or a 100% loss. If his first venture is a loss, he loses 100%. He is finished, because he cannot gain by making 100% on nothing. However, if the first venture is successful and he then uses his entire capital including the new profits again, on the same terms, and the second venture is a failure, he will be wiped out completely. No matter how many successes he may have, he stands to lose everything on his first failure.

In a lesser degree this is the situation we are speaking of. You would not risk all of your capital on a basis of doubling your money or losing all. But suppose you were extended, continually, to a point where you were taking the risk of a 40% net loss on each transaction, with the hope of a 40% net gain. Should you start with $1,000 and have a succession of ten losses, you would wind up with about six dollars. Now suppose the very next ten transactions were all successful. You would finally come out, after ten losses and ten gains, each of 40%, with capital of less than $100. It would not be necessary either that these ten losses and ten gains come in the order given. You might have the ten gains first, or three gains, four losses, seven gains and then six losses. The result would be the same. After ten gains and losses, in any order, you would have lost more than 90% of your capital.

On the other hand, if you risked your entire capital each time on twenty ventures, in ten of which you took an 8% net gain and in ten an 8% net loss, your $1,000 after the ten gains and losses would be reduced only to $937. You would still have about 94% of your original capital. Therefore, in this case (and 8% is a fair average figure for short-term transactions resulting in a loss, in fact a rather liberal figure according to extensive tabulations of actual transactions) you would have a handicap due to this paradox of only about ⅓ of one percent on each trade.

Now it is conceivable that ten successive trades might go wrong, though that would be an unusual condition. There was one period of ten months between the actual turn of the market and the Dow signal for a reversal of the Primary trend. True, the resulting new trend, once established, ran far and long, and would have made up all losses and produced fine profits. But during the ten hard months, allowing the fair average time of 30 days per transaction, it is possible that ten successive wrong-way trades might have been stopped out for losses, reducing the original $1,000 to $434.

The important thing here is that the next ten successful trades would have brought this $434 back to $937; in other words you could have righted the boat and sailed right on if you were working on the 8% basis, whereas if you had been following the 40% basis we gave previously as an example, you would have been sunk without a trace, a victim of over-trading.

Therefore, by maintaining a sane Composite Leverage Index and letting the law of averages work for you and with you, you will be on solid mathematical ground. Your technical studies will have every opportunity to make you a profit. Otherwise you can, simply by unwise over-extension of your trading, prevent even the best technical analysis from producing a net profit.

COMPOSITE LEVERAGE INDEX OF A SINGLE STOCK

If you keep a record of sensitivity as outlined in Chapter XXIV and have computed the Sensitivity Indexes for your stocks (or you can use the table in

Appendix B if your stock is one of those listed), then you can set down the Composite Leverage of any purchase or short sale as follows:—

Let S represent the Sensitivity Index of the stock.
" N " " Normal Range-for-Price from table in Appendix B, based on the price at the time of the original commitment.
" T " " Total net amount paid or received on the original transaction.
" C " " Capital reserved to finance this Commitment. In the case of outright cash purchases or 100% margin short transactions, this figure cancels out against T in the numerator.

Then

$$\text{Composite Leverage} = \frac{SNT}{15.5 \times C}$$

(15.5 is the Normal Range for a stock selling at a price of 25, and is simply an arbitrary selection to serve as a fixed point of reference in determining ratios.)

COMPOSITE LEVERAGE ON AN ENTIRE PORTFOLIO

The Composite Leverage on the entire account is a summation of the risks on the component stocks and can be figured in this way:—

$$\text{Total Composite Leverage} = \frac{\text{Sum of SNT*}}{15.5 \times \text{Total Capital or Net Worth}}$$

Let us add one more striking example of the importance of Composite Leverage. At a time when stocks could be bought on a 30% margin it would have been possible to buy, with $1,000, $3,300 worth of a highly speculative stock, Standard Gas and Electric $4 Preferred, then listed on the New York Stock Exchange. Let us assume that the price at that time was 25 dollars a share. The Composite Leverage then on your $1,000 capital would be 693% using the methods we have just outlined in determining this Composite Leverage. At this same time, using the same methods of figuring, an outright purchase of $1,000 worth of Celanese 4¾% 1st Preferred at 106 would give a Composite Leverage of only 11.8%. Comparing these two transactions, your purchase of SG Pr provided a leverage of 693 to 11.8 as compared to the purchase of CZ 1st Pr or approximately 60 to 1 (58.7 to 1). Presumably,

---

* Sum of SNT means that you figure S × N × T for each stock in the portfolio separately, and add all these figures together.

and based on the past history of the stocks, your chances of capital gain or loss were about 60 times as great in the **SG Pr** as in the **CZ 1st Pr.**

The method proposed here gives you a means of knowing at least approximately how much risk you are assuming in a stock or in a group of stocks. It can help you to avoid exposing yourself unwittingly to an inordinate degree of risk or on the other hand restricting unduly your opportunities for gain.

INVESTMENT ACCOUNT POLICY

Ordinarily investment account management is based largely on considerations of the "fundamentals," and not to any great extent on technical indications. Furthermore, such accounts would normally be set up on a more conservative basis, and would not try to use Bear Markets for short sales.

Nevertheless, the matter of Composite Leverage figured on the entire account is a help in determining the over-all nature of the investment. It would be a help in determining whether the account should be placed in a more conservative position, or whether it could stand a change in the direction of somewhat more speculative holdings. These decisions would, naturally, depend on the size of the account, the condition and requirements of the owner, and on the general condition of business and the market itself. However, the Composite Leverage Index will provide a useful gauge for appraising the character of the account as a whole at any particular time.

NEGATIVE COMPOSITE LEVERAGE

From what we have said about the "insurance" function of short sales in a Bull Market (and purchases in a Bear Market), where these "contrary" transactions are used to achieve balance by means of an Evaluative Index, it must be clear that such short sales or protective purchases must tend to reduce the Composite Leverage or total risk of the account; which is exactly why they would be used.

It might seem that by considering the contrary transactions as negative, and those in line with the presumed Major trend as positive, this sum could be reduced to zero, or at least to a point where there was no substantial total risk at all. This is not quite possible, since we are dealing, at best, with rough approximations, and also because we are dealing with more-or-less independent variables which may and will at times make erratic moves.

However, it is true that we can greatly reduce the total risk and that the contrary moves do, in a real sense, "subtract" risk from the total account.

This "subtraction" of risk appears in commodity accounts, where it is customary for brokers to reduce the margin required on total commitments if some of these commitments are "contrary," that is if there are some shorts along with a majority of long positions, or vice versa.

CHAPTER XLII

STICK TO YOUR GUNS

IT HAS often been pointed out that any of several different plans of operation, if followed consistently over a period of years, would have produced consistently a net gain on market operations. The methods we have discussed in this book (representing the technical approach) are a case in point.

The fact is, however, that many traders, not having set up a basic strategy and having no sound philosophy of what the market is doing and why, are at the mercy of every panic, boom, rumor, tip, in fact of every wind that blows. And since the market, by its very nature, is a meeting place of conflicting and competing forces, they are constantly torn by worry, uncertainty and doubt. As a result they often drop their good holdings for a loss on a sudden dip or shake-out; they can be scared out of their short commitments by a wave of optimistic news; they spend their days picking up gossip, passing on rumors, trying to confirm their beliefs or alleviate their fears, and they spend their nights weighing and balancing, checking and questioning, in a welter of bright hopes and dark fears.

Furthermore, a trader of this type is in continual danger of getting caught in a situation that may be truly ruinous. Since he has no fixed guides or danger points to tell him when a commitment has gone bad and it is time to get out with a small loss, he is prone to let stocks run entirely past the red light, hoping that the adverse move will soon be over, and that there will be a "chance to get out even," a chance that often never comes. And, even should stocks be moving in the right direction and showing him a profit, he is not in a much happier position, since he has no guide as to the point at which to take these profits. The result is he is likely to get out too soon and lose most of his possible gain, or overstay the market and lose part or all of the expected profits.

If you have followed the preceding chapters carefully, you will have realized that none of the technical formations and signals is certain and unfailing. The chart action of a stock discounts and records *all presently known* information about that stock (which *includes* all matters of dividends declared or expected, split-ups and mergers that are known to be planned, political angles as they affect the market, world affairs, management, earning records, etc.). The chart does not and cannot forecast unforeseeable events, matters that are completely unknown to anybody. In a majority of cases the charts are dependable. If you are not satisfied that this is true you should study further, or else not plan to use charts at all.

On the other hand, if you have satisfied yourself that the charts are, for you, the most dependable indication of the probable future course of stock prices, then you should follow explicitly the signals given on your charts, either according to the rules we suggest here, or according to such other rules and modifications as your experience dictates. But while you are following any set of rules and policies, follow them to the letter. It is the only way they can help you.

If you do this, you will have certain large advantages, right at the start: (a) You will never be caught in a situation where a single stock commitment can wipe out your entire capital and ruin you; (b) you will not find yourself frozen in a market that has turned against you badly, with a large accumulated loss and your capital tied up so that you cannot use it in the reversed trend to make new and potentially profitable commitments; (c) you can make your decisions calmly, knowing exactly what you will be looking for as a signal to take profits, and knowing also that your losses at the very worst will be limited to a certain definite amount.

All of this means that you will have peace of mind. You will take losses and you will make gains. In neither case will you have to take your notebooks home and lie awake worrying. You will have made certain decisions. If developments prove you were right you will, at the proper point, take your profit. And if it turns out that you were wrong, then you can take your comparatively small loss, and start looking for a better situation, with your capital still largely intact, liquid and available.

Your job, as a speculator, is to provide liquidity in the market; and to counteract the irrational excesses of market-in-motion. Part of that job is to keep yourself free to become liquid whenever it is necessary, in order to reverse your position. And to keep yourself free from irrational and excessive emotional actions. If you do this, intelligently and consistently, you will be performing a useful and necessary service to the general economic welfare, and you will find that the market offers as good or better returns for your efforts as any other line of endeavor.

APPENDIXES

APPENDIX A

TEKNIPLAT CHART PAPER

IF YOU have never kept charts on this type of paper, known as semi-logarithmic, ratio, or proportion, these instructions will help you to read and understand the charts more easily, and they will help you in getting started if you are setting up charts of your own.

There will be no problem here for the engineer or the experienced chartist, but many people who have not kept charts before, or who are familiar only with the arithmetic price scale where the intervals are uniform throughout, may be puzzled at first by the continually changing vertical spaces. As you will discover, however, this very feature makes for easier and faster charting, because the various prices always lie at the same point in one of the "banks," and the eye becomes adept in placing the point needed automatically, without reference to the index figures along the left margin.

On many simple charts, showing hours of work, temperature changes, depth of water, etc., it is perfectly satisfactory to use ordinary cross-section paper, so that each "hour," "degree," or "foot" is represented by the same vertical distance on the chart. The difference between 5 feet and 10 feet is the same as the distance between 105 feet and 110 feet.

But this is not a good way to represent the differences in stock prices. It is perfectly true that the difference in market value between a stock selling at 5 dollars a share and one selling at 10 dollars a share is 5 dollars, or $500 on a block of 100 shares. And that the difference between the value of a stock selling at 100 and one at 105 is also 5 dollars, or $500 on a block of 100 shares. But in this latter case there is a great deal more of your capital involved.

For example, if you put $1000 into a stock at 5 you would get (disregarding commission) 200 shares. And if you sold these at 10 you would receive $2000. You would have a profit of $1000, or 100%. But if you put your $1000 into a stock selling at 105 you would be able to buy only 9 shares. And when you sold five points higher at 110 your profit would be only $45, or 4 1/2%.

It will give you a better comparison of the percentages of profit in various stock transactions if the price scale of your chart is designed to show equal *percentages* of advance or decline as equal vertical distances, regardless of the

433

DIAGRAM 11 A sheet of *TEKNIPLAT* chart paper cut away to show six price scales most frequently used.

price of the stock. This is exactly what the *TEKNIPLAT* charting paper does. A certain vertical distance on the paper will always indicate the same *percentage change*, and a trend moving at a certain angle will always indicate the same *rate of percentage change*, no matter what the price of the stock may be.

Obviously one point of advance or decline is much more important to you in a stock selling at 5 or 6 dollars a share than in one selling at 100. So it should not surprise you that the interval between 5 and 6 is much larger than that between 100 and 101. And since the stocks at lower prices make larger percentage moves for each point, or half point, or one-eighth point, these moves will show up more plainly on their charts. Actually it is not possible on the *TEKNIPLAT* paper to show a single eighth of change for a stock selling as high as 100. But this is just another way of saying that a single eighth is not important at that price. You might well be concerned about the difference between $1\frac{1}{4}$ and $1\frac{3}{8}$. But you would not care too much whether you sold at 103 or $103\frac{1}{8}$.

Since all your stocks will be plotted on a proportion basis you can compare directly the action of any one stock with any other as to pattern, trend, etc. Thus, a stock selling at 16 can be compared with a stock selling at 56. However, although the percentages moves will be strictly comparable, it should be pointed out that typically the very high-priced issues make smaller percentage moves than the low-priced ones.

THE PRICE SCALE

The price scale on *TEKNIPLAT* paper consists of two "banks," occupying the upper and lower halves of the main chart space. These two banks are exactly alike. Each represents a doubling of prices from its bottom to its top, so that whatever value is assigned to the center line, the top line will be twice that figure and the bottom line will be half of it. Let us say the center point is marked 20; then the top will be 40 and the nine intermediate lines will be 22, 24, 26, 28, 30, 32, 34, 36 and 38, reading from center to top, with each of the smallest spaces representing $\frac{1}{4}$ point. In the lower half of the chart the bottom line will be 10, the intermediate heavy lines to the center will be 11, 12, 13, 14, 15, 16, 17, 18 and 19, and each of the smallest spaces will be $\frac{1}{8}$ point. Since the spaces get smaller as one goes up the chart, one bank shades into the next, making a continuous scale. Obviously, you could have 20 at the top, 10 at the center and 5 at the bottom; or 10 at the top, 5 at the center and $2\frac{1}{2}$ at the bottom.

At first you may have some trouble with the different values assigned to the small spaces at different price levels; you may wonder whether a single small space represents $\frac{1}{4}$ or $\frac{1}{8}$ or perhaps a full point. Do not let this bother you. You can see from the scale where 19 is and where 20 is, and obviously $19\frac{1}{2}$ is the mid-point, $19\frac{1}{4}$ is one-quarter of the way up, and so on. Very quickly you will find that your mind and your eye adjust almost instantly without any conscious thought or effort.

Where a stock goes off the top or bottom of the paper, it is a simple matter to re-scale by moving the chart scale down one bank. If the chart runs off the top at 40, mark the center of the paper 40 from then on—the top becomes 80 and the bottom, 20.

For uniformity, and because the paper is so ruled that you can divide either bank of the heavy intermediate lines into ten parts, with smaller spaces representing standard stock-trading fractions of these main divisions, you *must* use the figures 5, 10, 20, 40, 80, etc., as the values for the center lines, tops and bottoms of charts. For selection of scales on stocks for which you are starting new charts, use this table.

If the stock now sells between		Center line will be	Top	Bottom
224	and 448	320	640	160
112	" 224	160	320	80
56	" 112	80	160	40
28	" 56	40	80	20
14	" 28	20	40	10
7	" 14	10	20	5
3½	" 7	5	10	2½
1¾	" 3½	2½	5	1¼

(This table can, of course, be continued up or down as far as necessary by multiplying or dividing the key figures by two.)

THE TIME SCALE

The paper provides for a full year of charting. The sheet is divided into 53 weeks, each consisting of six days in which the heavier line represents a Saturday, and this is ordinarily left blank since the major markets are not open on Saturday. However, the heavier line will serve to make it easier to locate a day within a week, quickly. The omission of the Saturday will not perceptibly affect the trend of the technical patterns.

Holidays, when they occur, are skipped. Usually a small "H" is inserted at the bottom of the chart to note the holiday and explain the break in the chart.

Many technicians start their charts as of the first of a calendar year, filling in the dates of Saturdays marking the end of each week at the bottom of the paper in the spaces provided, and immediately above these dates, the months. There is no reason, however, that charts cannot be started at any time, and if you keep a large number of charts it may be a help to start some of these in each calendar quarter. Thus, you might start all charts from A to F in January, from G to M in April, from N to S in July, and from T to Z in October.

THE VOLUME SCALE

The volume scale that has proved most satisfactory is arithmetic, that is, each unit measured vertically represents the same number of shares traded. Space for volume entries is provided in a special section above the dates. At one time a logarithmic volume scale was used, but it was given up because the highly significant volumes on very active days tended to be compressed, while low volume in periods of dullness was given too much emphasis.

It is necessary to determine the proper figures for the volume scale. No rule for this can be suggested. It is simply a matter of trial and error. With a little experience you will be able to estimate, from your knowledge of the stock you are about to chart, about how much volume is likely to appear on very active days; and you can set up a volume scale that will allow for the maximum expected peak. What you want to avoid is the situation where volume too frequently runs beyond the top of the volume section; it should do this only at times of unusual activity.

Where a stock is new to you and you have no knowledge of its habits it may be best to mark a tentative volume scale, lightly and in pencil, and keep the volume on this scale for a few weeks. Then if it is necessary to change the scale you can do so without having to draw the entire chart over.

EX-DIVIDENDS AND SPLIT-UPS

When a stock goes "ex-dividend," "ex-rights," etc., the price will usually drop approximately the amount of the benefit that was "ex". A note should be made on the chart on this day and this can be entered conveniently at the very bottom, below the dates, showing the amount of the dividend, approximate value of the rights, or other benefits. If the amount involved was substantial and the price drop is large enough to require explanation a dotted line may be drawn vertically on that date from the old price to the "ex" price, showing that this drop was not a market fluctuation but merely the adjustment of price to the distribution.

In the case of a split-up, spin-off, or other capital change, a similar procedure is followed. If the stock is split three-shares-for-one, for example, the price level will change and the chart will be continued at a new level. A dotted vertical line plus an explanatory note will make clear what happened. In order to get continuity of the chart in such a case the previous price pattern can be traced and then transferred with carbon paper in the correct position to give a continuous chart adjusted to the new basis for as far back as you need it.

However, if a stock is split two-shares-for-one or four-for-one you will not have to make any change in the chart except to note the fact of the split, and to change the scale by dividing all figures by 2 or 4 as the case may be. In other words, if a stock has been selling at 80 and is split two-for-one, we

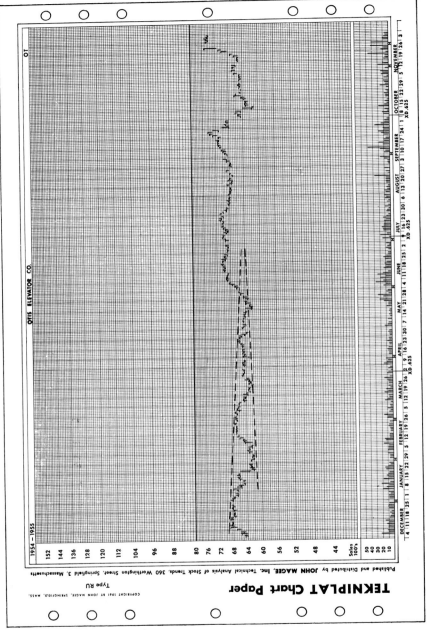

FIGURE 230. A typical stock chart on *TEKNIPLAT* charting paper. Allowing for ex-dividends "OT" never significantly violated the apex of the Triangle. The advance ultimately added 60% to the value of the stock.

simply re-scale the chart with the price at 40 and carry on.   Very often it will help to rule a vertical red line through the date on which a split-up or other capital adjustment takes effect.

NOTE: In case there should be difficulty in obtaining the TEKNIPLAT Charting Paper through local sources it may be ordered directly from the publisher, John Magee, Inc., 360 Worthington Street, Springfield, Massachusetts 01103, who will furnish samples, prices, or other information on request.

FIGURE 230 (preceding page).   This chart, in its long mostly sidewise movement is a good example of the importance of making allowance for the ex-dividend drop in the price.   During the first five months shown we see an almost perfect Symmetrical Triangle.   The first critical point would be on the slight breakdown in the middle of May.   The lower border of the Triangle was violated just a trifle, even if we had allowed for the 62½¢ March dividend.   If one had sold the stock here who could blame him?   And no great or immediate harm would have been done.   However, an experienced technician might have taken into account the insignificant volume at this point and waited a bit; with a stop at, say, 60.   (See the somewhat similar situation in the chart of "LA," Figure 217).   If "OT" had been held, the volume pick-up on the rally would have shown that the trend had not yet reversed itself.   The second critical point came in late September and early October at the time of the president's illness.   However, if we allow for the two dividends which went ex in July and October, the break did not violate the May bottom. Furthermore, it was on relatively light volume.   If the stock was still held there was no valid reason for selling on this decline.   From here on, breaking upward sharply from the October-November Island, "OT" resumed the Major advance interrupted by this long period of consolidation and advanced to the equivalent of over 100 (adjusted for two-for-one split) in 1956.

APPENDIX B

NORMAL RANGE-FOR-PRICE INDEXES

THE figures in this table represent that particular component of the Composite Leverage of a stock which is a function of its price level. They are based on actual tabulations from 3,800 stock charts. They state the *relative* proportion or percentage range of movement of a stock in each price range through an average six-month period.

Price	Normal Range	Price	Normal Range	Price	Normal Range
1¼	38.0	23	15.9	50	12.7
1½	35.0	24	15.7	51	12.7
1¾	33.0	25	15.5	52	12.6
2	31.5	26	15.3	53	12.6
2¼	30.0	27	15.2	54	12.5
2½	29.2	28	15.1	55	12.5
3	27.6	29	14.9	56	12.4
3½	26.5	30	14.7	57	12.4
4	25.3	31	14.6	58	12.3
5	24.0	32	14.5	59	12.2
6	22.8	33	14.4	60	12.1
7	22.0	34	14.3	61	12.0
8	21.2	35	14.2	62	12.0
9	20.4	36	14.1	63	11.9
10	19.8	37	14.0	64	11.9
11	19.2	38	13.9	65	11.8
12	18.7	39	13.8	66	11.8
13	18.4	40	13.7	67	11.7
14	18.0	41	13.6	68	11.7
15	17.6	42	13.5	69	11.6
16	17.3	43	13.4	70	11.6
17	17.0	44	13.3	71	11.5
18	16.8	45	13.2	72	11.5
19	16.6	46	13.1	73	11.4
20	16.5	47	13.0	74	11.4
21	16.3	48	12.9	75	11.3
22	16.1	49	12.8	76	11.3

Price	Normal Range	Price	Normal Range	Price	Normal Range
77	11.2	85	10.9	93	10.7
78	11.2	86	10.9	94	10.6
79	11.1	87	10.9	95	10.6
80	11.1	88	10.8	96	10.6
81	11.1	89	10.8	97	10.5
82	11.0	90	10.8	98	10.5
83	11.0	91	10.7	99	10.5
84	11.0	92	10.7	100	10.4
150	9.0	200	8.0	250	7.0

APPENDIX C

SENSITIVITY INDEXES OF STOCKS

Prepared by Cynthia Magee and Paul B. Coombs of the Technical Staff of John Magee, Inc.

ALTHOUGH it is not possible to predict the advance or decline of a stock over the years in the future it is possible to make a reasonable estimate of the most likely "degree" of advance or decline, based on its long-term market history. Barring major changes in corporate structure or in the nature of the company's product we can assume that the relatively conservative stock will usually continue to move conservatively, and that the relatively speculative stock will continue to be subject to wide swings of advance or decline.

This new table of Sensitivity Indexes shows the approximate relative sensitivity of stocks, based on the percentage price range of each stock for each year over the period from 1964 to 1973 inclusive, and the median price of each stock in each year. The values are adjusted for major split-ups and price level, and also for the overall range of the market in each year. For this correction we have used a Market Reciprocal which is inversely proportional to the total price range of all the stocks considered, and this makes it possible to set up the annual Sensitivity Indexes from which the ten-year figures used in the table are obtained.

Since some students may want to work out their own relative sensitivity figures or use this data in other ways we are giving here the Market Reciprocals used for each of the years in these computations:

1964	1.544	1969	.953
1965	1.320	1970	.861
1966	1.089	1971	1.075
1967	1.027	1972	1.238
1968	1.122	1973	.786

INDUSTRIAL STOCKS

Abbott Laboratories	.948	Armco Steel Corp.	.736
ACF Industries, Inc.	1.095	Armstrong Cork Co.	.939
Adams Express Co.	.535	ASA Ltd.	1.509
Addressograph-Multigraph	1.593	ASARCO Inc.	1.090
Aetna Life & Casualty Co.	.967	Ashland Oil Inc.	1.022
Air Products & Chemicals	.844	Associated Dry Goods	1.094
Airco, Inc.	.842	Atlantic Richfield Co.	1.399
Akzona, Inc.	1.031	Automatic Data Processing	1.473
Alcan Aluminum Ltd.	.889	Avco Corporation	1.154
Allegheny Corp.	1.084	Avery Products Corp.	1.087
Allegheny Ludlum Industries	1.192	Avnet Inc.	1.409
Allied Chemical Corp.	.916	Avon Products, Inc.	1.278
Allied Stores Corp.	1.045	Babcock & Wilcox Co.	1.172
Allis-Chalmers Corp.	1.195	Baker Oil Tools, Inc.	1.192
Alpha Portland Industries	.922	Barber Oil Corp.	1.299
Aluminum Co. of America	1.069	Bath Industries, Inc.	1.538
AMAX Inc.	.830	Bausch & Lomb, Inc.	2.287
AMBAC Industries	1.184	Baxter Laboratories	1.197
Amerada Hess Corp.	1.332	Beatrice Foods Co.	.788
American Air Filter	1.365	Beckman Instruments Inc.	1.362
American Airlines Inc.	1.440	Becton Dickinson & Co.	1.148
American Brands Inc.	.724	Bell & Howell Co.	1.501
American Broadcasting Cos.	1.401	Bendix Corporation	1.143
American Can Company	.834	Beneficial Corp.	1.092
American Chain & Cable	.746	Bethlehem Steel Corp.	.768
American Cyanamid Company	.874	Black & Decker Mfg.	1.145
American District Telegraph	1.238	Boeing Company	1.705
American Home Products	.888	Boise Cascade Corp.	1.563
American Hospital Supply	1.050	Bond Industries	1.006
American Motors Corp.	.972	Borden, Inc.	.766
American Standard Inc.	1.112	Borg Warner	.833
American Sterilizer Co.	1.056	Braniff Int'l	1.649
American Stores Co.	.956	Briggs & Stratton Corp.	.975
Ametek, Inc.	1.087	Bristol-Myers Company	.961
AMF, Inc.	1.429	British Petroleum	.878
AMP Inc.	1.011	Brunswick Corp.	1.315
Amstar Corp.	.958	Bucyrus-Erie Co.	1.170
Amsted Industries	.886	Budd Company	1.047
Anaconda Company	1.260	Bulova Watch Co., Inc.	1.172
Anchor Hocking Corp.	1.078	Burlington Industries	1.076
Anderson Clayton & Co.	.860	Burlington Northern, Inc.	1.033
ARA Services, Inc.	1.418	Burroughs Corporation	1.683
Archer-Daniels-Midland	.928	Campbell Soup Co.	.677

Canadian Pacific Limited	.502	Continental Oil Co.	.787
Capital Cities Commun. Inc.	1.195	Control Data Corp.	1.847
Carborundum Company	1.044	Cooper Industries	1.451
Carnation Company	1.090	Corning Glass Works	1.353
Carpenter Technology	.916	CPC International, Inc.	.956
Carrier Corporation	1.284	Crane Company	1.037
Caterpillar Tractor Co.	1.078	Creole Petroleum	.841
CBS Inc.	1.724	Crown Cork & Seal Co., Inc.	.931
Celanese Corporation	1.201	Crown Zellerbach Corp.	1.050
Cenco Instruments	1.221	CTS Corporation	1.022
Central Soya Co.	.710	Cummins Engine Company	.911
Cerro Corporation	1.221	Curtiss Wright Corp.	1.373
Champion International	1.062	Cutler Hammer Inc.	1.245
Champion Spark Plug Co.	.789	Cyprus Mines Corp.	1.000
Chase Manhattan Corp.	.735	Damon Corporation	1.644
Chemetron Corporation	1.034	Dana Corporation	.796
Chesebrough-Ponds, Inc.	.986	Dayco Corporation	.905
Chessie System Inc.	.869	Deere & Company	1.056
Chicago Milwaukee Corp.	1.938	Delta Air Lines, Inc.	1.373
Chicago Pneumatic Tool Co.	1.047	Diamond International	.783
Chicago Rock Island & Pacific RR	1.406	Diamond Shamrock Corp.	.860
Chrysler Corporation	1.393	Digital Equipment Corp.	1.566
Cincinnati Milacron Inc.	1.195	Disney (Walt) Productions	1.867
CIT Financial Corp.	.819	Distillers Corp.-Seagrams Ltd.	.753
CITICORP	.856	Dr. Pepper Company	.919
Cities Service Company	.947	Dome Mines Ltd.	1.376
Clark Equipment Company	.961	Dow Chemical Company	1.012
Clorox Company	1.530	Dow Jones Rail Averages	1.434
Cluett, Peabody & Co., Inc.	1.069	Dresser Industries, Inc.	1.072
Coastal States Gas Corp.	1.312	du Pond (E.I.) Inc.	1.050
Coca-Cola Bot. Co. of N.Y.	1.253	Eastern Air Lines, Inc.	1.669
Coca-Cola Co.	.983	Eastern Gas & Fuel Associates	1.396
Colgate-Palmolive Co.	.867	Eastman Kodak Company	1.098
Colt Industries, Inc.	1.724	Echlin Manufacturing	1.253
Combustion Engineering Inc.	1.218	Eckerd (Jack) Corp.	1.170
Commonwealth Oil	1.140	Eltra Corporation	1.209
Communications Satellite	1.577	Emerson Electric Company	.872
Conrac Corp.	1.633	Emery Air Freight Corp.	.989
Consolidated Foods Corp.	.952	Englehard Minerals & Chem.	1.253
Consolidated Freightways, Inc.	1.198	Esmark Inc.	1.014
Continental Air Lines, Inc.	1.557	Ex-Cell-O Corp.	1.019
Continental Can Company	.880	Exxon Corp.	.772
Continental Corp.	.727	Faberge, Inc.	1.303

Fairchild Camera & Instruments	2.640	Great Western Financial Corp.	1.253
Fansteel Inc.	1.459	Greyhound Corp.	.777
Federal National Mortgage	1.055	Grumman Corp.	1.376
Federated Department Stores	.961	Gulf Oil Corporation	.774
Fibreboard Corp.	1.187	Gulf & Western Industries, Inc.	1.523
Firestone Tire & Rubber Co.	.830	Halliburton Co.	1.379
First Charter Financial	1.103	Hammermill Paper Co.	.942
Flintkote Co.	.956	Harris Corporation	1.176
Fluor Corporation	1.276	Helca Mining Co.	1.104
FMC Corporation	.835	Helmerich & Payne, Inc.	1.267
Ford Motor Company	.903	Hercules Inc.	.927
Foremost-McKesson, Inc.	1.067	Hershey Foods Corp.	.735
Foster Wheeler Corp.	1.236	Hewlett-Packard Co.	1.420
Freeport Minerals Co.	1.388	High Voltage Engineering	1.488
Fruehauf Corporation	.872	Hilton Hotels Corp.	1.613
Gamble-Skogmo, Inc.	1.143	Holiday Inns, Inc.	1.610
Gardner-Denver Co.	.908	Homestake Mining Co.	1.349
Gen. Am. Investors Co., Inc.	.919	Honeywell Inc.	1.532
Gen. Am. Transportation Corp.	.878	Houdaille Industries, Inc.	.903
General Cable Corp.	1.195	Household Finance Corp.	.872
General Dynamics Corp.	1.362	Howard Johnson Co.	1.399
General Electric Co.	.914	Howmet Corp.	1.315
General Foods Corp.	.757	Hudson Bay Min. & Smelt. Co.	.875
General Instrument Corp.	1.393	Ideal Basic Industries, Inc.	.718
General Mills, Inc.	.874	Illinois Central Industries, Inc.	1.271
General Motors Corp.	1.020	Imperial Oil Ltd.	.866
General Portland Inc.	.939	INA Corporation	1.268
General Signal Corp.	1.106	Ingersoll-Rand Co.	.947
General Tire & Rubber Co.	.994	Inland Steel Company	.677
Genesco Inc.	1.270	Inspiration Consol. Copper	.869
Genuine Parts Co.	1.050	Interco Inc.	1.062
Georgia-Pacific Corp.	1.086	International Bus. Machines	1.811
Getty Oil Co.	1.427	Internat. Flavors & Frag. Inc.	.864
Gillette Company, (The)	1.127	International Harvester Co.	.903
Goodrich (B.F.) Company	.948	Internat. Minerals & Chem.	.900
Goodyear Tire & Rubber Co.	.810	International Nickel Co. of Canada	.813
Gould, Inc.	1.147	International Paper Company	.846
Grace (W.R.) & Co.	.955	International Tel & Tel. Corp.	1.033
Graniteville Co.	.931	Jefferson-Pilot Corp.	.934
Grant (W.T.) Co.	1.343	Jewel Companies, Inc.	.931
Great A & P Tea Co., Inc.	.875	Johns-Manville Corporation	.919
Great Northern Iron Ore	.566	Johnson & Johnson	1.299
Great Northern Nekoosa Corp.	.867	Jones & Laughlin Steel Corp.	1.070

N.L. Industries, Inc.	.792	Republic Steel Corp.	.878
Norfolk & Western Ry. Co.	.951	Research-Cottrell	1.714
Northrop Corp.	1.139	Revco D.S., Inc.	1.203
Northwest Airlines, Inc.	1.599	Revlon Inc.	.995
Northwest Industries	1.285	Reynolds (R.J.) Industries Inc.	.927
Norton Simon Inc.	1.256	Reynolds Metals Co.	1.126
Occidental Petroleum Corp.	.948	Richardson-Merrell Inc.	.945
Olin Corp.	1.067	Rio Grande Industries Inc.	.978
Otis Elevator Co.	1.011	Rite Aid Corp.	1.858
Outboard Marine Corp.	1.312	Robertshaw Controls Co.	1.062
Owens-Corning Fiberglas Corp.	.936	Rockwell International Corp.	.775
Owens-Illnois Inc.	.992	Robins (A.H.) Co.	1.214
Pacific Petroleums Ltd.	1.058	Rohm & Haas Co.	1.215
Pan American World Airways	1.510	Rosario Resources Corp.	1.239
Papercraft Corp.	1.218	Royal Crown Cola Co.	1.314
Pasco Inc.	1.332	Royal Dutch Petroleum Co.	.878
Peabody Galion Corp.	1.490	Ryder Systems Inc.	1.209
Penn-Dixie Industries	1.126	Safeway Stores, Inc.	.743
Penney (J.C.) Co.	1.037	St. Joe Minerals Corp.	.888
Pennwalt Corp.	1.016	St. Louis-San Francisco Ry. Co.	.972
Pennzoil Co.	i.326	St. Regis Paper Company	.763
PepsiCo, Inc.	.980	Santa Fe Industries Inc.	.807
Perkin-Elmer Corp.	1.147	Schering-Plough Corp.	1.034
Pfizer, Inc.	.869	Schlitz (Jos.) Brewing Co.	1.125
Phelps Dodge Corp.	.827	Schlumberger N.V.	1.309
Philip Morris, Inc.	1.023	SCM Corporation	1.275
Phillips Petroleum Co.	.885	Scott, Foresman & Co.	.980
Pillsbury Company	1.008	Scott Paper Co.	.816
Pitney-Bowes, Inc.	.961	Scovill Manufacturing Co.	1.137
Pittston Co.	1.100	Seaboard Coast Line Industries	1.256
Polaroid Corp.	1.588	Searle (G.D.) & Co.	1.209
Ponderosa Systems, Inc.	2.588	Sears, Roebuck & Co.	.947
PPG Industries, Inc.	.909	Sedco, Inc.	1.298
Prentice-Hall Inc.	1.137	Shell Oil Co.	.880
Procter & Gamble Co.	.870	Sheller-Globe Corp.	1.377
Pullman Inc.	1.045	Sherwin-Williams Co.	.902
Quaker Oats Company	.948	Signal Companies, Inc.	.986
Quaker State Oil	1.223	Simmons Company	1.006
RCA Corp.	1.047	Simplicity Pattern Co.	1.356
Ralston Purina Company	.704	Singer Company	1.153
Rapid American Corp.	1.176	Skelly Oil Co.	.978
Raytheon Company	1.416	Smith (A.O.) Corp.	1.058
Reed Tool Company	1.323	Smith Kline Corp.	.884

Winn-Dixie Stores, Inc.	.700	Florida Power & Light Co.	.732
Woolworth (F. W.) Co.	1.030	General Public Utilities Corp.	.616
Wrigley (Wm.) Jr. Co.	.791	General Tel. & Electronics Corp.	.725
Xerox Corp.	1.909	Gulf States Utilities Co.	.657
Xtra, Inc.	1.359	Houston Lighting & Power Co.	.713
Zale Corp.	1.259	Idaho Power Co.	.619
Zapata Corp.	1.725	Lone Star Gas Co.	.780
Zenith Radio Corp.	1.264	Long Island Lighting Co.	.602
Zurn Industries	1.494	Middle South Utilities, Inc.	.683
		Mississippi River Corp.	.866

UTILITY STOCKS

		New England Electric System	.544
		Nevada Power Co.	1.041
Alleghany Power System, Inc.	.534	Niagara Mohawk Power Corp.	.465
American Electric Power Co., Inc.	.607	Northern Natural Gas Co.	.746
American Natural Gas Co.	.744	Northern States Power Co.	.557
American Tel. & Tel. Co.	.591	Ohio Edison Co.	.548
Arizona Public Service Co.	.777	Oklahoma Gas & Electric Co.	.693
Arkansas Louisiana Gas Co.	.707	Pacific Gas & Electric Co.	.635
Baltimore Gas & Electric Co.	.580	Pacific Lighting Corp.	.510
Boston Edison Co.	.554	Panhandle Eastern Pipe Line Co.	.780
Brooklyn Union Gas Co.	.498	Pennsylvania Power & Light Co.	.597
Central & South West Corp.	.651	Peoples Gas Co.	.658
Cincinnati Gas & Electric Co.	.565	Philadelphia Electric Co.	.499
Cleveland Electric Illum. Co.	.557	Public Service Electric & Gas Co.	.610
Columbia Gas System, Inc.	.552	Southern California Edison	.696
Commonwealth Edison Co.	.630	Southern Company	.599
Consolidated Edison New York	.538	Southern Natural Resources, Inc.	.977
Consolidated Natural Gas Co.	.529	Tenneco Inc.	.747
Consumers Power Co.	.693	Texas Eastern Transmission Corp.	1.075
Delmarva Power & Light Co.	.599	Texas Utilities Co.	.641
Detroit Edison Co.	.532	UGI Corp.	.696
D. J. Utility Average	.613	Unitel Inc.	.722
El Paso Natural Gas	.649	Virgina Electric & Power Co.	.716
Florida Power Corp.	.933	Western Union Corp.	1.317

SUPPLEMENTARY CHART EXAMPLES

YOU HAVE read that "history repeats itself," and if we take this to mean that we can find significant parallels in historical events at different times and in different places, then in that limited sense, it is true. And the more history we know the better we can see the similarities and anticipate the probable consequences of certain situations. But we know that history never precisely, absolutely, "repeats" itself.

In the same way the stock market "repeats itself" to a degree. To be sure, no two stocks have ever acted exactly the same way for any considerable period of time. There are always some differences. But there are also some striking similarities between the behavior of one stock and another at a given time, or between stocks at very different times. We see similar patterns, trends, support and resistance, and price and volume relations, much as they were last year, five years ago, fifty years ago.

Several additional charts have been added in this printing of *Technical Analysis of Stock Trends* to show various typical market actions in the period from 1957 through 1963. Also included is the unique classic Broadening Top in the 1957 Dow Industrial Average.

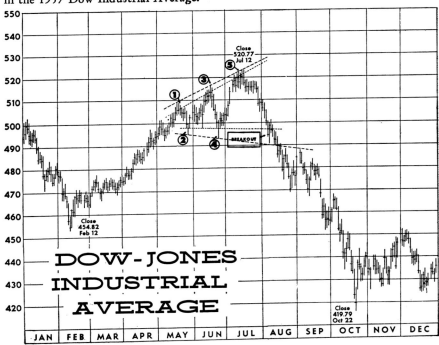

FIGURE 231. The Broadening Top in the Dow-Jones Industrial Average which formed in May, June, July, and August, 1957. Although Broadening Tops have appeared many times in individual stocks and as a rule have carried out their bearish implications, such a chart pattern has never before been completed in the Industrial Average. In 1929 on two occasions there were patterns which began to show broadening tendencies, but since these were interrupted by continuation moves about all one can say of them is that they may have indicated a growing technical weakness in the market.

The 1957 situation, on the other hand, was very definite and was fully completed. During the early stages of the pattern several of our friends wrote, calling attention to the possible Broadening Top, among them Charles E. Carden of Fort Worth, Texas, who has handled Dow Theory comment and analysis for the Fort Worth Star Telegram. The chart shown above is adapted from one of Mr. Carden's charts and is reproduced with his per-mission.

The first significant point after the February 12 bottom was the Minor peak of Tuesday May 21, marked (1). The Minor decline from this point to Tuesday, May 28 (2), was quite normal, as was the renewed advance to Monday, June 17 (3).

The first sign of a broadening tendency was when the average closed on Monday, June 24 (4), below the May 28 bottom. However, this by itself did not indicate a reversal. The advance was resumed and surmounted the May 21 and June 17 Minor tops, reaching a high closing figure of 520.77 on Friday, July 12 (5). The broadening picture was now quite evident, and the completion of a Broadening Top required only a close below the June 24 bottom.

On Tuesday, August 6 the Industrial Average closed decisively below the June 24 bottom, signalling the completion of the Broadening Top. This, of course, was an indication of Major weakness, a warning not to be taken lightly.

The Broadening Top, as we have pointed out previously, is an indication of a wildly gyrating market, a market without leadership or definite trend. The presumption is that heavy distribution is going on under cover of the rallies; and the breakout move is seldom a false one.

Since we are dealing, here, with an average rather than a single stock, we would consider that *any* closing below point (4) after the peak at (5), regardless of how slight the margin might be, would constitute a valid break-out, since averages are less sensitive than individual stocks and it is customary to consider even slight penetrations at signal points (as in Dow Theory) as perfectly satisfactory. You will notice also that although it would be possible to draw the Broadening Top through the extreme ranges of the price, as we have done with the wide-dashed line, we have used the closing prices as marked by the narrow-dashed line. This, too, is in line with Dow Theory practice, where only closing prices are considered.

The implication of the pattern here was bearish for the "market-as-a-whole." As might be expected, a majority of stocks showed weak patterns or trends at this time. However, as always, it was necessary to examine each stock separately on its merits, since, as we will show in the following pages, not all stocks behaved alike even in this extremely weak market situation.

FIGURE 232.   1957 bearish trend in Industrial Rayon.   At no time did this stock show significant strength.

FIGURE 232. Averages do not tell the whole story. Each stock has to be considered on its own merits. Long before the formation of the 1957 Broadening Top in the Industrial Average, Industrial Rayon was moving down in a Major decline. You will find many cases where it is difficult to "see" what a stock is doing, or to determine its Major trend. But in such a situation as this (and this is not a rare case) it is perfectly obvious that the trend is down. Although there were a number of Minor rallies and consolidations during the decline, the entire pattern was so obviously part and parcel of the same big decline that no one who was even slightly familiar with typical stock behavior would have been tempted to buy the stock, even to cover shorts.

On Monday, July 29, there was a sharp downward break with a gap on climactic volume. This would have suggested the probability of a Minor bottom; and for three and a half weeks the stock did stabilize at around 24. But even during this consolidation the continuing weakness showed up on the small Descending Triangle that was formed, and ultimately on Wednesday, August 21, the price broke sharply to continue the Major decline.

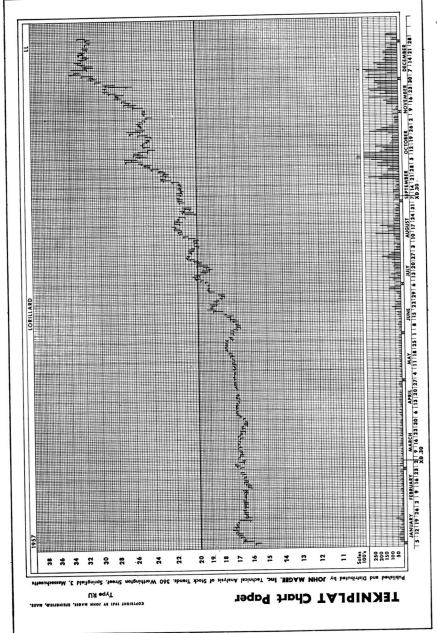

FIGURE 233. 1957 bullish trend in Lorillard. Although most stocks declined in 1957 there were a number of strong issues like this one which appeared to be totally unaffected by the general pessimism.

FIGURE 233. Averages do not tell the whole story. It will come as a shock to many readers who rightly regard the latter half of 1957 as a Major Bear Market to see Lorillard making a typical Bull Market advance. Lorillard moved up from 15-5/8 to 34 during the year—and reached 54-1/8 during the first three months of 1958. It is hard to believe that this chart and the Industrial Rayon chart we just looked at cover the same period, that is, the year 1957.

The majority of stocks did suffer severe depreciation. But there were a good many issues which, like Lorillard, enjoyed a generally bullish trend all year. Among the important stocks that moved up consistently in 1957 were American Chicle, Anchor Hocking Glass, Colgate-Palmolive, General Foods, General Cigar, Grand Union, National Biscuit, Parke Davis, Penick & Ford, Plough, Inc., Proctor & Gamble, Ruberoid, Vick Chemical, Winn Dixie Stores, and Zenith Radio.

Whatever theories we may have as to the condition of the "market-as-a-whole," we must always realize that we are buying and selling individual stocks. We may get a picture of extreme bullishness or extreme bearishness in the "general market," but if this picture conflicts with the clear evidence in a particular stock, we must recognize that it is the stock, not the average, that we have to deal with. We cannot assume that a stock "must" follow the average. And it is often possible to obtain greater stability and safety by buying a few strong stocks in a Bear Market or by selling short a few weak stocks in a Bull Market, than by attempting to maximize profits with an "all-out" position one way or the other.

FIGURE 234. During the latter nine months of 1961 some well-known market averages continued to show new all-time highs. However, the Evaluative Index (see Page 412), in this period, did not indicate any such overall strength: many stocks were in almost continuous decline for the nine months. These included such important issues as Air Reduction, Allied Chemical, Allis-Chalmers, Aluminium, Ltd., Fansteel Metallurgical, Flintkote, Heyden Newport Chemical, Sperry Rand, Texas Instruments, Trans World Airlines, Universal Match, and many others. At such times one cannot "buy the averages," and it is best to choose stocks selectively and maintain adequate liquid reserves.

FIGURE 235.   A familiar top pattern.   From the end of 1957 to the spring of 1961 Burndy Corporation moved from below 10 to 37 in a generally bullish trend.   The advance accelerated sharply on the post-election rally of late 1960 and early 1961.   But with Burndy, as with many other stocks, the rally ended in the early months of 1961.   Here we have not only a perfect example of the Head-and-Shoulders top in the price action, but we have the typical volume confirmation.   The early April rally was on heavy volume.   The rally in the last week of April was on somewhat disappointing volume although a new high was made at that time.   We have a definite increase of volume on the retreat from this peak, and practically no enthusiasm in the final rally of the first week of June.   The breakdown on Monday, June 19, accompanied by heavier volume and a definite gap in the price track, confirmed the top formation.   Although Burndy held around the 30 level for a time, and after a further drop recovered to 31, the Major trend had definitely been reversed. By June, 1962 Burndy was selling at 11¾.

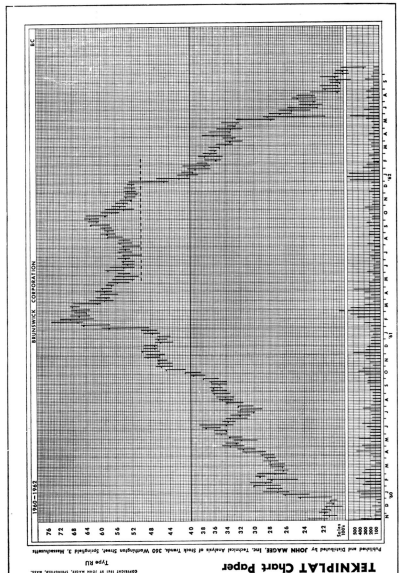

FIGURE 236. Weekly chart of BRUNSWICK CORPORATION showing the final stages of the long Bull Market in "BC," the climactic top in March, 1961, the distributive phase through December. 1961, and the ultimate breakdown.

FIGURE 236. For five years, from 1956 into early 1961 Brunswick advanced in a great Bull Market surge. During this period the stock was split four times. In the first week of March, 1961, terminating the post-election rally, "BC" made a new high on extraordinary volume; but closed the week nearly at the bottom of the weekly range. This One-Week Reversal might well have served as a warning to the market trader.

However, assuming that the owner of shares in Brunswick was not a trader, and was interested in the stock from a long-term point of view, he might have held the stock through the breakdown from the Symmetrical Triangle formed in March and early April. He might have continued to keep his shares through the summer and fall of 1961 and the rally of September and October. If so, and if he had been watching the action of the stock, he would realize that the 50-52 level was a critical area. That a break through this previous bottom would represent a serious failure of support. And certainly the decisive violation of the 50 level in the first week of January, 1962 (with heavy volume) could be recognized as a very dangerous reversal signal calling for immediate sale of the stock regardless of capital gains tax or anything else. Although this move preceded the general collapse of the market by several months it was a clear technical indication of extreme weakness and extreme danger in Brunswick, regardless of the action of other stocks at that time. If an investor had noted the break but decided to "wait for a rally" to sell his stock, he would have had no chance to get out. Brunswick never recovered, never rallied, and by October, 1962 it was selling at 17.

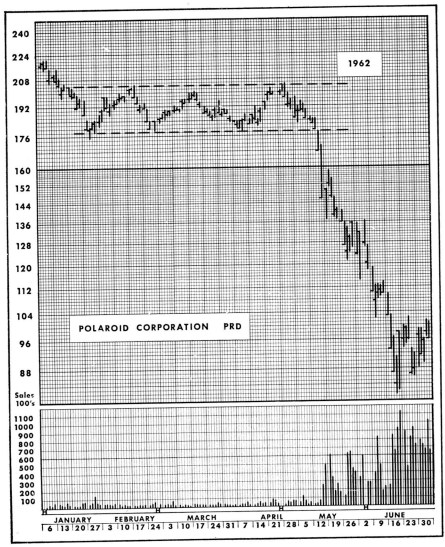

FIGURE 237. A beautiful example of a Rectangle in Polaroid. Notice the low-volume fluctuations between (approximately) 178 and 202. On Thursday, May 10, on the highest volume of the year to date, Polaroid broke support and plunged to 168. This was a clearly bearish move. It would have been fatal to "hold for a rally," for there was no rally. It can be very expensive to hold onto a stock wishfully when the situation has changed radically, no matter how good it may have looked previously. Note that this break came more than two weeks before the "near-panic" of May 28. By that time "PRD" had dropped fifty points and was headed for still lower levels.

FIGURE 238. At a time when a majority of stocks were already showing signs of serious weakness, early in 1962, Copper Range was making vigorous new highs. Actually, the move did not get far; it never substantially broke above the 1961 top.

The evidence of weakness in "CPX" did not become apparent until, after the relatively weak April rally, the stock broke through 19 on Monday, April 30, and closed at 17¾. This was, of course the completion of a well-marked Head-and-Shoulders top. In this case there were three days of rally before the downward move really got under way, but it might have been dangerous to count on a rally after the clearly bearish signal.

Incidentally, this top formation was completed well before the precipitous drop of May and June.

FIGURE 239. Like practically all stocks, "UV" went into a tailspin in the spring of 1962. After the "bad day," May 28, it continued to slide throughout the month of June. At this point there started what could be considered no more than a technical rally in a Bear Market. This rally stopped at 29 and was followed by a dull decline lasting about two weeks.

The next move, in the second week of August was marked by considerable volume and while there was no obvious, clear-cut pattern, it seemed significant that the 29 level, briefly touched on May 23, May 28, and July 12, was penetrated on August 6.

Whether to regard this August 6 closing as an immediate buy signal, or to wait for the completion of the breakout move and look for an opportunity to buy on a reaction, would be a problem. In this case it would have paid to wait. Notice that the late August reaction came back to the 29 level where it found support and then continued its upward move.

Considering the weakness of most stocks in this period the action of "UV" is remarkable. The important thing to recognize here is that individual stocks do not necessarily follow "the main trend" of the averages.

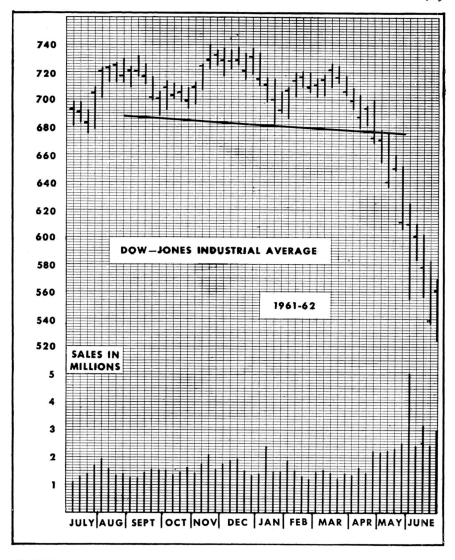

FIGURE 240. Weekly, July, 1961–June, 1962. This chart shows the Head-and-Shoulders top formation in the Industrial Average which preceded the collapse of April, May and June, 1962. Normally, and especially in the charts of individual stocks, there would tend to be considerably heavier volume on the left shoulder. However, the price pattern alone is sufficient to mark the pattern as a dangerously toppy situation. Furthermore, during the entire period in which this formation took shape, many individual stocks representing large and important companies, were showing top reversal symptoms, as might be expected. Note that so far as this Head-and-Shoulders pattern is concerned the reversal signal is not definite until the neckline has been penetrated.

FIGURE 241. Daily, April–September, 1961. Here is a rather confusing and complicated chart, but one which contains several points of interest worth a bit of analysis. Notice the beautiful little Head-and-Shoulders top in April and May, especially the volume weakness on the final rally before the down-side breakout. Notice also that this stock was split 2-for-1 in June, but that such a split does not materially affect the technical action of the stock, except that since there are now two shares of stock (at half the market value) for each share of old stock, there may be some increase in the average number of shares traded per day. Notice also that once the down trend was established the rallies (especially the mid-July rally) do not penetrate the trendline drawn through the April and May peaks. This trend continued down for over a year after this, reaching a low of 11¼ in October, 1962.

FIGURE 242. Daily, January–June, 1963. Here is a good example of a Symmetrical Triangle, as a continuation pattern. Triangles of this (Symmetrical) type may mark consolidations in a Major trend, or may constitute a reversal formation. The characteristics in either case are an active move to the first turning point of the Triangle, and then in generally diminishing volume as the price fluctuates in a narrowing pattern. During this period it could be said that the stock was in *both* an up trend, marked by the lower boundary of the formation, and a down trend, indicated by the upper boundary. Notice the increase of volume on the breakout, which in this case was on the up side. Also notice the reaction to the "cradle point" defined by the intersection of the two boundary trends of the Triangle. The advance of the stock from April to June measures just a little more than the height of the open side of the Triangle. The attainment of this "objective" does not necessarily mean the termination of the Major trend, however, and by August, 1963, CERRO had reached 33¼.

FIGURE 243. Daily, March–August, 1963. Here is a good example of an Ascending Triangle, in which the rallies advance repeatedly to a given level and the reactions find support at gradually higher points. Such a pattern normally indicates a potentially bullish situation in the making, just as the reverse (Descending Triangle) implies a bearish tendency. Notice the higher volume on the various peaks near 22; and the very high volume on the break-out move in August. If any further evidence of the strength of this move was needed, the breakaway gap at the opening, Monday, August 12, would supply it. After a breakout of this sort it would be quite normal for the stock to suffer some profit-taking reaction, usually on light volume, and such a reaction might run back to 22 or even a little below this without altering the essentially bullish nature of this picture.

FIGURE 244. Daily, June–November, 1962. Before commenting on the November breakout here, we should call attention to the fact that "SOC" was one of the stocks that held up fairly well during the Cuban crisis in October; and did not make a new low under the June bottoms. This chart picture is an excellent example of a Double Bottom. It is not necessary that the two bottoms be at exactly the same level if they are reasonably close. The important thing is that the stock has found support once, has rallied, then declined again, and has found support at nearly the same point. The bottoms should be some distance apart; there should be at least six weeks between them, preferably more. Also, the rally between them should be definite and should amount to at least a 15% gain at its peak. The formation does not acquire significance as a Major bottom pattern until the level of the top of the rally is penetrated on substantial volume. This penetration took place on Tuesday, November 13, and from that time continued in a Major bullish trend, reaching 1559 in May, 1963, an advance of over 500 points from the close on the day of breakout.

Double Tops have an opposite significance; are similar to the Double Bottoms, but consist of two tops at approximately the same level, separated by some weeks or months, and with a decline between them, which must be penetrated to validate the top formation.

FIGURE 245. Daily, November, 1962–April, 1963. To the average person, unfamiliar with the usual behavior of stocks in the market, the price fluctuations appear meaningless and entirely fortuitous. If they are aware of general trends lasting months or years, they are often inclined to consider only the trend of "The Averages," and are not conscious of the fact that many stocks may be making large advances at the very same time that others are sliding lower and lower. It is not always possible to lay a steel edge ruler along the trend and show that it makes a perfect straight line (though this does sometimes happen) but, as in the case of General Steel Industries, there is no question but what the advance is fairly consistent over a long period of time, barring the relatively unimportant reactions, consolidations, etc. along the way. You will notice, too, that the two-for-one split in early March did not materially affect the upward trend except to show somewhat more volume as might be expected with a greater number of (new) shares. For a contrasting (downside) trend, see the chart of Avnet Electronics.

FIGURE 246. Daily, February–August, 1963. An interesting study of support and resistance phenomena. Incidentally, also an example of a bearish stock (and not the only one by any means) in what was generally considered a bullish market, during the spring and summer of 1963. We would point out several rallies to 31 in March and April, and the breakdown in early May. In May and June the stock rallied, but stalled at about the level of the March low. Then there was another drop, and in the rally this time came back to the late April low. The next drop, in July, was followed by a little rally to the June bottom at 25. This is fairly typical support resistance behavior. The price level which has been a support tends to become a resistance once the support has been substantially broken. Vice versa, an overhead resistance, after it has been broken, tends to serve as a support level.

FIGURE 247. January–June, 1963. Sometimes a move happens all of a sudden and does not result in a continuing long trend. In this case it is not possible to say whether long-term trend will be up or not; the purpose of showing this chart is to point up the remarkable action that can follow a break through an important support or resistance level. You will notice that the entire period from mid-January to Tuesday, May 14, can be regarded as a Rectangle on the chart; with bottoms at about 10⅛ or 10¼, and tops at about 11¾. Notice the increase of activity on the several rallies during the formation. The move, which was a "situational" thing in Sugars, affected all Sugars in May, and turned out to be somewhat of a Flash in the Pan. Nevertheless it was a spectacular one, and a trader with courage and acuity might have picked up this stock as a speculation after the close of Tuesday, May 14. The next five trading days advanced the price from Wednesday's opening at 12, to Tuesday, May 21 close at 17½; an advance of 46%. This is a type of market trading we would not recommend generally; it calls for courage, experience, and the willingness to take a number of small losses in order to secure one substantial gain. However, the in-and-out trader who observed the action on May 21 and noticed the One-Day Reversal with abnormal volume and a gap, could have secured maximum quick profits either by selling his stock at the opening the next day, or by placing a stop-loss order just under the close, say at 17⅜.

FIGURE 248. There were some warning signs in "CDA" in the Minor breakdowns of late March and early May. What seems especially significant, though, is the nature of the recovery move in May and early June, 1965. The two convergent boundaries of the recovery trend form an up-sloping Wedge, which has rather definite bearish implications. If the Wedge had been pointed down it would strongly suggest the possibility of a decisive upward breakout. Notice that on the two days when the highest prices were attained during this Wedge pattern, the stock closed near the bottom of the day's range. The subsequent history here, the collapse on heavy volume, shows clearly how dramatic a break from this not-too-common formation can be.

FIGURE 249. Here is a chart that shows several interesting technical features. In July, August, and most of September "UV" was in a period of dormancy. The breakout of September 27 was followed by a week of in-action, and then a strong continuation of the move on big volume. Notice the October–November consolidation, which took the form of a large Symmetrical Triangle. If we draw the upper boundary of this Triangle, and the lower, we see that the breakout signalling a continuation of the move, on Wednesday, December 1, was decisive both in price and volume action. At no time during the advance from 28½ to over 62 was there any indication of potential weakness.

FIGURE 250.   The weekly chart of Livingston Oil from January, 1965 into January, 1966 is a good example of a Major bottom.   Just how weak the stock was during the early months of 1965 can be judged by the clear downside gap during the month of May.   Also you will notice that the volume on this whole headlong collapse was rather heavy.   However, from July to the middle of October the trading activity "dried up," and the stock fluctuated in narrow and narrower swings, forming a Symmetrical Triangle.   The pickup of volume on the October breakout was spectacular; and an observant investor would have had a "second chance" to buy on the reaction in the first week of November when the stock drifted back to the top of the Triangle.

FIGURE 251. Here is a beautiful picture of technical market action in Packard-Bell Electronics from August, 1965 into January, 1966. The first point of interest is the Flag consolidation in September and October, a classic example ("The Flag flies at half-mast") and on the resumption of the up move the stock did duplicate the earlier move, and a bit more. (Compare with the 1945 chart of Martin-Parry on Page 169). Notice the nearly flat tops and the rising bottoms from October to January, with generally declining volume (Ascending Triangle), and the magnificent breakout move in the second week of January, 1966. In this case we can see no evidence calling for selling the stock, all the way from September into January.

475

FIGURE 252. This could be regarded as a very flat Head and Shoulders top or as a long Rounding top. The breakdown through 66 was a warning; and certainly the sharp break below 60 in February was a definitely bearish signal.

476

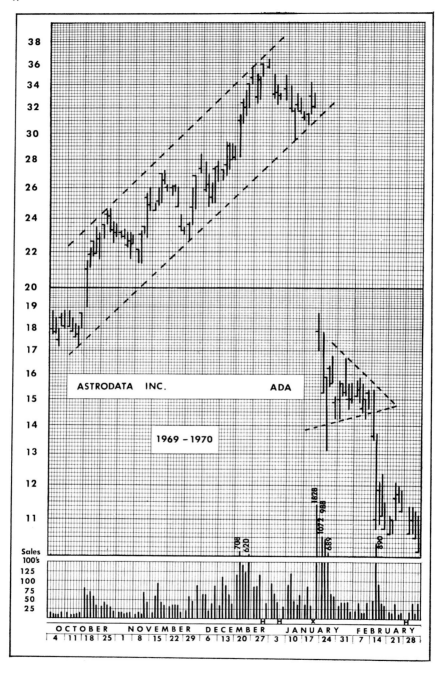

ASTRODATA INC.   ADA

1969 – 1970

FIGURE 253. A complete collapse in one day, Astrodata in January, 1970. Not the sort of action you see every day, or every month. But it is "normal" in the sense that it is a phenomenon we have seen many times in the past and which will undoubtedly be seen many times in years to come. When it does happen it should be heeded. It means trouble. "ADA" was doing well in what appeared to be a typical and perfectly healthy up trend. After a one-day suspension on January 15 it re-opened many points lower and never recovered. Trading was halted in late September. Some readers may remember other downside moves of this nature in the past. In Mack Trucks, in Fifth Avenue Coach, and some may even recall, many years ago, a break like this in American Woolen. Such a break is, of course, due to some sudden development or change in company affairs; but it is not necessary "to know the reasons"; the chart speaks for itself. As Lady Macbeth put it (in another connection), "Stand not upon the order of your going, but go at once." There was a good example of this type of a "gap move" in Villager Industries on April 30, 1971, when the stock dropped 42%, from 7⅜ to 4¼ in one day. Such moves as we are discussing here are nearly always on the *down* side; we do not often see comparable *upside* gap moves. And after this type of break, although there may be brief rallies, the stock nearly always resumes the down trend and in many cases is delisted from the exchange. Anyone caught holding such a stock should not feel that he had made a mistake in buying it, nor should he look for evidence of weakness before the big break-down; for ordinarily there is none. But he should get out immediately to avoid further loss. And by way of reassurance it can be repeated that this kind of collapse is a rather rare occurence.

FIGURE 254. A typical electric and gas Utility stock. There are a great many stocks in this group, serving various municipalities or regions. They tend to show similar market behavior because they are basically similar in nature.

FIGURE 254. There is, of course, a relation between the earnings of a
company and the dividends paid, and the market price of the shares. However, neither earnings nor dividends alone are sufficient to constitute a complete determination of "value," since there are many others factors that can
affect the "value" considered from different angles, such as dependability of
earnings, future prospects, taxability, research and development investment by
the company, and so forth.

The electric and gas companies, enjoying a regulated monopoly position in
most communities, have a sure and steady source of income; and they are also
in a definite "growth" situation because of the constantly increasing demands
for power by users. Most Utilities will show a record and pattern of trading
over a period of years very similar to that of "PEG." You will notice that
reported earnings have been larger each year from 1959 through 1970. Also
the dividend rate has been increased each year except in 1970 when it was
unchanged from the year before. Anyone basing his estimate of "value" on
a simple index such as "price-earnings ratio" would conclude that the stock
was 2½ times as good a buy in 1970 as it had been in early 1965.

Obviously, there is more to it than that. The big funds and other large
holders of stocks are not giving up "bargains" of that sort lightly and for no
reason. The depressed chart is undoubtedly reflecting the whole thorny outlook facing the Utility industry, including costly new facilities, anti-pollution
devices, and other problems.

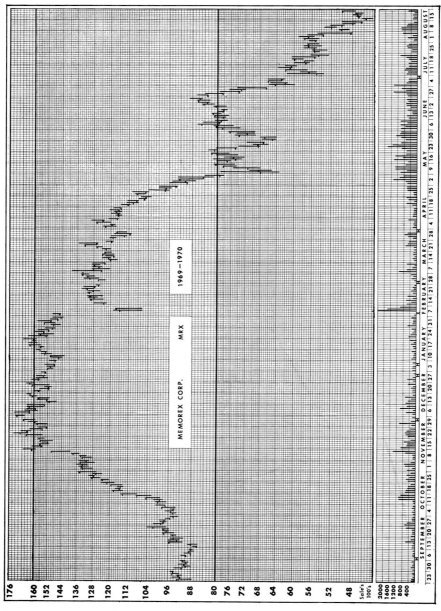

FIGURE 255. Although 1969 was bearish for most stocks "MRX" was enjoying the final fling of a dramatic four-year advance. Notice the Island-like top in November, December, and January, and the low volume all through this period. The breakaway gap in early February speaks for itself. See also Figure 253.

FIGURE 256. From a 1967 high of 48½, "FLY" started a down trend that lasted two years and took the stock down to 11¼. But during the spring and summer of 1970 the stock found bottom, made a Head-and-Shoulders reversal and took off in a skyrocket move that by February 1971, had recovered nearly all of the two year drop.

FIGURE 257. Here is a familiar pattern you have seen many times before in the pages of this book or in your own charts. Here we see a large Ascending Triangle in the daily chart of Action Industries, formed in December of 1971 and January of 1972. Notice the typical breakout and reaction moves and the continued up trend into April of 1972.

INDEX

Principal references are given in italic type

PUBLISHED AND DISTRIBUTED BY JOHN MAGEE, INC.
103 State Street, Boston, Mass. 02109, (617)367-0250